'This highly original, readable and illuminating
clarity what exactly has gone wrong with our m

Sir Anthony Seldon, *Ur*

'Bill Jones draws upon a wealth of knowledge and evidence to produce a truly fascinating book. He addresses some key questions which are rarely satisfactorily answered. Why do some people want to become politicians? What do they hope to achieve? How do they negotiate (or fail to) a game of political promotions akin to snakes and ladders? Is the old adage that all political careers end in failure really true? Avoiding lazy cynicism or unsupported assertions, Jones draws upon numerous astute political observations and examples spanning several decades to explain what makes politicians tick and whether they really do make a difference. This is a must-read book for anyone interested in politics.'

Jon Tonge, *Professor of Politics, University of Liverpool, UK*

'JUST LIKE US'?

Informed by interviews with key political figures and commentators, this entertaining and enlightening book exposes the influences, processes and motivations behind ministerial promotion in British government.

It identifies and analyses the political sinews that have influenced the selection and upward progression of our rulers since the middle of the last century. Given that politics is fuelled by ambition, it provides commentary on how this often-criticised emotional drive can work positively in practice, motivating politicians to strive constantly for advancement in their quest for power and achievement. Drawing upon many biographies, it explains how politics is essentially about the strengths and frailties of the people who occupy positions of power. It illustrates that climbing up that greasy pole is dependent upon a number of key character traits of politicians: their strength of desire; their abilities/skills as communicators, managers and administrators; the ways in which fate throws up opportunities; and the raw courage of politicians in confronting these challenges. Ultimately, the book illuminates the abiding obsessions of that tiny but potent minority in democratic societies who dare to dream they can rule over us.

This book will be of key interest to scholars, students and anyone interested in British political history, biography and the politics of executive government.

Bill Jones is Honorary Professor of Political Studies at Liverpool Hope University, UK.

Routledge Studies in British Politics

This series aims to promote research excellence in political science, political history and public policy-making, whilst addressing a wide array of political dynamics, contexts, histories and ideas. It will retain a particular focus on British government, British politics and public policy, while locating those issues within a European and global context.

Series editors: *Patrick Diamond and Tim Bale of Queen Mary University, London, UK.*

'JUST LIKE US'?: THE POLITICS OF MINISTERIAL PROMOTION IN UK GOVERNMENT

Bill Jones

An analysis of the abiding obsession of that tiny but potent minority in democratic societies, who dare to dream they can rule over us.

LONDON AND NEW YORK

Designed cover image: © Getty Images

First published 2024
by Routledge
4 Park Square, Milton Park, Abingdon, Oxon OX14 4RN

and by Routledge
605 Third Avenue, New York, NY 10158

Routledge is an imprint of the Taylor & Francis Group, an informa business

British Library Cataloguing-in-Publication Data
A catalogue record for this book is available from the British Library

ISBN: 978-1-032-52072-8 (hbk)
ISBN: 978-1-032-52075-9 (pbk)
ISBN: 978-1-003-40508-5 (ebk)

DOI: 10.4324/9781003405085

Typeset in Sabon
by Newgen Publishing UK

Soon after becoming an MP Estelle Morris asked a Cabinet friend what her colleagues were like, Her reply was:

'The good news is they are all like us; the bad news is they are all like us'.

This book is dedicated to a number of people: my truly fabulous wife, Carolyn, whose help has been vital during some difficult times; my lifelong friends and siblings, Pete and Liz; my children, Mandy and Markus; my former students in Manchester and Liverpool; the NHS staff who treated me so well, especially my oncologist, Dr Raheem Bashir; and in memory of my brave and wonderful mother, Doris Mary Jones.

CONTENTS

PREFACE

I was always intrigued by Senator Eugene McCarthy's view that 'Being in politics is like being a football coach. You have to be smart enough understand the game and dumb enough to think it's important' (Green, 1982, p.20). A witty epigram maybe but in reality politics *does* matter a great deal in determining the framework within which we live our lives, as, indeed, are the kind of people who come to be in charge of this process. Politics is essentially about people: fellow citizens armed with the vote and a political elite with ambitions and rather variable qualities. But it is also, as the American senator suggests, very much like a game with rules to be obeyed by most and ignored by some. Getting promoted in UK politics is accordingly a competitive 'game' played at Westminster and it is one that is of interest, sometimes great interest, to every voter in the country. As far as I am aware, this is the first study of its kind of this aspect of British politics.

As a student of British politics, most of my writing up to the present has taken the form of textbooks aimed at undergraduates, good A-level students and teachers of politics. Because such books require constant updated editions – *Politics UK* is now approaching its eleventh – a favourite project of mine found itself sitting on the back burner, I'm slightly ashamed to say, for two decades. Then a period of ill health intervened in 2021 when I was diagnosed with prostate cancer and so I decided to 'exhume' my projected research topic on ministerial promotion and use it as a distraction from the none too pleasant treatments to which my body was necessarily subjected. My professorial inaugural lecture at Liverpool Hope University in 2010 had drawn upon this research and an article accordingly appeared in *Political Quarterly*, but the book remained patiently on that back burner until that life- changing diagnosis.

Why ministerial promotion? I suppose I've always been interested in the 'democratisation' of political personnel. In medieval times appointments were mostly drawn from the aristocracy, members of whom regularly fought each other for the spoils of themselves becoming the monarch. This changed with the Tudors when Henry VIII first established Thomas Wolsey, son of a butcher, as his effective second-in-command, followed by Thomas Cromwell, whose father was a publican. Elizabeth I followed a similar strategy of preferring administrative ability to social rank by employing the non-aristocratic William Cecil as her principal adviser, followed by his son Robert who also served during the first nine years of James I's reign. Later, in the mid-nineteenth century, based upon the recruitment selection procedures of the East India Company, proven merit became the selection criterion for the nation's administrators and, once representative democracy and a curbed constitutional monarchy emerged, popularity in electoral contests became the main criterion for setting the political direction of our national governments.

The aim of this book is to direct what I hope is a penetrating eye into the body of British democratic government to identify and analyse the sinews that have grown to influence the selection and progression of our rulers in the period roughly since 1950 (though I do dip back before that occasionally). At the same time, given that politics is fuelled by ambition, it provides some insight on how this oft-criticised emotional drive works in practice, motivating politicians to strive constantly for advancement in their quest for power and recognition.

My purpose throughout is to show that progressing up that greasy pole, and staying there, depends so much upon the strength of desire, the abilities of the politician as communicator and administrator, the ways in which fate or the wheel of fortune throws up the opportunities, and the courage of politicians in taking them. I recognise that my focus mostly excludes the lively politics of the Scottish Parliament and the other two devolved assemblies, but their inclusion would have rendered the project so formidably large I suspect it would have remained on that back burner indefinitely.

I'm aware the book may seem a bit 'anecdote heavy' and there's a reason for this. I love political anecdotes and, being true to my *title* 'Just Like Us'?, politics is about lots of things – justice, belief, progress, equality depending on one's agenda – but essentially it's about the strengths and frailties of human beings usually trying very hard to achieve their objectives. Stories that illustrate the manner of this, sometimes amusingly, I think are as informing and, yes, educational, as the sometimes boring foundation facts of political processes.

I did briefly consider exploring the more psychology-based literature on 'ambition in politics' but realised it was too extensive and too far outside my comfort zone to undertake. Fred Greenstein's work is a good introduction for anyone wishing to venture where my feet feared to tread and, in particular,

Donald Searing's more accessible *Westminster's World: Understanding Political Roles*. Two points about the necessarily limited scope of my book. First, I recognise that my study is no more than my own single perspective: promotion is something that can be influenced by an infinite number of factors and elements of the political process, from gossip in the tea room, to the luck of coming top in the ballot for Private Members' bills. Second, while I fully appreciate the value of statistical analysis of the progress of Members of Parliament through their careers, I've tended to draw upon biographies, diaries, press articles and private interviews as my primary sources.

Whilst the focus of this book is on ministerial promotion, this kind of study is inevitably concerned with the system in which these political adventurers ply their trade. It follows that the book also provides analyses and updates useful, I hope, for the study and teaching of UK government, both its mainstreams and its eddies. Whilst this is not a textbook, I still hope students will find it of interest and value in their studies of how this country is governed. Finally, my central aim is to illuminate the qualities and abiding obsessions of that tiny but potent minority in democratic societies who dare to dream they can rule over us. My 'usual' health warning whenever giving a lecture is that politically I was a passionate Remainer and would describe myself as a left of centre 'progressive' but reckon I make every effort to be fair and balanced in my judgements.
Bill Jones, Beverley, 2023

Reference

Green, J. (1982) *The Book of Political Quotes*. Angus Robertson.

ACKNOWLEDGEMENTS

As I explained in my preface, this book has been a long time in the writing and along the way I have incurred a few debts which I'd like to acknowledge. First, I must thank my commissioning editor at Routledge, Andrew Taylor, who is the most relaxed, professional and fun publisher with whom I have worked in a long writing career; also big shout out for Sophie Iddamalgoda for coming in to save the day with her usual calm competence. On the resources side, I have to thank the Nuffield Foundation for funding part of my now substantial collection of biographies, memoirs and diaries; also former top politics student Angela Coleman, who, along with Maeva Zimmerman, undertook some useful statistical research on Cabinet membership funded by the University of Liverpool Hope when I served there as a professor of politics and history. For his insightful reading of draft chapters I have to thank my friend and colleague, Richard Kelly, former head of politics at Manchester Grammar and himself a widely published and astute student of British politics and history.

Grateful thanks also to those present and former politicians, journalists and civil servants – some of them sadly now no longer with us – who agreed to be interviewed for my study: Lord Andrew Adonis, Lord Kenneth Baker, Gyles Brandreth, Lord Carrington, Lord Grocott, Lord Roy Hattersley, Lord Dennis Healey, Professor Peter Hennessy, Lord Heseltine, Anthony Howard, Lord Roy Jenkins (who kindly shared a half bottle of claret with me), Gerald Kaufman, Sir Peter Kemp, Nigel Lawson, Lord David Lipsey, Professor the Lord (Philip) Norton, Sir David Omand, Lord Cecil Parkinson, Lord Charles Powell, Sir Peter Riddell and Baroness Shirley Williams. Finally, and he'll know why, I'd like to thank my former colleague, John Appleby. And a final,

final word on my wonderful copy-editor Sally Quinn who has demonstrated to me how vital a good copy-editor is to any non-fiction work.

Thanks are also due to the staff of that wonderful cornucopia of delight to political history scholars, the National Archives at Kew, where I benefitted from exploring Number 10's Prem 5 papers. Several colleagues have also been generous with their comments and suggestions, especially Lord Andrew Adonis, Lord David Blunkett, Lord Peter Hennessy, my friend and co-author Dr Isabelle Hertner, Professor Dennis Kavanagh, (co-author of *Politics UK*) Lord Philip Norton, Sir Peter Riddell and Professor Kevin Theakston. Oh, and special thanks for insights in his work to Steve Richards and Tim Bale. Baroness Estelle Morris kindly gave permission for one of her quotations being used in the title of this book. Those to whose writings I feel indebted, I'd like to add certain journalists. There are potentially many but I would single out: from the *Guardian*, Jonathan Freedland, Rafael Behr and Martin Kettle; from the *Observer*, Andrew Rawnsley; in the *Sunday Times*, Mathew Seyd; and from *The Times*, someone who has migrated from political 'retirement' in the House of Lords to becoming a truly outstanding columnist, Lord William Hague.

More widely I'd like to thank (I get a bit legitimately effusive here) all those politicians who have committed their experiences to memoirs or diaries – they have proved fascinating as well as invaluable. As for secondary sources, I have to thank the inspiring brilliance of Peter Hennessy's books and his BBC Radio interview series embodied in his book *Reflections*, the hugely insightful works of Sir Peter Riddell and the biographical products of Sir Anthony Seldon's unbelievably Stakhanovite energies.

Needless to say, despite the substantial volume of advice and comment on this work, I take the traditional full responsibility for any of the inevitable mistakes of fact or judgement within it.

Finally, and most importantly, for being a constant loving support during the sometimes fraught health conditions under which much of this book was written and for carefully proof reading and commenting on successive drafts, I must tender a few trillion thanks to my beloved wife, Carolyn, to whom this book is warmly dedicated along with the others mentioned.

INTRODUCTION

> Only a very small number of us would ever make it into the Cabinet. Perhaps that was why Parliament so often felt like a chamber of hungry ghosts in which no one was at ease.
>
> (Rory Stewart, in Stewart, 2023)

> Sometimes I wish I had stuck to my proper job but ambition ... is a terrible thing.
>
> (former lawyer Clement Davies to the *Montgomeryshire Express* when feeling some disillusion with being an MP; Wyburn-Powell, 2003, p.240)

> Self-interest is and ought to be the wellspring of human conduct. The world continues to offer glittering prizes to those who have stout hearts and sharp swords.
>
> (Lord Birkenhead quoted in *Times Leader*, 22 March 2023)

A young Jewish boy grew up with an ambition to be a comic actor. After completing a law degree he set up a production company and then starred in a popular soap opera called *Servant of the People*, in which he played an ordinary guy who, almost accidently, became president of his country. As you've already guessed, I'm writing about Volodymyr Oleksandrovych Zelensky, who was so angry at the corruption in his native Ukraine, that he stood for president against sitting president, Petro Poroshenko (2014–19), and commanded such public support that he won with a landslide 73.23 per cent of the vote in the second round. I do not open with this story simply to show how life can imitate art – though it clearly can – but to point out that in democracies, people way beyond the fringes of traditional power

DOI: 10.4324/9781003405085-1

elites can suddenly break through supposedly impossible barriers and find power bestowed upon them. Zelensky proved he was more than equal to the challenge he had taken on: fortunately, no recent British politician, let alone Prime Minister (PM), has had to face anything equal to it.

This book is about British politicians and how they claw their way up the famous 'greasy pole', as Benjamin Disraeli described it. We, the public, often think of politicians as rather odd, not especially nice people, usually drawn from the ranks of a British traditional rich 'ruling elite'. As with Zelensky, this has not always been the case but my 'Just Like Us' title derives from the answer given to a question posed by Estelle Morris when, as a new Labour member of Parliament (MP), she asked a colleague already a member of that august committee: 'What are members of the cabinet really like?' The memorable reply she received was, 'The good news is, they are just like us; the bad news is, they are just like us' (Jones, 2010, p.). But are such senior politicians indeed *so* similar to us? This study tries to offer an answer to this teasing question and from different perspectives examines the qualities ministers require to progress up that singularly insecure gradient. Two scholars of Australia's Westminster model system, cite the view, equally true of our own political system, that:

> the job of minister is complex and challenging, requiring different skills for the diversity of roles performed: administrator, politician, publicist and advocate, frequently all at once ... Some ministers were indeed highly effective, while others struggled, frustrating their colleagues, their officials and, occasionally, themselves.
>
> *(Tiernan and Weller, 2010, pp.1–2)*

This description defines the parameters of my study: I'm seeking to analyse the kind of people who enter the jungle-like world of politics, what qualities they require and the often fraught journeys they make en route to Cabinet level and beyond to Downing Street itself.

Candidates putting themselves forward for election do so in the hope, if not expectation, that they will eventually become close to the levers of power operated by government ministers. But with two major parties, some candidates *have* to accept that, even if they win their own constituency election, their party has to win a majority, either directly or in coalition with others; if not they will be forced to serve some of their career, or, if in a small minority party, all of it, in opposition. Such a period of political purgatory during the twentieth century would have proved relatively short for Conservatives but Labour MPs had to suffer longer periods of up to 13 (1951–64) and later 18 years (1979–97 and 2010–?). For smaller parties, like the Liberals and Liberal Democrats (Lib Dems), an indefinite period had to be endured until a hung Parliament offered the chance of a coalition, as occurred 2010–15.

Serving in opposition, however, offers a chance of studying the workings of departments and the government machine, the issues of the day, listening and participating in debates as well as being on select committees, investigating and occasionally contributing to the production of their influential reports. Incoming opposition MPs, as we learn in Chapter 2, usually seek to establish themselves in groupings of some sort: these could be socio-political dining/ debating clubs or ideological factions like Tribune (Labour) or Bow Group (Tory). Below follow some examples of how political progression can begin in opposition – sometimes slowly but steadily, sometimes surprisingly quickly.

British political parties did not start as tiny opposition groups that then evolved and expanded. The Conservative and Liberal parties emerged, along with the extension of the franchise, from *within* Parliament: the Conservatives out of groupings that traditionally supported the monarchy, empire, business, trade and the existing socio-economic status quo. When it became necessary from the mid-nineteenth century onwards to court voters for electoral purposes, this broad grouping of MPs, under the leadership of Robert Peel, sowed the seeds of an organised political party with declared policies and local branches to encourage activism. The Liberals too emerged from a coalescence of different factions – the eighteenth century Whigs, disillusioned Conservatives and the new 'Radical Liberals' like Richard Cobden and John Bright – that became organised under the eventual leadership of William Gladstone; once a Tory, who went on to become PM for four separate periods, advancing Liberal ideas of regulating free enterprise economic activity and promoting free trade.

Labour, by contrast, emerged from *outside* Parliament along with the extended franchise, from an alliance of trade unions with left-wing societies like the Independent Labour Party, the Fabian Society and the Marxist Social Democratic Federation. Keir Hardy started work as a miner at the age of seven and soon became a spokesperson for his fellow workers. He was first elected for West Ham South in 1892 but went on to lead the Independent Labour Party and help form the Labour Representation Committee, the founding organisation in 1900 of the Labour Party. From the first decade of the twentieth century those democratic pioneers who wished to realise their ideas through control of government, sought to do so via the agency of political parties, founded in nationwide memberships and the competition of rival party candidates for membership of the House of Commons. It follows that ambitions for ministerial roles were, and mostly remain, dependent on developments affecting political parties.

For Labour, the First World War offered opportunities for some MPs to serve as ministers in the wartime government. Even more advantageous to Labour was the bitter feud between Lloyd George and Herbert Asquith, which established a deep split in the hitherto dominant Liberal Party. This lost Liberals their role as the official opposition and enabled Labour to rule briefly as a minority administration under its Leader, Ramsay MacDonald, 1923–24. Furthermore, the extension of the right to vote to all men, and indeed finally women in 1928, opened up new recruiting opportunities for Labour. MacDonald led another minority government 1929–31 but its failure meant the party remained out of government throughout the 1930s. The split between MacDonald's national government – an alliance with the Conservatives – and the rump of his former party (Labour had only 52 MPs of which the shy unassuming Clement Attlee was among the most senior) kept the party out of power during this decade. He it was who succeeded the pacifist, George Lansbury, in 1935. Hugh Dalton, as a highly respected rising star in the party, would have had cause for regret that he lost his seat in 1931 and was not available as a leadership candidate in 1935 when Attlee, who did survive the 1931 cull, was elected Leader. Pimlott's biography of Dalton reveals how he supported Herbert Morrison as the new Leader, becoming 'in effect, Morrison's campaign manager'. This probably did Morrison more harm than good. A 'secret' canvassing meeting in Dalton's flat leaked to the press added to the reputations of both Dalton and Morrison for backstage plotting: while Dalton's noisy declarations that, apart from Morrison, the choice was between a 'nonentity and a drunk', may have helped bring Attlee (the 'nonentity') and Greenwood (the 'drunk' – he did indeed have a drinking problem) together. 'It was the first time that there had been any organised lobbying for the Party leadership and some MPs felt it improper' (Pimlott, 1985, p.231).

It was the Second World War that finally brought Labour into the wartime Coalition government Winston Churchill formed in 1940: Attlee became Deputy PM and established a reputation for tough, efficient administration, especially when Churchill was away from Number 10. Dalton was plucked from being an opposition MP and made Minister for Economic Warfare and later President of the Board of Trade. Against the expectations that Churchill's wartime leadership would ensure him a big majority in the 1945 election, it was Labour that emerged with the landslide and suddenly the opposition became the government, claiming, of course, all the major offices of state plus all the smaller portfolios as well. Dalton, aided by his high status in his party and his time as a senior minister in the wartime government, became Chancellor of the Exchequer – though an ill-advised chat to a journalist before delivering his 1947 Budget speech to the Commons (revealing his budget's contents), forced his early resignation. The other star Labour wartime minister, Ernest Bevin, became Foreign Secretary, later acclaimed for his roles in facilitating the Marshall Plan and the formation of the North Atlantic Treaty Organization in 1949. The war had elevated leading Labour MPs into candidates for high office. Even the most strident Labour critic of Churchill's wartime government, Nye Bevan, was made Minister of Health and engineered the birth of the remarkable National Health Service (NHS) in 1948. Morrison, whom Dalton had once favoured as Leader, became Home Secretary. Harold Wilson, of course, who had shone as a wartime civil servant was almost immediately given ministerial office and soon afterwards was in the Cabinet; something similar happened to Hugh Gaitskell, another high-performing wartime civil servant.

My opening chapter offers some analysis of why and how ordinary citizens decide they want to become professional politicians by 'promoting' themselves electorally to the House of Commons. Motives vary but most, on the basis of biographies and memoirs, seem to be driven either by a sense of duty or a desire to 'make a difference'. Chapter 2 looks at how MPs negotiate the system they have joined to advance themselves towards ministerial office and thence into the country's most important committee, the Cabinet. This usually begins with a spell as a Personal Parliamentary Secretary where MPs can learn the business of government via their minister boss. It proceeds with junior ministerial office as a Parliamentary Under Secretary of State (PUS) where they will usually be assigned specific duties by their Secretary of State; next step on the ladder will be as the more *senior* junior minister – Minister of State where they will be expected to take legislation through the Commons, speak from the Despatch Box for their departments and defend the government in the Commons and the media.

Chapter 3 examines the key part in promotion played by members of the Whips' Office: their role is to ensure government business is passed into law and a dozen whips on both sides of the House look after a cohort of MPs, being a protean sort of confidant, friend, even social worker, to ensure each MP under their care is happy and able to express views on all important issues. This intelligence network enables the Chief Whip to acquire knowledge of what their respective parties are prepared to support on key issues. Whips also monitor performance of their MPs in the House, committees and on the media. During reshuffles, the Chief Whip is a key source of advice on who will best fit in where and do the best possible job. Chapter 4 elaborates on the related role of reshuffles, which promulgate promotions, demotions and sackings involving the whips, aides and civil servants. In both these related chapters, biographies are extensively consulted and quoted. Chapter 5 looks at the role played by the ever-changing two-way mirror of the media, at Tony King's assertion that the print press is still the most influential branch of the media, at the vital role of television as a shop window for ambitious MPs and junior ministers and at the emergent role of social media in communicating views from MPs and government alike.

Chapter 6 examines that relatively new but key protagonist in the quest for ministerial promotion – the special adviser or 'spad'. These are increasingly often the young tyro 'career politicians' who, like Jack Straw, make their mark as advisers – rather like PPSs, they learn the business of government as 'apprentice ministers' – go on to enter Parliament and often rise quickly up the promotion ladder into the Cabinet and then, in the case of David Cameron, to become PM. Chapter 7 reminds us that promotion often begins when parties are in opposition. Being elected to a major party defeated at an election enables MPs to establish themselves as future ministerial candidates.

Smaller parties, like the Lib Dems face a long wait for office but when both big parties are unable to form a government, as in 2010, then the possibility of a coalition can bring office into view. Chapter 10 examines how women, LGBTQ+ (lesbian, gay, bisexual, transgender, queer/questioning, plus) and ethnic minority politicians fare in the competition for ministerial portfolios.

Chapter 8 focuses on the skills ministers require to climb the promotion ladder and Chapter 9 takes the promotion story up to the very top when UK politicians 'dare to dream' of Downing Street. Chapter 10 examines how women, LGBTQ+ and ethnic minority politicians fare in the competition for ministerial portfolios. Chapter 11 studies how rapidly ('promotion velocity') politicians rise from first entering Parliament to making it up to Cabinet level and goes on to examine the special case of Boris Johnson who was elevated to the Cabinet and then the premiership via his celebrity status and the mistaken belief of Tory Party members that he had the makings of one of our great PMs.

My concluding Chapter 12 considers some more unorthodox and often overlooked routes up the ladder, plus recent changes to the promotion process, plus a few recommendations to make it more effective.

Benjamin Disraeli's concept of the greasy pole suggests sharp and slithery competition, both up and down, for the top political prizes. However, researching the National Archives at Kew, I found a rather extraordinary letter that challenges such an assumption and offers an offbeat and rather amusing scene-setter for my study. It was a two-page handwritten missive from the Scottish Secretary, James Stuart – later Viscount Stuart of Findhorn – to the then PM, Anthony Eden. It was quite common for MPs to indicate to incoming premiers their availability for office – the Prem 5 collection contains several 'job applications' – but this one bucked the trend remarkably. It began with a claim that he was not 'trying to hang on to office' and continued:

> Indeed, I would be glad to be relieved as I know nothing of many tiresome subjects which come under me here- e.g. Education, Health Service etc. I had thought Tom Galbraith might relieve me here but has gone to the Lords at my own instigation.... Now, the 'Scotsman' recalls the name of Walter Elliott and this may be the answer to the problem. After all, although a few years older, he has much experience in addition to an alert and original brain. He retains lots of energy and he doesn't *hate* speaking as I do: he can also work hard and appears to be in excellent health. I was never a hard worker by nature and haven't been well of late although I admit to being rather better now. Watkins' seat is wobbly (Majority 1,431)

> – and I don't imagine that you want to make any changes just now. … This expects no reply until you wish to act: if at any time, you should wish to act, please do not bother about me or my feelings because I am fortunate in possessing none!
>
> *(Stuart, 1955)*

Despite his plea to be sacked in a job (at which, arguably, he confessed he was hopeless), he continued in post until January 1957! Interestingly Stuart titles his idiosyncratic memoir *Within the Fringe* (1967), suggesting – perhaps with aristocratic diffidence – he was a politician who operated at a distance from the centre of decision-making whilst, in fact, apart from serving in Cabinet, he had also served at the heart of government as Chief Whip during most of the war years. Stuart's recommendation of his possible successor marks another tendency of politicians to advise PMs on possible promotions. When I interviewed Michael Heseltine he was delighted to be given a copy of Peter Walker's letter to Edward Heath in October 1970 urging him to make Michael Heseltine Transport Secretary (Walker, 1970).

References and further reading

Note: I use the Harvard notation system; the reading list also serves as a guide to further reading.

Bale, T. (2023) *The Conservative Party after Brexit: Turmoil and Transformation*. Politico's.

Jones, B. (2010) 'Climbing the greasy pole: Promotion in British politics'. *Political Quarterly*, Vol. 81, issue 4, 616–626.

Pimlott, B. (1985) *Hugh Dalton*. Cape.

Stewart, R. (2023) *Politics on the Edge: A Memoir from Within*. Cape.

Stuart, J. (1955) 'Letter to the prime minister regarding his appointment as Scottish Secretary'. Prem 5, National Archives, 25 April.

Stuart, J. (1967) *Within the Fringe*. Bodley Head.

Tiernan, A. and Weller P. (2010) *Learning to Be a Minister: Heroic Expectations, Practical Realities*. Melbourne University Press.

The Times (2023) 'The Times view on Sunak's Brexit deal: Beyond the fringe'. 22 March.

Walker, P. (1970) 'Letter to Edward Heath'. Prem 5, National Archives, 13 October.

Wyburn-Powell, A. (2003) *Clement Davies: Liberal Leader*. Politico's.

1

BECOMING A PROFESSIONAL POLITICIAN

> They don't put up statues for journalists.
>
> (Boris Johnson's explanation of his desire to go into politics; quoted in Rawnsley, 2022)

> Not at all, if they made him Pope he would want to be God.
>
> (Mrs Gillian Waddington on whether she was surprised at her husband being promoted to Home Secretary in 1990; quoted in Waddington, 2012, p.182)

> They didn't spend university trying on new accents and personas ... They were climbing the greasy pole before most students had even located it.
>
> (Kuper, 2022b)

> Politics can look, from the outside, like a high stakes game of snakes and ladders, played out by alpha personalities with sharp elbows.
>
> (Leadsom, 2023, p.x)

> A talent for small talk with strangers should come high on the list of gifts for which a life of a politician in a democracy demands.
>
> (Cooper, 1953)

'He knows nothing; and he thinks he knows everything. That points clearly to a political career', wrote George Bernard Shaw in *Major Barbara*. The novelist Irvine Welsh even suggests: 'Going into politics is a self-glorifying, self-flagellating career move rather than a serious attempt to make the world a better place' (Potton, 2023). Cynical quotations abound, yet without people

DOI: 10.4324/9781003405085-2

prepared to take the plunge into political life, any democratic endeavour is neutered before it has begun.

Human nature is frail, and we have to make so many allowances, but the persistence of those bold young initiates – fuelled usually by an admixture of personal ambition or genuine altruism – is in reality the sine qua non of our British way of life. There are downsides to any political career, especially when under the cosh of tabloid or social media pursuit, but, instead of further maligning what I consider a generally misunderstood profession, we should perhaps allow expression of some gratitude to those willing to place their future on that roulette wheel of a life in politics. Yes, the system is flawed and should be greatly improved, but as Winston Churchill famously quipped in a Commons speech (11 November 1947) '*democracy* is the worst form of government, except for all those others that have been tried.' It's not always a popular view these days but I argue that ensuring citizens can throw out governments via free elections is the foundation of our national polity and, accordingly, requires our support.

Any political career begins with a realisation by someone that this is the course he or she wishes to follow. Such a decision might arrive as a sudden 'light-bulb' moment but more usually it is the eventual product of several years of 'learning' political experience at a non-professional level; or, as we shall see later on, some recruits are channelled in directly from other professions, ennobled for the purpose according to the constitutional rule that all ministers must be MPs, which, it is sometimes forgotten, includes the Lords. For example, from engaging in local politics and acquiring a taste for its triumphs and tragedies, the constant impetus is ambitiously upwards to achieve the next level: the first glimmerings of the desire for career betterment – yes, *promotion*! Typically a career might begin as a party foot soldier delivering leaflets, moving up maybe to local constituency officer – secretary, treasurer or perhaps chair.

Once rated by the party faithful, the next stage might be as candidate for a councillor's seat. Having made a name as an effective local politician, wider ambitions can cause new horizons to beckon. Inevitably, as explained in my Introduction, the most usual route into the Commons would be via membership of one of the big parties: Labour, Conservative and Lib Dems all provide training programmes for their parliamentary candidates. Aspirant MPs often remain on an approved list before they must persuade a local selection meeting that they are their particular ideal candidate. Others, of course, might not be attracted by politics at the local level and decide to enter having achieved success in a career – maybe law, journalism or business (though it has to be said the proportion of such recruits are diminishing). Searching for a winnable seat might take years of trailing around constituency parties making one's pitch as a servant of party and local community. Betty Boothroyd, the famous former dancing Tiller girl, tried for 17 years to convince over a dozen Labour constituency selection panels of her suitability as a candidate and fought three elections without success before winning her West Bromwich by-election in 1973. Boothroyd was not alone in her obsessive pursuits but what underlies such lifetime dedication to this goal? What are the requirements for flourishing in the world of politics? Much depends on the degree of public participation in the democratic process.

Participation in UK politics

Voting

For most people their sole political participation is passive – 'watching' the political world unfold via the media. Their most active participation will be voting, either at the local or national level; over 80 per cent of all voters in the 1990s (Parry et al., 1992, p.44) had voted at least once in a local or general election. In 1950, turnout in general elections was a remarkable 83.9 per cent; in 1959 turnout was down to a still respectable 78.7 per cent and then a gradual decline set in so that by 2001 the figure was a worrying 59.4 per cent. After that nadir there was a sharp recovery – 68.7 per cent in 2017 – but figures over 70 per cent during the period 1959–97 were only rarely experienced.

Average voting turnout for devolved legislatures since they came into being have been substantially lower:

Northern Ireland (2019)	64%
Scottish Parliament (2021)	64%
Welsh Assembly (2021)	46.6%

Euro-elections were even lower: the last in 2019 registered a mere 37.2 per cent. However, the lowest electoral turnout in the UK was for local elections in 2018: 34.5 per cent. But this is not necessarily a reflection of political apathy: the turnout in the 2014 Scottish Independence Referendum was 84 per cent and in the 2016 'Brexit' one, 72 per cent. (For a study of why participation in democratic politics has declined see the 2006 Helena Kennedy chaired 'Power to the People' report.)

Other types of participation

The major study by Parry et al. back in 1992 showed only very small percentages engaged in party campaigning (5.2 per cent fundraising, 8.6 per cent attending a rally), contacting an MP (9.7 per cent), councillor (20.7 per cent), town hall (17.4 per cent). However, 14.6 per cent attended a protest meeting, 63.3 per cent signed a petition, only 5.2 per cent went on a protest march, 4.3 per cent engaged in a political boycott and 0.2 per cent engaged in political violence. That last figure is very low but in absolute terms 0.2 per cent of the population is around 67,000 people: violence requires only a determined few or even the single killer – think of Jo Cox and David Amess – so that danger is always with us.

Politicians: the nature of the beast

(This section draws upon my earlier article: B. Jones (2010, 1 October) 'Climbing the greasy pole', *Political Quarterly*.) Why do aspiring politicians embark on such a perilous journey, involving hugely long hours, no real job security and, on occasions, high degrees of self-abasement, just to have the chance of making it to the first rung of the ladder? What kind of person, then, wants to become a professional politician? The answer is as old and as opaque as human nature itself – a topic from which any author would shrink from offering definitive answers whether a political scientist or, indeed, a psychologist. Yet we must make some attempt to comment on the essential nature of politicians, if only to set the scene for any examination of ministerial promotion.

I'm not sure the answer to Estelle Morris's question about the nature of Cabinet members was wholly correct in saying they are 'just like us'. Maybe the response referred to fellow politicians? This group certainly differs from shall we say the 'ordinary' and 'normal' in all kinds of ways. For starters, most people engaging in a professional career aim for competence in their chosen area – medicine, law, engineering or whatever: politics is not really like any of those. Political activity is essentially about the winning and retaining of power to change the way other people live their lives. Some would say – and this is the dangerous bit given the vagaries of human nature – it is also about the acquisition of power for its own sake.

Understanding politicians involves some kind of plunge into the study of that opaque and much disputed area – *human nature* – and, by extension, the *psychology of the political mind*. A fair amount of specialised research has been undertaken in this field, much of it in American universities, especially by Fred Greenstein, and in the UK by Ashley Weinberg in his much more accessible book, *The Psychology of Politicians*. I have not personally taken any plunges into this area of scholarship but have tried to indicate where it might be found. Inevitably the quality of ambition features strongly in any study of promotion and the qualities required to make one's way in the political jungle.

One of the better attempts to elucidate the topic is made by Jeremy Paxman in his entertaining and perceptive book, *The Political Animal: An Anatomy*. Paxman – and who would know the political species better than he? – finds it very hard to penetrate the mindset but adduces some irreducible and familiar characteristics:

- The first requirement he identifies is, obviously, *self-confidence*. Party politicians come to believe, within themselves at least, that they have identified key issues, for example the single best way to run public services, set taxation levels, deal with other nations. Politics also entails high performance skills. For example, Nick Clegg's first appearance in the televised debates on 15 April 2010 made it imperative he was on top form. Many 'ordinary' people might have quailed at the thought of what depended on one's debut TV debate, but ex-Westminster public school boy Clegg had the confidence to carry it off with impressive aplomb and even initiated a media-dubbed 'mania' suffixed to his name – sadly for him only short lived.
- The second requirement is fierce persistence in the face of all setbacks; I've mentioned Boothroyd but Paxman quotes the case of Caroline Spelman (made Secretary of State the Department of Environment and Rural Affairs, May 2010) who endured 27 selection interviews before landing a winnable constituency.
- Third, in order to reach the top, politicians need immense energy and good health. Sleep suffers, and many politicians do not require what 'normal' people would regard as the minimum. Napoleon and Margaret Thatcher thrived often on a mere three hours sleep a night, and at the very end of the 2010 election campaign David Cameron managed to keep going non-stop for 36 hours. Once in office, moreover, ministers put in 18-hour days quite normally as their diaries frequently testify. And still they have time and energy to appear on *Question Time*, do major interviews or, in Edwina Currie's case, have a four-year affair with a future PM and even write the occasional romantic novel. When Harold Wilson felt his powers beginning to fade during the mid-1960s as dementia took hold, he wisely stood down. Michael Heseltine suffered a heart attack when 60 years old but after four months' recuperation he returned to the fray and, at the time of writing, aged 90, is still displaying remarkable vigour.
- The fourth requirement is *unfailing optimism*: to win that hopeless seat, to believe one's party can win from a 20-point deficit in the polls, to hear that phone call from Number 10 with the offer of office. Michael Barber, one-time head of the Delivery Unit in Tony Blair's office, stood in 1987 for Labour in rock solid Tory Henley-on-Thames; he lost heavily but recalled that: 'Incredibly, I remember convincing myself that I could win in the last few days' (Jones, 2010).
- Fifth is the ability to absorb huge amounts of information and *distil* just those items that buttress a party position.

- Sixth is *loyalty*, sometimes to the point of humiliation, as characterised by many Boris Johnson supporters during his Partygate travails 2021–22.
- Paxman's final quality is a *long-suffering and endlessly supportive family*, one willing to accept long periods of separation and secondary status to an unquenchable obsession (Paxman, 2002).

Additionally, I would add my own gloss to Paxman's of at least two more characteristics. Politicians can be just a little *odd*, that's right, *odd*. Churchill wrote to his wife Clemmie, before the outbreak of the First World War: 'Everything tends towards catastrophe. I am interested, geared up and happy. Is it not horrible to be built like that?' (Jones, 2010). Even odder, regarding Churchill, is this snippet of his early teenage vision as told to a Harrovian schoolmate: 'The country will be subjected somehow to a tremendous invasion ... but I tell you that I shall be in command of the defences of London and I shall save London and the Empire from disaster' (ibid., 2010). It is perhaps significant that Boris Johnson admires Churchill inordinately as his biography of the great man reveals and, I have come to believe, even tries to imitate some of his characteristics.

Furthermore, an ever-present quality in many, but not all, politicians would appear to be a near *narcissistic interest in themselves*. Edwina Currie captures some of this in her commendably honest but revealing diary comment:

> This evening I went out to dinner at a flat in Smith Square. As ever with dinner parties, which were not part of my upbringing, I found it very hard work, just trying to be sparkling and interested in my companions. I'd much rather be the centre of attention!
>
> *(Jones, 2010)*

So many politicians clearly yearn for and revel in the *public attention* this profession entails. Glenda Jackson recalled an early grumble from one MP when she entered the Commons was 'What do you want to come here for? You're famous already' (Times Diary, 2023).

People are infinitely complex, of course, and we can find other qualities like, for example, the ability to self-persuade, being *so* sure that personally one can make that crucial difference on behalf of us all and that one is motivated purely by concern for others and by principle. Examples of this mode of thinking are legion. Indeed, David Owen, former medical doctor, Labour Foreign Secretary and founder member of the Social Democratic Party, has diagnosed both the aforementioned condition and in addition suggested that Thatcher and Blair both suffered from an excess – indeed an intoxication – of power, or, to quote the title of his book, *The Hubris Syndrome* (Owen, 2007).

Yet all these conditions for succeeding only offer a rough guide to the type of person who tends to fill the often oddly shaped shoes of a politician. Churchill, for example, spent much of his life being an outcast from his own party and to some extent had seriously underachieved, until mere chance – Johnson spoke in his own case of a 'ball appearing out of the rugby scrum' (Mason, 2013), which he could snap up and sprint into Number 10 – or, perhaps for Churchill, destiny itself, arriving in 1940 courtesy of Adolf Hitler. Hundreds of others, although winning the lottery of a seat in a general election, have had to accept the bleak reality of such a fate. Lost to history, moreover, are those thousands, possibly with both ambition and ability, who fell at the first fence and never even made it past the candidate stage. This cohort is not necessarily lacking in ability: it includes, for example, Robin Day and Ludovic Kennedy – failed candidates who went on to achieve great distinction in other professions.

In my lifetime's experience of studying politics and meeting its practitioners, politicians, for the most part, do not fulfil the negative characterisation of power-mad monomaniacs. They usually enter politics not because they are venal, egotistical or ruthlessly selfish, though there are several who might deserve such labels, but because they genuinely believe they can 'make a difference' and fulfil an idealistic sense of service to the local or national community. I believe many start out like the fictional Hamer Shawcross in Howard Spring's *Fame is the Spur*, someone whose poverty-based idealism has progressively leaked away leaving him open to the seductions of the baubles of power, the comfortable life, the capacious social and physical furniture of the ruling class. Most think of Ramsay MacDonald as the model for the Shawcross character, but there are many other possibilities. Fiction loves this possible subversion of decency and commitment to the common good by inner selfishness and the limitless seductions of power. Along with Shawcross we have the Michael Dobbs's ruthless character in his novel *House of Cards*, Francis Urquart, and, in the American dramatised version, Frank Underwood, played by Kevin Spacey.

So success in politics seems to be an admixture of driving ambition, narcissism, genuine idealism with, perhaps, a dash of daring and necessary ruthlessness. Murdering one's political rivals and enemies in real life is a practice fortunately reserved for non-democratic regimes. Charles Powell, foreign affairs aide to Margaret Thatcher, marvelled at their perseverance with this key insight:

> I think there is a quality that separates politicians from the rest of us. It is the scale, the depth of the ambition and what they have to go through to realise it. For a politician you have to be prepared to spend anything up to twenty years of forlorn existence on the back benches, being whipped through the lobbies on subjects you know little about and care less about … in order even to aspire to the dizzy heights of being a parliamentary secretary or minister of state.
>
> *(private interview)*

These then are strange, special people about whom we wonder, criticise and love to bitch, often because we have agreed to give them power over us and are not sure about our wisdom in doing so. However, they are quintessentially still human beings. Political scientists have a more prosaic take on why people engage in politics at even the most basic of levels. Geraint Parry's survey-based study (Parry et al., 1992, pp.9–15), identifies four theories of participation.

i. *Instrumentalism* argues that people enter politics because they believe, quite rationally, that it will be a means of achieving their objectives, whatever they might be: ideological, policy based, maybe even nationalistic. The 'social-psychological' subsection of this approach adduces, further, that certain groups develop 'civic' attitudes: that political activity is both effective and a 'duty'; an *obligation* to participate. These groups are usually drawn from the better-off sectors of society, are better educated and well endowed with the skills necessary to succeed in this activity, especially self-confidence, articulacy, plus a thorough knowledge of political issues and systems. The democratic irony of this tendency is that it is the rich who take naturally to politics and the less well off – who have a much greater need for politics to deliver them benefits – lack the resources to acquire the necessary skills and knowledge in the first place and tend to abstain from participation as not worth the effort.
ii. The *communitarian* theory suggests the impulse to political action can be concern for one's community, leading to an emphasis on decentralisation of decision-making.
iii. John Stuart Mill was an early proponent of the *educative* theory, which suggests political participation helps develop a range of useful skills while promoting a wider awareness of broader interests in society and their responsibility to others.
iv. The *expressive* theory of participation argues that it manifests a desire to show feelings or opinions on issues. This might take the form of joining a march, a demonstration or even singing a protest song or national anthems. An unusual, not primarily political recruit to the political arena, was the former Czech president.

The thoughts of Václav Havel on the profession of politics

In his 1991 acceptance speech for the biennial Sonning Prize for his contribution to European civilisation, Havel added to our knowledge by focusing on the very human desire to acquire power (see Wanis, 2020). He saw the motivation to enter the world of politics as being threefold: ideas, self-affirmation and the material advantages of power.

Ideas

Clearly of major importance in politics, ideas originate often as refinements of philosophical analyses. Early political philosophy focused on the relationship between citizens and government – its nature, content and limits. Later emphasis shifted to concern for how government impacts on society – its economic and environmental welfare viewed through the prisms of general principles like equality, justice and liberty. For his part, Andrew Adonis adds to the observation of political ideas that often people are drawn as much, or often more, not by the ideas but by those who most effectively express them. He quotes Jonathan Freedland who suggests 'people do not believe in ideas: they believe in people who believe in ideas'. He points out that 'most of the world's ideologies and religions are named after their founder, sometimes a champion or interpreter'. Christianity, Buddhism, Marxism, Leninism, Keynesianism all hail from individual leaders or writers (Adonis, 2021, p.2). And, of course, we have 'isms' attached to individual's names: 'Thatcherism' 'Blairism'.

Self-affirmation

This term, used by Havel, is 'the natural longing every human has for self-affirmation' – in other words, ambition – and mirrors the oft-made criticism of politicians that they are mostly motivated by the selfish pursuit of their own glory. 'Is it possible', Havel asks us:

> to imagine a more attractive way to affirm your own existence and its importance than that offered by political power? In essence it gives you a tremendous opportunity to leave your mark in the broadest sense on your surroundings, to shape the world around you in your own image, to enjoy the respect that every political office almost always automatically bestows upon the one who holds it.
>
> *(Wanis, 2020)*

Given this is true, one is moved to ask why so few are interested in the business of politics; the downsides of such a life, already mentioned, clearly offers a partial answer.

Perks of office

Along with ambition, this advantage is often cited as a major failing of politicians. Dr Johnson opined in the eighteenth century that it was not just *a* failing but actually *the* main reason for people becoming politicians in the first place: 'Politics are now nothing more than the means of rising in the world. With this sole view do men engage in politics and their whole conduct proceeds upon it' (Green, 1982, p.6). It needs no more than a glance at history to see how rulers and their cronies have sought to live (and die) in the most fabulously luxurious fashion – the vast pyramidal mausoleums of the pharaohs, the extravagant beauty of Versailles for Louis XIV, Hampton Court for Henry VIII's Cardinal Wolsey, later seized jealously by Henry himself. On a lesser level, modern-day politicians in 2009 reinforced this negative public perception of UK lawmakers by exploiting the generous expenses MPs were allowed. Even on the mundane level of a junior minister, the perks are hard to lose: such politicians often mourn most the use of a chauffeur-driven car at one's beck and call. Even a humble back-bench MP, moreover, has the chance – often called 'jollies' – to travel, first class, to exotic locations on parliamentary delegations.

Havel, the former poet, playwright and dissident who eventually became president of the Czech Republic 1993–2003, sums up wonderfully well, from a decade's experience, the seductively dangerous temptations of political power.

> There is something treacherous, delusive, and ambiguous in the temptation of power. On the one hand, political power gives you the wonderful opportunity to confirm, day in and day out, that you really exist, that you have your own undeniable identity, that with every word and deed you are leaving a highly visible mark on the world around you. Yet within that same political power and in everything that logically belongs to it lies a terrible danger: that, while pretending to confirm our existence and our identity, political power will in fact rob us of them.
>
> *(Wanis, 2020)*

Catching the political bug

Many politicians talk of 'catching the politics bug', becoming obsessed with the world of politics. Disraeli candidly confessed to his Shrewsbury constituents that, 'I love fame; I love public attention; I love to live in the eye of the country' (Jones et al., 2022, p.15). Lord High Chancellor, F.E. Smith, gloried in the 'endless adventure of governing men'. Michael Heseltine enthused in similar vein: 'Politics is a life sentence. It's an obsessive, all demanding, totally fascinating, totally committing profession – stimulating, satisfying, stretching' (Jones et al., 2022, p.10). I also remember David Ennals (Labour Secretary of State for Social Services 1976–79) after elaborating the difficulties of a political life, staring at me wide-eyed, saying: 'But politics is so *very fascinating*!'

Almost always we hear politicians claiming that their objectives are honourable, altruistic and, for many, especially at the start of their careers, this is probably genuine. Yet, at the same time, according to Havel – shades of Hamer Shawcross again – there is the seductive reality of the all-enveloping appeals of self-affirmation and the wonderfully comfortable accoutrements of power: think of the fabulous palaces built by Putin and Erdogan. In consequence he reckons that 'politics is work of a kind that requires especially pure people, because it is especially easy to become morally tainted' (Wanis, 2020): another word for this, of course, is *corruption*. Lord Acton famously stated that 'all power tends to corrupt, and absolute power corrupts absolutely'. It is not the purpose of this study to travel along such well-worn lines of enquiry, but it might be noted that desire for advancement or *promotion* in politics could, in some sense, mark a progress point along this road. Instead I wish to continue this chapter by delving into political biographies to study the points at which a variety of noted politicians decided to enter their trade and, if the question can be answered, why?

Just occasionally we learn of politicians, who, when quite young set their sights on being PM and actually got there. The most famous must be Harold Wilson who, aged eight in 1924, had a photo of himself taken in front of Number 10. When, aged 12, Margaret Thatcher visited London, Downing Street was included among all the sights seen but, unlike Wilson, she did not have the prescience to have her picture taken outside the famous door. Another famously ambitious politician, according to Oxford contemporary, Julian Critchley, actually planned out his career on the back of an envelope – acquiring wealth, marriage, MP, PM by 1990s – in his memoirs Heseltine claims to have no recollection of this. And, as we know, it so very nearly happened.

Harold Wilson (1916–95), PM 1964–70 and 1974–76

The photograph of the boyhood Wilson outside Number 10, has served to create something of a myth about Wilson's ambition and sometimes formed part of a negative narrative about a scheming, ambitious but rather shallow man behind the avuncular façade. His biographer, Ben Pimlott, rather doubts 'the fantasies of childhood' can be accurately dubbed 'ambition', though traces the origins of what was truly an idée fixe to the occasion when on holiday in Scotland. His father took him to see a statue in Stirling of Sir Henry Bannerman, Liberal PM 1905–08 and the town's former MP. According to his first biographer, Leslie Smith, Wilson's father explained at some length the growth of the Labour Party, the radical history of Colne Valley and the careers of Mann, Grayson and Snowden' (Pimlott, 1993, p.21). Smith reckoned the effect was 'dramatic: politics became the only career Harold wanted to pursue. Henceforth, he felt an inner certainty of destiny, an absolute conviction about his future mission and his unique fitness to undertake it' (ibid., p.22). Like so many successful politicians, he always thought he was headed for big things in his life and in his individual case he was right.

David Owen (1938–), Foreign Secretary 1970–79 and Leader Social Democratic Party

Owen was born into an upper-middle-class Welsh family in Plymouth, that social group which always forms the 'long list' for entry into any UK elite. He used to think his entry into politics was an 'accident' but, given his background was infused with both medicine and politics, it is unsurprising he first qualified and worked as a doctor before leaning towards a political career. An early influence was his family's veneration of David Lloyd George but a bigger influence on the young Owen was listening 'spellbound' to Nye Bevan at Exmouth Hall addressing a huge audience 'for 85 minutes without a script' (Owen, 1991, p.15–16). His mother, a charismatic Devon county councillor, was 'the major influence in my life' and he suggests in his memoir she made his 'going into politics' something of a 'natural development'. Influential moments for him arrived in 1956: Suez plus the Soviet invasion of Hungary, but at Cambridge he was put off by the mannered style of the Union debates; he did not join the Labour Party until 1960 at which time he was ready to scale the promotion terrain.

Harold Nicolson (1886–1968), leading journalist and diarist

Never a senior minister but a very well-connected journalist and latterly famous for his diaries, he was another product of Britain's upper-middle class and, being the son of a senior diplomat, Lord Carnock, he was born into a family already highly political in culture and outlook. After public school and Balliol College, Oxford, he entered the diplomatic service. Interestingly his wife, Vita Sackville West's family only assented with reluctance to their marriage as they wanted her to marry an aristocrat from a long and noble lineage. After serving in the Middle East for a number of years he resigned from the service in 1929 to become a journalist. His first entry into politics was to join Oswald Mosley's New Party – its ideas and charismatic leadership were initially attractive to progressives – and he even stood for it as a parliamentary candidate but quickly left when Mosley's infant organisation evolved into the Nazi-aping British Union of Fascists; he subsequently entered the Commons representing National Labour in 1935.

William Hague (1961–), Leader Tory Party 1997–2001, Foreign Secretary 2010–14

Hague was born into a family who owned a small soft-drinks business. Educated at Wath Comprehensive School, which retained many of its grammar school traditions, he excelled academically and even as young as 13 years old declared he intended to study politics, philosophy and economics (PPE) at Oxford and become an MP by the time he was 30. Despite being brought up in a Labour voting area he, perhaps predictably for the scion of a small business family, leant towards the right rather than the left. He soon began to assist in campaigns, acquiring a nerdish interest in politics, rote learning its complex statistics and, unusual for any reasonably sane person, becoming addicted to reading Hansard. At the age of 16 he gained national attention by making an impassioned ultra-loyal speech to the Conservative Party conference, with Mrs Thatcher looking maternally down on her prodigy protégé. Here's a snatch of the gist and content of his precocious performance:

> Through the long, proud history of the Conservative Party runs a golden thread. That thread stretches out through the decades, linking each one of us to the great men and women who have led this Party. It is that we are a Party which draws its inspiration from the character of the British people; it is that we cherish the precious traditions and freedoms of our island home; it is that we found our programme on the experiences of the people, not the abstract theories of purists and ideologues.

Ever after, Hague's sister used to jokingly address him as 'Tory Pig!' Michael White, (2000).

Betty Boothroyd (1929–2023), Speaker of the House of Commons 1992–2000

She saw it as her 'great good luck to be born into a working class Yorkshire family', which 'insisted on a disciplined approach to life and gave me the confidence to fulfil my ambitions'. As the only child of relatively comfortably off working-class parents, they 'poured all their ambitions into me'. However, Betty found it impossible to succumb to her father's Victorian parental values requiring total obedience to father's word, something that caused rows when he found himself unemployed in the 1930s. When Betty joined the Tiller Girls dancers at the end of the war, they were not best pleased; for her part, Betty recalled, 'it was just like politics – damned hard work' (Boothroyd, 2002, p.42). Her Mum and Dad were both staunch trade unionists and Labour Party members. It was her Mum who provided the political inspiration: 'She made it possible for me to think politically, and to understand the importance of argument and debate and of communicating one's beliefs to other people' (ibid., p.42).

Neither parent was especially 'socialist': they had 'no time for theorising'. It was her mother who took her along to party meetings and to listen to party leaders when they came to speak in Yorkshire: Nye Bevan 'almost knocked us off our feet with the strength of his convictions' (Boothroyd, 2002, p.43). Membership of Labour's League of Youth enabled her to represent Dewsbury at London meetings and she was active in organising rallies, hikes and galas: she won a beauty contest at a rally in Filey and in 1952 became a full-time Labour Party staff member. Later she became Commons secretary to the legendary Barbara Castle who helped draw her within the inner currents of the Parliamentary Labour Party and supported the long pilgrimage mentioned earlier before her victory in West Bromwich in 1973.

Gillian Shephard (1940–), Secretary of State for Education and Employment

Shephard claims her entry into politics was related to her lifelong fascination with 'power and who exercises it'. Born into a garage and haulier business family she was brought up in rural Norfolk aware of an ever-present 'us' and 'them' but also of a certain secretiveness about political sympathies:

> there was a whole tranche of opinion which regarded politics as something you did not talk about. Your views were your own business and no one else's. ... I wondered at the courage of those who were so open about their beliefs and so prepared to be publicly defeated that they actually put themselves up for election.
>
> *(Shephard, 2000, p.10)*

Education for this bright young Norfolk girl was grammar school and then Oxford, not so very different from that of Margaret Thatcher, her nearby neighbour in Grantham: 'Deciding which political party to attach myself to was never a problem. I had been born a Conservative, and if I had any doubts Margaret Thatcher would have dispelled them' (Shephard, 2000, p.12). Having served on Norfolk County Council she was elected to the Commons in 1987 for Southwest Norfolk. Starting as a Personal Parliamentary Secretary to Peter Lilley she soon ascended through the Tory ranks into the Cabinet.

Norman Tebbit (1931–), Cabinet member 1981–87

Tebbit is interesting because he was born into a working class background – his father famously 'got on his bike' to look for work in 1931 – and Norman's first rung on an upward social ladder was to acquire a place at Edmonton County Grammar School, where 'it was Miss Rudwick, who in teaching me the history of Europe from 1830 to 1914, most excited my mind and may have set me on the path to politics'. By 1942 and 'mainly by intuition', the future Tory Cabinet minister had come to:

> believe in what we would now call capitalist non-interventionist economic theories and to discard completely the fashionable paternalistic and socialist doctrines of the mid-1940s. So even at fourteen years of age I had

> conceived a distrust of socialism and sympathy with the liberal free market views, which unknown to me, Professor Hayek was expressing in *The Road to Serfdom* – a book I was not to read for almost 40 years.
>
> *(Tebbit, 1989, p.13)*

So the already fully formed ideological Thatcherite went on as a teenager to strongly oppose the 'closed shop' when he joined the *Financial Times*. He joined the Royal Air Force as his national service, becoming a pilot and then flew commercial flights for BOAC in the early 1960s where he became a trade union official in the airline pilots' trade union, BALPA, a move initiated essentially by the 'incompetence of management in BOAC'. His interest in politics at that time was awoken by frustration with the self-serving stasis of Harold Macmillan's government, disbelief in the 'myth of John Kennedy' and frustration with the inefficient conduct of his own state-owned employer. At work he acquired (unsurprisingly, perhaps) 'a reputation as an abrasive committee member and a ruthless chairman' but it was the spectre of a 'socialist' government, as the Macmillan government crumbled, which led him away from BALPA and 'towards politics' (ibid., pp.74–76). Deciding to escape from his well-paid career, aged 34, he wrote to former friend, now an MP, Peter Walker, who warmly encouraged him. In 1970, he was elected for Epping.

James Prior (1927–2016), Cabinet minister 1970–72 and 1979–84

Prior was born into an upper-middle-class family, his father having some aristocratic connections. After public school and Cambridge he was elected MP for Lowestoft and soon became a minister. His memoirs attest to the fact that he'd always, ever since his early days at Charterhouse, started down those 'slippery slopes' towards politics. His headmaster, Robert Birley, was clearly influential: 'this man whose powerful intellect and strong social conscience placed duty to others very high in the order of obligation and he gave a liberal twist to my entrepreneurial intent' (Prior, 1986, p.9). Prior also makes an interesting point that his generation was perhaps less rebellious than the previous First World War generation: 'We did not experience life in the trenches which 25 years earlier had lead [*sic*] men of Harold Macmillan's generation to dedicate themselves to a better society' (ibid.). He also expresses great warmth towards trade unionists whose support Tories have always needed to attract: 'they did more to help my political education than they ever could have realised'. But his actual initiation into the professional ranks was remarkable, to say the least: it deserves full quotation.

> To my astonishment, a little after the general election of 1955, I was driving a tractor along the road when someone stopped me and said they

> were looking for a new candidate for Lowestoft. 'You're a young man; you are just the type of person we want. Why don't you let your name go forward?' I didn't even know they needed a candidate. ... Almost immediately I found myself the prospective candidate for Lowestoft constituency. Everything had happened so quickly that I was selected as their candidate without having been approved by Conservative Central Office.
>
> *(Riddell, 1993, p.84)*

Ernest Bevin (1881–1951), Minister of Labour and National Service 1940–45, Secretary of State Foreign Affairs 1945–51

This titan of the Labour Party was born into abject poverty, being effectively orphaned aged eight years and receiving only a rudimentary primary education but, unlike so many of his peers, able to read and write. Additionally he was a healthy, well-built, ebulliently outgoing young lad who made the most of the few opportunities available to him. Early on as a youngster earning a pittance, he became aware of the great differences in the conditions in which people lived. His first contact with politics was probably via attendance at Baptist chapel – his 'university of life' – where he found in himself a readiness to preach persuasively and to discuss the subject of politics. His attendance at Workers' Educational Association classes gave him access to the socialist texts of the day and enriched his ability to argue the progressive case. In 1910 he formed a union for unskilled workers in the docks and became a full-time union official. As his biographer notes 'The penniless 13-year-old orphan who arrived in Bristol with nothing more than his brothers' addresses was now embarked on the career that would take him to fame and political fortune beyond his wildest boyhood dreams' (Adonis, 2020, pp.8–21). Bevin's life trajectory rose on his building of the biggest trade union in Europe, the Transport and General Workers' Union, and elided quite naturally into prominence within the unions' political arm, the Labour Party.

Angela Raynor (1980–), Deputy Leader Labour Party 2020

Educated in what Alistair Campbell might have called a 'bog standard comp' (possibly even 'less than') she left school at 16 with no qualifications and also pregnant. Her subsequent evolution into a national politician is extraordinary. She studied at Stockport College for a social work qualification and began work in this area. However, her lifeline proved to be joining the trade union Unison of which she became a local representative and then for the whole northwest region. Her assertively extrovert personality quickly caused her to stand out and she became nominated in September 2014 as Labour candidate for Ashton under Lyne, being elected in 2015, becoming Deputy Leader in April 2020.

Alan Johnson (1950–), held several Cabinet offices including Home Office, Health, Education, Trade and Industry, and Work and Pensions

Like Raynor, another remarkable back story. Johnson was born to a philandering pub pianist who abandoned his family and was effectively orphaned when his cleaner mother died of a heart condition when he was only 13 years old. His elder sister, Linda, proved to be his lifeline – she successfully argued with council officials to be allowed to bring up her brother in a council flat. After a period trying to succeed as a musician and future rock star, he became a postman, joined the Union of Communication Workers and, encouraged by the bewhiskered Tom Jackson, quickly rose up the hierarchy. In 1971 he joined Labour, though reckoned that at the time he was closer to Marxism in his thinking and the policies of the Communist Party of Great Britain (Johnson, 2013). He was elected as MP for Hull West and Hessle in May 1997, going on to serve in the Cabinet and be considered a candidate for the leadership.

William Whitelaw (1918–99), Home Secretary 1979–83 and other Tory Cabinet posts and de facto Deputy Leader of party 1975–91

After his landed-gentry father died when he was a still a baby, Whitelaw's local councillor mother was able to give him a comfortable and very privileged upbringing. Educated at Winchester School, a 'shy' boy, his school days taught him 'whatever your basic ability you have to work. That valuable lesson has enabled me over the years to withstand all the immense pressures which Senior Cabinet Minister have to bear' (Whitelaw, 1989, p.4). His housemaster, Major ('Bobber') Robertson gave him huge support, both at school and with sustained correspondence way into his later life. His Cambridge experience took place under the shadow of imminent war. However he 'emerged from Cambridge as one of those rare subsequent members of the House of Commons who had never been inside the Union or joined any political party' (ibid., p.8). It seems the traumatic experiences in the war, where he was a tank commander at a very early age and saw some fairly bloody action in 1944, provided him, along with so many others of that wartime generation – including Ted Heath – with a determination to prevent another European war. Having returned to Scotland after the war he found an amazingly compatible life partner and 'embarked on a career in politics', standing in a then Labour-held seat, East Dunbartonshire. He withstood the hostility of big Clydeside audiences: he lost by over 4,000 votes but reduced that figure by 1,000 when he fought the seat again in 1951 when Labour's redoubtable David Kirkwood had stood down. He finally made it into the Commons for Penrith and the Border in 1955.

Margaret Thatcher (1925–2013), PM 1979–90

At the 1948 Llandudno Conservative Party conference, fresh out of Oxford, the future PM was chatting to John Grant MP whom she had known at university, when he asked if she would like to become an MP.

> 'Well, yes,' was my reply, but there's not much hope of that. The chances of being selected are just nil at the moment. I might have added that with no private income of my own there was no way I could have afforded to be an MP on the salary then available. I had not even tried to get on the Party's list of approved candidates'
>
> *(Thatcher, 1995, p.63)*

Grant later met the chair of the Dartford Conservative Association who was actively looking for a candidate and suggested the 'very good' Roberts but was told that for a 'real industrial stronghold, I don't think a woman would do at all'. Thatcher comments, 'This was quite definitely a man's world into which not just angels feared to tread' (ibid., p.63). So, for a woman seeking her way in politics, in the wake of the Second World War, her ambitions were locked within the restrictions of finance, and, even more crucially, the widespread prejudice, after a war fought and won chiefly by men, against the idea that women could succeed in politics.

But she showed up well in the selection process and was adopted as candidate to fight a 20,000 majority. Though not a natural public speaker she was both composed and impeccably well prepared. As one of her rivals on the day, Bill Deedes, recalled, 'Once she opened her mouth, the rest of us began to look rather second rate.' The media took up the fact that she was both the youngest and only female candidate. At her formal adoption meeting, where a new candidate seeks to impress the rank-and-file party activists, her father also spoke – for the first time they were on the same platform. He explained that he had always been Liberal but 'now it was the Conservatives who stood for the old Liberalism' – little did he know how true that was going to be of his daughter. A few weeks later fate was again on the march when Margaret Roberts attended a dinner party in her honour: there she met the managing director of the Atlas Preservative Company, which made paint and chemicals: Dennis Thatcher. They bonded over 'his professional interest in paint and mine in plastics' and, as for politics? She 'discovered that his views were no-nonsense Conservatism'. She was elected to the Commons for Finchley in 1959.

Tony Blair (1953–), PM 1997–2007 and Labour Leader 1994–2007

Born into what had become an upper-middle-class family, Blair must have absorbed quite an awareness of politics whilst attending Edinburgh's Fettes

School (known as Scotland's Eton). Moreover, his barrister father – born out of wedlock to two entertainers – was highly political and desperately wanted to become a Tory MP (yes, a *Tory* MP). To complete his unusual provenance his mother was the daughter of an Orange-supporting butcher who settled in Glasgow in 1916. His father's ambitions – once a communist in his youth, Leo became a 'huge supporter of Margaret Thatcher' – crashed when he suffered a major stroke aged 40. On entering Oxford, Blair thew himself into becoming a student pop star but, once cured of that, began to shift in a political direction and after leaving Oxford he joined the Labour Party at the same time becoming a barrister pupil of the leftish barrister, Derry Irvine. Through him, he met senior figures in the Labour Party including John Smith. His barrister wife to be, Cherie, was also a committed Labour member and she exerted more left-wing influence upon him. But the real political epiphany occurred for Blair when he first entered the House of Commons – it was the drama of British politics! He was

> thunderstruck. It just hit me. ... This was the place I wanted to be ... to be a Member of Parliament, to be one of the legislators of the land, to walk unhindered through those hallowed corridors and chambers; what excitement, what an adventure, what a sense of arrival a new and higher level of existence.
>
> *(Blair, 2010, pp.34–35)*

An interesting footnote to Blair's journey into politics is confided in his brilliant BBC interview with Peter Hennessy where he recalls a powerful trigger point occurring when he read the Deutscher trilogy of Trotsky, noting 'a very, very, odd thing, just literally it was a like a light going on ... the notion of having a cause and a purpose and one bigger than yourself or your own ambition'. Who would have believed Blair had been led into politics by Leon Trotsky! (Hennessy and Shepherd, 2009, p.418). He was elected for Sedgefield in June 1983.

David Cameron (1966–), PM 2010–16

Born into a wealthy, privileged upper-middle-class family, Cameron was educated at Heatherdown prep school (Princes Andrew and Edward both alumni) then the exclusive politician's 'nursery', Eton College. Initially he did not shine academically, receiving only moderate O-level grades, but during the next two years he underwent a kind of upsurge of ambition: 'I realised that I needed to stop moping around behind my brother and make my own way. Crucially, instead of drifting academically I needed to make a greater effort. It was time to pull my finger out' (Cameron, 2019, p.24).

His biographers discerned:

> an awakening of interest in politics, a steely ambition and an academic facility flowered within him, seemingly simultaneously, just in time for his A' levels. As long as the will is present, Eton's teaching support – in his case his Tutor Tim Young – is clearly very impressive.
>
> *(Elliott and Hanning, 2012, p.37)*

After his first year of A-levels, he won Eton's Trial Prize for Politics and later another prize for work on the Spanish Civil War followed by a strong interest in the politics of Northern Ireland. 'Had Cameron ... decided on a career in politics from an early age?' ask his biographers. He had not, but his second tutor, John Clark, disagrees:

> I'm pretty sure I viewed him as politically ambitious even then. He was articulate and politically motivated and interested. He was interested in the business of politics as a profession, even at that stage. I don't think he'd planned it out the way Heseltine is supposed to have done. He found politics stimulating, in a good pragmatic Conservative way. He was intrigued by politics as an art, as a way of resolving problems.
>
> *(ibid., p.39)*

However, a close friend in Cameron's House doubted he was headed for a political career: 'We were convinced there would never be an Etonian prime minister again. I certainly didn't think Dave would have a go at it. His only acting roles at school were as a serving man and as a girl. He was never outrageously extrovert' (ibid., p.40). Interestingly though, given his passionate leadership of Remain in 2016, he was known to rail passionately against the shortcomings of the European Union. A final apercu made of Cameron when at Eton was the comment in class, 'You are as tough as nails and no one realises it' (ibid., pp.35–42). He entered Brasenose College for PPE in 1985 but had already spent a highly 'political' gap year researching for Tim Rathbone MP and attending debates in the Commons. His Oxford tutor, Vernon Bogdanor, reckoned him 'one of his ablest' ever students. After winning his first in PPE in 1988 he discovered a welcome home in the Conservative Research Department, where he found a group of friends – wealthy, privately educated, Oxbridge later to be dubbed 'The Notting Hill Set'. Now with a future career as a professional politician clearly established, Cameron was elected for the safe Oxford seat of Whitney in 2001. What did he plan to do with the premiership if he were able to win it? Cameron must have been one of the least ideological PMs in power post 1945. George Osborne once answered a question on why Cameron wanted to be PM at a conference I attended, thus: 'Because he thinks he'd be good at it.' Something an Eton education probably instils into most of its pupils. Cameron was certainly highly skilled politically but his judgement over Brexit brought him down until his renaissance as Foreign Secretary courtesy of Rishi Sunak in 2023.

Assessing the 'trigger points' and related social status

The above biography 'grabs' reveal how really varied the 'trigger points' are for entering the political arena and how social background is critical in each case in determining when and where allegiance is permanently placed. My upper-middle-class recruits – Whitelaw, Nicolson, Prior and Cameron – all with links to well-established families and fringes of the aristocracy, were all brought up in environments fully freighted with British political culture. Anyone attending Eton had to be very aware of the huge input its alumni have made to political personnel for centuries past: currently 20 out of Britain's 57 PMs have worn its top hats. Nicolson not only benefitted from an excellent education but his spell in the diplomatic service plunged him into practical politics and set him up well for his future journalistic and political careers once he made the transition after 1929. When his gamble that Mosley's New Party was to be a progressive initiative evolved into the British Union of Fascists, he quickly retreated into the mainstream.

The well-educated and solidly upper-middle-class David Owen and Nick Clegg flirted with careers respectively in medicine and Brussels administration before succumbing to the seductions of the 'politics bug'. Next down the hierarchy were the maybe predictably Tory-inclined offspring of small-business-owning families, Shephard and the precocious Hague, both encouraged by mothers active in local politics and civil society. Hague's famous conference speech catapulted him into politics, even though he had no idea he would be allowed to deliver it. Betty Boothroyd typified the adventurous northern working-class female who made it to London and did all she could to find that way into a political career.

Then at the bottom of the occupation pile come Johnson, Raynor and the extraordinary Ernest Bevin. If the above people are drawn from social categories AB, C1/C2, then all three of these are close to the DE categories. Their personal experience and ambition to change social conditions must have been sustained to extraordinary degrees to overcome the hurdles that did not confront those higher up the social hierarchy.

A final note on the tough backgrounds of entrants to the legislature is demanded by a member of the nationalist group of MPs: Steven Flynn who became Commons leader of the SNP (Scottish National Party) group in December 2022. This (at the time of writing) 34 year old is of working-class provenance and suffered 17 years of severe ill health from avascular necrosis, a poor blood circulation condition that causes a disintegration and collapse of bone tissue. Much of his time was spent in hospital involving surgery and painful traction procedures. Nevertheless he acquired a Dundee university degree in history and politics followed by an master of arts. He told the News Agents podcast, that when he first entered the Commons he was on crutches but an artificial hip enabled him to move normally for the first time since early childhood. Overcoming such early hardships and then rising so quickly to party leadership, sets a standard of resilience and determination for which it is hard find an equal.

Public schools

One institution that is ubiquitously present in the CVs of successful politicians is the British 'public' school system of private education. The Clarendon group of top fee-paying schools – Eton, Harrow, Westminster, St Pauls, Merchant Taylors, Shrewsbury, Rugby and Charterhouse – bestow a very many times more likelihood to become members of the British 'elite' than the products of any other school. These schools charge fees of upwards of £30,000–40,000 for boarders so it is essentially members of the rich upper-middle classes whose children populate these elite schools. To put it another way, the children of this demographic represent the 'long list' for membership of British elites, whether it be Parliament, the Cabinet, the judiciary, the armed forces, business or any other elite grouping. The Clarendon schools are the top tip of a privately educated 7 per cent sized iceberg of the population: boarders comprise only 1 per cent. In June 2019, 39 per cent of the Cabinet were privately educated compared to 9 per cent of Labour's Shadow Cabinet. Inevitably Britain's social mobility is reflected in patterns of recruitment to elite positions. In theory anyone can enter the Commons and become PM but, on average, it requires more than the energy and talents mentioned in this opening chapter (see Jones et al., 2022, ch. 8).

The Oxford Union

'If you can speak in this country, you can do anything' – Churchill to future Tory minister Quintin Hogg when visiting the Oxford Union (Kuper, 2022a, p.60).

Founded in 1823, the Oxford Union is separate and independent of the university and, despite only allowing women to join in 1963, it has a significance for ambitious politicians that precedes entry into Parliament. In his entertaining and perceptive 2022 study *Chums: How a Tiny Caste of Oxford Tories Took Over the UK*, Simon Kuper entitles one of his chapters, 'The Children's Parliament'. It mimics the adult equivalent in its procedures, style and ambience, including a late bar, and offers a smooth transition for those privately educated scions of the upper-middle classes into an extended 'rehearsal' for the real thing. Harold Macmillan found the Union: 'fun because it was an opportunity to learn something of the parliamentary system, to which I always had ambitions' (Kuper, 2022a, p.59). Michael Heseltine, who had occupied the president's chair – which sat on a raised dais like a throne – called it ' "the first step to becoming prime minister'. Once you ascended the Union, Downing Street felt within your grasp' (ibid., p.62). The top public schools, especially Eton, of course, offered discussion and debating societies (for example Eton's Political Society and Debating Society) providing practice in speaking in public, reinforced by the burgeoning personal confidence that such an education usually bestows. Rachel Johnson judged such pupils are 'given a huge head start; you'd get incredible heavy hitters going to address "Polsoc" and talking to the boys' (ibid., p.65).

Kuper comments further: 'The Union was a reason for politically inclined students, especially Tory public schoolboys, to choose Oxford over Cambridge'. Elections for Union officers can be so intense 'some students could be described as "virtually professional politicians, complete with support staff" ' also provided practice for the core activities of such people in the beckoning adult world. Not only could speakers pirouette and pose in their white or (if speaker) black ties, they could face off against 'senior ministers and parliamentarians up close' as Christopher Hitchens noted, adding 'and be amazed once again how ignorant and plain stupid were the people who claimed to run the country' (Kuper, 2022a, p.61). Edward Heath first met Churchill in 1936, chatting with him until 2.00 a.m.

Malcolm Turnbull, future PM of Australia, had this to say about his experience at Oxford:

> It was the first place that anyone asked me essentially 'what does your father do?'. People actually were hung up on how they spoke, their social background, where they went to school and so forth. It's [the Union] standard student politics, which is all about getting to the top of the greasy pole ... student politics is all about the game. And I think it's fair to say that some people who go from being involved in student politics are more enamoured of the game than they are of what should be the objective of politics, which is good public policy.
>
> *(ibid., p.63–64)*

SELECTION AS A CANDIDATE

When it comes to standing in front of a constituency selection meeting this imbalance of skills can become clear. Privately educated products tend to speak in a received pronunciation (RP) accent and tend to be well educated and confident to an extent much less common in comprehensive school products. The big parties have well-established selection procedures requiring acceptance on a 'candidates list' and then various stages of acceptance by party committees. But the main selection forum is usually an interrogatory forum of party members. Traditionally such gatherings have tended to favour men over women and native Britons over those with an immigrant background. These prejudices have been changing fast in recent decades – see Chapter 10 – but the privately educated still enjoy advantages. A crucial aspect of this process is that selection panels tend to choose someone who will effectively represent constituency and party in the House of Commons: crucially for this study, they do not necessarily choose a person who is going to make a good junior or Cabinet minister.

Extrovert or introvert?

Finally, returning, briefly, to who succeeds as a politician: outgoing extrovert or quiet introvert. Who performs better? There's a certain stereotype of a politician, possibly coloured by foreign examples, of a relentlessly extroverted 'in your face' kind of person. In UK politics, during my lifetime, we've had the likes of the hugely moustachioed Sir Gerald Nabarro of the 1950s and 1960s, the luxurious hair-flicking Heseltine (aka 'Hezza'), Boris Johnson and other unfazed characters like the aggressively vocal Speaker, John Bercow, not forgetting the student, guitar playing Tony Blair. All outgoing types you'd think? Maybe, but extroverts never wholly dominate the political scenery: we have the example of Clement Attlee ('a modest man with much to be modest about' quipped Churchill of his wartime deputy), Geoffrey Howe (whose anger routed his diffidence when delivering the coup de grace to Margaret Thatcher's reign) and Theresa May whose most rebellious exploit when younger was running through unharvested wheat fields. And there was, of course, the probably ill-selected Tory Leader, Iain Duncan Smith, who, despairing of shifting the polls growled, somewhat risibly, to the 2004 Tory conference, 'The Quiet Man is turning up the volume!' – he was dropped as Leader soon afterwards. The quiet men and women all have had their moments but it is probably the case that extroverted, confident characters have a better chance of surviving and prospering than the quiet and modest.

Height

It is often argued that politicians in the United States tend to be tall and that being tall is a factor in determining votes and, hence, political success. There might be something in this suggestion but probably only a smidgeon: of the 45 US presidents to date, 20 have been 6ft or over – Abraham Lincoln was 6ft 4 inches, Lyndon B. Johnson, Donald Trump and Bill Clinton 6ft 3.5 inches, but James Madison was only 5ft 4 inches and over half of the 45 presidents have been under 6ft. Maybe the origins of this tendency dates back to earlier conflicts between humans where height gave a marked advantage.

In modern times physical violence is mostly not personal for politicians, but when the researcher asked volunteers to depict leaders and ordinary citizens, they drew leaders taller. An article in *The Times* concluded height was no sine qua non of political success, citing Churchill (5' 6"), Napoleon (5' 5"), Volodymyr Zelensky (5' 7") and Rishi Sunak (5' 7"). Women of course tend to be less tall; Thatcher and Angela Merkel (5' 5") and Giorgia Meloni only 5' 4" (Malvern and Azoor, 2023).

Charisma

The concept of 'charisma' demands some attention. Max Weber, who popularised the role of charisma in human affairs admitted to its 'mysterious, elusive quality'. It has a quality of the mystical too, as if endowed by some spiritual power: a quality that inspires devotion, a willingness to be led. Anyone so blessed must surely have a few laps' start on rivals? One would think and expect so, but the problem is that the quality is so elusive that some people are credited with having it by some but hotly denied it by others.

Considering the role of charisma in UK politics is difficult. Who can be said to occupy this category? Lloyd George, Churchill, probably, but only once their careers were established. Freakish charismatics like Hitler, Ghandi, Joan of Arc are few in number in any case. Some people claim Boris Johnson has this magic quality but is he charismatic? Many, including this author, would deny it. Corbyn similarly has been awarded the quality by supporters but my visit to one of his rallies revealed, to me at least, a rather pedestrian politician, rehearsing hackneyed, decades-old lines – certainly not a future PM. Probably the closest to 'charismatic' we have seen in UK politics are Tony Blair and Margaret Thatcher. In US politics, John F. Kennedy stands out but supporters of Trump would claim their guy should be included. Awarding Donald Trump the 'charisma' label is not easy and I often think its connected to other factors: in Churchill's case, his use of iconic 'character' props like the cigar, the V sign; in Trump's case his fame as a allegedly successful uber business man as well as his media fame via television where he transferred from 'celebrity businessman' to 'celebrity politician'; in Thatcher's case? Her blazing conviction, her handbag of course but also her shining, immaculate self-presentation.

A key aspect of charisma is the way in which 'charismatics' are *perceived*. Nigel Farage, someone whose several attempts to become an MP have so far failed, became the focus of the successful campaign to take Britain out of the European Union. His props were usually a pint of beer, a fag (cigarette) and a cocky grin but he was able to appear charismatic to that key group of disenchanted lower income/education demographic who voted in such heavy numbers that the initial opinion poll majority for Remain was overturned on the day, albeit narrowly, in June 2016. Farage had extraordinary verbal skills, able to rouse apathetic non-voters to get up from their sofas and vote Leave. I watched his TV debate against Nick Clegg and, being a Remainer, thought Farage had been crushed. My mistake! Polls showed he won it 2–1. The BBC clearly valued his presence and invited him to be part of its *Question Time* panel a record 33 times from the 1990s onwards, despite not even being an MP or member of a party with a Commons presence (apart from the defecting former Tory MPs, Douglass Carswell and Mark Reckless).

Other possible charismatics? Enoch Powell was a spell-binding speaker with his burning, staring eyes and his near poetic rhetoric often drawing upon his great knowledge of the classics. I remember the superb lecture he gave to some hundreds of my students at a sixth form conference: mind you, an equally charismatic speaker, in my view, was the journalist Paul Foot. Another possibility? Alex Salmond, with his easy relaxed verbal style, was also someone who did much to build support for nationalism north of the border: to SNP supporters he proved a charismatic Leader for several years during which he poached Scotland from Labour for his nationalists.

Courage

This is possibly an underrated and underappreciated requirement in that politicians *being* politicians are taken so much for granted in the modern day. Winston Churchill served in trenches near Ypres in 1916 and, whilst his fellow officers, all Conservative supporters, at first treated him coolly, his bravery in the front line soon earned their respect. That kind of courage was again a requirement for some serving soldier MPs in the 1939–45 war and, indeed, a certain degree of physical courage is needed day to day for current MPs, especially since the murders of Jo Cox and David Amess plus regular death threats on social media. Another kind of courage is also needed to take up certain issues in the Commons and to brave what can be an intimidating atmosphere in the Commons chamber. Margaret Thatcher, for example, famously displayed courage throughout her time as an MP – raising sensitive and unpopular issues and leading the country though the Falklands War 1982–84. It also has to be said that female MPs have to survive and try to prosper in a Commons culture that is more male based than receptive to females. Finally, MPs recruited from working-class backgrounds also find the Commons intimidating given the large percentage of privately educated MPs on the Conservative side plus the domination of those educated at Oxbridge and other universities.

References and further reading

Adonis, A. (2020) *Ernest Bevin: Labour's Churchill*. Biteback.
Adonis, A. (2021) *It's the Leader, Stupid: Change Makers in Modern Politics*. Amazon.
Barber, M. (2007) *Instruction to Deliver: Fighting to Transform Britain's Public Services*. Methuen.
Blair, A. (2010) *A Journey*. Hutchinson.
Boothroyd, B. (2002) *Betty Boothroyd: The Autobiography*. Arrow.
Bowers, C. (2012) *Nick Clegg: The Biography*. Biteback.
Cameron, D. (2019) *For the Record*. William Collins.
Cooper, D. (1953) *Old Men Forget*. Faber.
Crick, M. (1997). *Michael Heseltine: A Biography*. Hamish Hamilton.
Crick, M. (2022) *One Party After Another: The Disruptive Life of Nigel Farage*. Simon & Schuster.
Currie, E. (2002) *Diaries 1987–92*. Little Brown.
Elliott, F. and Hanning, J. (2012) *Cameron: Practically a Conservative*. Fourth Estate.
Garnett, M. and Aitken, I. (2002) *Splendid! Splendid! The Authorised Biography of Willie Whitelaw*. Cape.
Green, J. (1982) *The Book of Political Quotes*. Angus & Robertson.
Greenstein, F. (1975) *Personality and Politics*. Norton.
Hennessy, P. and Shepherd, L. (2009) *The Complete Reflections*. Haus.
Heseltine, M. (2000) *Life in the Jungle, My Autobiography*. Coronet.
House of Commons Library (2006) 'Power to the people: An independent inquiry into Britain's democracy'. Chaired by Helena Kennedy.
Johnson, A. (2013) *This Boy: A Memoir of Childhood*. Bantam.
Jones, B. (2010) 'Climbing the greasy pole: Promotion in British politics'. *Political Quarterly*, Vol. 81, Issue 4, 616–626.
Jones, B., Norton, P. and Hertner, I. (2022) *Politics UK*, 10th edition. Routledge.
Kennedy, H. (2006) 'Power to the People: An independent inquiry into Britain's Democracy'. House of Commons Library.
Kuper, S. (2022a) *Chums: How a Tiny Caste of Oxford Tories Took Over the UK*. Profile.
Kuper, S. (2022b) '"A nursery of the Commons": How the Oxford Union created today's ruling political class'. Guardian, 19 April.
Leadsom, A. (2023) *Snakes and Ladders: Navigating the Ups and Downs of Politics*. Biteback.
Malvern, J. and Azoor, A. (2023) 'Rise of the "short kings": Can you guess how our leaders measure up?' *The Times*, 15 July.
Mason, C. (2013) 'Boris Johnson and the future PM question'. BBC News, 26 March.
Nadler, J. (2000) *William Hague: In His Own Right*. Politico.
News Agents Podcast, accessed 31 July 2023.
Nicolson, H. (1966) *Diaries and Letters 1930–1964*. Penguin.
Owen, D. (1991) *Time to Declare*. Michael Joseph.
Owen, D. (2007) *The Hubris Syndrome: Bush, Blair and the Intoxication of Power*. Politico's.
Parry, G., Moyser, G. and Day, N. (1992) *Political Participation and Democracy in Britain*. Cambridge University Press.
Paxman, J. (2002) *The Political Animal: An Anatomy*. Michael Joseph.
Paxman, J. (2002) 'Paxman's politics'. *Sunday Times*, 13 October.

Pimlott, B. (1993) Harold Wilson. HarperCollins.
Potton, E. (2023) 'I doubt that Trainspotting would be published in today's climate'. *The Times*, 11 May.
Prior, J. (1986) *A Balance of Power*. Hamish Hamilton.
Rawnsley, A. (2022) 'Boris Johnson clings to office like chewing gum to a shoe but he is becoming unstuck'. Observer, 24 April.
Reeve, A., Friedman, S. and Flemmen, M. (2017) 'The decline and persistence of the old boy: Private school and elite recruitment 1987–2016'. *American Sociology Review*, Vol. 82, Issue 6, 1–28.
Riddell, P. (1993) *Honest Opportunism*. Hamish Hamilton.
Searing, D. (1994) *Westminster's World: Understanding Political Roles*. Harvard University Press.
Seldon, A. (2007) *Blair Unbound*. Simon & Schuster.
Shephard, G. (2000) *Shephard's Watch*. Politico's.
Tebbit, N. (1989) *Upwardly Mobile*. Futura.
Thatcher, M. (1995) *The Path to Power*. HarperCollins.
The Times (2023) Times Diary, 16 June.
Waddington, D. (2012) David Waddington: Memoirs. Biteback.
Wanis, P. (2020) 'What really motivates politicians? Is it service, legacy or the temptation of power and perks?' www.patrickwanis.com/what-really-motivates-politicians-is-it-service-legacy-or-the-temptation-of-power-perks/.
Weinberg, A. (2011) *The Psychology of Politicians*. Cambridge University Press.
Whitelaw, W. (1989) *The Whitelaw Memoirs*. Aurum.

2

NEGOTIATING PROMOTION

> Attaining Cabinet rank is an enormously significant step for a minister, the promotion places him above the salt; there is huge gulf between the most popular and successful junior minister and the least known, least senior of Cabinet ministers.
>
> (James, 1999, p.3)

So, you've done it! You have won a seat in the House of Commons; intoxicated still, quite possibly, with the voice of your Returning Officer announcing your victory. But what do you do now? You haven't really won a career, only the opportunity to build one in one of the most competitive environments anywhere. The biographies suggest new MPs now pass through at least early two stages: *networking* with the new fellow MPs, especially those elected at the same general election, and then a whole-hearted attempt at 'learning the rules of the game'. I recall a former Workers' Educational Association tutor friend, Mike Noble, who made it into the Commons for Labour at Rossendale (1974–79), who amused adult audiences with his initial encounters. 'I was given a clothes hanger which I thought was useful. What's that tag fastened on the one side of it? I asked. Oh, that's to hang your sword through.' To say the least, being an MP entails a history-laden working environment like no other.

My first chapter examined the sort of people who decide to enter this minority activity – some of them ideologically committed, others fascinated or even obsessed by the risks and thrills of what has often been likened to a 'game'; and many who even genuinely mean they want to make a difference and leave the world a better place after their contribution. This chapter, drawing again on some of the dipped into biographies of the foregoing chapter, tries

DOI: 10.4324/9781003405085-3

to pick up on some of their stories once in the Commons. However a good place to start is with a quotation by Sir Harry Legge-Bourke, a former chair of the Conservative's 1922 Committee, which correctly suggests that some MPs are not necessarily interested in ministerial careers, as will be discussed in Chapter 3; this study's focus, of course, is on those who do have ministerial ambitions. Legge-Bourke explains the advice he gave to new members:

> I always ask them first to make up their mind whether they seek power or influence, because the two things are very different. There are some who want office and are ambitious from their career point of view. There are others who prefer to get into a position where they can exercise influence on those who have power. To me it's a much more sophisticated thing to exercise influence than it is to use power.
>
> *(Searing, 1994, p.80)*

Ministers in British government

'Ministers stand at the heart of British government' writes the constitutional authority Philip Norton. 'In legal terms they are the most powerful figures in government.' This is because an Act of Parliament specifically enables Secretaries of State to undertake action, not the PM, or Cabinet. The most senior rank is Secretary of State but there are different levels of junior minister who often comprise a team reporting to their Cabinet level superior. A team of civil servants staff each department, each headed up by a Permanent Secretary who will have spent a lifetime in government service, quite possibly in one department, guaranteeing intimate knowledge of its responsibilities and activities. Ministers work closely with senior people like this who, unlike their American counterparts, will usually stay in post even when governments change. Senior ministers have political advisers who provide advice independent of the civil service often from the party-political standpoint. Each minister will have a Private Personal Secretary (as opposed to the other PPS: Parliamentary Private Secretary), who will play a huge role in organising his or her daily activities. Most departments now have departmental boards chaired by its Permanent Secretary and his/her senior colleagues. Norton notes that in 1945 a department usually had two or three ministers. These days there are fewer departments but they are bigger and boast more junior ministers: the Department for Business and Skills had 11 ministers; the Home Office, eight (Norton, 2022, p.506).

'First rung' on the ladder: Parliamentary Private Secretary

This role is often dismissed as a footling, unimportant position: an 'unpaid aide de camp'. They are not even officially members of the government: they remain mere backbench MPs and are sometimes referred to as 'bag carriers', scarcely worthy of note. Adding insult to injury they are not allowed the single valued advantage of not being in government: their independence when voting – they are all expected to vote along with the paid ministerial or 'payroll' vote. They qualify for expenses but any overseas visits for Parliamentary Private Secretaries (PPSs) are only allowed after approval by the PM. So why was John Major so delighted to become Patrick Mayhew's PPS? Why was Gyles Brandreth so delighted when Stephen Dorrell asked him to become his PPS in February 1993? 'At Oxford', Dorrell recalled where both he and Brandreth attended at the same time, 'I used to sit at your feet at the Union. They told me I could have a PPS last year, but I didn't like the people they had on offer. I thought I'd wait for you' (Brandreth, 2000, p.157). Gyles confided to his diary, 'They say he's a coming man, a certainty for the Cabinet, a possibility as leader. I couldn't have been more pleased' (ibid., p.57).

The reason both men were so pleased is that this position is much more important than it might seem from the foregoing. If one's first step on a journey is the most important in determining one's destination then becoming a PPS is that first tentative step on the ministerial ladder. Political scientist Philip Buck points out that 90 per cent of MPs who won seats after 1918 and went on to become ministers began their ministerial lives either as PPSs or junior ministers. Technically PPS is indeed an aide but within a department; he or she joins in the daily ministerial conferences, helping to discuss policy and learning the position they have an ambition to later occupy (Buck, 1963, pp.624–632). An advantage of this role too is that a new MP might have joined the entourage of a minister headed for higher things and whose coattails might assist future promotions. When I asked Roy Jenkins the quickest route to promotion he answered 'Get yourself a senior minister as sponsor' (private interview). A final thought is that, whilst an individual PPS might not wield much clout, when it came to the vote on 22 April 2022 on the issue of whether Boris Johnson's possibly misleading comments to the House over Partygate should be referred to the Privileges Committee, it was the threat of 'at least a fair number of the 41 parliamentary private secretaries – the first rung on the ministerial ladder – who were prepared to resign', which caused the whips to call a U-turn on their three-line delaying amendment (Bond, 2022).

Junior ministers

PPSs are not really ministers. The formal hierarchy of authority within a government department starts at its lowest level with PPS, moves up to Parliamentary Under Secretary of State (PUS), continues with Minister of State (MoS) and is topped by Secretary of State, with the hoped-for ambition of most MPs, a seat in the Cabinet.

PUS

PUS is seen as the second rung on the ministerial ladder. The Ministerial and Other Salaries Act, 1975 lays down that there can only be 83 paid ministers (not counting Chancellor), up to 3 law officers and 22 whips. There is a ceiling of 50 on this number of ministers senior to a PUS: if 50 senior ministers are appointed then no more than 33 PUSs can be appointed. However, there is no limit on such appointments in the House of Lords.

The Duke of Devonshire, who became a PUS under Macmillan in October 1960 once said: ‘No one who hasn’t been a PUS has any conception of how unimportant a PUS is’ (Theakston, 1987, p.55). Macmillan, related by marriage to the Duke, promoted him to MoS in September 1962.

MoS

This is the next step up the ladder and one next to Cabinet. It is sought after for its status plus the expectation it carries of imminent Cabinet membership. (Kevin Theakston’s *Junior Ministers* is highly recommended on this subject.)

First day as a minister

Readers (especially students of politics) are highly recommended the two-part podcast by the Institute for Government entitled ‘Becoming a Minister’. It features recollections from former ministers, Estelle Morris, Jim Murphy, George Eustice and Andrea Leadsom and stresses the need to clarify what they are expected to achieve and the need to study and absorb civil service advice, in particular the fat policy guide folder made up specially for them.

The Cabinet

The British Cabinet evolved during the sixteenth century and was essentially the monarch’s team of senior officials appointed by him, under the command of a head or ‘prime’ minister as he became known, to carry out his governmental wishes under a degree of control by Parliament. As the power of monarchs declined and the power of representative democracies grew, Cabinet assumed the role of the nation’s senior governing committee. As Simon James (1999) notes in his *British Cabinet*:

> Between the early nineteenth century, when the Cabinet assumed a form modern ministers might find familiar, and the First World War, the character of the system remained much the same. The span of business was relatively narrow. There was little administrative, as opposed to pre-legislative, work to be done. A minister’s life was relatively leisurely (Asquith’s Agriculture Minister put in two hours at the office each day).

> The Cabinet was small – average of fourteen members – and its meetings, held once or twice a week, were informal and discursive.
>
> *(ibid., p.2)*

Most members were usually well known to each other via school, university, blood or marital connections and shared similar social lives. However it's surprising that this rather cosy informality represented the governing peak of an empire covering a quarter of the planet's surface and a fifth of its inhabitants. This relaxed approach had to be abandoned however during the First World War when Lloyd George introduced a Cabinet Secretary and Cabinet Office, creating a proper administrative support for the mountain of complex tasks government took on during the war. During the Second World War, which entailed the total mobilisation of the country, the number of departments burgeoned in number and size. The size of the Cabinet – tiny during the war – subsequently grew to number over 20 and 'ministerial life became frantic and high pressured and several of Attlee's colleagues literally worked themselves to death' (ibid., p.2). These days, Cabinets have become more of a forum for reporting on work in progress – much of its work carried out via a network of Cabinet committees – but, as James notes:

> This does not mean that the Cabinet has ceased to matter. It is still the supreme tier of British government and an aura of importance still surrounds it. Attaining Cabinet rank is an enormously significant step for a minister, the promotion that places him above the salt; there is a huge gulf between the most popular and successful junior minister and the least known, least senior of cabinet ministers.
>
> *(ibid., p.3)*

Sitting at the Cabinet table

Gaining membership of this supreme elite committee represents the holy grail for ambitious MPs. Rising from humble backbencher to Cabinet member is the probable ambition of most new MPs but only a small percentage make it; for others the journey proves too onerous or an election takes them out of the game maybe for a while or for good. I start my analysis of how these ambition-driven politicians fared in the rough and tumble of parliamentary politics, with someone from very humble beginnings who ended up in Downing Street.

John Major (1943–)

When he first entered parliament, John Major joined other new members, forming alliances. Perhaps proving that the Commons is indeed the 'best dining club in London', Major records that:

> within weeks, like-minded Conservative colleagues established or joined existing dining clubs. The *Blue Chips* included those new MPs with most experience of the inner ring of government, often through working at Central Office or as a front bench aide – Waldegrave, Patten, Cranbourne and Garel-Jones foremost amongst them: It was the Praetorian guard of the 1979 intake.
>
> *(Major, 1999, p.67)*

As someone used to working out of Central Office, Major obviously had also given himself a flying start. Initially he joined the Guy Fawkes Club (stars included David Mellor, Brian Mawhinney and Graham Bright) but after 1983, he settled into the Blue Chips grouping.

When discussing ambition, during an early meeting, Major had confessed to colleagues his emphatic goal: 'Chancellor!' while Bright offered 'PPS to the PM'. Entering the Commons with a reputation already built carried with it an expectation of 'early promotion'. Major notes this was not for all: 'Others chose the tortoise's strategy and set out painstakingly to learn the way Parliament worked' (ibid., p.67). It has to be said that Major, as a former employee of the Standard Bank, must have been well aware of the processes whereby one ascends the corporate ladder – not too exotically different in essence, after all, from the famous greasy pole of politics: exhibit competence, and if you've got it, flair, and make damn sure it is noted by one's seniors.

Major was also aware of the different forums and workshops of parliament:

> The Chamber of the Commons is the display cabinet for the world at large, but committees and backbench groups are where worth is often recognised by the cognoscenti within Parliament and especially the all-seeing Whips Office who hold Members' fates in their hands as surely as any prime minister.
>
> *(ibid., p.67)*

Elections for the 1922 Committee, the equivalent of a Tory MPs' trade union, were an early initiation into the tribal currents of the new MP's daily life. Elected as joint secretary of the Backbench Environment Group, he acquired the vital office space, supported by the services of a trusted former secretary from his days in Lambeth who transferred to him from John Patten. His first real leg-up arrived in 1981 when he was invited to become PPS to Patrick Mayhew and Timothy Raison, Ministers of State at the Home Office. He revealingly states of them: 'They both had the solid common-sense instincts of traditional Tories, with a fine distaste for ideology' (ibid., p.73). Major's initiation into the Commons was short and successful: 'As a new backbencher I was as happy as Bunter in a bakery' (ibid., p.70). He soon added the post of a junior Environment whip to his CV and in October 1984 was made a senior whip ('that bit closer to the chancellorship'; ibid, p.83–84) from where he became the recipient of some surprising, counterintuitive luck: he had a serious row with the PM herself.

It was at a dinner where whips reported on backbench feeling to their collective boss, the PM. 'They don't like some of our policies', Major stated bluntly. 'They're worried that capital expenditure is being sacrificed to current spending.'

> Margaret did not like the message at all and began to chew the messenger. I thought her behaviour utterly unreasonable and repeated myself. 'I'm astonished at what you're saying,' she snapped. I made it clear I was merely reporting the views of many Members but she continued to attack me. I became increasingly annoyed and said, 'That's what colleagues are saying whether you like it or not – it's my job to tell you and that's what I'm doing.' Her tirade continued. By now I was past caring about tact, shaking with anger, and nearly walked out ... I was almost beside myself with fury and made no attempt to hide it. Aware that I might be wrecking my career.... I might not be promoted, I thought, but I'm not going to be humiliated.
>
> *(Major, 1999, pp.84–85)*

The next day he was astonished to be sought out and engaged in a friendly discussion by his fierce boss. A few weeks later he was reshuffled into his first departmental post: junior minister for Social Security. 'Not for the first or last time, Margaret Thatcher had surprised me' (ibid., p.85). Interestingly – see below – something similar had happened to David Owen after a row with Harold Wilson. An intriguing approach, ascribed to Dick Crossman, quotes Nye Bevan telling him: 'There are two ways to promotion Dick, you can either crawl on your belly or you can kick them up the arse. But for God's sake don't mix the two' (Jay, 2001, p.37).

Margaret Thatcher (1925–2013)

Thatcher stood for Dartford in the 1950 and 1955 elections and lost both times to Norman Dodds, a Labour MP whom she found to be kind and charming. It's a mistake to view Thatcher exclusively through any combative 'Iron Lady' prism. For example she was an admirer of Attlee: 'He was a serious man and a patriot. Quite contrary to the general tendency of politicians in the 1990s [she was writing in 1995] he was all substance and no show. His was a genuinely radical and reforming government' (Thatcher, 1995a, p.69). It is also worth mentioning that Thatcher maintained cordial relations with certain Labour MPs, especially the old-fashioned socialist types. One of these was Eric Heffer whose funeral she attended, somewhat bravely as the church was packed with scouse militants. Tony Benn later recalled that at the start of the service, Thatcher was 'clearly tearful'.

Despite her losses she reduced the Labour majority by 6,000 in 1950 and then by another 1,000 in 1951. And it's clear from her memoirs and biographies, that she had learnt a huge amount about the daily quiddities of the political life from her electoral blooding. It is often overlooked that as well as studying science at Oxford, she also trained as a barrister, passing her bar finals in December 1953 and going on to practise alongside Airey Neave and Robin Day (Moore, 2013, p.125). Being a barrister is probably the best preparatory occupation one can enter for a career in politics: it requires an aggressive approach from the outset and a skill at thinking on one's feet. Elected for Finchley in 1959, her parents were able to see their daughter enter the House. As the uber-assiduous student who was into all things, she eagerly absorbed the initial talk she received from the Chief Whip on the rules of the House and the whipping system. She also noted the (sound) advice from 'old stagers' that, as well as focusing on the big issues like finance and foreign policy, she should seek out one or two relatively minor topics to make her own and have associated with her name. She quickly established a 'pair' for when voting was not possible, with Labour's Charles Pannell ('exactly the sort of good humoured, decent Labour man, I liked'; Thatcher, 1995a, p.108).

She initially, unsurprisingly, found the Commons building 'bewildering' – it has three miles of corridors – and it took her a while to 'find my way with ease around it' (ibid., p.108). She inevitably homed in on the Tea Room and the Library. She was not seen in the Smoking Room and makes no mention of frequenting the plentiful provision of bars within its ancient precincts – though later in her career she was seldom averse to the odd tot or two of whisky. In 1959 there were only 25 women MPs and they shared desks in a collective 'Lady Member's Room'. The House, she noted, was 'a very masculine place', manifesting itself, 'above all, in the sheer volume of noise'. She also soon made an interesting observation likely to influence a new woman MP's willingness to speak in the chamber:

> In different ways I had on occasion been made to feel small because I was a woman in industry, at the bar and indeed in Tory constituency politics. But in the House of Commons we were all equals; woe betide ministers who suggest by their demeanour or behaviour that they consider themselves more equal than the rest. I soon saw with appreciation that sincerity, logic, and technical mastery of a subject could earn respect from both sides of the House.
>
> *(ibid., p.109)*

She was impressed by the range of expertise reflected in the membership as a characteristic central to an MP's future ministerial career:

> Almost whatever the subject, there would be some figure on either side of the House who would bring massive, specialised knowledge and obvious intuition to bear on it - and be listened to with respect by front and back benches alike.
>
> *(ibid., p.109)*

A stroke of luck which must have proved very educational for the future Cabinet and PM was that very soon into her term of office she came second in the Commons poll for Private Members Bills; 'never previously having so much as won a raffle' (ibid., p.109). At first she intended to offer a law weakening the closed shop: a current case was before the courts courtesy of a 'brilliant young Tory barrister' – and her later nemesis – 'called Geoffrey Howe' (ibid., p.110). However, conferring with her whips she learnt the then Tory leaders' 'ethos ... was still one of accommodating and appeasing the unions' (ibid., p.110). Instead she lasered in on the loophole used by some Labour-controlled councils to deny journalists reporting on sensitive matters.

The press had a statutory right to full meetings of the council but not its committees, so by resolving to 'go into committee' the press could thereby be excluded. Ending this loophole would seem to be something a Tory government might welcome but she discovered this was not quite the case; opposition lay not with the Minister of Housing and Local Government, but with senior officials – a case right out of the *Yes Minister* casebook one might conclude. But the new MP for Finchley was not easily deterred and she was aided by a future ally and disciple, the minister appointed as her supervisor, Sir Keith Joseph. Not only did she get to know this influential politician through delving into the intricacies of the measure: 'I learned a great deal in a very short time from the experience of devising, refashioning and negotiating for my Bill' (ibid., p.111).

She learned the power of pressure groups and how they can be played against each other but 'in the end', concluded in characteristic style:

> there is no substitute for one's own efforts ... I have always believed in the power of a personal handwritten letter – even from someone you barely know. So just before the Second Reading [of her Private Members Bill] I wrote 250 letters to government backbenchers asking them to attend and vote for my measure.
>
> *(ibid., p.112)*

Given that each letter took 10 minutes to write, her Stakhanovite epistolary efforts must have absorbed the equivalent of a 40-hour week's work. As she had not yet delivered her maiden speech – by tradition uncontroversial – it seemed she was to do so by default and in a speech decidedly controversial, to introduce her own Bill. The future Iron Lady was not devoid of nerves but the presence of some 200 MPs spurred her on and she made a fine speech, which was capped by an easy passing of the vote. RAB Butler congratulated her fulsomely and she noted:

> It was clear from the press next day ['A new star was born in Parliament' *Daily Express*, 'A Triumph', *Daily Telegraph*] that the speech had been a success – I was, for the present at least – a celebrity ... I had learned a lot and gained a good deal of confidence.
>
> *(Thatcher, 1995a, p.113)*

The Public Bodies (Admission to Meetings Act) entered the statute book in 1960.

With the gleaming new law on her CV, she stepped a little to the right in joining a rebellion on the 1961 Criminal Justice Bill in favour of introducing birching or caning for young offenders: the 'only occasion in my entire time in the House of Commons when I voted against the Party line' (ibid., p.117). Her act of rebellion did not harm her advancement. When fellow MP Pat Hornsby Smith decided to stand down from her post, Margaret heard the government was keen to maintain female ministerial numbers and that she was probably in line for something bigger than being a mere PPS, probably in 'Pensions'.

She dug out her best sapphire blue outfit to receive her promotion to the all-important second rung on the ministerial ladder; PUS to the Minister for Pensions and National Insurance. Immediately she loved the complex detail of her new job and was given 'every opportunity' (ibid., p.119) by John Boyd Carpenter and his successors in the Cabinet post. She was impressed by the civil servants who served her but when at the Department of Education, she felt they were 'self righteously socialists' (ibid., p.166). While she continued to impress at her ministry, the political weather veered into stormy conditions after Macmillan's savage night of the long knives reshuffle, the rising threat of Harold Wilson, worries over joining the Common Market and the Christine Keeler scandal. At the party conference in 1963 Thatcher favoured RAB Butler as PM but when Douglas Home's name popped up as a compromise, she quickly told whips she agreed he was 'the right person' (ibid., p.130; see Chapter 9 for more on leadership contests). Labour's narrow victory ended her stay at Pensions; she now moved to cover housing in opposition where she developed her soon to be famous 'right to buy' policy. In 1966 she moved to join the Treasury bench: clearly now seen as a substantial front bench talent. When Ted Heath won his surprise victory in 1970 she was catapulted into Cabinet as Secretary of State for Education. Entering the Commons in 1959 it had taken her a decade to traverse the distance between PPS and full Cabinet. But if the years are counted when her party had posts at their disposal, it was merely an impressive five years. Through luck, hard work and genuine talent, she had quickly hit the political big time.

Gillian Shephard (1940–)

Our previous account of this future Cabinet member ended in 1987, after she had been elected for Southwest Norfolk. How did she handle the promotion terrain? Her first step on the ladder was becoming PPS to Peter Lilley, then Economic Secretary to the Treasury. Viewing the political game from the backbenches is much different from watching it from the ministerial standpoint. Shephard notes how much she learnt as a member of the Health and Social Security Select Committee and was privy to all the gossip about Thatcher's leadership which, in the late 1980s, was just beginning to falter. But as she observed 'Power did not seem to reside on the backbenches' (Shephard, 2000, p.15). She was able to observe the passage of the Finance Bills and confront 'the immense amount of detail to be mastered for work in committee' as well as the often necessary 'sudden changes' (ibid., p.15). As PPS she also had to keep interested parties informed, especially fellow MPs. She clearly managed to impress, as in the summer of 1989 she was made PUS at Social Security. It seems quite possible that Thatcher was already aware of her near neighbour in a Norfolk constituency and confided to her that this was the job she had first been given and, no doubt, adding that she had enjoyed its detail and challenge.

It seemed to Shephard that she was not drinking 'deep of the cup of power' in her new job but she did not have long to wait; in November 1990, the new source of power in Number 10 summoned her to offer her a job where she had cut her teeth as a PPS: MoS, at the most important department of all, the Treasury. It seemed clear now that her next stop was going to be a seat in the Cabinet. This duly happened after Major's somewhat surprising victory in 1992 election. After a four hour wait – Major had encountered one or two appointment problems –she became Secretary of State for Employment with special responsibility for women's issues. After entering the Commons in 1987, Shephard's, promotion velocity, matched Thatcher's and had landed her in Cabinet after only five years.

Special factors favouring her, apart from being a hard worker and a quick learner, included her gender – women Conservative MPs were not numerous – and she had impressed senior ministers like Peter Lilley. The fact that Thatcher raised her up into the same post she had first occupied suggests the PM maybe took a special interest in the fortunes of the MP for Southwest Norfolk.

Willie Whitelaw (1918–99)

Whitelaw's promotion trajectory provides an interesting contrast to that of Shephard. Despite appearing to many at the time as the very epitome of the Tory establishment and an omnipresent member of the Tory top team, his promotion velocity was not exactly rapid. Elected in 1955 it took him 15 years to make it into the Cabinet – nine years if you subtract the years Labour was in power 1964–70. For Whitelaw the prospect of entering Parliament was both 'daunting' and 'awe-inspiring' but having an 'establishment' background must have helped soften the sharper edges of his early days in the Commons. His old golfing friend, the deputy Speaker Charlie McAndrew, set about educating him in 'Commons procedures'. Kith and kin helped too: 'I also knew Peter Thorneycroft, who is a relation of mine, and was at that time President of the Board of Trade' (Whitelaw, 1989, p.41) And who became his PPS, his 'first opportunity to learn about the working of government departments' (ibid., p41)? Willie, naturally. He got his maiden speech out of the way by addressing the needs of 'isolated country areas' – inevitably regions like his constituency.

In 1959 Willie was made an Assistant Whip, an indication perhaps of the role he was destined often to play: mediating, warning, negotiating, calming. He continued to sit on the front bench, either in government or opposition, for the next 30 years. The infamous night of the long knives, July 1962, caused much grief to those Cabinet members Macmillan so calmly despatched but for Whitelaw the slaughter 'provided a tremendous opportunity' (ibid., p.45). He was appointed PUS to the Minister of Labour, John Hare (later Lord Blakenham), whom he came greatly to admire for his sensitivity and his practice of trusting him to 'get on with' delegated work 'without interference'. Very soon he was competently 'taking complicated legislation through Parliament', a crucially testing process for any ingenue junior minister. He soon found his interest in those 'safety, health and welfare problems ... which vitally affect our economy' (ibid., pp.45–47).

His campaigning in the 1964 election illustrated for him one of the problems of ministerial collective responsibility. His constituency had suffered some rail closures, courtesy of Transport Minister Ernest Marples. He had opposed the closures but had not been able to highlight this in public because of the rule that all ministers, however junior, have to toe the official government line or face being sacked. After 13 years in power Conservatives were narrowly beaten by Labour in the 1964 election so Willie's promotion appeared to be stalled.

However, he suddenly became Douglas Home's Chief Whip. He was surprised because usually a move into a department after a short stint as a whip was not followed by a return to the Whip's cloister. Here again, as so often, luck was a factor. Martin Redmayne wanted to retire while his deputy, Michael Hughes-Young, had lost his seat. But why Whitelaw? It seems some senior Tories, including Selwyn Lloyd, had, to use a Toryish kind of term, liked the cut of his jib. Despite clashing with Redmayne back when the most junior of whips, he was happy to occupy one of the most powerful positions for any party in opposition. Whitelaw was the party's lead man for some crucial negotiations with the BBC and other broadcasting matters as well as delicate talks regarding that very sensitive issue for many Tory MPs, Rhodesia. His great talent was for being even-handed, quiet of voice and perceived as decent by all. He was the perfect example of the 'good chap' that Peter Hennessy famously suggests British political life makes possible in the absence of a written constitution (Blick and Hennessy, 2019). Some commentators have suggested Willie was the perfect exemplar of a senior politician with 'bottom': calm, consistent and, tempered by war, steady under fire.

After getting elected, Whitelaw moved his family to live in his constituency and he emphasised the importance of this in relation to political longevity. Being fully involved in the civil society of one's area was of key importance to becoming the widely perceived natural incumbent and therefore someone with a suitable foundation for those hoping to achieve those higher heavyweight political prizes. Such ambitions were fulfilled for Whitelaw when, in the wake of Heath's rather surprising victory in 1970, he flew down to London from Carlisle to assist his new PM in forming his first Cabinet. His prize was to be Lord President of the Council and Leader of the House of Commons. This was not such a senior position, but maybe appropriate for a key in-house mediator and member of the Tory inner counsels during six years of opposition.

David Owen (1938–)

Having joined Labour, Owen was poised to live one of the most colourful political lives of the last century. Born with many gifts, including dashing good looks, it began rather prosaically with him giving a talk to the drug industry, after which a number of those present – mostly female it seems – suggested his name be added to the selection list of prospective candidates for the Torrington constituency Labour Party. When the Southwest Regional Labour Party asked him if he had any objection to being shortlisted for the seat, he readily agreed: this occurring in the same week he became a newly qualified doctor. In his election message at the 1964 election he, ironically in view of his later political change of position, denied that the Liberals were 'a serious alternative': even more ironic, Mark Bonham Carter for the Liberals came second, Owen third and the Tories won it.

In 1966 Owen stood in his home city in the Plymouth Sutton constituency (originally the seat of the first woman MP, Mary Astor), remaining as its MP until 1992 when he entered the House of Lords. Walking into St Thomas's hospital after his victory (majority 5,222) he was 'greeted with a mixture of amazement and humour but even the most Tory of consultants seemed genuinely pleased' (Owen, 1991, p.92). On that first day a note from Defence Minister (Army) Gerry Reynolds (who had spoken for Owen during his campaign), presaged an invitation to become Reynolds' PPS. Reynolds, seen by some as a 'rising star in the Labour government' (ibid., p.93) and possibly even a future leader, was someone close (at the time) to 'big beast' George Brown. Owen thus found himself now perceived aligned with 'the right wing of the Labour Party' (ibid., p.94). Given his SDP future, this judgement might be seen as unsurprising.

Reynolds educated Owen into the 'the inner workings of the Labour Party, invaluable over the years' (Owen, 1991, p.94) and introduced him to 'The 1963 Club', a posthumous fan club of Hugh Gaitskell, thus pitching Owen into the inner circle of people who, 'at their mildest, were highly suspicious of Harold Wilson and, at their strongest, loathed his guts' (ibid., p.94). Owen makes an interesting point about these ubiquitous dinner clubs that flourished on both sides of the aisle. 'For a young backbencher, listening as we went round the table, each contributing to the discussion, it was fascinating, particularly hearing Roy (Jenkins) and Tony (Crosland) talk, often indiscreetly, about what was going on in the Cabinet' (ibid., p.94). Owen's closeness to Reynolds, his eyes and ears as PPS (his duties, according to him were 'pretty minimal'; ibid., p.95), had a marked impact on his promotion trajectory. Being a doctor had inclined him naturally towards the social policy departments – he had even written a book entitled *A Unified Health Service* – but he was soon on a route defined by defence and foreign policy. He relates in his memoirs how he was dining with Robert Maclennan (then a Labour MP but, like Owen, destined to defect and lead the SDP), discussing how to get rid of Harold Wilson, when a message came through from the man himself to see him immediately. When meeting Wilson by chance in a lift Owen had sharply told him to stop his staff 'briefing the press against Brian Walden, John Mackintosh, David Marquand and myself' (ibid., p.131). But instead of having 'completely burnt my boats' (shades of Major's row with Thatcher) Wilson made him PUS for the Navy – he was delighted, aged only 30, to be on his way up that famous greasy pole (ibid., pp.131–132). However, as someone who had argued for 'devaluation, defence cuts and withdrawal East of Suez', Wilson had ensured he would now 'defend and implement that policy at home and abroad' (ibid., p.130).

There can be no doubt Owen made an impact on the Ministry of Defence: as a young Assistant Principal (I think the last appointed before the system changed) briefly in the Navy department 1970/71, I heard senior civil servants talk admiringly of 'that young chap Owen we had as a Navy minister under Labour'. Owen was soon promoted to Foreign Secretary by Jim Callaghan but his memoirs reveal the interesting facts of his earlier promotion back in 1974. Anyone familiar with British political history will know that David Owen, at 38 years old, was the youngest Foreign Secretary for nearly half a century but of interest for the focus of this book is his leap from Defence PUS to MoS for Health. Owen explains he was so disillusioned with Harold Wilson by 1974 that he 'did not care very much' (ibid., p.126) regarding any possibilities of office being offered him.

But things did not quite work out as he expected. Barbara Castle, so close to Wilson, was made Secretary of State for Health and Social Services. Because she did not favour Shirley Summerskill as a team member and David Ennals was heading for another job, she responded to a suggestion by Peter Shore's wife, Elizabeth, also a medical doctor, that Owen might provide a good fit for a health portfolio. 'Barbara then proposed to Harold on the telephone that I should be appointed' (ibid., p.225). Owen recalled 'Harold's reply was, "I like the idea. Let me think about it" ' (ibid., p.226).

Wilson eventually offered him a PUS for Health but in their meeting Owen quibbled: 'I said I did not believe the job could be done effectively without the more senior status of Minister of State ... Harold was somewhat taken aback at 'a young pup who ought to have been grateful for the bone thrown at him' (Owen, 1991, p.226). Owen later explained to Castle that he wished to 'advance in seniority' compared to his previous job in government (ibid., p.226). Castle, who clearly wanted him in her team, suggested he visit her department and sit in on a meeting to reorganise the NHS along lines suggested by the outgoing Sir Keith Joseph; Owen, silent throughout the meeting though supportive of implementing the Tory plan was fascinated and 'hooked ... how could I give her this unpalatable message and then walk away from implementing it?' (ibid., p.226). After extracting the promise from Castle that he would not have to deal with her through MoS Brian O'Malley and become 'in effect the Minister of Health', Owen agreed to serve and later on in that summer Wilson, true to his promise, promoted him to MoS rank.

This little case study reveals how important matters of promotion can be influenced by: gossipy conversation; the exigencies of available talent; a genuine desire for advancing someone by a senior colleague; the *absence* of any Labour whip in the process; the confidence, if not arrogance, of the young MP concerned; but, ultimately, the decisive role played by the source of appointments – the PM (ibid., pp.224–227).

Norman Fowler (1935–), a political life at the top

'In politics, people tend to put on you the value you put on yourself – you need to take yourself seriously' (Fowler, 1991, p.17).

Somehow Fowler seems to have been active in UK political life forever; he only gave up his role as Speaker of the House of Lords in April 2021. His early career contains some fascinating evidence of how ambition can impact upon ministerial careers, making his one of the most impressive in the post-war period. He subtitles his memoirs by linking them specifically to the era of Margaret Thatcher, the person who dominated his early political life; she also played a role that reflects how, ultimately, personality plays a crucial role in the fulfilment of political ambitions. He notes that the possibility of her becoming PM seemed remote in the early 1970s – her discontinuation of school milk was not popular on the Tory backbenches – yet, she was able to emerge as a towering figure in British politics from the early 1980s onwards.

Elected for Nottingham South in 1970, Fowler spent two years as an unpaid PPS at the Northern Ireland office. During the post-1974 leadership campaign he originally favoured Sir Keith Joseph and urged him to stand but, when Joseph refused, he transferred his support to Thatcher, via the agency of Airey Neave who ran her campaign 'like a secret service operation' (ibid., p.14). An interesting note here is that Neave did not like Heath; in 1959 illness caused him to resign. Once recovered:

> he went to see the Chief Whip to receive the bleak message that his ministerial career was finished; Neave clearly did not forget the way he had been slighted. Anyone who doubts the effect of personal feelings in politics has only to examine this episode.
>
> *(ibid., p.13)*

Ted Heath's position, it is worth a small digression at this point, was even more vulnerable after he conceded a lead to Labour of 297–301 seats in the crucial 1974 election following the 'three-day week' industrial relations crisis. Worse, as a leader he was perceived as exhibiting that much disliked middle-class quality of being 'unclubbable'. Forced into the Commons Tea Room he'd relapse into moody silence. His handlers tried hard to socialise him into Conservative society but the shy son of a carpenter seemed devoid of social skills, so surprising for someone who served successfully as Chief Whip. Being cheerfully sociable is a hugely important quality in political advancement but poor Heath, so talented in intellect and music, was never able to channel his inner charm.

Frustrated ambition and personal animosity are all part of the warp and weft of political life. Thatcher offended Ted Heath terminally by standing against him and the rift was never healed. Fowler, despite operating on the fringes of Margaret's campaign actually voted for Ted, despite him being 'awkward and at times autocratic': the reason? It was partly 'a question of loyalty' (Fowler, 1991, p.10): Ted had appointed Norman to his Front Bench opposition team in November as a junior spokesman on Home Office affairs. Unusually, for such appointments Fowler was already well up on the detail: he had been the correspondent on Home Affairs for *The Times* for four years during the 1960s.

Fowler also vouchsafes to us yet another ploy of the 'promotion game'. Enoch Powell observed that 'potential candidates for the leadership could leave their visiting cards' (ibid., p.16) by achieving a respectable vote in the second round. Such candidates would also be well placed for good positions in the new Shadow Cabinet. Within hours of the first vote it became clear that a small group was backing Jim Prior, not with the aim of wining but of making him a strong man in the new regime. 'A number of us decided to do the same for Geoffrey Howe' (ibid., pp.16–17). Despite his exceptionally shy and modest demeanour – Healey described debating with him as 'being savaged by a dead sheep' (Press Association, 2015) – Howe was perceived as not just dogged but as a highly 'creative' politician who 'delighted in new ideas' (Fowler, 1991, p.18). Howe had been a junior member of the Heath Cabinet. On the evening of Thatcher's first round victory, a group of Howe's admirers met at his house in Lambeth – Leon Brittan, Ken Clarke, David Walder, Tony Buck and Ian Gow – and in the small hours they persuaded him to stand. By the following Monday, Tony Buck was able to report that Howe had 25 firm pledges, 'providing a cautionary tale for would be candidates in leadership elections. Estimates of support can be appreciably amiss' (ibid., p.18) On the day Howe only managed 19 votes.

Thatcher	146
Whitelaw	79
Howe	19
Prior	19
Peyton	11

Following Thatcher's victory Fowler held no high hopes for the Shadow Cabinet; after all, he had not voted for the new leader in either ballot. He was therefore astonished after a couple of days to receive a note asking him to see the future PM; even more so when she invited him to 'take over social services' (ibid., p.19). As Howe had been in charge of this area, Fowler assumed he'd be working to him. But no, Howe was to be elevated to Shadow Chancellor and Fowler was to be in charge. He notes:

> Significantly, all Margaret Thatcher's opponents in the leadership elections were to be given Shadow Cabinet posts and these included two which were entirely crucial for the Thatcher revolution. Willie Whitelaw was appointed Deputy Leader of the party and, in total vindication of our 19 vote campaign, Geoffrey Howe was made Shadow Chancellor.
>
> *(ibid., p.20)*

Fowler, of course, was delighted to join them, at 37 years old the youngest member of Thatcher's first Shadow Cabinet. When assuming power in 1979 Fowler was made MoS for Transport, a portfolio he had shadowed, but attended all Cabinet meetings before becoming a full member. In 1981 he became Secretary of State for Health and Social Services, the second of yet more senior positions he was destined to hold.

Ernest Bevin (1881–1951)

On 12 May 1940, Ernest Bevin was appointed Minister of Labour and National Service, a key personnel position that involved the nation's foremost trade unionist being put in charge of the 'home front'. When the new PM asked him to go to the Ministry of Labour, Bevin at once accepted, characteristically saying only that he must first get the agreement of the Executive Committee of his union and the Trades Union Congress General Council, since he would be valueless without the support of 'his people' and adding that he only wished he were ten years younger (Williams, 1952, p.217).

Bevin was not an MP so a by-election was choreographed whereby Bevin was elected unopposed for the actual constituency of Wandsworth Central: his promotion velocity, therefore, albeit during wartime conditions, from MP to Cabinet was thus the highest possible: instantaneous. His transition from trade union leader into the Cabinet – and for the next hugely eventful decade it was a giant step – as befits a giant, of course, of the trade union movement. Mostly promotion to the Cabinet is at the behest and calling of the monarch, primed by the PM: in Bevin's case the summons was delivered by the fraught contingencies of the time – arguably by Adolf Hitler rather than Winston Churchill, though the PM was sure that Bevin was the most able Labour politician of his time, as experience went on to prove. However, whilst Bevin was a natural communicator and a very effective speech maker, he was not quite so much at home in the Commons; this perhaps was a similar experience for others later brought in from outside – Frank Cousins and, from the world of business, John Davies and Digby Jones – to face the unique challenges of the political world.

Tony Blair (1953–)

In Chapter 1 we left Blair chosen as Labour candidate for Sedgefield. His experience after that achievement was in opposition, as a promising, highly articulate and rather good-looking young backbencher, in lockstep with his closest political friend and office mate, Gordon Brown. In 1987, Blair became front bench shadow spokesman for Trade; in 1988 it was Energy, in 1989 Employment, in 1992 Home Secretary. He certainly seemed to be

FIGURE 2.1 'All behind you, Winston'. The caption of David Low's famous cartoon in the *Evening Standard*, 14 May 1940.

Source: Low (1957).

shinning up that greasy opposition pole when one of those sudden events occurred, as it did to Bevin, which transformed his career and that of his country: Labour's much-loved leader, John Smith, died 12 May 1994 of a heart attack, foreshadowed by the serious attack he'd suffered in 1988. Blair reckons he initially assumed and wanted Brown to be leader: 'I actually rejoiced in it. I didn't want the job. I was high enough to espy its responsibility and its pain. No, if someone else could do it, I would be the supportive and loyal lieutenant' (Blair, 2020, p.65). Much has been written and speculated upon what happened to Blair's ambition in the months and years following. His memoir displays his ambition for Labour's top job beyond doubt. Blair's second memoir chapter vividly reveals how ambition can work below the surface of political activity and in an almost unconscious way.

Blair became convinced that the steady-as-you-go approach of Neil Kinnock was essential for establishing an electable foundation; plus, following the tantalising 1992 defeat followed by John Smith's stolid but unimaginative leadership, a radical approach was required.

> In my view, we needed a complete top to bottom reorientation of our programme and policies. In particular we needed to separate conceptually a commitment to our values (timeless) from their application (time bound). So, of course we should and always fight for social justice; but in today's

> world that didn't mean more state control. And on issues like defence and law and order, being tough was not striking a pose but a sensible reaction to the threats of the modern world, whether globally or on our street corners.
>
> *(ibid., p.49)*

In the wake of the 1992 defeat, Blair was making his case to the party and country. The party had lost, he said, 'because we had failed to modernise sufficiently and we now had to do so, not by shades but by bursts of vivid colour' Blair reckoned he had 'planted my banner firmly on the terrain of radical change'. Though he wasn't aware of it at the time, 'party members recalled the thought of me as leader stemmed from that morning' (ibid., p.50).

Third, Blair's friendship and wish that Brown would be the future leader of the party began to fade in the wake of defeat and his elevation to Shadow Home Secretary. Blair's brilliant slogan, summarising an essentially Labour solution to crime – 'tough on crime, tough on the causes of crime' – was in fact coined by Brown. However, Blair by degrees was becoming a little disillusioned with his talented colleague; he learned from Smith, that in the wake of defeat in 1992 Brown would not challenge for the leadership from which Kinnock had resigned. Smith felt, however, the deputy position should be either Brown's or Blair's – they should decide who. Blair felt that two Scots at the helm would be 'a problem, especially as it was precisely in the south of England that our support was thinnest'. Chief Whip Nic Brown took soundings and reported the 'strong consensus it should be Gordon' (ibid., p.54). Blair's response?

> I knew this was not true. It couldn't be. Not even the PLP at its daftest was that daft. From that moment I think I detached a little from Gordon; just a fraction, imperceptible to the eye … unaccompanied by any diminishing of affection. The seed was sown of my future insistence that I should be leader, not him.
>
> *(ibid., p.54)*

'I was out in front taking risks, and this was the time for risk takers. I spotted that; he didn't' (ibid., p.59). Blair reckoned his friend, and not yet perceived rival, preferred to:

> reframe the question rather than acknowledging the need for the hard answer. He was brilliant, had far more knowledge of the party than me, with an acute and, even then, well-honed brain; but it operated essentially within familiar and conventional parameters. Within the box he was tremendous but he didn't venture outside it.
>
> *(ibid., p.60)*

Blair's account of the aftermath of Smith's tragic death reads almost like the script of an emotive film biography of Tony Blair; perhaps the most vivid expression of political ambition in practice ever written. Back down in Parliament from Aberdeen he found 'a state of turmoil' (ibid., p.62). Mo Mowlam told him directly, 'It's got to be you. Do not on any account succumb.' Cherie's advice was even more emphatic. 'They hadn't needed to tell me. My mind was made up' (ibid., p.60; see also Chapter 7).

It had taken the decade of the 1990s, and more especially the traumas of the 1992 defeat and the death of Labour leader John Smith, to distil Blair's nascent ambition into something powerfully explicit. He had reached a conclusion on what Labour needed to do to win and another one on who should lead the fight – and it was not his elder, more experienced close political colleague. It was now clear in his own mind: it was to be Blair himself. It was not destined to be an easy journey – indeed it would be marked by toxic feuding with Brown and his camp followers. But as the 1997 election approached, once the prize was in Blair's mind, his future was clear. On 2 May 1997, Blair walked into Downing Street as PM. 'I had never held office, not even as the most junior of junior ministers. It was my first and only job in government' (Blair, 2010, p.1). He had entered the Cabinet, not after years of apprenticeship understudying a Secretary of State but in one giant leap; and rather than being beholden to anyone within the most senior committee in the land he was about to decide who should comprise it. It was hardly surprising that without any reassuring inbuilt memories of executive experiences, the 'predominant feeling was fear, and of a sort unlike anything I had felt before, deeper even than the fear I had felt taking over the leadership of the Labour Party' (ibid., p.1).

David Cameron (1966–)

Elected leader in 2005, Cameron had another five years to wait until he walked through the door of Number 10. He used those years to very good effect, seeking to detoxify the Conservative brand. Theresa May's accusation at the 2002 conference had silenced her audience: 'You know what people call us? the nasty party' (White and Perkins, 2002). Seldom can a senior member of a political party have served it so well; she spoke the unpalatable truths that are so often ignored while their damage continues to be wreaked. Mrs May, so mocked in her later career, had mustered characteristic candid courage – later, during Brexit negotiations, Michel Barnier testified to this quality – to explain why the Tory polls had flatlined on 30 per cent for over a decade. Cameron had instantly been spotted, along with his close friend George Osborne, as talented young stars of the future. They both recognised May's critique as accurate – Lord Ashcroft's 'Smell the Coffee' research-backed pamphlet argued something very similar – and, once leader of the opposition, Cameron set to work. At his first Prime Minister's Questions (PMQs) Cameron attacked Blair – whom both he and Osborne admired – quipping wittily, 'You were the future once' (Jeffrey, 2005). Then began a relentless series of photo ops: visits to the Arctic to display environmental bona fides and his 'hug a hoodie' speech to demonstrate his understanding of young people. All these themed PR events to demonstrate 'Dave' and his friendly party were not bogey men hiding under the beds of our children but sensible caring types, desperately concerned about the environment, fighting against homophobia, fighting for gender equality: on the progressive side of virtually every cause except immigration and relations with the European Union.

When it came to the 2010 election the Tory seat numbers, via Cameron's efforts, were hugely improved but no party had overall control. In response Cameron made Lib Dems that famous 'big, open and comprehensive offer' and, during the resultant talks on policies, both Lib Dems and Tories shed the (in practice very few) unacceptable to either side and a deal was done. William Hague, who led the Tory side and is an acclaimed historian, suspected Clegg and company were unaware that historically Liberals had always come out badly from coalitions. He 'staggered back home at 1.0 am and told his wife Ffion "Well, we've formed a government ... but may well have destroyed the Liberal Party."' Even after the formation of the Liberal Democrats, Tories still called them 'Liberals' (Seldon and Snowdon, 2015, p.25).

Cameron had initially been opposed to a coalition but realised a minority government would have been hostage to his Brexiteer wing and finally supported a course of action that would lead him to become, like Blair before him, without any ministerial experience, PM of the United Kingdom; a post that he believed he'd 'be good at' (ibid., 2015, p.36). Did he live up to his own Etonian confidence? He succeeded in keeping a not wholly happy coalition running for a full term with no real threats to its stability but his career and reputation were both shredded after his expectation that the 23 June 2016 referendum would vote Remain proved catastrophically wrong. Reading the public mood correctly is the most important judgement a party leader has to make: no matter how accomplished they may be, those who call it wrongly end up in the wrong side of history.

References and further reading

Ashcroft, M. (2005) *Smell the Coffee: A Wake Up Call for the Conservative Party*. Politico's Media.

Blair, T. (2010) *A Journey*. Hutchinson.

Blick, A. and Hennessy, P. (2019) *Good Chaps No More? Safeguarding the Constitution in Stressful Times*. Constitution Society. https://consoc.org.uk/publications/good-chaps-no-more-safeguarding-the-constitution-in-stressful-times-by-andrew-blick-and-peter-hennessy/.

Bond, A. (2022) 'The inside story of why the government U turned on Partygate vote'. *Standard*, 21 April.
Brandreth, G. (2000) *Breaking the Code*. Phoenix.
Brazier, R. (1999) *Constitutional Practice: The Foundations of British Government*. Oxford University Press.
Buck, P.W. (1963). 'The early start toward cabinet office, 1918–55'. *Western Political Quarterly*, Vol. 16, Issue 3, 624–632.
Fowler, N. (1991) *Minister's Decide*. Chapmans.
James, S. (1999) *British Cabinet Government*, 2nd edn. Routledge.
Jay, A. (2001) Political Quotations. Oxford University Press.
Jeffrey, S. (2005) 'You were the future once'. *Guardian*, 13 July.
Leadsom, A. (2023) *Snakes and Ladders: Navigating the Ups and Downs of Politics*. Biteback.
Low, D. (1957) *'All Behind You, Winston' in Low's Autobiography*. Simon & Schuster. Internet Archive. https://archive.org/details/lowsautobiograph017633mbp/page/n356/mode/1up?view=theaterv
Major, J. (1999) *John Major: The Autobiography*. HarperCollins.
Moore, C. (2013) *Margaret Thatcher, The Authorised Biography*, Vol. 1: *Not for Turning*. Allen Lane.
Norton, P. (2022) 'Minister, departments and civil servants', in B. Jones, P. Norton and I. Hertner, Politics UK, 10th edn, pp. 504–527. Routledge.
Owen, D. (1991) *Time to Declare*. Michael Joseph.
Press Association (2015) 'Denis Healey's 10 most celebrated quotes'. *Guardian*, 3 October.
Searing, D. (1994) *Westminster's World: Understanding Political Roles*. Harvard University Press.
Seldon, A. and Snowdon, P. (2015) *Cameron at 10: The Inside Story 2010–2015*. HarperCollins.
Shephard, G. (2000) *Shephard's Watch*. Politico's.
Thatcher, M. (1995a) *The Path to Power*. HarperCollins.
Thatcher, M. (1995b) *The Downing St Years*. HarperCollins.
Theakston, K. (1987) Junior Ministers in British Government. Blackwell.
White, M. and Perkins, A. (2002) '"Nasty party" warning to Tories'. *Guardian*, 8 October.
Whitelaw, W. (1989) *The Whitelaw Memoirs*. Aurum Press.
Williams, F. (1952) *Ernest Bevin: Portrait of a Great Englishman*. Hutchinson.

3

THE RECRUITMENT POOL AND THE ROLE OF THE WHIPS' OFFICE

> There is no HR policy for ministers really. But if I were going to construct one I would make it the case that, as far as possible, most people should start government in the Whips Office. It just gives you an understanding of how parliament and government works.
>
> (Murphy, 2022, p.3)

> The prospect of promotion to ministerial office is one of the few things that keeps a lid on parliamentary dissent.
>
> (James Forsyth; Forsyth, 2022)

Is there a 'promotion system'?

Let me begin this chapter by referring to two interviews I had with retired politicians on ministerial promotion. In an extended telephone interview, Lord (Tristan) Garrel-Jones, a former Tory Deputy Chief Whip, told me there *is* an actual 'promotion system' and it's called the Whips' Office. However, this was contradicted in my interview with Sir Geoffrey Howe who insisted there was no system: it's done subjectively on the 'whim of the Prime Minister' (private interview). This poses an interesting, yes, and maybe opportune, fundamental question to debate in this chapter on the Whips and those occasions when their personnel advice is allegedly crucial: those regular reshuffles. But first some attention is required to the question of who is available to be promoted, the recruitable pool from which promotions can be made?

DOI: 10.4324/9781003405085-4

The 'recruitable talent pool'

A central question regarding promotion is, who can the PM potentially promote? Sadly, perhaps, for a British PM the options are limited. The biggest restriction is the 'strong convention that members of the United Kingdom Government should be a member of either the House of Commons or the House of Lords. This convention ensures that ministers are directly accountable to one or other House of Parliament' (Public Administration Select Committee [PASC], 2010, p.6). Given that the Lords ceased to be the dominant chamber of government after the 1911 Parliament Act, most ministerial appointments are drawn from the Commons, though a few peers have been allowed membership plus a small number of junior ministers. My interview on ministerial promotion with Garel-Jones, left me in no doubt that such resources are always distinctly finite. These figures are approximations but, according to Garel Jones it is usually assumed that a third of a governing parliamentary party is not available by virtue of their total unsuitability: excessive drinking; inability to run anything, let alone a ministry; too old and enfeebled; too young and inexperienced; too ideologically extreme; or too much of a risk to any government because of bizarre attitudes or personal habits. There could be other reasons.

Depending on the size of its majority a government might therefore have a couple of hundred MPs who can realistically be put in charge of Whitehall departments and fill the 20–25 Cabinet posts and the remaining 100 or so posts any PM currently has at his or her disposal. ('As of 24th April 2023, there [were] 133 ministerial posts, held by 124 people – some individuals hold multiple posts'; White, 2023.) In addition there is the extensive gaggle of PPSs appointed who effectively act as unpaid trainee ministers and as conduits between their minister and the parliamentary party. Philip Norton has pointed out to me that 'The number of ministers now exceeds the number that can be paid, so several ministers serve as unpaid ministers' (private interview). As Garel-Jones also told Jeremy Paxman on the subject of ministerial appointments: 'Once you've eliminated the bad, mad, drunk and over the hill, you've got rid of a hundred. You then have to pick ninety people out of a pool of 250. Is it any wonder the calibre is so low?' (Paxman, 2002, p.209). Indeed any employer would blanch at the idea if only just over two candidates for important jobs turned up for interview. The principle of accountability is a cornerstone of democracy but is to a degree in conflict with the one expecting the best possible people to serve the nation in government.

The number of available candidates depends on the size of a government's majority but this is a smaller group, for sure, than most voters would assume was available. Given that ministers need time to prove themselves in the job and display signs they are suitable to go on to higher things at Cabinet level, even this number has to be qualified in that a PM has to be mindful of other considerations, such as: representing Welsh and Scottish interests, especially in their respective ministries; number of women, racial minority and LGBTQ+ MPs, given their under-representation generally in Parliament; as well as the major ideological or 'tribal' interests in the parliamentary party. Put like this, Sir John Hoskyns' jibe that governments are formed from a talent pool that 'could not sustain a single multi-national company' (Kavanagh, 2014) seems less a spiteful swipe than a bleakly accurate analysis. William Hague, former Tory Leader and Foreign Secretary turned distinguished columnist, underscores these analyses:

> A governing party rarely has more than 100 members who will be highly capable ministers, able to run things well, not just comment and campaign. And the number who have the intellect, decisiveness, resilience and drive actually to run the country at the very top is much smaller. ... Our politics depends on a thin layer of outstanding talent.
>
> *(Hague, 2023)*

Despite New Labour's huge majority of 179 created by 419 seats, Blair did not find it easy to discover sufficient talent within their number. Astute columnists often attested to this fact.

Andrew Rawnsley, whose *Servants of the People*, chronicled Labour's early years, recalls a conversation with a senior official from Number 10 about: 'the shallowness of the junior ministerial gene pool and how few really good people there were available to the Prime Minister for promotion to the top table' (Rawnsley, 2004).

The situation is even worse than Garel-Jones implied as the number of ministers has increased from the 90 he cites to closer to over 130. Moreover, senior former Labour whip, Lord Bruce Grocott, suggested to me that the reality is yet *more* desperate as the number of MPs wishing to *be* ministers is less than commonly realised. He argued such 'ministerialists', who wish to serve in the government are in the minority. There are MPs, according to him, who are happy merely to serve their constituents – see Legge-Burke's comment in my Introduction – others who focus on select committees like Tony Wright (who turned the PASC into an ongoing top-level professorial seminar on UK government) and still others who choose to be gadfly ideologues, like Dennis Skinner: the natural rebels written about so eloquently by Philip Cowley from Queen Mary College University of London (Cowley, 2005).

One means of accessing more talent emerged in the form of coalition governments. This unusual British arrangement in May 2010 saw David Cameron have at his disposal a number of highly talented and experienced politicians in the form of Nick Clegg, of course, but also Vince Cable and over a dozen others. Perhaps the most able of the lot, David Laws, was lost to the crucial post of Chief Secretary to the Treasury after only 17 days, due to breaches of the parliamentary expenses rules.

Notwithstanding this perhaps rare, new development, it might seem a little surprising that PMs ever succeed adequately in fully staffing their governments. Not so much a talent pool, more, as I have written a 'talent puddle'. Riddell comments: 'The UK has narrowed its pool of potential ministers to a *much*, *much* smaller group than in almost any other country where being an existing member of the legislature is not required to qualify for most posts' (Riddell, 2020, p.123; my italics).

In addition to the scarcity of available ministerial talent, there is the fact that they don't really serve long enough to be of much use. Ken Clarke – holder of eight Cabinet posts 1985–2014 – made the following lament:

> When you first arrive you are overwhelmed. All this stuff, people talk to you about all kinds of things – and if you are not careful, you will get a moment of panic. The next stage, after six months is you have got an agenda. You know exactly what you are going to do. The next stage after two years, you are really on top of it – you are really comfortable, you are doing things. And then the phone rings and the Prime Minister is having a reshuffle and you move on to the next department and you are back at the beginning; there you are panicking again.
>
> *(Riddell, 2020, p.xix)*

Riddell emphasises that the service span of the average minister in office is shorter than in virtually any other leadership position in Britain. By the beginning of 2019 barely a quarter of ministers in the Commons had been in the same post only 18 months earlier when Theresa May reshuffled her administration following the 2017 election. 'In the Brown years, the average tenure for individual ministerial posts was 1.7 years, rising to just 2.2 years for members of the Cabinet' (ibid., p.3). In fact there is a good case for saying our constitution has a serious flaw – something reformers have tended to neglect perhaps – and that thought ought to be given to removing the (quixotically British) restraint upon recruitment imposed by the requirement that ministers also be members of the legislature (see my concluding Chapter 12).

The career politician

Riddell, building on Anthony King's concept of a 'career politician', drew attention to this phenomenon in his book, *Honest Opportunism*. Such a political player is a political obsessive with no substantial employment outside the world of politics – having worked for example for MPs, think tanks, pressure groups, trade unions and the like – and, thus, having little experience of what might be described as 'real life'. The term probably embraces most prominent past politicians we can think of: Disraeli, Gladstone, Churchill, Lloyd George. The modern versions start on their quest very early on in their lives and, maybe because of their acquired expertise, in recent years have dominated senior positions in British government: Cameron, Osborne, both Milibands, Matt Hancock, Ed Balls and Alan Milburn are all examples of the 'professional politician'.

Being such a person, argues Riddell, 'is unquestionably an advantage in gaining ministerial office' (Riddell, 2020, p.34). The problem is that such political recruits may prove to be fluent policy wonks and supremely savvy about how political processes work but they lack the kind of lifetime experience and knowledge of an earlier generation of politicians who established themselves in their professions – the law, business, agriculture, academia or been hardened by experience of war – before entering the insecure world of politics. Nigel Farage neatly summed up, with typical exaggeration, the critical attitude towards such players of the political game:

> They all go to the same schools. They all go to Oxford. They all study PPE. They leave at 22 and get a job as a researcher for one of the parties and then become MPs at the age of 27 to 28 – we are run by a bunch of college kids who've never done a day of work in their lives.
>
> *(ibid., p.32)*

Richard Kelly also makes the point to me that the increased numbers of such 'young Turks' means they are more likely to be:

> impatient about promotion … given that these young MPs are conscious that while they might languish on the backbenches earning not much more than schoolteachers, their university contemporaries will be commanding far more in the City and private sector generally – as well as being in jobs that are rather more secure than many MPs' constituencies.
>
> *(Kelly, private email)*

As a newly elected MP told Richard:

> I don't want to be like Ed Balls, frittering away years of high earning power before being humiliated on election night. In other words, this MP wanted promotion and wanted it fast – otherwise what was the point of being a 30 something full-time politician rather than a 30 something hedge-fund manager?
>
> *(ibid.)*

Possibly Sunak's early promotion into the Cabinet after only four years of becoming an MP reflected a fear that, if 'exiled to the backbenches, the party would be denied one its brightest talents' (ibid.).

Ministers from the House of Lords and the Goats initiative

When Gordon Brown became PM in 2007 he attempted an enterprising new approach to appointments popularly dubbed, the 'government of all the talents' (Goats). The PASC undertook a useful study of how this worked in practice (PASC, 2010). Outside appointments to ministerial posts have been rare – only three during the twentieth century one of whom was General Smuts in 1917. Brown's appointments were six in all: former United Nations Deputy Secretary General, Lord Malloch Brown; Lord Digby Jones, former CBI Director-General; City financier Lord Myners, former Admiral Lord West; Shriti Vadera, an investment banker; and Sir Ari Darzi, surgeon and academic. Only one of these had any links with Labour and the drop-out rate was high. Jones – never a Labour member – lasted only 16 months. In his memoirs Jones reflects on the differences between business and politics with some bitterness:

> I had learnt something rather important too – that business is essentially honest in its endeavours – or at least transparent in its endeavours in what it strives to do, which is to make money. ... But what struck me was the basic dishonesty of the political driver. Politics is, as one former Prime Minister said, about the acquisition, maintenance and use of power.
>
> *(Jones, 2011, pp.83–124)*

Digby Jones records the details of his appointment: Brown explained 'how he wanted to get some experienced non-politicians into government where their specific skills could be brought to bear for a limited period to the benefit of the country; a new way of delivering in key areas' (ibid., p.85). The businessman heartily agreed with this objective, confessing to his rage when trade ministers had to cancel a mission he had also been on 'because there was a vote in the house of Commons deemed of greater importance in the bubble that is Westminster' (ibid., p.85). At his first meeting with his PUS at the Department of Business, Sir Brian Bender told him he was, 'mad and that I wouldn't fit in at all. When I said I was in here to bring about a change in the way things were done at Trade and Investment, he just smiled' (ibid., p.89).

Reflecting on his experience in government, Jones complained it had been, 'one of the most dehumanising and depersonalising experiences a human being can have. The whole system is designed to take the personality, the drive and the initiative out of a junior minister' (PASC, 2009, p.84).

To be fair, Jones had expected his political sojourn to last only 12 months and he stuck it out for 16 but, by his own admission, it can scarcely be called a success.

Malloch-Brown and Darzi lasted just over two years but West stayed the course until the 2010 election. Interestingly, Lord Turnbull's evidence to the PASC contained the following encomium to at least one of the Goats: 'The Human Embryology and Fertilisation Bill was taken through the House of Lords by Lord Darzi and he made a million times better job of it than the person who took it through the House of Commons' (PASC, 2010, p.19).

Should government abandon such 'goat' recruitment in the future? Looking abroad, when in some countries the whole nation provides a potential ministerial talent pool, many 'outsiders' have proved adept at transitioning into the political world: Robert Macnamara, former president of the Ford Motor Company served successfully as Secretary of Defence, Henry Kissinger left academia to serve several years as Secretary of State (effectively foreign affairs) and, while Donald Trump was and remains hugely controversial, he made a transition to politics that placed him in the White House 2015–20 – though personally I'd argue that someone as flawed as the celebrity businessman–politician, should never be allowed anywhere near the White House or anything similar. Other countries reflect similar experience so it would seem the success of such incomers depends on the person, the job they are asked to perform and the length of time they serve.

Nick Raynsford, in his evidence to PASC, indirectly perhaps supported the idea of widening and deepening the expertise of the recruitable pool. He was impressed at international meetings how many ministers he met who had been appointed for the technical expertise they already had, unlike UK ministers. He added:

> We have a culture which rightly emphasises the importance of political accountability to Parliament, and that means the overwhelming majority of ministers come into the job without any technical expertise in the area they are responsible for.
>
> *(PASC, 2010, p.12)*

The PASC's report into Goats concluded:

> Appointing a small number of junior ministers directly, without requiring them to be members of either House, would resolve some of the problems resulting from appointment via the House of Lords. It would also provide a mechanism to place clear limits on the number of ministers that could be appointed that way and their role. Whilst not completely without

precedent, this would be a considerable constitutional innovation. It is an idea that deserves further consideration.

(PASC, 2010, p.25)

Given the widely accepted critique of our ministerial recruitment pool as too shallow and lacking in specialised expertise, something radical is required to attract those people of real ability into the insecure and relatively poorly paid profession; I return to this in my concluding chapter.

The House of Lords

After 1911, ministers from the Lords ceased to be appointed as before: the Commons was now the main fulcrum of political debate and accountability. However, they have still played and still do play an important role in government appointments, both directly and as a back door for new appointments favoured by the PM. Figure 3.1 shows that members of the Lords serving as ministers has averaged around 20 per cent since the 1960s, with the majority having been Conservative members.

Thatcher rather ignored these emergent conventions for excluding Lords in Cabinet with the appointment of Lord Carrington as Foreign Secretary 1979–82 and Lord Cockfield as Trade Secretary 1982–83. However, since her departure such a practice has ceased; apart from the government's Leader in the House of Lords, most appointments are at the junior level. But

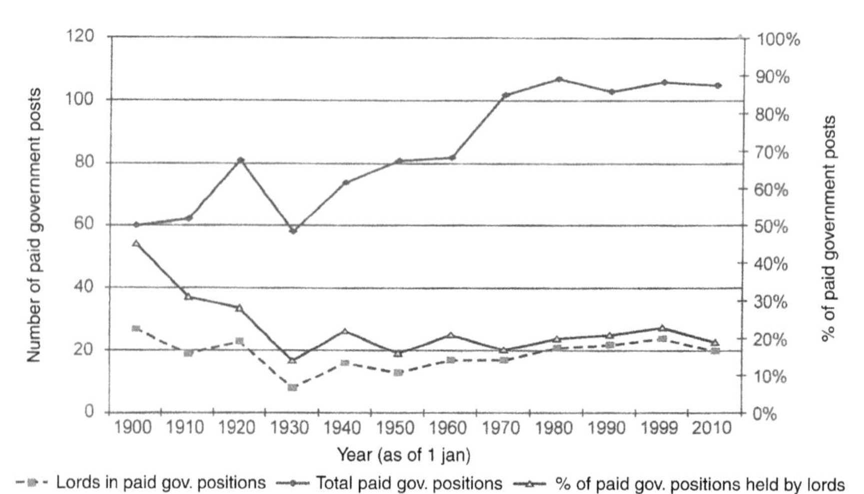

FIGURE 3.1 Members of House of Lords in paid government positions (1900–2010).

Source: PASC (2010, p.7), © Parliamentary copyright, 2010.

nevertheless, PMs have deliberately appointed life peers to serve as ministers, using the back door of the Lords to recruit life peers with much-needed specific skills: Wilson appointed Alun Gwynne Jones (Lord Chalfont) as Minister for Disarmament in 1964 alongside trade unionist, Frank Cousins, as Minister of Technology. Thatcher appointed businessman David Young as a Minister without Portfolio who went on to become Secretary of State for Employment and then Trade and Industry; and Lord Andrew Adonis was ennobled to become a junior Education minister, later appointed to the Cabinet in 2009 as Gordon Brown's Secretary of State for Transport. In 2008, Brown, surprisingly given their conflicted relationship, elevated Peter Mandelson to the peerage, then directly to the Cabinet as Secretary of State for Business. The PASC report made the additional point that at least two Goat peers were entitled to attend Cabinet: Lord Grayson and Lord Malloch Brown (PASC, 2010, p.16). The report also undermines the accountability argument against such appointments in quoting Adonis's willingness, when Secretary of State for Transport, to answer questions in the Commons if requested to do so. If this were established the accountability barrier against ministers in the House of Lords would disappear.

Tony Blair used the Lords' back door to fill sub-Cabinet roles including Lords Simon and Sainsbury: Rishi Sunak, of course, famously appointed David Cameron from the Lords to be his Foreign Secretary in November 2023. If truth is told a fair proportion of the above appointments were not especially successful. Business enables its leaders to make decisions that are then implemented: politics entails having to defend against hostile critics potentially every ministerial decision made with less certainty that they will ever be implemented in full.

The whips

Idealists of the left and advocates of a more 'pure' form of democracy, tend to view the Whips' Office with a degree of disfavour. After all, don't they ensure MPs vote with party rather than conscience or the bipartisan good of the country? Enoch Powell, that paragon of constitutional principle, once commented, 'whips in parliament were as inevitable as rats in sewers' (Renton, 2004, p.ix). Indeed, brief consideration of representative democracy leads one to the conclusion that independently elected MPs might prove so independent in their thinking and voting that collective decision-making might be rendered impossible. For parties to work in legislative assemblies, some nexus, or 'glue', is required to connect the UK's executive arm with the legislature that has been elected to form the government in the first place. Whips, it is maintained by Westminster enthusiasts, perform this essential task.

The Whips' Office moreover also provides its new members – and each big party's whips number over a dozen MPs – with an excellent education in the workings of the Commons as noted in Jim Murphy's title quote for this chapter; the Whips' Office is often a place where 'talent can be spotted' (Armstrong, 2019).

An amusing insight into the communist view of a whip's role is provided in Edward Heath's memoirs when he met Khrushchev and Bulganin in 1956. Antony Eden explained to the two visitors that his role as whip was to:

> persuade members of our party to support its leaders with their votes in the House of Commons. Both of the guests were 'nonplussed': How do you mean 'persuade then to support you? Surely you just tell them what to do?'
>
> *(Heath, 1998, p.164)*

Closer examination than these two communist leaders were able to make or understand reveals that whips perform three major functions relevant to the focus of this book:

1. *Voting*. Their name echoes the 'whippers' in and out – an old hunting term – of the voting divisions in the Commons. A 1980s Chief Whip reckoned his job formed 'an important part of the "usual channels"' entailing 'frequenting the various bars in the palace of Westminster trying to strike deals with the opposition to facilitate the progress of parliamentary business' (Waddington, 2012, p.166).
2. *Information feedback*. It is the whips' job to inform the leadership how the front-line voting troops are feeling about the measures they are asked to support and the leadership they follow. Myth has it that the whips often 'bully' recalcitrant MPs to desist from rebellion, maybe using threats or withdrawing favours if loyal support is not forthcoming. However, all the evidence – for example, consider the Radio 4 programme *Whipped* (24 March 2022) presented by Ben Wright – both whips and MPs interviewed all report that these days gentle persuasion and friendly management is the whips' modus operandi on all sides of the political divide. However, whips still can play hardball. Christian Wakeford, branded a 'traitor' by colleagues for sensationally defecting to Labour on 19 January 2022, claimed his former whips tried to smear him as a 'problem drinker': 'to try to use that as a way to discredit me when some of the work I am most proud of is my work on alcohol harm was quite a nasty trick to play' (Pidd, 2022).

   But whips are much more important for their intelligence role. They are the eyes and ears of the government – 17 on the Tory side in March 2022, 14 for Labour – able to feedback, with a high degree of accuracy, how every MP thinks and feels about the many and complex issues of daily governance. This role extends to monitoring the activities of MPs, in debates, committees and, indeed, just as importantly, on radio, television and the print press; whenever an MP speaks in the Commons or on the media, a whip will almost certainly be watching, listening and taking notes to report back. Crucially, when appointments are made by the PM, the Whips' Office provides their chief sources of advice.

3. *Appointments*. As John Major, who himself started his ministerial career as a junior whip, explains: 'The office … and the chief whip particularly, are crucial in advising the prime minister about the performance of ministers and backbenchers, which is vital for determining whether members climb the parliamentary ladder to senior positions, slip from high office, or remain for ever on the backbenches living in hope' (Major, 1999, p.78).

Former Chief Whip, Tim Renton, summoned a slightly more conspiratorial role for these well-staffed departments:

> The Whips are like the spies that kept Philip II's enormous empire together; they listen everywhere in H of C – in the tearoom, in the dining room, in the bars and on the front bench while ministers are speaking and questions are being asked and answered. They report back via notes or words of mouth on everything, and all this information is assessed by the whips collectively every day while the House is sitting.
>
> *(Renton, 2004, p.23)*

Rumours still circulate that the Tory Whips' Office keeps a black book containing details of what the KGB would have called 'kompromat' – items that could be used as none-too-subtle blackmail to enforce compliance. Both Whips' Offices currently deny such brutal tactics but instead describe their roles – calling to mind therapists or social workers – as friends to every MP, willing to listen and help in every way. Evidence of how close relationships between whips and MPs within their 'pastoral care' is provided in the case of former whip under David Cameron, Charlie Elphicke. When charged with sexual assault, four of his former 'flock' – those MPs assigned to him when serving as a whip under David Cameron – the senior Tory MPs Sir Roger Gale, Theresa Villiers, Adam Holloway and Bob Stewart, plus Elphicke's successor, his wife, Natalie (ringleader of this campaign) were disciplined for 'improperly trying to influence a judge'. They had all signed a letter 'pressing Mrs Justice Whipple not to disclose their character statements for Elphicke in his sex assault trial at Southwark Crown Court' (Pogrund, 2022). One might expect that relationships between a personable whip and his/her relevant MPs often to be close but the word 'flock' suggests a bond between whip and MP comparable with that between a priest and members of a congregation.

The *Sunday Times*, which had been engaged in a highly expensive libel case following its 2018 report that a former aide had reported that the MP for Deal and Dover had raped her, faced a court action. Elphicke's employment of the top Carter-Ruck legal firm caused the newspaper to run up bills of £500,000 even though Elphicke was sentenced to two years in jail for the assault. It sternly concluded: 'The Elphicke case emphasises the need for urgent reform. At present bullies can easily hire rottweilers like Carter-Ruck to kill off stories everyone should be able to read' (ibid.).

The intelligence gathering systems of the whips require the full-time employment of 30 or so MPs in all parties who are so engaged. Indeed, as noted earlier, some see the Whips' Office as a kind of nursery for assessing future talent. To be a good whip requires discretion, excellent people skills plus a profound understanding of the political scene and related issues. It's hardly surprising that so many future senior ministers started their ministerial careers as humble junior whips: John Major, for example, or, indeed, though it's seldom remembered, Nigel Lawson. The most important whip of all though is the 'Chief', as the Tory man in charge is traditionally known. Ted Heath of course founded his later career on his four-year stint as Chief Whip, April 1955 to June 1959. Studying the lives of every Chief Whip would be hard when so few memoirs are available but some consideration of reasonably recent incumbents of the office provides good insights as to how they can understand, interpret and manage the ambitions of their colleagues.

A classic example of the role Chief Whips play in promotions is revealed in a memo to Churchill from Patrick Buchan Hepburn late October 1953. 'I attach a list of names of MPs whom I think eligible, though not necessarily "ripe" for promotion.' The list gave age and year elected and picked out several of those destined for high office, including Edward Boyle, Robert Carr, Enoch Powell and Julian Amery (Buchan-Hepburn, 1953).

Finally an example of some bullying persuasion being used by a minister rather than a whip. On their joint podcast *The Rest Is Politics*, Alistair Campbell and Rory Stewart interviewed George Osborne in May 2023. When discussing Osborne after the interview Stewart recalled that just before he was about to vote against a government bill on the House of Lords, Osborne approached him and warned him that the promotion to junior minister he was considering would be withheld should Rory decide to vote against the government. Unlike many other MPs, one supposes, Rory ignored the 'bribe', if it can be so called, and in consequence suffered 'five wasted years' before promotion arrived (Campbell and Stewart, 2023).

Edward Short, Labour Chief Whip, October 1964 to July 1966

Short is one of those relatively unshowy politicians, of both parties, who often end up serving long periods in UK Cabinets: Short ended up as Deputy

Leader of the Labour Party. It followed that he was close to Harold Wilson who gave a speech in his constituency during the 1964 election campaign and following that meeting confirmed at that time he wanted Short to become his Chief Whip. Short was not immediately delighted by the offer – 'usually it [Chief Whip] is the dreariest and most frustrating chore in government' (Short, 1989, p.11). However, Wilson had sold the post as being 'the linchpin' of his future administration and this, perhaps, was not mere political rhetoric. Labour's minuscule majority of only four, ensured that the management of Labour's MPs would become the paramount consideration until a future election brought the chance of healthier figure. The Chief Whip is not automatically a member of Cabinet but, like Short and others on both sides of the aisle, he normally attends every one. The health of every MP carried acute political significance throughout Wilson's first administration with its tiny majority. Short records that he and Herbert Bowden, Chief Whip in opposition, prepared for government by:

> preparing a rundown of every MP of the PLP [Parliamentary Labour Party], as well as new candidates likely to be elected, assessing their suitability for ministerial office.
>
> We had discussed each one at length and set down the department for which he or she appeared best qualified and the ministerial level we felt was most appropriate: senior minister [Cabinet level], MoS or PUS.
>
> *(Short, 1989, p.17)*

Short notes that jobs were found for 'almost everyone' judging that an MP 'who could not manage at least the job of PPS ... would be very dim indeed' (ibid., p.17). The outcome of their Whips' assiduity however was disappointing: there was no evidence Harold had even read their document, placed before him 16 October 1964 on the Cabinet table. They discovered, moreover, to their chagrin and in support of Howe's argument, that appointments merely reflect the whim of the PM: Wilson had 'made a great many promises to a great many members. ... And that he received advice on appointments' from other sources: 'all his 16 appointments', thought Short and Bowden, appeared to have been 'promised long before the election'. Wilson was a regular habitue of the Tea Room where he loved to wander around, chatting small-talk and indulging his love of gossip. He seemed to rely on '*hunches*' when making appointments, rather than anything else (ibid., p.18, my emphasis).

Both Labour advisers, close to Wilson, even at this early stage in her career, worried about the role of Marcia Williams and her likely influence on the distribution of posts: they disbelieved her claim to have an 'encyclopaedic knowledge of the PLP'. (Much more on how Marcia's ambitions clashed sharply with those of other aides not to mention potential Labour ministers are dealt with in Chapter 6.) His first Cabinet involved dividing up ministerial responsibilities for economic policy: George Brown to the Department of Economic Affairs – a short-lived experiment as it turned out – while Callaghan became Chancellor: Short thought the latter would have been better placed at Education. Brown was effectively Deputy PM but the title was withheld: the opposite happening when Callaghan was awarded it a decade later in 1974.

The major problem associated with these early appointments for Wilson and Short was that Patrick Gordon Walker was made Foreign Secretary when not having been elected to the Commons. In 1964, Gordon Walker had lost his seat in a bitterly racist campaign: the Conservative, Peter Griffiths, had been elected in the general election on the slogan "If you want a n****r for a neighbour, vote Labour'. Labour's embarrassment was compounded when Gordon Walker, 'found' a safe seat in Leyton (Reg Sorenson had been happy to accept elevation to the Lords), suffered the occasional perversity of voters when they decided *not* to elect the candidate offered and returned the Tory, Ronald Buxton. The Foreign Secretary, still without a seat, then had to resign but finally won Leyton in the 1966 General Election. Once back in the Commons, Gordon Walker served as a Minister without Portfolio (1966–67) and then Secretary of State for Education (1967–68).

Short appreciated Wilson was obsessed, necessarily perhaps, with preserving the unity of what was always a potentially fragmented if not divided party. 'Every British PM must balance his appointments', he wrote:

> between the wings of his party. ... Wilson obsessed with achieving unity while Gaitskell 'wanted to fight for what he believed to be right'. ... Somewhere, Harold believed, in every conflict there was a formula, a solution behind which everyone could unite – one of the Wilsonian laws of politics.
>
> *(ibid., p.27)*

But by avoiding conflicts we get 'policies which are so anaemic and bereft of bite that they commanded little respect and achieved meagre results. He led by consent and compromise as opposed to Gaitskell's leadership by confrontation and conflict' (ibid., p.28).

Following that so very slim 1964 election victory, Short writes:

> 90 people were interviewed and appointed in 5 days. All were excited at the prospect of office, but by the time they got to No 10 the first flush of euphoria had been superseded by anxiety about the ministerial level at which they were to be offered jobs. And all MPs believe they are uniquely fitted to sit in the Cabinet, if not to occupy the PM's chair.
>
> *(ibid., p.29)*

Ted Heath, Chief Whip, 1955–59

Following Churchill's 1950 election victory, Heath was made up to a full member of the Whips' Office from being an unpaid junior. He was soon to witness to a strange anomaly whereby someone close to the top job actually played a role as PM, if only for a few weeks. It happened in July 1953 when the PM had a serious stroke after dining. Aware of his disability and hoping it was yet another illness from which he could recover, Churchill insisted news of his stroke be suppressed; even the Whips' Office itself was kept in ignorance. Son-in-law Christopher Soames and his secretary Jock Colville took care of the old man and RAB Butler took over as acting PM; a tiny consolation, perhaps, to reflect upon in his retirement for someone often dubbed the 'best prime minister we've never had'. (An additional consolation prize was derived when Butler resumed his acting PM role when Eden retreated to the Caribbean to recuperate following the Suez debacle.)

Slowly Churchill began to recover and resolved to make a speech at the Margate Conference that year. Heath recalls in his memoirs that at a certain point Churchill began to read from the wrong page of his speech. His eyes met those of the then Chief Whip, Patrick Buchan-Hepburn: after a tense few seconds, the PM realised his error and found his place again – both whips 'breathed a sigh of relief' (Heath, 1998, p.158). Churchill resigned shortly afterwards and Eden called an election, which he won with a majority of 59. Towards the end of the year, Buchan-Hepburn stood down and Eden asked Heath to become Chief Whip, advising in the reshuffle that saw Macmillan moved to the Treasury and Butler as Lord Privy Seal and Leader of the Commons. Heath saw his new role, essentially, as 'to hold the parliamentary party together'. He accepted the position with eyes open: he was 'fully aware that few Chief Whips had gone on to hold a Cabinet post and none had ever reached the summit'. Heath, however, adds a revealing afterthought: 'This did not however mean that I had given up all personal ambition. I felt from the start that if I could fill the post successfully, it would stand me in good stead for the future' (ibid., p.163). As part of this mindset he was 'determined to get away from the generally held view, constantly and graphically described in the press, that the Whips were a gang of ignorant bullies, forcing MPs to vote in certain ways, all too often against their wishes' (ibid., p.163).

Such a judgement, though unfair has achieved much traction in the media and public alike. He wanted 'much closer, friendlier and more personal contacts between each Whip and the Members for whom he was responsible' (ibid., p.163). To assist the feedback of intelligence regarding individual MPs, he introduced a system of writing pads whereby one copy was left for the whip concerned, another for the reporting whip and a third left for all whips to read: the system effectively provided immediate feedback on how the party was feeling on issues across the gamut. Heath's image, following his 'great sulk' (Ley, 2016) after being toppled by Thatcher as Leader is hardly consistent with the kind of intense empathetic persuasiveness required to lead the Whips' Office, yet it seems Heath created an excellent impression of a clubbable, caring and mostly cheerful Chief. No less a person than Tony Benn marvelled at 'How you manage to combine such a friendly manner with such iron discipline is a source of respectful amazement to us all'; of a later meeting Benn described him as a 'most amiable and friendly soul' (Ziegler, 2011, p.90). 'He had a heart full of kindness', according to Woodrow Wyatt who also noted 'an element of reserve an awkwardness' (ibid., p.90). Philip Ziegler sees Heath as 'less than perfect. He always suffered from a short temper and was apt to explode if opposed in any way which he thought pig-headed and unreasonable' (ibid., p.93). One Tory MP described him as 'fratchety; he can be very huffy if you don't agree with him' (ibid., p.93).

Such cheerfulness was to be sorely tested by events in November 1956: the Suez crisis. Heath was opposed to his government's reaction, and hugely upset by the lying about secret collusion with the French and the Israelis. His reaction reflects another aspect of political ambition: once having achieved power, no politician is content with relaxing back to any kind of prior normality. They all desperately want to continue to hold on to the means to determine events and to achieve their long-held political and personal goals. Heath explains that he chose not to follow colleagues Anthony Nutting and Edward Boyle, who both resigned, in terms of his obligation to democratic system itself.

> As this crisis developed, the feeling between the two sides of the House became so bitter that only the two Chief Whips were on speaking terms with each other. If that bond were ever to be broken, the parliamentary system itself would collapse.
>
> *(Heath, 1998, p.170)*

Heath also believed strongly in loyalty – Lord Kilmuir, recall, reckoned this to be the Conservatives' 'secret weapon' (Huhne, 2014). 'The Chief Whip's relationship with the Prime Minister is a special and personal one. He owes his complete loyalty to the prime minister, who is entitled to count on it' (Heath, 1998, p.172). Heath saw total commitment to his PM as the sine qua non of his job; perhaps explaining some of the bile he felt when one of his appointees in whom he had invested trust by elevating her political career, decided to mount the coup that toppled him in 1975. But, whilst solidly loyal, Heath was no feeble yes-man. His biographer explains that 'absolute and undivided loyalty' did not 'imply supine acquiescence' (Ziegler, 2011, p.91). Speaking truth to power was one thing but, given the Chief's key and intimate role, Heath knew that a Chief's resignation would direct 'a mortal blow to confidence in the government' (Heath, 1998, p.172). And maintaining the government in power – the primary aim of all Conservative MPs – was seen by Heath as his overriding duty. Faced with the disaster of losing the support of the USA and the potential collapse of sterling, Heath advised Macmillan during a break in Cabinet that, despite strong unhappiness in the party, the only available course was to accept the 'humiliating withdrawal from Egypt' (ibid., p.174–175).

The so-called Suez Group of MPs, including Julian Amery and Captain Charles Waterhouse, asked to speak to Heath when he was sitting at the Whips' table in the dining room. The latter assured Heath of full voting support of his group for the government in any division over the crisis, 'provided I would give an undertaking to bring about Eden's downfall as Leader of the Conservative Party. I told him to go to hell and, without further discussion went back to finish my dinner' (ibid., p.175). The government survived the resultant division with only six abstentions. Heath records that he received a 'number of notes thanking me for holding the party together during the crisis' (ibid., p.175). Eden, unwell for some time since an operation had not gone well, disappeared to the Caribbean in an attempt to restore his health (being famously looked after en route by ship's steward and future Deputy PM, John Prescott) but, predictably, speculation about the leadership went into overdrive: would it be Macmillan or RAB to take over from Eden?

Heath reports how he buried his head in his hands when he heard Eden lie to the House by 'denying any foreknowledge of Israel's invasion of Egypt' (Heath, 1998, p.177). Later he was told by the Cabinet Secretary, Sir Norman Brook, that Eden had told him to 'destroy all the relevant documents. I must go and get it done' (ibid., p.177). Accordingly he destroyed the Secret Sèvres Protocol and other evidence of collusion between Britain, France and Israel. It is clear Heath (rightly) thought this shameful together with the fact that for the rest of his life Eden 'never changed his position and always denied that any such agreement had ever existed' (ibid., p.177). By backing Macmillan, Heath perhaps ensured his survival in post and was well placed to continue climbing the Tory ladder in the post-1959 Tory election victory. His qualities as Chief Whip in retrospect seem to have been ideal but his later career revealed the emergence of the less attractive, rather imperious and short-tempered side of his nature. Perhaps he was fortunate to show up so well as Chief Whip where his record as a unifier and an understanding, yet efficient, manager laid the foundations of a career that ran the full gamut of promotion, though still managed to fall short of the ambitions he still hoped to fulfil.

Tim Renton, Chief Whip, July 1989 to November 1990

Renton was rung up, 26 October 1989, by Geoffrey Howe to tell him he was being offered the job of Chief Whip: his answer was 'Cor!' Renton's elevation was, to a degree, controversial because unlike so many previous

Chiefs, he had no prior experience of serving in their midst. However at that time in the late 1980s, there was a pervading sense of crisis caused by the poll tax, senior figures resigning and the perceived spectre of Michael Heseltine as a looming counter-revolutionary threat to Thatcherism. The provenance of this proposal had emerged via Kenneth Baker in a high-profile group of aides: Thatcher's Principal Private Secretary, Andrew Turnbull, (yes, it is often denied, but civil servants were and are still often involved in reshuffles), her Foreign Policy adviser, Charles Powell and her Press Secretary, Bernard Ingham. 'It was reckoned', his memoirs explain, 'That I would be good at knitting the different sides of the party together and particularly acting as a bridge between Margaret and Geoffrey Howe' (Renton, 2004, p.14; Renton had been close to Howe ever since serving as his PPS in 1983). It has to be allowed that over the decade he held this office, he made a substantial contribution to unifying Margaret Thatcher's government.

Renton did not think that, despite the almost monastic calling of the Whips' Office, his lack of experience was held against him (ibid., p.19). After his second Cabinet meeting, Defence Secretary Tom King, told him he thought that during Cabinet 'I was beginning to look like a Chief Whip' – clearly a reassuring comment. In other aspects of his role, Renton was aware that, despite appearing to be friends and confidants, whips occasionally had to play the 'heavy' with 'miscreants' (ibid., p.21). The classic anecdote on this refers to Michael Cocks, Labour's formidable Chief Whip who summoned Jack Straw after straying from the party line. Just when the dissident MP was not being convinced by Cocks' argument the Chief Whip seized him by the genitals, 'held onto them tight while Jack turned white in the face and finally released him with the comment, "Are you convinced now?"' (ibid., p.20). However, Straw makes no reference to such event in his own memoirs so maybe the story is apocryphal. Renton never went for anything so brutal but admits he 'sometimes used to bang his heavy ruler into my hand … and sometimes I saw a rebellious MP flinch' (ibid., p.21). The more modern story relates to Gavin Williamson's time as Chief when he used to keep a live tarantula, which he called Cronus, under glass on his desk and reckoned it would deter independent-minded MPs from rebelling against the party lines. His attempt to make Cronus a key feature of his 2017 conference speech, sadly for his career, fell a little flat.

> Trying to decide what treatment was appropriate and would be effective for each of our colleagues was a particularly difficult task. it inevitably meant a thorough knowledge of their circumstances, their ambitions and their likely reaction; made amateur psychologists of all of us in the whip's office.
>
> *(Renton, 2004, p.21)*

In the wake of Anthony Meyer's 'stalking horse' leadership contest, which he easily lost but in which Thatcher suffered 60 abstentions, 5 December 1989, Dennis Thatcher turned to Renton at the celebratory aftermath and underlined that fundamental element of the Tory MP mindset: 'Loyalty's the name of the game isn't it?' (ibid., p.32). Indeed, for Lords Commissioners of the Treasury, as whips are grandly titled, strict loyalty to the leadership is always the beginning and end of an MP's rationale for being part of the office. During reshuffles the Chief Whip is usually, but not always centrally, involved advising the PM. For example in the mini reshuffle, 3 January 1990, Renton oversaw the promotion of Michael Spicer to Minister of State at the Department of the Environment and Tony Baldry promoted to take Spicer's vacated role. Renton commented: 'Both had been on my shortlist for promotion and I was pleased she had gone along with those I recommended' (ibid., p.37).

Renton is frank in his memoir about the eventual decline in his relationship with Margaret Thatcher, around the summer of 1990. 'As the summer holidays passed', Renton's memoir notes, 'it went down with a speed that surprised me' (ibid., p.73). The reason? Peter Morrison had become Margaret's PPS. 'Thatcher very much wanted a friend as her new PPS, someone she could feel easy with. Mark Lennox-Boyd, her previous PPS had been a bit grand' (ibid., p.73). Renton was surprised at her choice of Peter Morrison, though. 'I wondered whether he was wise or firm enough and I was worried about his drinking habits' (ibid., p.73). Morrison, oddly, didn't see PPS as a downgrading but as 'the pinnacle of his career, a job of immense importance' (ibid., p.73), Whether Morrison was equal to its challenges is arguable when Thatcher relied upon his leadership of her campaign to remain party Leader. Why Morrison wanted so much to be PPS to the PM is unclear. Certainly some incumbents went on to senior office – Robert Carr, Tony Barber – but others, like Ann Coffey who laboured as PPS to Blair for several years, failed to move up to a departmental post; nor did Bruce Grocott who held the same post although he was later made Chief Whip in the House of Lords. Possibly Peter Morrison simply wanted to be the person recognised as being at the centre of things and constantly in demand, as well as serving someone he hugely admired.

Renton encountered a flurry of difficulty in the autumn of 1990 when Margaret Thatcher, looking for solid support within her less than wholly united Cabinet, tried hard to restore Norman Tebbit to the Cabinet as Education Secretary. Renton, was 'horrified' and told her the appointment would 'alienate the pro EU people' (which in practice included himself); she replied, 'You are always on the wrong side' (Renton, 2004, p.78). Alistair Goodlad, the Deputy Chief Whip, reported around this time a 'terrible' drinks party at Number 10 attended by Turnbull, Powell, Denis Thatcher and John Whittingdale who were all 'very gung-ho' about the Tebbit recall idea (ibid., p.79). To Goodlad's comment that Tebbit had been difficult about the proposal to allow special treatment to immigrants from Hong Kong, Denis said, approvingly, 'Quite right, he was against immigration' (ibid., p.79). Given Denis's frankly expressed opinions, usually even further to the right than Tebbit, it would seem likely he expressed views on appointments to Margaret.

On 2 November, Renton reacted to the PM's sustained enthusiasm for such a move with the remark that whilst 'it would show she was firmly in charge', it would make the task of uniting the party that much harder. To this came the thin-skinned reply: 'Who says I'm not in charge?' (ibid., p.79). On the phone to Tebbit shortly afterwards she asked him whether there would be 'open war' (ibid., p.80) on the European situation? The listening Renton assumed the answer was 'Yes' and Tebbit agreed to call in later to discuss the offer. When he did, he disappointed Thatcher when he explained his first duty was to care for his wife, crippled by the Brighton bombing. Eventually she agreed, with some reluctance, to accept the perceived left-leaning William Waldegrave as her new Education Secretary.

Gavin Williamson, Chief Whip, July 2016 to November 2017 – meteoric rise, catastrophic fall

Of all the Chiefs mentioned so far, Williamson is perhaps the most curious both personally and politically. Very much an outlier socially – he was manager of a Yorkshire fireplace company before becoming an MP in 2010 – he was appointed PPS to Cameron in October 2013 and was a Remain supporter when he led Theresa May's campaign to become Leader in 2016, being rewarded with the office of Chief Whip. When appointed Chief Whip it had taken him a relatively short six years from entering the Commons to achieving a Cabinet-level post. Stories of Cronus, his tarantula used allegedly to terrify rebel MPs into compliance, began to circulate but otherwise his term of office seemed unexceptional except in one respect: once Mrs May lost her majority in that infamous 2017 election Williamson was despatched to Belfast to negotiate a deal whereby the Democratic Unionist Party agreed to support May's government and provide it with the slim but vital edge needed to survive and fight another few months. Again he seemed to carry out his task with some skill: his reward? The Defence Secretaryship.

Williamson showed exceptional and ruthless guile and some good fortune in the people he decided to back politically. Again rewarded by May with the Defence portfolio until May 2019, his ludicrous declaration to Russia to 'shut up and go away' (Walker, 2021) over the Skripal attempted murders in March 2018 failed to impress. He was later dismissed from his post after a National Security Council leak enquiry named him as the source. Quickly changing sides he then helped Boris Johnson become Leader and was rewarded again in July 2019 with a Cabinet post: Education Secretary. His frequent errors over the timing of school closures and exams during the pandemic, not to mention poor performances in the Commons and the media, made him the most predictable sacking in the reshuffle of September 2021: predictions proved correct. Before the sacking, back in April, the *Daily Mail* ran a story that Williamson was 'begging' Johnson to be made Chief Whip again to save his career, on the grounds that the then current Chief, Mark Spencer, was under pressure and wanted to move to a departmental post (Tapsfield, 2021). His time as Chief, despite his failures and shortcomings, demonstrates the strength of the office as a platform for further promotion. My failed attempts to discover how effective Williamson (even from a formerly friendly Tory MP) had been as Chief reinforced the aura of omertà that surrounds the office.

However, an insight into Gavin's skills emerge in Seldon and Newell's book on the Johnson premiership. In the wake of Johnson's 2018 resignation from May's Cabinet, his focus was firmly on willing that rugby ball to emerge from the back of the scrum, plus Johnson's self-appointed supporters. This group included Williamson and James Wharton who introduced 'iron discipline' into the campaign. Johnson was told to allow 20 minutes to see a list of chosen MPs but his:

> willingness to say anything to anyone to gain their backing became a nightmare for his minders. Wild promises were made about seats in the Lords, public offices, ambassadorships, posts in No 10 and more. Williamson recalls 'we drafted in Grant Shapps [another shrewd judge of winners and losers in leadership contests] to sit in the room and make a careful note of what on earth Boris was promising'.
>
> *(Seldon and Newell, 2023, pp.48–49)*

Despite his poor public profile and being cast, once again, into the backbench wilderness, this time by Johnson, Gavin was still highly regarded for his political nous. Seldon and Newell recount how Sunak consulted him in early 2022 after the 'non-dom' crisis emerged. He was advised to hang on in to repair the damage before going for Leader after Johnson falls. 'Williamson's form in helping make May and Johnson Prime Minister made him the go-to man among leadership contenders' (ibid., 2023, p.531).

David Waddington, Chief Whip, 1987–89

This northern, barrister MP entered the Commons in 1979 for Ribble Valley and, after a two-year stint as a junior whip had risen to MoS level in charge of immigration. He expected to be moved after the Tory victory in 1987, either as Chief Whip or Solicitor General; Thatcher offered him the former and he accepted his return to the Whips' Office, this time as boss. Nigel Lawson subsequently told him he was only Margaret's second choice: she wanted John Major but Lawson insisted he join the Treasury team as Chief Secretary; given he entered Parliament in 1979, his promotion velocity was steady rather than meteoric. Waddington reflects, a little ruefully in his memoirs: 'Whether John Major would have become Prime Minister had he spent a sizable part of the 1987 parliament as Chief Whip is extremely doubtful. If I had been made Solicitor General I certainly would not have become Home Secretary' (Waddington, 2012, p.164).

The new Chief was immediately put to work completing the reshuffle with John Wakeham by settling the 'middle-rank and junior ministers' (ibid., p.164). Despite his subsequent reputation as a 'safe pair of hands', Waddington reflected he was unsure that Disraeli's view that a Chief Whip required 'consummate knowledge of human nature, the most amiable flexibility and complete self-control ... sounded like me' (ibid., p.165). However, he soon settled into the job, viewing it, during the Thatcher years as 'a training ground for those it was thought had the qualities to become departmental ministers' (ibid., p.166). He congratulated the fact that most of his team, including David Hunt, Bob Boscawen, Tristan Garrel-Jones and David Lightbown, 'soon got promotion' (ibid., p.166). There is no doubt the Chief 'has extraordinary influence with ministers' (ibid., p.67) – Waddington cites an occasion when he asked four Cabinet members to speak at an event in his constituency, expecting only one to say yes. In the event all four volunteered: not too surprising when one appreciates how central the Chief's judgement of them might prove to their future promotion in reshuffles.

Chris Heaton-Harris, Chief Whip, February 2022–

Chris Heaton-Harris replaced Mark Spencer as Chief Whip following the rocky period for Boris Johnson after the Partygate revelations in January 2022. The *Guardian* ran a piece in April 2022, when Partygate was again dominating the news following the fines handed out to Johnson, his wife Carrie, and Rishi Sunak for attending Whitehall parties during lockdown in 2020–21, alleging that the new Chief and his deputy, Chris Pincher:

> have said to have taken on a 'good cop, bad cop' approach to stop MPs rebelling in votes and voicing discontent publicly in the media. The pair organised a team dinner last month for all Conservative MPs to get together and restore some of the bonds of camaraderie that had become frayed during Johnson's lowest point in mid-January. While both have avoided making any public appearances they play an important backroom role: reassuring MPs who are sceptical of key government decisions, and,

> if needed, dangling the prospect of promotion to encourage them to stay supportive.
>
> *(Clinton and Mason, 2022)*

The article also points out that within the Cabinet, uber-loyal members Nadine Dorries and her persuasive colleague, Grant Shapps, were daily looped out around the media studios to argue the PM was genuinely unaware these social events were not work related and constituted a breach of the law. In addition recently demoted Cabinet members, Matt Hancock and Robert Jenrick, were both enthusiastically speaking up for Johnson, presumably in the hope it might help reboot their ministerial careers.

Extract from an interview with Keith Bradley, Deputy Chief Whip, July 1998 to June 2001

Keith Bradley suggested to me that a 'continuum' existed between Garrel-Jones's 'Whips' System' and Howe's 'No System' points of view.

> In my term in the whip's office we were contributors to discussions on who got promoted and when. We weren't in any shape of form the deciding factor. We were part of the centralised process that enabled the PM to make decisions: we fed into that process.

During the 1990s, posts were allocated according to annual PLP votes on their fellow MPs; in government there was some transference to opposition briefs but it was never total and other people were often preferred. During the first reshuffle in July, when Blair's preferred choices were put in post, whips were instrumental in suggesting who might be promoted to become a minister, especially who should be placed on that first rung of the ladder: PPS. Labour's huge majority created the need for MPs to play a role and whips acted to deploy MPs towards specific areas of departmental interest. His own appointment as Deputy Chief Whip came as a surprise to him as he 'had not displayed any wish to be in the whip's office but the PM, found out, through chatting around a bit, that there was a role for me in managing the huge parliamentary Labour party'. Interestingly Bradley suggests the location of one's interview with the PM is significant: 'If he wants to see you in the House, you're sacked. If he wants to see you in Number Ten, you will get a job.'

Bradley's insight on the clash between Frank Field and both the Chancellor, Brown, as well as Harriet Harmon at Social Security is that only the junior ministers, including his own contributions, were actually 'keeping what show there was, on the road'. Blair had told Field to 'think the unthinkable' but after the mega-fallout declared his thinking was in fact, 'unfathomable'.

Rivalry and promotion

Nobody in politics denies the intensity of the feelings engendered by the ambition for self-advancement. In her very readable memoir, Andrea Leadsom notes:

> Sadly, the tantalising prospect of promotion also creates jealousy and a strong sense that there is no meritocracy in politics: your preferment or otherwise is viewed too often as a result of voting as you are told to, or because you're part of the right clique ... Those who make it to the Cabinet face the spectre of being sacked at the peak of their performance, and those in the ranks of junior ministers are rarely satisfied with their lot, longing to reach the next rung of the ladder.
>
> *(Leadsom, 2023, p.22)*

When Cameron won an overall majority in 2015 and the jobs once performed by Lib Dems came up for grabs, Leadsom reports there were:

> a few tensions between those who got ministerial jobs and others who felt stuck on the back benches. Politics is a brutal business – while many MPs keep their views on promotions to themselves and carry on to forge brilliant careers on select committees, as government trade envoys or lobbying for major policy changes, there are definitely some who struggle with feelings of being overlooked.
>
> *(ibid., pp.22, 47)*

References and further reading

Armstrong, H. (2019) 'Whips reflect'. Institute for Government, 6 March.

BBC News (2012) 'The legacy of Macmillan's "night of the long knives"'. 6 July. www.bbc.co.uk/news/uk-politics-18722428.

Blick, A. and Hennessy, P. (2019) *Good Chaps No More?* Safeguarding the Constitution in Stressful Times. Constitution Society report. https://consoc.org.uk/publications/good-chaps-no-more-safeguarding-the-constitution-in-stressful-times-by-andrew-blick-and-peter-hennessy/.

Buchan-Hepburn, P. (1953) 'Memo to prime minister'. Prem 5, National Archives, 30 October.

Campbell, A. and Stewart, R. (2023) 'George Osborne: Austerity, Boris Johnson, and the UK's next prime minister'. *The Rest Is Politics: Leading*, Podcast, 15 May. https://pod.link/1665265193/episode/41e322f4b8167f84fc348b29a3c07457.

Clinton, J. and Mason, R. (2022) 'No 10 denies PM knew of Chris Pincher's misconduct claims before promotion'. *Guardian*, 1 July.

Cowley, P. (2005) *The Rebels: How Blair Mislaid His Majority*. Politico's.

Devine, D., Durrant, T., Britchfield, C. and Barr, B. (2023) 'Government ministers'. Institute for Government, 21 May. www.instituteforgovernment.org.uk/explainer/government-ministers.

Forsyth, J. (2022) 'Tories may never recover if they lose in 2024'. The Times, 20 May.
Hague, W. (2023) 'Too much localism gives us second rate MPs'. *The Times*, 25 April.
Heath, E. (1998) *The Autobiography of Edward Heath: The Course of My Life.* Hodder & Stoughton.
Hoskyns, J. (1983) 'Whitehall and Westminster: An outsider's view'. *Parliamentary Affairs*, Vol. 36, Issue 1, 137–147.
Huhne, C. (2014) 'Cameron's Tories are even more rebellious than Major's: Whatever happened to loyalty?' *Guardian*, 2 February.
Jones, B. (2010) 'Climbing the greasy pole: Promotion in British politics'. *Political Quarterly*, Vol. 81, Issue 4, pp. 616–626.
Jones, D. (2011) *Fixing Britain: The Business of Reshaping our Nation.* Wiley.
Kavanagh, D. (2014) 'Sir John Hoskyns: Plain speaking self made millionaire who headed Margaret Thatcher's Policy Unit but fell out with her'. *Independent*, 23 October.
Leadsom, A. (2023) *Snakes and Ladders: Navigating the Ups and Downs of Politics.* Biteback.
Ley, S. (2016) 'Margaret Thatcher hails Ted Heath as a "Great PM" '. BBC News, 9 July.
Major, J. (1999) *John Major: The Autobiography.* HarperCollins.
Moore, C. (2015) *Margaret Thatcher: The Authorized Biography*, Vol. 2: Everything She Wants. Allen Lane.
Murphy, J. (2022) *Ministers Reflect.* Institute for Government, 7 October.
Oakeshott, I. (2009) 'Gordon Brown wants Ed Balls as chancellor'. *Sunday Times*, 31 May.
Paxman, J. (2002) *The Political Animal.* Michael Joseph.
Pidd, H. (2022) 'Interview: Tory defector Christian Wakeford on crossing the floor: "All I was thinking was, please don't throw up"'. *Guardian*, 2 April.
Pogrund, G. (2022) 'Charlie Elphicke: Predator MP and his protection racket'. *Sunday Times*, 20 March.
Public Administration Select Committee (PASC) (2009) 'Good government'. Eighth Report of Session 2008–09, Vol. II, 18 June.
Public Administration Select Committee (PASC) (2010) 'Goats and tsars: Ministerial and other appointments from outside parliament'. Eighth Report of Session 2009–10, 11 March.
Rawnsley, A. (2004) 'Another one bites the dust'. *Observer*, 4 April.
Renton, T. (2004) *Chief Whip: People, Power and Patronage in Westminster.* Politico's.
Riddell, P. (1993) *Honest Opportunism.* Hamish Hamilton.
Riddell, P. (2020) *15 Minutes of Power: The Uncertain Life of British Ministers.* Profile.
Seldon, A. and Newell, R. (2023) *Johnson at 10: The Inside Story.* Atlantic.
Short, E. (1989) *Whip to Wilson.* Macdonald.
Stratton A. and Wintour, P. (2009) 'James Purnell quits cabinet and calls on Gordon Brown to stand aside now'. *Guardian*, 5 June.
Summers, D. (2009). 'Gordon Brown's reshuffle in crisis as John Hutton quits'. *Guardian*, 5 June.
Tapsfield, J. (2021) 'Gavin Williamson is pleading with Boris to make him Chief Whip as Tory MPs brand him a failure who should be forgotten'. *Mail Online*, 9 April.
Waddington, D. (2012) *David Waddington: Memoirs.* Biteback.

Walker, P. (2021) 'Gavin Williamson, the man who told Russia to "go away and shut up"'. *Guardian*, 15 September.
White, H. (2023) '2023: Institute for Government's year in review'. Institute for Government, 29 December. www.instituteforgovernment.org.uk/comment/institute-government-year-review-2023.
Ziegler, P. (2011) *Edward Heath*. Harper.

4

RESHUFFLING THE PACK

> If the PM makes you an offer and you are not in an exceptionally powerful position, take what you are offered or be ready to return to the back benches; dozens will be ready to accept what you rejected.
>
> (Kaufman, 1997, p.xix)

> I would say that Gordon is much better at reshuffles than Tony. Tony didn't enjoy them on the whole – well, neither of them enjoyed sacking ministers – but Gordon just brought an organisation to reshuffles.
>
> (Institute for Government, 2022, p.5)

Much of this book focuses on politicians' progress up the promotion ladder but it also includes an awareness that, once they make it to the top, PMs use a number of ploys to remain there, including the Whips' Office to monitor and encourage loyalty, patronage to incentivise it and reshuffles to reward it, plus improving the chances government objectives will be *delivered*. There is some evidence that PMs use reshuffles to plan strategically. David Cameron's approach, for example, was to be 'always thinking about the reshuffle after next' (Cole and Heale, 2022, p.85). In their biography of Liz Truss, Cole and Heale have a party grandee explain:

> Right from the beginning of 2010 when we got into power, there was a plan to accelerate some of the new kind of Cameron MPs as quickly as we could, so they could be in the cabinet for the 2015 General Election. But to do that you have really to push them on every level. They have to go

DOI: 10.4324/9781003405085-5

> MP to bag carrier to junior minister. You have to push, push, push, push, push. And then, when people fall by the wayside, not everyone makes it.
>
> *(Cole and Heale, 2022, p.85)*

Reshuffles always create some excitement in the media, both in anticipation and on the day, but usually not for much longer. There is a natural interest in how some will prosper – the 'winners' – and why, plus the slightly morbid interest in who will suffer – the 'losers' – and the associated pleasures of those who never liked the latter anyway. All these factors were present in one of the most infamous reshuffles in British democratic political history, engineered by Harold Macmillan in 1962; this and other reshuffle examples reveal the varying roles these events can play in the constant upward progress of those who make it in politics plus the downward movement of those who don't.

Before considering some of the more significant reshuffles it is worth remembering the way in which Cabinet appointments are initially made. Anthony Seldon points out that PMs' first Cabinets are appointed when conditions are exactly propitious.

> The most significant appointments may have been in the mind of a would-be prime minister for many months or years, but when the result of the general election is declared at dawn on a bleary Friday morning and they have had a night without sleep, PMs can rush out appointments to feed the hungry press.
>
> *(Seldon, 2024, p.183)*

Perhaps a sensible practice for incoming PMs is to beg a few days to recover and to assemble his or her Cabinet? Reshuffles, moreover, do not necessarily produce spikes in the polls. *The Economist*'s study in November 2023 concludes that their influence is 'negligible' (*The Economist*, 2023) but recognises that dispensing with poor performing ministers and recruiting new talent waiting on the back benches is a very necessary process. Seldon recommends that although most PMs shy away from reshuffles, they must screw up their resolve and be 'ruthless' when they have to be done (Seldon, 2021, p.164). Attlee managed to wield the knife with an aplomb few of his successors were able to manage.

The night of the long knives

This event, named after Hitler's bloody elimination by the SS and Gestapo of a supposed threat to Nazism from its paramilitary Brownshirts section led by Ernst Rohm, bore no real resemblance to Macmillan's Cabinet changes in 1962. However, the fact that someone assumed to be a moderate, kindly Edwardian figure, had sacked an unprecedented third of his Cabinet was a form of political brutality that led the media to make the comparison. Why did he do it and snuff out the careers of his closest colleagues? His reasons were similar to those of most PMs when they feel their top team needs some rearrangement.

First, after his 1959 election victory, when he had been widely anointed 'Supermac', his government had lost much of its shine: it needed to be refreshed. Lord Hailsham reckoned the PM 'was losing his grip on public opinion and the party in general ... the party had lost its sense of direction and conviction' (Lewis, 1998, pp.219–222). The electoral hammer blow of the Orpington by-election occurred on 14 March 1962 when a 22 per cent swing from the Tories in the safe seat of Orpington landed the Liberal's Eric Lubbock in the Commons. Second, Macmillan himself had lost faith in some of his ageing colleagues: he felt his Chancellor, Selwyn Lloyd, did not have the appearance of 'a man with fire in his belly ... we wanted a less tired mind'. For his part Selwyn thought 'things were going rather well' (BBC News, 2012).

Third, and maybe closest to home, he suspected his long-time rival, the able RAB Butler, widely seen as the probable next in line as PM, to be plotting against him. However, Macmillan's reshuffle bombed. Instead of appearing wise and firm of decision, his ploy appeared more like desperation with a strong element of malevolence. And yet, as Peter Oborne observed, it could have been perceived as a 'masterstroke of political renewal', ushering in the next Tory generation of talent: Maudling, Thorneycroft, Joseph – average age 50 years, compared with the despatched seven of 59 years old. Instead Macmillan's government slowly expired via De Gaulle's veto, poor economic growth and the Profumo affair (Oborne quoted in BBC News, 2012).

PMs and reshuffles

Few PMs enjoy reshuffles. That most headmistress-like of PMs, Margaret Thatcher, shared her view early on in Number 10 with Robin Day: '"I'm not a good butcher ... but I've had to learn how to carve the joint", implying this traditionally male role was not to her taste' (Moore, 2015, p.66). My interview with Charles Powell provides a graphic account of how much she hated these unwelcome but necessary procedures:

> She hated reshuffles. She would not think about reshuffles. She wouldn't talk about reshuffles until jolly nearly the day before and as desperate private secretaries drew up lists and tried to engage her attention so that there was some structured thought beforehand, she would dismiss them all and the papers would come back unread in the box, because she really didn't like the business of getting rid of some people and appointing others. She would only focus under great pressure. So the idea, as one

> reads in the paper, months ahead that so and so was going to advance in the next reshuffle was just a laugh, because where would they come from? We couldn't persuade her to give a moment's thought to it and so we knew that these things were not official leaks – inspired usually by the candidates for advancement, who were determined to put their own names into the ring.
>
> *(personal interview)*

Adding to this evidence, her biographer Charles Moore records, she realised 'good people sometimes have to be moved just to let new blood through the system, but she hated it, claiming: "Reshuffling was the worst and rottenest job a PM ever has to do"' (Moore, 2015, p.429). She also realised demotions and sackings were not just unpleasant confrontations to be endured: they also created enemies. For politicians the future is a space in which they dream of longed for achievements: anyone damaging such dreams is launching a spear into the heart of the person concerned. A good example of this is provided by the Thatcher's leadership campaign manager, Airey Neave, later tragically murdered by the Irish Republican Army.

When a junior minister in 1959, Neave was told by the then Chief Whip, Ted Heath, that his political career was over. Norman Fowler recalled that Neave 'deeply resented the way he had been discarded and the way it had been done' (Fowler, 1991, pp.13–14). Fifteen years later Neave got his 'revenge', running Margaret Thatcher's campaign almost along military lines and achieving a success that probably disguised a major element of his motivation. Sir Geoffrey Howe was another Cabinet member with rather conflicted views on reshuffles. Following the 1985 party conference he regretted the absence of Patrick Jenkin, whom Thatcher had asked to stand down 'to give her room for new faces in the Cabinet' (Howe, 1995, p.445). Jenkin wrote to Howe: 'You and I have soldiered together for so long that is difficult to believe that we can no longer do so – at least in the same way' (ibid., p.445). Howe comments:

> I was dismayed to see him go, since I saw him as one of a number of colleagues whose ability to shape the collective wisdom of the government had been diminished by frequent job changes and premature disposal. A government that is long in office, of course requires refreshment from time to time. And loyal, sometimes long-suffering back benchers need to see credible prospects of advancement.
>
> *(ibid., p.445)*

Mrs Thatcher's first few years in power were dominated by Cabinet rows: the 'wets' like Jim Prior and Ian Gilmour were very concerned by the direction of the 'dry' economic policies of Thatcher and Chancellor Geoffrey

Howe, which were causing widespread bankruptcies and unemployment. After her Falklands-inspired triumph in 1983, she was determined, and felt strong enough to install a more supportive Cabinet. The key question was who would replace Howe. Patrick Jenkin was regarded as the most likely candidate to succeed but Thatcher chose someone she regarded as more dynamic, with a 'creative mind': Nigel Lawson.

Her biographer comments that by this time it now looked like the 'economic doctrines of Thatcherism could be boldly applied in what was beginning to look like prosperity' (Moore, 2015, p.66). To achieve this she needed disciples in Cabinet, not people prepared to argue in the wider party and public. Appointing John Wakeham as the new Chief Whip, whom she described as 'another of my boys' (ibid., p.67), she called him in to discuss the reshuffle. Perhaps expecting to give the advice Chief Whips traditionally feed into such discussions, he must have been surprised to be handed 'a complete list of her proposed changes which she had already worked out with Whitelaw, Parkinson and the outgoing Chief, Michael Jopling' (ibid., p.67). She had had to recognise that her favourite, Cecil Parkinson, could not become Foreign Secretary because of the scandal surrounding Sarah Keays – she passionately felt he should *not* leave his wife, Ann – but agreed to his suggestion that he head up an amalgamated Department of Trade and Industry.

Denied the Chancellorship Jenkin was shifted to Environment to deliver 'a really big job' (ibid., p.67): the abolition of the Greater London Council. Immediately a typical reshuffle downside occurred: Norman Tebbit was miffed by Parkinson's appointment as he had hoped for something similar after Employment. Moore notes that 'as young Conservative activists in Hemel Hempstead in the early 1960s, they felt rivalry as well as friendship' (ibid., fn p.67). It seems Thatcher was following the advice of her unpaid Chief of Staff, David Wolfson, that 'The crucial battle of the next five years will be with the unions' and that Tebbit was the best person to fight it (ibid., p.67). Nevertheless, her biographer notes, Tebbit's 'lack of promotion marked the beginning of increasingly fractious relations between Mrs Thatcher and her toughest public defender' (ibid., p.67).

The downside of reshuffles returned in the case of its major casualty, Francis Pym. During the election campaign, he had been sufficiently unwise to warn against a 'landslide majority' (ibid., p.68). One suspects her hand did not hover long before the red line was applied to his name; 'he was soft' (ibid., p.67) she remarked of him and he was consigned to the back benches. She had tried to compensate him by suggesting the Speakership (his ancestor John Pym had been one of the five MPs who had stood up to Charles I) but Pym, furious at being sacked (read the first chapter of his hastily written *Politics of Consent*, to see how angry) 'absolutely refused' (ibid., p.68) the offer which in any case was not in her gift.

Another problem in this reshuffle arose over Leon Brittan whose promotion was something of a leap from Chief Secretary of the Treasury to Home Secretary. Within the party, according to her biographer Charles Moore, Brittan was seen as a creature of the PM as well as a pro-European with liberal, and hence unconservative, social views, along with the so-called Cambridge Mafia group containing Norman Fowler, Norman Lamont, John Gummer and Ken Clarke. Moore also suggests that

> contained in the adverse reaction to Brittan's appointment was a submerged element of antisemitism: the belief that it was all very well for Jews to take 'clever' ministries to do with money but in matters of law and order the Tory party tended to prefer someone 'more English'.
>
> *(ibid., p.70)*

My interview with one of her senior aides confirmed this possibility. Noting that Thatcher had included in her Cabinet a number with a Jewish East European background, Harold Macmillan had joked that these days there were 'more Estonians in the Cabinet than Etonians' (Delingpole, 2014). Moore rejects any idea Thatcher sought to create 'a defined Jewish group among her ministers', judging that her 'sympathy with Jews was part of her anti-establishment instincts and her belief that conservatism was a creed of opportunity' (Moore, 2015, p.70). Thatcher ideally wanted to be surrounded by 'her boys' and was prepared to back them when they made mistakes. Nick Ridley was someone with whom she shared a warm common bond of agreement on most issues: he was one of the original 'hardcore' Thatcherites (ibid., p.70). In a July 1990 interview with Nigel Lawson's son Dominic, Ridley let fly at the European Community and Germany in particular:

> This is all a German racket designed to take over the whole of Europe. It has to be thwarted. This rushed take-over by the Germans on the worst possible basis, with the French behaving like poodles to the Germans, is absolutely intolerable.
>
> *(Wasps Nest, 2011)*

His bleak view on Germany's post-war economic miracle was attributed, insultingly – given their high productivity and winning efficiency – to 'their habits' (ibid.). With the UK an important member of the derided European Economic Community, these statements were dynamite. Heseltine, immediately he saw the article, rang through to Number 10 to say Ridley should be sacked at once. Thatcher was extremely reluctant to do so as she had such a high regard for someone Renton describes as 'one of the last of the faithful around her' (Renton, 2004, p.64). She took a fair bit of coaxing to realise she had no choice but to ask him to resign: he duly obediently did so.

The resultant reshuffle is remarkable for another reason. The PM invited Renton and his wife Alice to Chequers so that the matter could be discussed. After dining, the PM looked at Renton's prepared list of appointments and suggested they retire to the drawing room for this purpose, adding that Alice should accompany them. Renton instantly noted one of Mrs Thatcher's foibles when discussing reshuffles – further evidence of Powell's comments above and perhaps a reflection of how fraught such a process is – a tendency to slip 'away at a tangent':

> This was the hallmark of all conversations about reshuffles. One would start at a fixed place but find, within seconds, that she had darted all over the scenery, and pieces that had been elaborately woven into the tapestry a day or two before would fall apart in the most haphazard manner. I went through my suggestions, continually trying to bring her back to my draft list. She interrupted, jumped from one department to another and then – worst of all – occasionally leaned back and fell asleep for some seconds.
> *(ibid., p.66)*

They duly moved and began their discussion but 'after a while Alice, sitting on the opposite sofa and amazed at the confusion, suggested that she should act as secretary and make a list, a compilation of our various suggestions' (ibid., p.66). Mrs Thatcher provided pens and paper and Alice 'faithfully wrote down all the different computations and possibilities, occasionally observing that we were giving two people the same job' (ibid., p.66). On Sunday, Renton reports, his wife set out on her word processor a precise scheme of how and where every existing minister stayed where he was, left the government altogether or moved across to a slot in a different department. 'This put everything in order in a number of different columns, but it took us much of the day' (ibid., p.67). They were able to correct mistakes where they 'had moved one PUS into two departments at once or moved him or her out of a department but provided no other job' (ibid., p.67). Turnbull subsequently made three copies and the reshuffle 'followed the exact format that Alice had created' (ibid., p.67). In a research interview on promotion with a senior civil servant I was told it would not be 'proper' for a civil servant to be involved in promotion issues: this I thought curious as the biographies mention how frequently they were in fact involved. However, the participation of a wholly external, unelected person – a minister's wife – surely raises some important issues?

The pivotal Thatcher reshuffle, July 1989

Thatcher's position had been weakened by the poll tax travails, plus the gradual tiring of Tory MPs and large sections of the public at her imperious style. The Iron Lady's views on Europe had hardened, especially regarding the idea of a common currency, and her tolerance of the Cabinet's most enthusiastic pro-European, Geoffrey Howe, had reached an end. The reshuffle entailed replacement of David Young, John Moore and Paul Channon by Peter Brooke, John Gummer and Norman Lamont. It also saw the promotion to Cabinet of rising star, John Patten. However, the reason why this reshuffle was pivotal is because of what produced its main headline: the sacking of Sir Geoffrey Howe.

Concerned about his Minister of State, Howe rang Waddington on 23 July to lobby for the retention of Lynda Chalker as his Minister of State for Europe. The Chief Whip kept quiet on this as the PM had already informed him confidentially that Howe was pencilled in for the sack. Howe later complained Waddington should have told him of his soon-to-be fate but he explains 'my first loyalty was to the Prime Minister' (Howe, 1995, p.586): Howe understood this, but their relationship never really recovered. On 24 July 1989, Howe was summoned to Number 10 but 'had no special anxiety regarding any change of post as either sensible or likely' (ibid. p.586): 'I'm making some changes Geoffrey', the PM told him, 'and they will involve the Foreign Office' (ibid., p.586). He was offered the Home Office as an option, which did not appeal: he asked for time to consider the Leadership of the House offer (plus the Lord Presidency). As an afterthought sweetener she said she was asking Lawson to 'give up Dorneywood [the grace and favour residence for the Chancellor] so that you can move there from Chevening [the equivalent for the Foreign Secretary]' (ibid., p.587). The mild-mannered Howe was dumbfounded: 'The word "shock" cannot do justice to my feelings at the way in which this was sprung on me, after ten years as one of her closest Cabinet colleagues' (ibid., p.587). Leon Brittan and Lawson were both 'greatly shocked' by his sacking (ibid., p. 587), with the latter advising he refuse both the Home Office and the Leadership of the House.

Brittan, his friend Richard Ryder and Howe's wife, Elspeth, advised resignation as Howe's best option; his private secretary Stephen Wall and his special adviser, Anthony Teasdale, advised that as 'a natural insider' he would be 'stronger' if staying within the government rather than on the back benches (ibid., p. 587). They argued resignation would 'seriously damage the government and would not be understood or forgiven, even by some of my own supporters'; the latter concern suggests Howe's team had his possible future leadership ambitions in mind here (Howe, 1995, p.588). They advised he ask to be given 'proper authority' as Deputy PM (ibid., p.588). Howe then asked Waddington to call and see him. He arrived, 'ashen faced', to be shown the text of Howe's planned resignation letter (ibid., p.589). The Chief Whip, aware Howe was ready to resign, did his best to dissuade him. Howe mentioned his Deputy PM requirement, stressing that the 'terms on which he held the Deputy Prime Ministership would be of crucial importance' (ibid., p.590). Again discussing with the PM, Howe asked that he wanted to assume 'the role previously occupied by Willie Whitelaw' (ibid., p.590). She replied that would depend on how far they 'were able to create confidence in each other, for Willie has been a very special kind of person'. Howe said such confidence had been 'greatly damaged by today's events' (ibid., p.591).

She explained she could not tell Howe who would replace him 'since I haven't yet warned his boss' (ibid., p.590). Back in his old office Teasdale worked out that the only minister with a 'boss' was the Chief Secretary to the Treasury, John Major. To be replaced by a complete foreign policy novice must have added yet an extra layer to the humiliations heaped upon poor Sir Geoffrey. He quotes Richard Ingrams, editor of *Private Eye* on his dismissal:

> Perhaps in ordinary times it would not matter very much who is Britain's Foreign Secretary. But we are not living in ordinary times but amid momentous events. All the more extraordinary that our man on the world scene is ... completely lacking in any experience of, or even evident interest in, foreign affairs, by comparison with a predecessor who now seems a giant of statesmanship.
>
> *(ibid., p.595)*

John Major noted in his memoirs that he would not have been surprised if Geoffrey had resigned a year earlier in 1989,

> when he was removed from the Foreign Office to become Leader of the House and nominal Deputy Prime Minister, it was a blatant demotion. But he had stayed on to be treated with increasing intolerance by the PM. Her general tone towards him was sharp, occasionally even cruel. If he felt aggrieved, he would certainly have been justified in doing so.
>
> *(Major, 1999, p.177)*

Clearly it was with a heavy heart that Howe accepted the package deal of titles and responsibilities awarded by Thatcher as a consolation for losing the job he loved. He was subsequently infuriated by the suggestion appearing in the press that he had 'only agreed to stay when the PM had promised to take Dorneywood from Nigel Lawson' (Waddington, 2012, p.174) – Howe and Elspeth had loved Chevening but always realised it was a lease on limited time – and even more annoyed by Bernard Ingham's briefing to the Lobby, which 'rubbished' the Deputy PM role as a 'courtesy title with no constitutional status' (Howe, 1995, p.594). It was clear Ingham reflected the views of his boss – Waddington comments that Thatcher 'was far too honest to pretend that the title of Deputy Prime Minister meant anything very much when it clearly did not' (Waddington, 2012, p.175). His unexpected, and for him wholly undeserved, sacking was hugely consequential as it hid a history of humiliating treatment of Sir Geoffrey by Mrs Thatcher in Cabinet meetings especially when European matters were discussed. The final straw was to occur later on 30 October 1990 when she indulged her hostility to any future plans for European institutions with her cries of 'No, No, No!' at the Despatch Box. Two days later came Howe's historic resignation speech, which effectively opened the door to the leadership contest that Thatcher was destined to lose.

The night of the blunt knives

Gordon Brown's major reshuffle in June 2009 instantly prompted comparisons with Macmillan's infamous ministerial rearrangement in 1962, dubbed by the press as the night of the long knives. In Brown's 2009 case, the word 'blunt' was substituted by *The Times* (see Oliver et al., 2009). Brown's political trajectory was always aiming to become Labour Leader and PM. Back in 1994, after John Smith died, Brown was forced to realise that despite his own intellectual and especially financial brilliance, Tony Blair had been the more gifted political persuader and preferred by his party as Leader. His refusal to accept Blair's authority marred the New Labour years but, ironically, once he finally became PM, he seemed not to know what he wanted to do. Initially he sought a mandate from a general election but when opinion polls suggested a Tory revival, his boldness melted away and his reign was beset with problems and failures, many of them stemming from his apparent loss of any winning style as a communicator. The expenses scandal damaged both parties but, as the party of government, Labour came in for an undeserved share of the blame. The 2009 reshuffle came less than a year after the October 2008 reshuffle occasioned by the resignation of Ruth Kelly from the Cabinet, to 'spend more time with her family' (Summers, 2008), often the excuse given by ministers who have become disillusioned with their jobs (she has another job, at the time of writing, as Chair of Water UK). The biggest surprise of this ministerial rearrangement was the return to the Cabinet of Peter Mandelson, after four years of serving as European Trade Commissioner. The appointment caused great surprise as Mandelson was widely seen as a disciple of Brown's arch-rival Tony Blair; this was the third time Mandelson had been awarded a Cabinet post. He admitted he had not expected to be asked but dismissed any former feud as mere 'ups and downs': he was 'very proud to have been invited to serve in this government' (Wintour, 2008). A more cynical analysis of this appointment was that Brown was becoming desperate at his lack of progress as the next election became imminent.

Moreover, disillusion with Brown's leadership reached a critical phase by the summer of 2009. Children's minister, Beverley Hughes, had resigned for personal reasons, according to her allies because she 'could not see a reason to continue in ministerial office' (*Manchester Evening News*, 2009b). Next a bitterly disappointed Hazel Blears, the Communities Secretary, had resigned following Brown's comment that her expenses claims were 'totally unacceptable' (*Manchester Evening News*, 2009a); the media went to town on Labour's travails on the eve of important local and European elections. On the same day, the first ever female Home Secretary, Jacqui Smith, resigned having suffered the humiliation of having claimed on expenses the cost of two 'adult' films for her husband.

There were rumours that an email campaign had revealed that a substantial group of Labour MPs were plotting Brown's downfall. As if all this were not enough, more rumours abounded that Labour activists were not enthusiastic about their Leader. Seldon's study of Brown notes that Downing Street 'despaired at the deep pessimism that infected some Labour ministers' regarding the looming general election. Brown's distant relationships with his three Secretaries of State is one reason why the National Security and International Development committee was not a success. Members complained that he often turned up late, created an atmosphere of hostility and was distracted by scribbling to himself or receiving notes passed to him by his private secretaries, which attendees found degrading (Seldon and Lodge, 2010, pp.299–300). Perhaps Brown's poor ratings were undeserved, given his performance in the wake of the 2008 economic meltdown when, if he did not 'save the world' (ibid., p.190) by successfully recapitalising British banks, he certainly saved the UK economy. But economics is so complex, it's possible his exceptional statecraft passed by unnoticed by most voters. Arriving as a body blow to his government – acknowledged by Brown as 'an attempt to dislodge me' (Brown, 2017, p.352) – was the resignation of the Work and Pensions Secretary, James Purnell. In case anyone should doubt his real intentions he asked that Brown 'stand aside to give Labour a fighting chance of winning the next election' (Stratton and Wintour, 2009).

Purnell had become increasingly disillusioned with Gordon Brown and intended his resignation to be a rallying cry to Cabinet colleagues to do the same; he was also annoyed at the false rumour emanating from Number 10 that he was gay, possibly the work of a deliberate smear. The final hammer blows to Brown were delivered by Labour's poor showing in the local elections: a loss of 327 councillors plus the long-held Labour-controlled Derbyshire, Lancashire and Staffordshire county councils. Piling on the agony Labour slumped to their lowest in the Euro elections of 8 June coming third behind UKIP with only 15.2 per cent of the vote and having lost 1.5 million votes. So, as in the case of his Tory predecessor in 1962, Brown tried a similar tactic to refresh his government and strengthen it for the coming general election. Could a reshuffle save the beleaguered Brown?

Winners and losers

One of Brown's main intentions was to move Ed Balls from Children's Secretary to his long-held ambition of Chancellor (Brown, 2017, p.352). However, this move was stymied when Alistair Darling refused to be moved from his post as Chancellor, thus becoming a major winner from the disputed process. Ed Balls had been confidently expecting to fulfil his foremost ambition and had even been packing his things to exit his department; he was left furious, frustrated and humiliated especially as his wife Yvette Cooper had been promoted to the biggest spending department of Work and Pensions. David Miliband, seen by many as the leading candidate to replace the weakened Brown, remained as Foreign Secretary, though questions about his interest in the job remained unanswered; some said he lacked the resolve to stand. Purnell, Blears and Jacqui Smith had all resigned, thus effectively ending their Cabinet careers. Glenys Kinnock's elevation to Minister for Europe via a seat in the Lords to replace Caroline Flint caused some surprise and criticism. Flint herself, along with Balls, was seen as one of the sore losers from this reshuffle. Brown had offered her promotion by raising her to Minister of State status to enable regular Cabinet attendance. Quite possibly she expected a more substantial promotion and vented some self-regarding anger at being treated as 'female window dressing' and being the subject of 'constant pressure, this negative bullying'. Flint had allegedly caused a few waves in the Foreign Office and Number 10 by featuring in a glamorous photoshoot for the *Observer*, perhaps explaining her criticisms of Brown, rumoured, according to one report, to 'have a problem with women' (Day, 2009).

Mandelson, stayed on as Business Secretary – some suggested he might have coveted one of the big offices of state – but had to be satisfied with the title of First Secretary of State, a grand-sounding badge sometimes awarded to a Cabinet member indicating seniority and perhaps a role according with that of a Deputy PM, itself an occasional and not especially meaningful title. The biggest winner of this none-too-successful reshuffle was Alan Johnson who was promoted from Health to Home Secretary. Johnson in fact played a crucial role in the political game being played behind the changing musical chairs of the reshuffle.

Just like Macmillan in 1962, Brown feared for his political life as his ministers fell from his employ like autumn apples from their trees. Brown's mention in the *Sunday Times*, on 31 May, that he planned to appoint his closest political ally, Ed Balls, to the office of Chancellor had caused consternation. The theory behind the move was that Darling, though he had performed well – astoundingly so in my opinion – during the financial meltdown, was 'associated in the public mind with the darkest days of the recession'. It was hoped a 'younger rejuvenated team' would perform better against Osborne as election day approached (Brown, 2017, p.352). But, as

Isabelle Oakeshott noted in her article, 'Brown's authority has become so weakened that some ministers are openly defying Downing St.' Balls was a divisive figure and much distrusted by major 'Blairite' Cabinet figures: David Miliband, Jack Straw and Alan Johnson, it was reported, had indicated they would resign if Balls became Chancellor. Other ministers phoned through to Number 10 to make the point how it would 'look terrible to ditch the man responsible for dealing with the recession when there were signs that its worst effects were over' (Oakeshott, 2009). It seems Brown was prepared to ignore these objections but Purnell's resignation was the grenade that exploded into the middle of the reshuffle calculations. This was the most serious challenge to Brown and with Labour's poll rating at only 21 per cent, his position was on the point of collapsing.

However, it seems this is where Mandelson's role in hitting the phones became crucial. David Miliband, who had been making some signs of wanting to be PM (in my view), rashly spurned his opportunity and declared Purnell had 'made a mistake' (Watt and Wintour, 2009). Other ministers seemed able to swallow their private doubts about Brown's faltering leadership and followed suit: Yvette Cooper, who took over Purnell's Cabinet post followed Miliband's example, as did Harriet Harmon and the Schools minister, Jim Knight. Jim Murphy (Scottish Secretary), Pat McFadden (Employment Relations minister), Douglas Alexander (International Development), Hilary Benn (Environment Secretary) and finally the man viewed as possibly the next PM, Alan Johnson (*Washington Examiner*, 2009).

When asked whether he had no ambition to be PM, he replied, 'never say never' (Hattenstone, 2013). Faced with an opportunity of which most politicians could only dream, Johnson decided to allow it to pass by. Having expressed a desire to stand as Leader in 2006, Johnson's ambition had ebbed dramatically by 2009. Why? Johnson's back story in terms of the Labour Party: orphaned in his teens and brought up by his elder sister, was, politically, to die for. Perhaps seeing at close hand how the pressures of government can inhibit and damage one's life was a factor; perhaps his lack of a traditional education eroded his confidence that he could cope with such a job. When the leadership was contested in 2010 he decided not to stand: he backed David Miliband instead and when in opposition and made Shadow Chancellor he seemed unable to cope with the complexity of the role and soon stood down.

John Major's first Cabinet and subsequent reshuffle, May 1993

'Politics is sometimes a despicable business' (John Major, 1999, p.185). A PM's first Cabinet often resembles a reshuffle as sitting shadow incumbents all offer some kind of a case either for retention or reallocation to another Cabinet-level post. John Major's accession to the top job was unlike that of Tony Blair in 1997, or David Cameron in 2010, who entered Number 10 without *any* previous ministerial experience: all the other PMs since 1945 began their term of office having served in senior positions. Moreover he was taking over an existing Cabinet team selected by his predecessor. As Margaret Thatcher's favoured heir, Major had led a charmed ministerial life: junior whip, PUS and then MoS Social Security, Chief Secretary to the Treasury, Foreign Secretary and then Chancellor. Thatcher was keen that Major should experience as many senior roles as possible to strengthen his CV for when a future leadership contest might take place.

Major was not surprised by his victory in 1990 – his campaign and expert predictions had appeared strong from the outset. On the very night of his accession to power, he began to create his first Cabinet; deciding that 'As we were near to a general election I did not want wholesale changes. Most of Margaret's ministers could stay in their jobs' (Major, 1999, p.205). Should he give a job to Margaret? He did consider this – after all Heath had made Alec Douglas-Home Foreign Secretary – but Thatcher was a completely different bundle of qualities to the diffident Earl: he decided against having someone who claimed she was a 'good back seat driver' sitting in one of the front seats (BBC News, 1999). But a brand-new chancellor was obviously a necessity. He identified four candidates: John Macgregor, John Patten, Ken Clarke and Norman Lamont (Major, 1999, p.205). Major thought Chris Patten was a candidate for Chancellor but was now unavailable after his surprise loss of his Bath seat. 'After the turbulence of recent weeks', he consequently reasoned, 'we needed stability. So Norman became chancellor' (ibid., p.206). Major recognised this was 'the controversial appointment of my premiership' (ibid., p.306). In an article for the *New Statesman*, Julia Langdon analysed their uneasy relationship; during an interview in October 1990 Lamont unwittingly disclosed his personal bitterness about the ambitions of his boss, the then Chancellor, John Major.

'They were not friends', observes Langdon. 'Even then they did not much like each other. They are very different characters. They did not share an ideology, beyond a commitment to the Conservative Party' (Langdon, 1999). In a move highlighting how political expedience conjures up such strange bedfellows, Lamont became Major's campaign manager and helped him win. Lamont claimed it was not his idea: 'John Major's team had begged him' to lead them and Norman Fowler too (ibid.). Certainly their backgrounds could not have been more different: Lamont the son of a Scottish surgeon and public school/Cambridge alumnus; and Major, son (astonishingly) of a circus performer and later garden gnome entrepreneur. 'Lamont is a man who attracts French adjectives: suave, a little louche, somewhat outre perhaps. Major does not attract French adjectives' (ibid.). Lamont was solidly upper-middle class, and a likely tip for any elite membership in the United Kingdom; Major's class, difficult to be precise given his father's occupation is probably closer to 'lower middle' (ibid.). Lamont, only a year older than Major, entered the

Commons (Kingston upon Thames) in 1972; Major in 1979 (Huntingdon). Lamont took 17 years to make Cabinet level: Major only 8 years. In a highly competitive professional milieu, it is hardly surprising there was rivalry and that the also ambitious Lamont might well have felt unhappy his political contemporary was outperforming him; age was a keen catalyst of rivalry as politicians are keenly aware of their peer group's prospects.

Once in post, Lamont faced a number of big problems, the most fearsome being the crisis on 16 September 1992, when a crippling run on sterling prevented Britain from being able to prevent the value of the pound from falling below the lower limit laid down by the European Monetary System, which the UK had joined at DM2.95 to the £1 in October 1990. Major demanded a remedial but panicky hike in interest rates, Lamont was forced to appear before cameras outside the Treasury (his adviser David Cameron lurking in the background), looking definitely panicky too, to announce that after a day of 'much market turbulence Britain has suspended membership of the ERM [European Exchange Rate Mechanism' (BBC News, 1992). After this disaster, doomed to resonate with voters for at least a decade, Major considered resigning – something that would put Norman out of a job – but realised also that sacking Lamont would greatly weaken his own position. The press – notably Max Hastings, editor of the *Daily Telegraph* – called for Lamont's head. Major decided Lamont had only been loyally following a policy he had inherited from Major himself: 'he scribbled a note telling him not to resign' (Major, 1999, p.335). Further thoughts of standing down himself soon faded once Stephen Wall, his sister Pat and Douglas Hurd insisted – 'You've only just been elected, you can't go' – he should stay (ibid., p.336). Major's political longevity, of course, extended until 1997 – Lamont's however, had only less than a year to survive.

His Spring Budget in 1993 was another big hurdle posed by the national indebtedness following the recession caused by the ERM debacle. Treasury advisers reckoned taxes should be raised by £7 billion, although cleverly to be announced three years in advance; VAT (value added tax) was to be increased on fuel from 8 per cent to 17.5 per cent from April 1995. Together with tax increases on cigarettes and beer and a reduction in the mortgage interest rate relief, this was a tough and not very popular budget – though in retrospect has been seen as a brave and effective one. However, that fickle but so often decisive factor, gossip, intervened against Lamont and the press, so often fuelled by gossip, loved the story that Lamont had let out his basement to a lady offering 'sex therapy' sessions – instantly given the name of 'Miss Whip Lash' by the tabloids. He was also rumoured to have not paid a hotel bill after a party conference and been spotted shopping in a seedy part of Paddington and then accused of having credit card arrears. All of these press stories were without any foundation but, as we know, once the UK tabloid press has even the faintest breath of scandal in high places they cannot be restrained: as Major observed, 'the damage to Norman and the government was cumulative ... Norman's credibility plummeted' (Major, 1999, p.679). The satirists piled in and speculation about whether he could survive was constant. His credibility seemed to vanish according to Major not just in the City and industry but amongst colleagues reacting to his name with raised eyebrow, rolling eyes and dismissive gestures. 'My sympathies were with him as more sinned against than sinning, but I had no choice but to make a change. As the reshuffle approached, I consulted senior colleagues; they all believed Norman had to go' (ibid., p.679).

The interview on 27 May did not go well. Major offered Lamont:

> a major departmental job, urging him to stay in the Cabinet at Environment with the sweetener that he would keep the chancellor's official country residence at Dorneywood. Pale faced and tense, he refused. I pressed him, he refused again. I expressed my regrets. Still he refused. My offer was genuine but it seemed he could not bear to do so if he left the Treasury. It was a stilted series of exchanges that illustrated the cloud that had descended upon our relationship and the depths of Norman's hurt. 'Yes Prime Minister, No Prime Minister, thank you Prime Minister, I wish to leave the Cabinet.' Were the only words he spoke. He turned and left. We have never spoken since.
>
> *(ibid., pp.679–680)*

To be fair to Lamont, Environment would have been perceived as major, and maybe humiliating, demotion. Lamont subsequently told Peter Hennessy in his 2014 Reflections interview that the grim silence had been broken but it seems clear the bitterness ran deep, and intensely so (Hennessy, 2020, pp.107–125). Lamont claimed, wrongly says Major, that he was refused an extension in post until November, nor had offered to him Leadership of the House, a job he would have liked. Major argues Lamont had refused 'a serious and substantial appointment'. Major agreed when Lamont in his resignation speech, argued the recession had not been caused by membership of the ERM but by the fall in output 1990–91 after the boom in 1988–89. But it was Lamont's cruel swipe at the end that clearly cut his former boss: 'Norman closed his statement with a soundbite which was sadly better than any he coined in government: 'We gave the impression of being in office but not in power'; Lamont's memoir is entitled 'In Office'. In the light of history it is hard not to sympathise with Lamont and to feel Major sacked him on the basis of a rather thin rationale.

Surprising and unusual reshuffles

To conclude this chapter are examples of how reshuffles can be surprising and unusual and one where expectations far exceeded likelihood.

Richard Marsh

This example occurred in 1969: after heading back from the Brighton conference, Harold Wilson, Joe Haines and others discussed a forthcoming 'substantial reshuffle in the government, dropping a large number of elderly ministers and bring on new blood'. Haines recalls:

> My outstanding memory of those changes was a personal one. On the Thursday of the Labour conference I had lunch with Richard Marsh, the minister of Transport and, at 41, thought to have a glittering career before him. Marsh had risen rapidly from being a local union official and Wilson greatly admired his speeches in opposition. He was witty, cheeky, irreverent even about Labour's establishment and Wilson saw him as a future star.
>
> *(Haines, 2003, p.20–21)*

So what happened to this laden-with-promise young prospect?

> He marked himself down as a recipient of the black spot when he came one night to see the Prime Minister. After he had gone, Wilson said to me: 'He is always bringing me problems to solve instead of coping with them himself' [an interesting insight into how PMs hope their appointments rise effectively to fulfil their responsibilities].
>
> Like so many bright young features of the political firmament, Marsh was better at opposing, a meteor, not a star. At the lunch Marsh spoke warmly of Wilson adding that 'if Harold were to drop me tomorrow, I could have no complaint'. I sat there knowing that on the following Sunday I would be announcing to general surprise – and in Marsh's case astonishment – that Harold had indeed dropped him. When I did so, Marsh loudly and publicly complained ... and never forgave Wilson.
>
> *(ibid., p. 21)*

Haines adds a partisan swipe that 'in 1981 Marsh was ennobled by Mrs Thatcher and became a supporter of her policies, which Wilson would have seen as a vindication of his judgement' (ibid., pp.20–21)

David Mellor

This account comes from Charles Powell and relates how a new Minister for the Arts was appointed. Powell suggested to Thatcher and Chief Whip Waddington that John Patten might be good. Powell phoned him, told him of the vacancy and he didn't want to do it. 'I said I couldn't go back in and tell them he had said no. Just down the corridor from me is another minister of state, David Mellor and he has the biggest record collection in Britain. I went back into the study and told them. David Mellor was appointed' (private interview).

Alan Clark

Clark is famous for his 'coven' of lovers, and infamous, when a junior minister, for being challenged by Clare Short for being drunk when answering Commons questions. There are two parts to this item: the first in Charles Moore's biography when it seems Alan Clark was becoming 'impatient' for office. His wish was granted – PUS in Employment (1983–86) – but via a very unusual route. A copy of a letter he'd written to the PM was found by a Commons copier and was handed in to Chief Whip John Wakeham; in it Clark told her he was 'running ... a "Shadow Cabinet" to keep her government up to the mark with right-wing policies' (Moore, 2015, p.71). 'Wakeham showed the letter to Thatcher who said "Oh dear, I'll speak to him." No! exclaimed Wakeham, that would be too dangerous. Make him a minister! Mrs Thatcher, who had a soft spot for Clark, agreed' (ibid., p.71). It transpired that few Cabinet members wanted this self-promoting junior minister but Tebbit finally accepted him, commenting 'I don't really mind who my junior ministers are as long as they keep out of my hair' (Tebbit, 1989, p.71). Clark eventually made MoS in the Ministry of Defence (1989–92) but always harboured hopes of a Cabinet seat. Moore reveals that when he asked Clark about the 'nature of his love for Mrs Thatcher', said, 'I don't want full penetration – just a massive snog' (Moore, 2013, p. 436). Moore adds to his footnote that 'quite large numbers of men fell for her' including Kingsley Amis (ibid., p.437).

My question to Charles Powell and his reply provide an emphatic answer to his unlikely ambition.

> In any organisation, not just government, the idea of raising your career prospects with the Chairman's office or whatever, is a natural human instinct. I don't think there was a great influence. Dear Alan lived in a fantasy world. The idea that Alan ever had the flimsiest chance of being a cabinet minister was completely wrong. He wouldn't want to hear it. I regarded Alan as rather a good thing in many ways, a good leveller of the government, who wanted to see a spread of views and Mrs Thatcher used to feel that she needed one or two of 'my people' – there weren't very many of them.
>
> *(private interview)*

The 'root and branch reshuffle' that never happened

The section in Anthony Seldon and Raymond Newell's wonderful study of Boris Johnson on his Cabinet formation in 2019 begins as follows:

> Johnson became Prime Minister without any understanding of what Cabinet was for, what domestic departmental ministers did, who his talent to draw on was or what skills they would require in office. It was as if

> a gifted visionary on the staff was suddenly appointed to run a multinational company.
>
> *(Seldon and Newell, 2023, p.154)*

The book recounts that while Johnson had over 100 ministerial posts to fill, 'he had told dozens more that they would get a job if they gave him their support' (ibid., p.155). Writing names on a whiteboard with his team of aides plus Chief Whip Mark Spencer, he made sure his political friends were rewarded – Conor Burns, Jake Berry and Amanda Milling for example – plus campaign helpers Oliver Dowden, Robert Jenrick and Rishi Sunak. Gavin Williamson, another enthusiastic campaign helper, was clearly up for something too. However, Mark Sedwill vetoed any appointment for him involving 'sensitive intelligence' following his dismissal from May's Cabinet for leaking information: he got Education (ibid., p.155). Grant Shapps, another skilled insider and key communicator, was given Transport. Sajid Javid became Chancellor because of his campaign help and also because 'Carrie Symonds loved him' (ibid., p.156; who it seemed was centrally involved in the Cabinet making). Rishi Sunak was slotted in as Chief Secretary to the Treasury; fellow Brexiteer Priti Patel became Home Secretary. When aides questioned some of the names he was reading out from a list, he replied 'this is only temporary. As soon as we get Brexit out of the way I'll do it properly' (ibid., p.155).

Johnson hesitated over Ben Wallace as he suspected him of leaking confidential material to the *Sunday Times* and gave him Defence on the understanding 'any leak on security matters would result in automatic dismissal' (Seldon and Newell, 2023, p.157). Michael Gove was a problem – clearly the most able minister available for appointment, Johnson was still 'simmering with anger and distrust' over Gove's 2016 betrayal when he had withdrawn his support to coincide with the launch of Johnson's campaign (ibid., p.158). Instead of becoming Chancellor, as would have happened if Johnson had been PM in 2016, he had to be satisfied with Chancellor of the Duchy of Lancaster, preparing for a possible no-deal Brexit.

This first Cabinet was praised for its diversity – 'the most minority friendly in history' (ibid., p.159) – but was it as temporary as Johnson had envisaged? Seldon and Newell think not:

> Over the next three years, Johnson was never to initiate his root-and-branch reshuffle, as originally foreshadowed. He hated the very idea of reshuffles and was content to leave tame loyalists in post. The lower the risk of an up-and-comer challenging him for the throne the better. 'We don't want hungry young lions' [he is reported as saying in reaction to Sunak's successful furlough scheme], 'we want old, tired lions'.
>
> *(ibid., p.159)*

Reshuffling the Lords

A good insight into reshuffles in the Lords is provided by a note on 4 October 1968 when Labour's Lord Shackleton – Leader opposition in Lords and former Paymaster General – met with the PM, Harold Wilson, the Chief Whip, John Silkin, and a Mr Gregson (probably a civil servant), to discuss the composition of the House of Lords' front bench. According to the memo in the National Archives, Wilson wanted to delay his reshuffle of junior ministers 'for a few months' but was happy to listen to the Paymaster General's advice that Lord Beswick was 'not an ideal Chief Whip in the Lords and that he would be more suitable as a Minister of State' (National Archives, 1964); Lord Winterbottom would be 'an able replacement' (Brook, 1953). What might have been a factor here is that Beswick had a working-class background while Winterbottom a public school and Oxford one. Various possible recruits to the front bench were discussed including Ritchie Calder and the Latvian wife of the former Labour Leader, Dora Gaitskell. Lord Beswick got the job. One senior civil servant I interviewed for this book, denied that he and his ilk participated in promotion processes. This point of view is hard to defend as the memoirs of aides and the National Archive documents prove otherwise. A memo signed by Cabinet Secretary Norman Brook made a series of far-reaching suggestions to the then PM, regarding the staffing of the Board of Trade. He strongly urged that the department should not be subject, as suggested by the Chancellor, to 'an artificial separation between production for exports and production for the home market' and that it be led by a 'single president' and 'two strong Under Secretaries' (ibid.). He went on to suggest appropriate berths for Sir David Eccles, Geoffrey Lloyd and Derek Heathcoat Amory (Brook, 1953).

Johnson's caretaker Cabinet

For details on Johnson's caretaker Cabinet, see Chapter 9, 'Events leading to Liz Truss becoming PM for 49 days'.

Sunak's sensational reshuffle

Sunak's November 2023 reshuffle announcement caused quite a stir and deserves a mention. Insiders had expected a reshuffle for several months to provide Sunak with the team to fight the 2024 election. An additional factor, however, had entered the political equation in that Sunak's Home Secretary, Suella Braverman, had been making a number of statements on immigration, homelessness and marches in favour of Palestinians involved in the Israeli–Gazan war that were seen as incendiary and divisive; many saw such statements as part of a campaign to win the Tory leadership after the expected Labour victory in 2024. Due to the delicacy of Braverman's position (given her effective leadership role on the right-wing of the party in that it was her appointment as Home Secretary in October 2022 that made secure Sunak's election as Leader), Sunak had been willing to overlook some of these transgressions. However, by early November, with feelings over the Gazan war becoming intense, he realised he had to act decisively.

On 13 November he announced Braverman's sacking, to be replaced by Foreign Secretary, James Cleverley, who apparently only agreed to the move with reluctance. However it was his replacement which caused the sensation. Sunak had sounded out former PM, David Cameron, on making a comeback to frontline politics to take Cleverly's place. He willingly agreed, turning up on the morning of 13 November, wholly unexpected by the media (the secret had, remarkably, been retained by Number 10 without leakage). The last time a former PM had been reappointed to Cabinet was Alec Douglas-Home in Heath's 1970 Cabinet, also as Foreign Secretary (for more background on this see Swindford et al., 2023). The shock took some time to settle with some applauding the recruitment of an experienced talent but with critics pointing out that, by appointing Cameron, Sunak had shunted his Cabinet towards the centre, thus causing much disquiet on the right of his party; he had also opened up a flank to Labour to attack Cameron's shameful lobbying activities on behalf of the failed Greensill Bank.

References and further reading

BBC News (1992) 'UK crashes out of ERM'. 16 September.
BBC News (1999) 'Major damns "intolerable" Thatcher'. 11 August.
BBC News (2012) 'The legacy of Macmillan's "night of the long knives"'. 6 July.
Brook, N. (1953) 'Memo the Prime Minister'. Prem 5/225, National Archives, 20 August.
Brown, G. (2017) *My Life, Our Times*. Bodley Head.
Cole, H. and Heale, J. (2022) *Out of the Blue: The Inside Story of the Unexpected Rise and Rapid Fall of Liz Truss*. HarperCollins.
Day, E. (2009) 'The day I interviewed a feisty Caroline Flint for that photoshoot'. *Guardian*, 7 June.
Dellingpole, J. (2014) 'Estonians, Etonians and women in the cabinet'. 17 July. https://pvewood.blogspot.com/2014/07/promoting-women-become-they-are-women.html.
Fowler, N. (1991) *Ministers Decide*. Chapmans.
Haines, J. (2003) *Glimmers of Twilight*. Politico's.
Hattenstone, S. (2013) 'Alan Johnson: The prime minister we almost had'. *Guardian*, 28 April.
Hennessy, P. (2020) *The Complete Reflections*. Haus.
Howe, G. (1995) *Conflict of Loyalty*, 2nd edn. Pan.
Institute for Government (2022) 'Ministers reflect: Jim Murphy'. 7 October.
Kaufman, G. (1997) How to Be a Minister. Faber.

Langdon, J. (1999) 'The Major–Lamont relationship'. *New Statesman*, 4 October.
Lewis, G. (1998) *Lord Hailsham: A Life*. Pimlico.
Major, J. (1999) *John Major: The Autobiography*. HarperCollins
Manchester Evening News (2009a) 'Blears stands firm at Brown's criticisms'. 21 May.
Manchester Evening News (2009b) 'Beverley Hughes to quit'. 3 June.
Moore, C. (2013) *Margaret Thatcher, The Authorised Biography*, Vol. 1: *Not for Turning*. Allen Lane.
Moore, C. (2015) *Margaret Thatcher: The Authorized Biography*, Vol. 2: *Everything She Wants*. Allen Lane.
National Archives (1964) 'Harold Wilson'. Prem 5/500, 16 October.
Nevett, J. (2022) 'Chris Pincher: Tory whip resigns saying he embarrassed himself'. BBC News, 1 July.
Oakeshott, I. (2009) 'Gordon Brown wants Ed Balls as chancellor'. *Sunday Times*, 31 May.
Oliver, J., Oakeshott, I. and Wolf, M. (2009) 'Blunt knives out for Gordon Brown'. *The Times*, 7 June.
Paun, A. (2012) 'Shuffling the pack: A brief guide to government reshuffles'. Institute for Government, 31 August.
Payne, S. (2022) *The Fall of Boris Johnson: The Full Story*. Macmillan.
Pogrund, G. (2022) 'The protection racket'. *Sunday Times*, 27 March.
Pym, F. (1984) The Politics of Consent. Hamilton.
Renton, T. (2004) *Chief Whip: People, Power and Patronage in Westminster*. Politico's.
Seldon, A. with Meakin, J. and Thoms, I. (2021) *The Impossible Office? The History of the British Prime Minister*. Cambridge University Press.
Seldon, A. with Meakin, J., Thoms, I. and Egerton, T. (2024) *The Impossible Office? The History of the British Prime Minister*, 2nd edn. Cambridge University Press.
Seldon, A. and Lodge, G. (2010) *Brown at 10*. Biteback.
Seldon, A. and Newell, R. (2023) *Johnson at 10: The Inside Story*. Atlantic.
Stratton, A. and Wintour, P. (2009) 'James Purnell quits cabinet and calls on Gordon Brown to stand aside now'. *Guardian*, 5 June.
Summers, D. (2008) 'Ruth Kelly: I am quitting to put family first'. *Guardian*, 24 September.
Summers, D. (2009) 'Gordon Brown's reshuffle in crisis as John Hutton quits'. *Guardian*, 5 June.
Swindford, S., Wright, O., Smyth, C. and Scott, G. (2023) 'Cameron warmed to idea during fireside chat in Downing Street'. *The Times*, 14 November.
Tapsfield, J. (2021) 'Gavin Williamson begs Johnson to make him chief whip'. *Daily Mail*, 9 June.
Tebbit, N. (1989) *Upwardly Mobile*. Futura.
The Economist (2023) 'Will Rishi Sunak's reshuffle make any difference in the polls?' 14 November.
Trevor-Roper, H. (1947) *The Last Days of Hitler*. Macmillan.
Waddington, D. (2012) *David Waddington: Memoirs*. Biteback.
Washington Examiner (2009) 'Brown defies calls to step down as British Premier'. 4 June.

Wasps Nest (2011) 'July 1990: Nick Ridley on the EU and the Germans'. 19 November.
Watt, N. and Wintour, P. (2009) 'Miliband: Yes, I thought about resigning. Now I want to save the party'. *Guardian*, 13 June.
Wintour, P. (2008) 'Third time lucky: Mandelson brought into Brown's economic war cabinet'. *Guardian*, 4 October.

5

THE ROLE OF THE MEDIA

> If you turn out to be good minister, make sure everybody knows about it. Only the press, television and radio can tell them: there is no message without the media.
>
> (Gerald Kaufman; Kaufman, 1980, p.151)

In all modern democratic countries the media is central to political activity in carrying the spoken words of politicians to the public, especially those empowered with the vote. Accurate reflections of critical popular opinion are not always reciprocally delivered: the more autocratic 'democracies', for example Turkey – where scores of journalists have been imprisoned – exert distorting self-interested control. As mentioned in Chapter 8 on ministerial skills, politicians have quickly accustomed themselves to new technologies and have harnessed them to their causes; the spoken words that once only reached a face-to-face audience of at most a few thousand, are now carried forth to touch millions domestically and indeed potentially billions internationally. Any aspirant politician, even within autocracies, needs to master the art of communicating via the media to have any hope of advancement or survival. This chapter explains why the media is crucial to MPs' appointments as ministers and their success or failure. It also analyses some of the changes affecting the way in which the modern media now works.

John Hutton and Leigh Lewis open their chapter on the media in this way: 'Most ministers, if they are being frank, would probably concede that trying to manage the media is one of their biggest challenges and one that takes up a huge amount of time and effort' (Hutton and Lewis, 2014, p.65). Such management might be on advancing their key policies, their own

DOI: 10.4324/9781003405085-6

political cause or, as so often, both at the same time. A policy successfully delivered is wholly consistent with buffing up one's own credentials for a step up the promotion ladder. Despite the time it might take, Hutton and Lewis insist any minister:

> would be right to assume from the outset that perhaps your most important job as minister is to be absolutely on top of your personal and departmental communications. You are, after all, there to tell the public what you are trying to achieve and why you want to change things for the better.
>
> *(ibid., p.67)*

The authors delineate a number of things to which ministers should attend:

- To be successful they advise a little humility: after all becoming a minister shifts one up several rungs in your importance to the media: 'You are now the person under the spotlight and every aspect of your personal as well as political life will now be under scrutiny. Nothing you do – from the most important to the most utterly trivial – will be off-limits as far as the media are concerned' (ibid., pp.67–68).
- They mention how some ministers spend their whole careers courting the media, with little positive outcome – one might think of Matt Hancock here – or others, like Ken Clarke, who 'seem to be able to spend no time at all on this endeavour and instead get on with the job of running their departments very effectively without apparently losing anything in the process' (ibid., p.67).
- Trust your press officer and allow him/her to speak for you 'with absolute authority and a clear understanding of what you want to say and why' (ibid., p.68).
- Before big announcements – which should be carefully planned and managed – make sure you are prepared and have anticipated the really difficult questions you might be asked. Make sure too your special advisers are on good terms with your civil service press office. In other words take responsibility: big announcements can turn into big disasters.
- Prepare policy statements by making sure related professionals are on side beforehand. Try to counter alternative arguments in advance so that their thunder is stolen – pre-emptive rebuttal!
- Don't rush in front of the cameras before you are ready to do so and in the event of an alleged mistake be extra thorough and careful: 'Once the facts have been established and when it is clear your department is at the centre of the storm or the allegation, you need to make one fundamental decision – whether you can go on the offensive or whether you need to say you are sorry' (ibid., p.74).

- If you are feeling angrily traduced by media coverage, 'it is generally a good idea to keep these sorts of emotions under wraps'.

Gerald Kaufman's chapter on the press in what might now be described as his seminal work on *How to Be a Minister* begins with this rather obvious but important point: 'If you turn out to be good minister, make sure everybody knows about it. Only the press, television and radio can tell them: there is no message without the media' (Kaufman, 1980, p.151). Indeed, once embarked on their political journey, politicians have to give the media a fair slice of their time and, if possible, make them allies. Further, on the crucial performative side, they must learn or use their inherent common sense to sound engaging, caring and interesting when talking on the radio or on television. Throughout their careers, being good on the telly is a constant requirement for becoming known by the public and brought to the attention of the party leadership who make the key promotion decisions. Once promoted these skills are required both to consolidate their position and take their career even further up the greasy pole. As Kaufman advises:

> You will meet the press wherever you go: in the House of Commons, in your department, when you travel. Learn to know them and try to make the most of what they can do for you. The most junior minister will get a packed house when he calls a press conference at his department.
>
> *(ibid., p. 151)*

He encourages MPs to get to know the sketch writers who:

> treat Parliament like a theatre and write reviews of the debates. They are very selective and very capricious. ... If you speak well in a debate you may have a chance with them, but do not rely upon it. One snappy response to a supplementary question can get you more coverage than a major speech over which you have slaved for days.
>
> *(ibid., p.152)*

Kaufman observes, however, that the elite of the journalists in Westminster are the 'Lobby Correspondents': especially those with bylines like: Political Editor, Political Staff or Lobby Correspondent. They have special privileges when it comes to access to such places as the Members' Lobby and other protected areas (ibid., pp.152–154). In exchange for speaking off the record, so they won't be named in quotations, inside information can be elicited, which journalists might use or store away for a later occasion. Politicians have to be invited to enter the Press Gallery. A smaller group of journalists belong to The Lobby, which is supposedly a secret organisation but which receives daily briefings from Downing Street and are the journalists closest to the nerve centre of political activity at any given time. Astute politicians make friends with key figures and provide discreet information, which might reflect malice towards rivals or the leadership or might just be part of their regular self-promoting activities. If a minister, such conversations might prove to be 'leaks' of confidential information regarding policy, personnel or even security but leaking is a dangerous game. Gavin Williamson was sacked in May 2019 by Theresa May after she found 'compelling evidence' that he was the person who leaked information about Huawei's potential role in helping construct the UK's 5G network (McGuiness, 2019). When PM Jim Callaghan quipped to another politician: 'You leak, I brief', he was indicating that only the PM has the real authority to inform the press and that breaching this rule, if discovered, can carry heavy penalties (Odugbemi, 2015).

Since the 1960s, television has dominated UK politics as it has in the USA and throughout Europe (though see below for the views of Anthony King). Added to the requirement of sounding good on the airwaves is that of appearance: Granada Television once captured a clip of David Owen discreetly self-adding some hairspray just before going on air. Great care is now taken by politicians in terms of their hair and clothes, indeed every aspect of how they present themselves.

Margaret Thatcher was the first leading UK politician to take a wholly professional approach to image-building under the mentorship of Gordon Reece. Peter Mandelson, Labour's premier spin doctor of the 1980s and 1990s, commented in an interview with me: 'By the mid-1980s, every part of her had been transformed: her hair, her teeth, her nose I suspect, her eyebrows. Not a part of Mrs Thatcher was left unaltered' (Jones et al., 2022, p.224). Lance Price, one-time senior spin doctor in Number 10 reflected on Tony Blair's vanity in one of his entries:

> He's started wearing glasses for reading but doesn't want ever to be seen in them! So we are devising a glasses strategy – some friendly profile writer 'spotting' them on his desk by chance. The trouble is TB thinks it's cool that they are made by Calvin Klein and AC [Alistair Campbell] wants to get him a pair on the NHS.
>
> *(Price, 2006, pp.142–143)*

Tony Blair's televisual skills were on display in the leadership election in 1994. Nick Jones's excellent *Soundbites and Spin Doctors*, records how his relaxed manner and ability to speak to the cameras was a major factor. Henry Porter, writing in *Daily Telegraph*, observed that neither of his two rivals in that contest, 'displayed the same attentiveness as Blair did when in front of the camera. He listens, then says what people want to hear, and even when delivering unpleasantness allows a smile to play at the corner of his mouth' (Jones, 1996, p.156).

Jones cites Andrew Marr in emphasising the crucial importance of media skills to modern politicians in an article in the *Independent*:

> politicians who perform badly on television have to recognise that they could be a liability to their parties because they might end up jeopardising the support of millions of potential voters. Failure to communicate effectively through television is not an endearing personal flaw but an act of lethal political incompetence.
>
> *(ibid., p.156)*

Almost certainly Marr's comment would have been shared then and now by whips on both sides of the aisle.

Blair, however, was superbly equipped as a political communicator. He was a past master at hitting the right notes in his speeches. Simon Hoggart, the *Guardian*'s late political sketch writer noted the tricks employed:

> This Big Brother smiles a lot in a self-deprecating kind of way. He uses 'um' and 'well' as a rhetorical device, to convince us he's not reading out a prepared text, but needs to pause to work out exactly what he means. There is a prepared text of course but he adds to it a phrase such as 'I really think' and 'you know I really have to tell you' and 'in my view'. This is the new oratory. The old politicians told us they were right, and that there was no room for doubt, the new politician is not telling us truths but selling himself ... his message is that you should take him on trust; you should believe him because you love him.
>
> *(Hoggart, 1999)*

Gordon Brown by contrast was shy in public and often not looking especially well dressed, unable to project the warmth and quick wit his friends saw in private.

This easy facility with the media almost certainly explains why Blair bested Brown when it came to popularity within the party and the voters. Cameron, too, shone in the media. In the 2010 first ever televised election campaign debate Cameron was below par but by the final debate he had learned the new rules and, arguably, came out top. Cameron also showed great media savvy in the 2005 leadership contest when he addressed his annual conference wholly without notes or autocue. Coming over so direct and strong probably gave him the substantial edge in the final vote over his rival David Davies whose speech was comparatively lacklustre: appearance and confident delivery are essential in the advancement of political careers. Michael Foot, a compelling public orator, was not effective on television through his tendency to address the camera as if it were a public meeting. Liz Truss's monotonous delivery, moreover, was just one reason why her sojourn in Number 10 was so short.

Soundbites and slogans

Content is also hugely important and the skill with which words are used. However, the attention span of the voting public is not great and, in recognition of this, broadcasters impose strict time controls; they hate 'long rambling replies or discursive extracts from speeches' (Jones, 1996, p.27). Both sides have a common interest in demanding replies which encapsulate 'arguments in brief, self-contained statements or answers' (ibid., p.27). Whilst longer than the seven seconds jokingly attributed to goldfish, studies have found attentiveness to be shrinking, placing more importance on short 'soundbites'. According to studies in the USA, in 1968 soundbites lasted on average 47 seconds but by 1988 they had shrunk to a near goldfish-like nine seconds. The advance of social media has increased the need for vibrant brevity and so creating such slogan-sounding political messages has become a kind of art either for election materials or being inserted into speeches for that purpose.

Nick Jones gives examples of a soundbite that triumphed for Margaret Thatcher and one that bombed for Harold Wilson. Thatcher's was composed by playwright Ronald Millar for her 1980 speech to her party conference. She was determined to ignore the many critics of her counter-inflationary policies and imperiously declared 'To those waiting with bated breath for that favourite media catch phrase, the U turn, I have only one thing to say. You can turn if you like: the lady's not for turning.' Millar's soundbite had its provenance in the popular play by Christopher Fry, a success decades earlier in 1948, entitled *The Lady's not for Burning*. The next day, five of the national dailies led with the quote.

At the other end of the spectrum, Wilson's disastrous soundbite came in a party political broadcast in 1967 following the devaluation of the pound.

> From now on, the pound abroad is worth 14 per cent or so less in terms of other currencies. That doesn't mean, of course, that the pound here in Britain, in your pocket or purse or in your bank, has been devalued.
>
> *(Harari, 2017)*

Even those who do not follow politics carefully spotted the falsity of such a claim: devaluation, for a start, makes imports more expensive to buy so of course it would have an impact on the nations' wallets. Wilson, quite rightly, was the butt of much damaging press criticism and ridicule.

Another slogan that seemed by mid-2023 to have become a liability rather than an asset, was Boris Johnson's 'Levelling up'. In the December 2019 election this concept helped turn 42 Labour stronghold 'red wall' seats into Tory wins. However, in January 2023 focus groups appear to have reported the phrase had lost any magic it might have had and 'Conservative MPs in marginal seats have been told to shun the phrase and instead use "stepping up" or even the rather opaque "gauging up"' (Scott, 2023).

Soundbites then, as catchy slogans, are important when they contain compressed complex messages, especially during elections: the 2016 referendum was a good example. The Remain campaign was essentially saying: 'stay as we are', a cautious and perhaps unglamourous message, while the Brexiters' 'Take Back Control', despite its straightforwardness, in the context of the referendum sounded dynamic, radical, even exciting. Dominic Cummings, the leader of the Brexit campaign, is credited with coming up with this slogan as he did for the 2019 'Get Brexit Done'; again, a simple enough message but in the heightened atmosphere of an election occurring after three years of polarising strife following the referendum result, it had the virtue of expressing the frustrated fatigue millions experienced and therefore triumphed over the Remain camp's somewhat muddled position.

Newspapers still the dominant medium?

Despite the dominance of television as a public medium and especially its blanket coverage of the big elections, Professor King argued that it is not the most influential medium. That honour, he claimed, still rests, in the UK, with the print media:

> Despite the rise of the electronic media and their own declining circulations, the most powerful media in Britain are almost certainly still the national newspapers – that is, the newspapers published in London and distributed across the country. Politicians read those papers, even if fewer and fewer others do, politicians believe that the views of voters, and the news agenda of many of the other media, including those of the main television and radio broadcasters, are influenced by the papers' agendas. ... In political terms newspapers matter more than other media, certainly more than television and radio.
>
> *(King, 2015, pp.148–149)*

The *Sun* and Daily Ma*il* are by far the most widely read newspapers and senior politicians try hard to court their good opinion, queueing up especially to woo the *Sun*'s owner Rupert Murdoch; before the 1997 election Tony Blair flew across the world to address his staff conference. Lance Price, former press spad to Blair has written revealingly that: 'His presence was almost tangible in 10 Downing St and it was as if he was the 24th member of the Cabinet. In fact, more than that' (Price quoted in King, 2015, p.150). He went on to claim: 'No big decision could ever be made inside Number 10 without taking account of the likely reaction of three men – Gordon Brown, John Prescott and Rupert Murdoch' (ibid.).

Cameron was equally assiduous, flying in October 2008 to join Rupert on his yacht in the Med and becoming very close to the magnate's favourite editor, Rebekah Brooks of the *Sun*. Gordon Brown was not to be outdone, attending Brooks's wedding and trying hard to become a confidante of Paul Dacre, editor of the *Mail*, inviting him to watch *Hamlet* at Stratford starring David Tennant (Brown, 2017, p.118). Blair was similar regarding Rupert Murdoch, traveling across the world to speak at a conference of the Australian's company conference in July 1995. Such extraordinary, sycophantic deference signals how important PMs reckon the tabloids are to winning elections, especially when they are close-run things.

Another factor making the tabloids crucial to electoral success was the gradual de-alignment of voter loyalty from their traditional class-related parties. Voters no longer vote automatically for Labour if working class or Tory if middle class, and consequently their votes are more winnable, 'up for grabs'. Given the relatively lower levels of education of tabloid readers, their bold and perhaps simplistic analyses are designed to direct their voting intentions according to the publications' preferences. In 1992, 40 per cent of *Sun* readers voted Conservative leading it to claim in the wake of the Tory victory, 'It's the Sun wot won it.'

In his provocative polemic, *The Triumph of the Political Class*, Peter Oborne, provides an analysis of New Labour's take on the media. According to him, management and control of the media was a top priority for Blair and his ministers. The role of the Chief Whip was made secondary to the PM's press secretary or, as Oborne expresses it: 'The position of enforcer which had formerly belonged to the chief whip [he cites Michael Cox and his deputy Walter Harrison as examples] was grabbed by the Prime Minister's press adviser' (Oborne, 2007, p.236). He argues that 'control was exercised though the media' and that it was strict:

> The press machine ensured only favoured ministers or MPs were allowed on the airwaves while others were frozen out and found themselves subject to hostile briefings behind the scenes. Cabinet ministers who suffered this fate included Mo Mowlam, Clare Short, David Clark, and intermittently ... Gordon Brown.
>
> *(ibid., p.235)*

Oborne also claims that:

> The characteristic method of attack used against errant or unpopular ministers was to privately brief they were mentally unstable and on the verge of cracking up, though the charges concerning sexual profligacy or drinking problems were also used to undermine the public standing of targeted individuals.
>
> *(ibid., p.235)*

Oborne adds that the pivotal influence of the Chief Whip was reflected in Michael Dobbs's *House of Cards* and claims other dramas, e.g. *The Queen* and *The Deal*, 'have laid comparable stress on the role of the press secretary, Alistair Campbell' (ibid., p.236); he was also said to be the model for Malcolm Tucker, the foul mouthed spin doctor in the satire, *The Thick of It*. Aspirant ministers can benefit from good press write-ups. Press reports that praise politicians can certainly turbo-charge their careers. Delving back into history Harold Wilson was given a positive leg up when the *News Chronicle* served up this glowing encomium: 'He is outstanding among the really "new" men on the Labour benches' and a 'brilliant young civil servant ... regarded by Whitehall high ups as one of the great discoveries of the war' (Pimlott, p.92–93).

However the press can often decide to be critical, sometimes brutally so.

'Monstering'

What role do newspapers play in ministerial advancement? It depends on which newspaper and why there is coverage. A Tory MP, one might think, has little to fear from the likes of the *Sun*, *Mail* or *Telegraph*? This is generally the case but if his or her departure from the paths of 'righteousness' as these papers see it, is sufficiently in excess, a point can be reached when any newspaper will consider coverage to be fair game. King points out that the tabloids can decide to 'monster' someone and politicians always have public figures like politicians in their sights. Whether guilty or innocent, the MP being monstered:

> suffers intense personal embarrassment, possibly physical harassment and sometimes public humiliation. He or she is made to look foolish – or worse – in the eyes of both colleagues and constituents. His or her political career can come to a juddering halt.
>
> *(King, 2015, p.154)*

King lists examples:

- Tony and Cherie Blair over their property ownership and the latter's relationship with her personal trainer, Carole Caplin, and her boyfriend, who proved to be a convicted conman.
- David Blunkett over his affair with an American publisher.
- Chris Bryant who was exposed for using a gay dating site.
- Robin Cook who was having an affair with his secretary.
- Liam Fox for taking with him on foreign trips a close friend who posed as an official aide.

- Chris Huhne who became involved in a strange stand-off with his wife over his speeding fine, which she had illegally claimed was her fault.
- Neil Kinnock who received a barrage of undeserved sniping criticism from the *Sun* and *Mail* culminating in the infamous 1992 headline: 'If Kinnock wins today, will the last person to leave Britain please turn the lights off' (ibid., pp.154–158).

In most of these cases the invasive publicity caused personal pain and career injury; enough to deter ambitious politicians from mouthing any criticism of their persecutors.

Tabloid monstering was not, of course, confined to left-wing targets. The *Sun* waged a huge campaign against Conservative Cabinet minister, David Mellor, when it was discovered he was having an extra-marital affair with an actress, Antonia De Sancha. Every lubricious detail was recorded and when nothing new was available the *Sun* simply made up the story of him making love to Da Sancha wearing a Chelsea shirt: that was denied by De Sancha, along with the spanking and toe-sucking (Low, 2012). King also mentions an occasion in August 2016 when a Cabinet minister, Ed Balls, faced a negative threat to his career from Rebekah Brooks, editor of the *Sun* newspaper. It concerned the London Borough of Haringey's head of children's services in a row over the death of 17-month-old 'Baby P', who had died as a result of neglect and abuse. The *Sun* called for the sacking of Sharon Shoesmith, the head of children's services in the borough. When Ed Balls, then Education Secretary, did not immediately respond, Brooks repeatedly rang Balls and demanded the sacking, on one occasion adding ominously that 'We don't want to turn this thing on you' (King, 2015, p.163). The story ended with Balls sacking Shoesmith, the Court of Appeal ruling that sacking unlawful and her receiving compensation of £600,000; but it has to be said Brooks's phone call did sound suspiciously like a threat by the *Sun* to monster Ed Balls (ibid., p.163).

Even when they died, Labour politicians were not free of the *Sun*'s monstering style. One of their leading attack dogs, Richard Littlejohn, chose to debunk the reverential obituaries that followed Foot's death in February 2010: he called him a 'coward' for not fighting in the Second World War and accused him of being a 'Soviet stooge' (Littlejohn, 2010). Evidence of the tabloid papers' fast and loose way with the truth is not hard to come by. In his book *The Establishment*, Owen Jones quotes a former *Daily Star* journalist, Richard Peppiat, who had camped outside a Chelsea townhouse being used to accommodate asylum seekers. The next day his news editor confronted him with a quote attributed to the father of the refugees: Peppiat said 'He never said that, I was there all day' and received the reply, 'That's not the point. You've got to be more canny' (Jones, 2014, p.86). Peppiat came to realise there was a pattern:

> 'Someone is always to blame for our social ills and to me it stops you questioning what the real causes of a lot of social ills are. You can just go, "Well it's all the bloody immigrants or it's all the bloody Muslims". They stop you questioning "Well is it really?" When actually those readers should have more fundamental issues with the whole system we live in. I very much felt I'd sold myself down the river; I hated what I was doing.' He drowned his despair in alcohol.
>
> *(ibid., p.86)*

Michelle Stanistreet, now General Secretary of the National Union of Journalists, told Jones of her attempts when at the *Daily Express* to complain to the Press Complaints Commission (PCC) in 2001, about her paper's coverage of asylum seekers. 'Our own editor sat on the PCC at that time, so we just got a ridiculous note back from [former PCC Chairman] Christopher Meyer saying he didn't believe there was a problem' (ibid., p.87).

Jones's comments, in my view accurately, regarding the tabloid press:

> The experiences of Peppiat and Stanistreet are illustrative of a culture of endemic dishonesty and myth making within the media. Rather than providing an honest view of British society, media organisations relish hunting down extreme examples that might be used to tap into widespread prejudices and insecurities – and in doing so work in tandem with the political consensus.
>
> *(ibid., p.87)*

He points out how many fallacies are believed by the public: for example, YouGov's January 2013 poll revealed the perception that 27 per cent of social security is claimed fraudulently, compared with the government's own figure of 0.7 per cent and that 41 per cent of social security flows into the pockets of the unemployed while the real figure is 3 per cent.

Ambitious politicians, then, have to be wary about consorting with the tabloid press: it can give a boost to a career with favourable publicity but only on its own terms. It can also decide to attack and damage the careers of those who might criticise them or those whose views are deemed unacceptable. Whilst the quality press does generally respect true reportage and the principles of democracy, the tabloids aim their copy at the gut level of the readership, calculating, in my view, that people tend to enjoy having their prejudices endorsed, however ill-founded they might be.

Crises and the media

Politicians have to be able to handle crises well if they want to advance their case for further promotion: political crises are invariably played out via the media. Riddell's chapter on how politicians deal with crises is especially authoritative as it draws upon evidence from former senior ministers (Riddell, 2020, pp.218–227). Alistair Campbell makes a distinction between the countless 'media frenzies' and genuine crises of which, during his ten years as Blair's right-hand media man, he reckons there were only six. The first one was the lorry drivers' strike in summer 2000 over petrol levies. As Riddell notes 'For a time, the government appeared to have lost control as the blockades – aided by mobile phone communication between the pickets – threatened everyday supplies' (ibid., pp.221–222): followed by the spring 2001 outbreak of foot and mouth disease. The huge and alarming extermination of animals thus caused and their burning pyres all over the country fostered a sense the government was not able to control the situation: the key requirement for political stability. But things became even worse when there were a number of prison breakouts in 1966 including that of the Soviet spy, George Blake. Roy Jenkins as Home Secretary came under severe pressure. 'My nerve was a bit shaken', he confessed. 'I ought to have been steadier under fire but it is easier to say this in retrospect than it was to sustain during the barrage of daily bombardments' (ibid., pp.219–220).

But, true to his high calibre as a politician, he turned in a brilliant performance in the ensuing Conservative censure motion. 'It was all slightly farcical. For it neither helped to recapture Blake nor to make me a better (or worse) Home Secretary. Nevertheless it was by far the greatest parliamentary triumph I ever achieved' (ibid., pp.219–220). But, from the promotion point of view 'It also made him a leadership contender' (ibid., p.220); thus demonstrating how debating victories in the Commons can change little but, crucially for the victors, they can confirm and burnish reputations, leading on to greater things (though not ultimately for Jenkins who sought the top job via the route of a new short-lived political party: the Social Democratic Party).

A much more serious crisis was when, on 11 October 2008, Chancellor of the Exchequer, Alistair Darling took a call from Sir Tom McKillop, chairman of the huge Royal Bank of Scotland telling him 'the bank would collapse within hours. What was I going to do about it?' (Darling, 2011, p.12). In retrospect, he explained the full gravity of the crisis:

> The [Royal Bank of Scotland] was the biggest bank in the world at that time. If it had shut it would have brought the entire banking system with

> it. And you think about it: no money, no food, no petrol, not just here but across Europe, America – so the stakes were pretty high!
>
> *(ibid., p.224)*

This crisis had been preceded by the problems of Northern Rock, a small but important bank that threatened to fail, causing ominously long queues of people desperate to withdraw their savings. The crisis escalated and Darling said:

> I found myself having to make a statement at short notice. I had to reassure the public in a way that would stop the panic escalating further. It was a critical moment and I knew we had only one chance. If it failed, the panic might spread to other banks. So I announced the guarantee and, to my immense relief, it worked.
>
> *(Darling, 2011, pp.29–30; see also Weinberg, 2011, chs 7 and 8, who suggests 'the job of politician should carry a government health warning')*

In retrospect, Darling stressed the importance of:

> media management – if you let things get out of control, you're ruined. ... Do you sound calm and measured, even if inside you may think 'Goodness, I'm flying by the seat of my pants here'? But how you come across is terribly important. And no doubt you can think of umpteen examples of ministers who have done a really bad Today programme and the grim reaper is at the door within hours.
>
> *(Riddell, 2020, p.224)*

Social media

Tom Baldwin's splendid book on the modern media and politics singles out March 1989 as a significant turning point in media history: it's when:

> Tim Berners-Lee found a way to connect hypertext with the internet to create, as he put it 'ta-da' – the World Wide Web. If the immediate reaction from his boss was less than effusive, scrawling the words 'vague but exciting' on the proposal, such technology would soon be heralded as an engine of progress, breaking down borders, connecting people and opening minds.
>
> *(Baldwin, 2018, p.8)*

Reflecting some of this spirit, once Facebook and Twitter were transforming political relationships with the media, Blair's spin doctor Alistair

Campbell noted in a 2012 *Times* article how politicians were now able to 'communicate directly without having to rely on elites of the old media. That is both emancipating and democratic' (Jones, 2014, p.155). This early optimism about such beneficial effects was soon forced to enter a shadowy world created by the US President elected in 2016. All those hopes of progressive journalists that the 'new information age' would mean the 'future belonged to' them were proved 'horribly wrong' (Baldwin, 2018, p.2). Donald Trump claimed he hated 'Big Tech'. Yet, as James Clayton pointed out, 'He has loved using Twitter. He's used it as a way, for more than 10 years, to bypass the media and speak directly to voters' (Clayton, 2021). Communicating directly with voters sounds 'democratic' in normal times but the new breed of populist politicians exploits such access by shamelessly lying. Shortly before Twitter banned Trump in January 2021, he had nearly 90 million followers. His tweets were given 'official' status by the White House and he used the platform to inform and motivate his core supporters, especially in the run up to the riotous assault on Capitol Hill, 6 January 2021.

As in so many cases Britain tended to follow American political practice: Twitter became a virtual automatic and powerful element of MPs' communication capacity and the means whereby they conducted their business activities, whether, if a minister, it was government policies, or otherwise their own personal advancement. Writing in *Wired* (but now with the *Daily Telegraph*), journalist Ben Gartside explained the phenomenon of MPs' WhatsApp groups 'a politician's best friend'. The vexed problem of Lady Hallet's efforts in extracting huge numbers of WhatsApp messages between ministers and officials during the pandemic, illustrates how central this form of communication has become at the highest levels of government. 'Government by WhatsApp' is a condition the presenters of the *The Rest Is Politics* podcast fear might soon become a reality (7 June 2023).

Coups and leaks

The most infamous factional group, that of the Brexiter European Research Group, used their platform to put pressure on the pro-Remain David Cameron ahead of the 2016 referendum.

Back benchers lacking the profile to interest the print press in their comments can slip 'outlandish texts' into the group chat 'knowing they will inevitably be passed on to journalists and published as a "leak"' (Gartside, 2019).

Social media, of course, has performed a far more important role in the general politics of the UK, affecting for good and often ill, the careers of politicians and indeed journalists: in other words the two main professions supporting democratic functions.

Whilst in theory social media opens up and democratises political activity, it also releases a dangerous destructive germ into the body politic. As Joshua Tocker of New York University observes:

> Prior to social media, if you were the only one in your county supporting extremist views regarding the overthrow of the US government, organising with other like-minded but geographically dispersed compatriots would be a costly activity. Social media drastically reduces costs and allows such individuals to more easily find each other to organize and collaborate.
>
> *(Tucker, 2021)*

In his *Times* column, February 2023, David Aaronovitch observes: ‘Whereas 30 years ago the warriors against evil were lonely figures, occasionally meeting in pubs, now they have a playground to romp in and the billionaire funded new TV channels to give them validation and sell them things’ (Aaronovitch, 2023).

Alt-right and alt-left

Baldwin notes that the biggest exploiters of social media have tended to be the extremes of left and right, which became respectively known as the ‘alt-right’ and ‘alt-left’. The term alt-right was coined by Richard Spencer, a leading white supremacist and it was given a huge boost by the candidature in 2015 of Donald Trump. Websites sprung up like 4chan and 8chan, defining themselves in opposition to the hated mainstream media and the so-called corrupt ruling elites propagating messages and memes about white supremacism, neo-Nazism, racism, as well as hate crimes and mass shootings, not to mention the nonsensical but widely believed conspiracy theories of QAnon. The most important website was Breitbart, funded by hedge-fund tycoon Robert Mercer with Bureaus in Los Angeles, Washington, London and Jerusalem (Baldwin, 2018, pp.200–218).

While these sites fed their right-wing poison into the political cultures of the USA, UK and other developed nations, counter organisations emerged on the alt-left: in the UK, especially the Canary, Another Angry Voice, Evolve Politics and Squawkbox. As Baldwin notes: ‘Much of the material being pushed by these groups in the 2017 election included highly effective Youtube videos produced by the [then Corbynite] Labour Party and the [Corbynite cheerleaders] of Momentum which reached well beyond the alt-left cave’ (ibid., p.204). Canary seemed obsessively concerned with Laura Kuenssberg’s alleged pro-Tory bias: ‘The Canary has seen her booed, jeered and shouted down for asking perfectly reasonable questions at Labour events. After receiving specific threats, the BBC decided she needed a body-guard when she went to the party’s annual conference in 2017’ (ibid., p.206).

Yes, you might object, this extremism is awful but does it directly affect ministerial promotion? I would argue that it does and profoundly so. The erosion of democracy by extremists who do not share its underlying liberal consensus deeply affects the lives and careers of politicians seeking to advance themselves in British political life: it also surely deters some able potential politicians from entering the fray so essential to our good governance. As the former Tory Leader has written: 'In the social media age, MPs are subjected to much more intemperate, misogynistic, antisemitic and hateful abuse. Two of them have been killed in recent years by fanatics' (Hague, 2022). However, within the Westminster village, WhatsApp groups have been increasingly used for communications between MP factions, most notably the European Research Group. There is some evidence to suggest participants believe such messages are wholly confidential while experience suggests they most certainly are not. In March 2023, Isabelle Oakeshott released a vast haul of WhatsApp messages she had accessed via a book collaboration with Matt Hancock. These revealed the casually disdainful language used by both civil servants and ministers in their references to their fellow ministers and indeed the general public. It seems as if this more informal mode of contact encourages a less inhibited (or 'professional'?) expression of views compared with written memos or even emails.

In 2019, BBC Scotland ran an article on four MPs who had suffered abuse. Joanna Cherry was an Scottish National Party MP who received more abuse than most. She tries to explain: 'A lot of abuse I receive is misogynistic, but it's also homophobic, anti-Catholic, and also people resent me because they see me as a strong voice in favour of Scottish independence' (Campbell, 2019).

Kirstene Hair, a Scottish Tory MP, explains how abuse and threats – mostly received on social media – affect her: 'I can deal with it – the problem is I don't want to deal with it', she said. 'I do ignore it – I would go insane if I didn't' (ibid.). She believes it would be a mistake not to take the threats seriously:

> The thing I say back to everyone who says 'you're just a snowflake', or 'you need to man up', is you don't know when someone writes something ... on social media if they are actually capable of doing something much worse and we don't know that therefore ... we do have to have additional security and support.
>
> *(ibid.)*

Events have demonstrated, she says, that the hatred directed at politicians can have real, harmful consequences. 'It's not just a threat on social media, we've seen people go further. I can't just say "that won't happen to me"' (ibid.).

One of the worst aspects of social media abuse has been the anti-Semitic abuse directed at Jewish MPs – especially if female – during the time Jeremy Corbyn was Leader. Baldwin lists some of the awful social media messages she received – here's a sample of two:

> Hang yourself you vile treacherous Zionist Tory filth. You are a cancer of humanity.
>
> The gallows would be a fine and fitting place for this dyke Yid shit to swing from.
>
> *(Baldwin, 2018, p.208)*

Given the murder of two MPs – Jo Cox by a far-right extremist 16 June 2016 and David Amess on 15 October 2021 by an Islamic State sympathiser – MPs are understandably deeply concerned about their safety. Louise Ellman, a senior and highly respected Jewish Labour MP, tired of the anti-Semitic abuse stood down from the party as did Luciana Berger on 18 February 2019 for the same reason. The harsh partisanship and polarisation caused by issues like Brexit plus the divisive populist political style of Boris Johnson fuelled the extremism – most obviously expressed on social media – which has soured UK politics. Several Tory MPs have decided to end their political careers: one veteran ex-Cabinet member still with a chance of high office, Sajid Javid, and another, Cloe Smith, another former Cabinet member, at 30 years old with a whole career in politics ahead of her, has also announced she will not contest the next election.

Podcasts

As a footnote to this chapter the recent innovation of political podcasts should be mentioned. These are usually 30–60 minute 'programmes' uploaded on to the internet and cover a huge gamut of subjects. The political ones offer MPs and ministers, not forgetting overseas visitors, a platform to advance their views. My favourites begin with *The Rest Is Politics*, hosted by ex-Tory minister Rory Stewart and former Blair spin doctor and political activist on many fronts, Alistair Campbell. They engage in witty but very well-informed debates on political issues – managing, given both their respective chemistries – to disagree very agreeably in, according to one reviewer 'a radically disgruntled brand of centrism' (Marriott, 2023). So successful has the podcast become that when they offered their followers a public performance in December 2022, they managed to fill the Albert Hall. It has to be said, however, that the podcast might not be so attractive to those not sympathetic to centrist viewpoints.

Others worth listening to include *Americast* on US politics, plus on the UK scene the BBC's *Newscast* and the *Newsagents* featuring ex-BBC journalists, Emily Maitlis and John Sopel.

Concluding comment

The various branches of the media provide the means whereby democratic politics is carried out. MPs use it to get attention, to enhance their profiles, to become popular and noticed by their party leaders when considering fitting ministers into available political jobs. Boris Johnson, for example, used his wit and performative skills to become a 'celebrity politician' and thence PM; Tony Blair's brilliance as a communicator on the broadcast media also carried him into Number 10; Nadheem Zahawi revelled in media popularity, with its promotion potential soon to be realised, when delivering the vaccination roll-out to manage the Covid pandemic. However, Johnson's manifold transgressions from the truth and decent behaviour led the media to finally claim his head in July 2022. Blair too, once the media's darling, found how easily it can turn negative when he insisted weapons of mass destruction existed in Iraq when intensive and long-standing investigations revealed they did not. And Zahawi, also briefly loved by the media, discovered how brutally cruel it can be when it researched his tax history and brought about his sacking.

References and further reading

Aaronovitch, D. (2023) 'No limit for this web of conspiracy theorists'. *The Times*, 2 February.
Baldwin, T. (2018) *Ctrl Alt Delete: How Politics and the Media Crashed Our Democracy*. Hurst.
Brown, G. (2017) *My Life, Our Times*. Bodley Head.
Campbell, G. (2019) 'MP abuse: "I had a police escort after a death threat"'. BBC Scotland, 28 November. www.bbc.co.uk/news/election-2019-50549432.
Clayton, J. (2021) 'Trump's Twitter downfall'. BBC News, 9 January. www.bbc.co.uk/news/technology-55571291.
Darling, A. (2011) *Back from the Brink: 100 Days at Number 11*. Atlantic.
Ellery, B. (2023) 'How junior doctors "took over" the British Medical Association'. *The Times*, 14 January.
Gartside, B. (2019) 'The scheming MPs guide for WhatsApping in Westminster'. Wired, 4 September. www.wired.co.uk/article/mps-whatsapp-guide-westminster.
Gregory, A. (2023) 'Matt Hancock: What do the leaked WhatsApp messages reveal?' *Guardian*, 1 March.
Hague, W. (2022) 'Would I still go into politics? That's an easy one'. *The Times*, 27 December.
Harari, D. (2017) '"Pound in your pocket" devaluation: 50 years on'. Insight, House of Commons Library, 17 November.
Hoggart, S. (1999) 'Blair lays on the therapy for the terracotta army'. *Guardian*, 3 November.
Hutton, J. and Lewis, L. (2014) *How to Be a Minister*. Biteback.
Jones, B. and Norton, P. (2014) *Politics UK*, 8th edn. Routledge.
Jones, B., Norton, P. and Hertner, I. (2022) *Politics UK*, 10th edn. Routledge.

Jones, N. (1996) Soundbites and Spin Doctors. Indigo.
Jones, O. (2014) *The Establishment: And How They Get Away with It.* Allen Lane.
Kaufman, G. (1980) How to Be a Minister. Faber.
King, A. (2015) *Who Governs Britain?* Pelican.
Lensch, J. and Witter, L. (2020) '10 things politicians should be thinking of right now'. Innovation in Politics Institute, 24 April. https://innovationinpolitics.eu/coping-with-the-crisis-article/10-things-politicians-should-be-thinking-of-right-now/.
Littlejohn, R. (2010) 'Good old Footy? No, a dangerous, deluded hypocrite'. Daily Mail, 5 March.
Low, V. (2012) 'Antonia: The truth about Mellor'. *Standard*, 12 April.
Marriott, J. (2023) 'At least they're not talking about football'. *The Times*, 3 February.
McGuiness, A. (2019) 'Calls for police investigation into leak after Gavin Williamson sacking'. Sky News, 2 May .
Nelson, F. (2023) 'The importance of exposing Matt Hancock's WhatsApp messages'. *Spectator*, 1 March.
NPR (2011) 'The incredible shrinking sound bite'. 5 January.
Oborne, P. (2007) *The Triumph of the Political Class.* Simon & Schuster.
Odugbemi, S. (2015) '"You leak, I brief": who is the scoundrel?' LinkedIn, 13 July.
Price, L. (2006) *The Spin Doctor's Diary.* Hodder & Stoughton.
Riddell, P. (2020) *15 Minutes of Power: The Uncertain Life of British Ministers.* Profile.
Scott, G. (2023) 'Levelling up is so 2019 … Rishi Sunak's Tories are now gauging up'. *The Times*, 18 January.
The Times (2012) 'Mellor attacks tabloids over Chelsea football shirt claim'. 27 June.
Tucker, J. (2021) 'How does social media impact democracy?' Koch Foundation, 3 March. https://charleskochfoundation.org/stories/how-does-social-media-impact-democracy/.
Weinberg, A. (2011) 'Should the job of national politicians carry a health warning?' In A. Weinberg (ed.), The Psychology of Politicians, pp. 123–142. Cambridge University Press.

6

SPECIAL ADVISERS

The new 'apprentice ministers'?

> Compared to the total Senior Civil Service (SCS) the political and politically appointed policy makers remains small – 250 compared to the 400 plus in the whole SCS. But that comparison can be misleading. It might be more appropriate to compare the politically-appointed elite with the very top of the civil service – maybe 200 strong. This group has arguably equivalent status to the political elite - and is slightly smaller in number.
>
> (Professor Colin Talbot, quoted in Stanley, 2022)

> Thea and George's other special adviser, Ramesh 'Mesh' Chhabra were two of the good guys among the spads I would come to know during my ministerial career; kind, helpful and good at their jobs. Mesh in particular was invaluable when press attacks came. Mesh's sound (but very difficult to heed) advice not to pour fuel on the fire by responding to media accusations would stay with me over the years.
>
> (Leadsom, 2023, p.36)

One of the most potent additions to our political personnel has been in the field of special advisers or spads as they have come to be called. It's fair to say that they began as non-parliamentary advisers to PMs but in the recent era have been extended to most big Whitehall departments, which now usually have spads advising ministers. Before the democratic age, monarchs often relied upon a kind of 'prime minister' in the form of a trusted adviser. Those which spring to mind – and mentioned in the preface – include the right-hand man of Henry VIII, Cardinal Wolsey (son of a butcher), who demonstrated the king's preference for raw ability over the plentiful supply of eager blue-blooded aristocrats. Thomas Cromwell, Wolsey's successor (born

DOI: 10.4324/9781003405085-7

to a publican and brewer), was probably the most able and naturally gifted public servant employed by any British monarch hitherto. Queen Elizabeth I echoed her father's preference for avoiding the nobly born by employing the two Burghleys, William and later his son Robert, not commoners but born into the landed gentry rather than the traditional aristocracy.

Roy Hattersley, a biographer of Lloyd George, claims it was Lloyd George who 'invented' spads by drawing a number of businessmen into government when PM during the First World War. He also created a ' "Prime Minister's Secretariat", aka "The Garden Suburb" comprising six advisers based in huts behind Downing Street during the First World War' (Cardwell, 2020, p.6). But it's fair to say all PMs, past and recent, relied for advice, quite naturally, upon a small number of close political allies. Stanley Baldwin, for example, had John Colin Davidson (later a Viscount), a former civil servant and Tory politician, as well as William Bridgeman (also later a Viscount; Stanley, 2022). Churchill's close adviser was Professor Lindeman (later Lord Cherwell) who has been described as a brilliant but arrogant scientist and intellectual whose advice clearly Churchill valued very highly. Harold Macmillan relied upon a number of close political friends and depended greatly upon John Wyndham, his aristocratic private secretary, who accompanied him on many overseas visits and offered constant advice and support; he described his role as that of 'a classic court jester who lightened the tone of the place but this is to vastly underplay his influence as Macmillan's right hand man advising Supermac on fundamental issues daily' (Cardwell, 2020, p.4). But it was Harold Wilson who began to appoint spads from outside the civil service 'in significant numbers', not just in Number 10 but in government departments as well (Stanley, 2022).

Critics of spads sometimes argue PMs and ministers should rely solely on the advice of the civil service: lifelong professionals and hugely knowledgeable in their departmental specialisms. Sir Robin Mountfield, former Cabinet Office Permanent Secretary, reckons, 'A good special adviser is gold dust but they can be an awful nuisance ... many of them treating themselves as unaccountable ministers' (Yong and Hazell, 2014, p.1). Yong and Hazell add that through:

> much of the 20th century and into the 21st, special advisers have been seen as a malign development – at best a necessary evil and at worst a waste of public funds, whose potential for shady and pernicious behaviour had to be contained.
>
> *(ibid., p.1)*

Stories of internecine bickering and briefings were an integral part of the Labour years ... briefing behind the scenes, poisoning the relationship between ministers and civil servants, or as gatekeepers keeping them apart. Spads are often seen as adding to the concentration of power in the PM and his staff at the expense of Cabinet and also as wet-behind-the-ears, gaffe-prone youngsters (Number 10 has employed some in their 20s and 30s) with little or no experience or understanding of the world in which 'ordinary people live and work and who contribute negatively to what is often seen as the professionalisation of politics at Westminster' (ibid., p.2). Furthermore, they are often characterised as over-powerful and unaccountable incomers who exercise their minister's authority by proxy to an unjustifiable extent. The classic example cited is usually Blair's Communications Secretary, Alistair Campbell, satirised in the TV comedy *The Thick of It* by the foul-mouthed and irrepressible, Malcolm Tucker. Tory back bencher Ian Sproat told the Commons in March 1976 that it was 'totally repugnant that special advisers should be paid out of taxpayer's money' (Cardwell, 2020, p.9).

However, there are excellent reasons why spads came to be employed in relatively substantial numbers. Professor Lindeman, as a scientist, represented a specialism much neglected by top civil servants, who traditionally were (less so nowadays) educated in the arts or classics. Second, civil servants tend as a group to be prejudiced against change and in favour of maintaining the status quo. Harold Wilson worried that this tendency would dilute and delay the changes Labour wished to introduce and saw special advisers as the 'more politically committed and politically aware' advisers against civil service complacency (Constitution Society, 2010). Special advisers are usually already ideologically committed to the political aims of their employer and their presence ensures such objectives are not allowed to drift unacceptably. Ministers can become 'isolated in their departments and need aides who share a common commitment' (Yong and Hazell, 2014, p.3). Third, spads are often employed as specialists in managing the 24/7 modern media, massaging messages and firefighting bad publicity. David Lipsey advised Labour ministers and explained his role thus:

> As a special adviser, I could do all sorts of tasks that civil servants rightly thought weren't appropriate for them. If Tony was going to give a political speech, I could write it for him, whereas the civil service was inhibited, and anyway they hadn't got a clue how to write a political speech.
>
> *(Cardwell, 2020, p.5)*

These days spads are accepted as a regular feature of UK government and seen by ministers as an essential part of their career advancement. 'Our evidence', claim Yong and Hazell, 'suggests that special advisers are a valuable part of British government and, indeed, almost all ministers now regard them as indispensable' (Yong and Hazell, 2014, p.3). Sir Alan Walters, economic adviser to Margaret Thatcher, who had condemned the European Monetary System as 'half baked', thereby infuriated her Chancellor, Nigel Lawson, who then scathingly described Sir Alan as merely 'a part time adviser' (Fowler, 1991, pp.325–326). On 27 October 1989, Neil Kinnock asked PM Thatcher 'Who ruled, the minister or the adviser?' She replied, famously, 'Advisers advise, ministers decide' providing her disciple Norman Fowler with the title for his memoirs (ibid., p.326).

The Cabinet Office recognises the important role of spads and issues an annual report on them containing a clear description of their role:

> Special advisers are a critical part of the team supporting Ministers. They add a political dimension to the advice and assistance available to Ministers while reinforcing the political impartiality of the permanent Civil Service by distinguishing the source of political advice and support. Special advisers should be fully integrated into the functioning of government. They are part of the team working closely alongside civil servants to deliver Ministers' priorities. They can help Ministers on matters where the work of government and the work of the government party overlap and where it would be inappropriate for permanent civil servants to become involved. They are appointed to serve the Prime Minister and the government as a whole, not just their appointing Minister.
>
> *(Cabinet Office, 2022, p.2)*

In an interview I held with Charles Powell, he commented on this new cohort of players in the political firmament:

> The new breed of politicians, most of whom start as special advisers to ministers and then progress to being MPs in their late 20s or 30s, view politics as a full time career and although it would be disparaging to say they aren't inspired to a degree by a wish to serve, I think the career structure and the ambitions of that plays a much bigger part now than it did in the past.
>
> *(private interview)*

David Cowling, who advised Peter Shore at the Department of the Environment 1977–79 found the job enthralling as he had:

> an immensely privileged view of the upper echelons of the civil service. I got access to a Secretary of State that many of the brightest people in the country – would have spent a lifetime virtually trying to get to that degree of seniority, that kind of access, that I, swanning through the door got almost immediately.
>
> *(Cardwell, 2020, pp.10–11)*

The impact of spads on ministerial efficacy is cited below via analyses of recent important examples of their role.

Bernard Donoughue: 'Father' of modern spads?

Harold Wilson's desire for an alternative source of advice to the civil service also gave rise to a fresh institution within Westminster politics: the *Policy Unit*. Established in 1974 by one of the first well-known spads, former London School of Economics academic and Wilson's Senior Policy Adviser, Bernard Donoughue, its role was to be the 'eyes and ears' of what is coming into the PM from the departments, to 'scrutinise papers' and be aware of political backgrounds to policy areas as well as 'feed in new policy ideas' (Donoughue, 2003, p.129). Donoughue faced opposition from the civil service and press criticism that unelected aides would be helping shape government policies. However, he was able to assuage the concerns of the Cabinet Secretary, Sir John Hunt, and agreed with him a 'concordat' establishing areas of responsibility and ways of working. Next he sought the agreement of the PM's private secretaries, gaining the trust of Sir Robert Armstrong. Wilson's formidable political secretary, Marcia Williams, was less easy to convince – I cover her extraordinary role as a political adviser below. Donoughue was able to staff the Policy Unit with a range of very able academics, civil servants and political advisers. The notion of additional 'political' advice to appointed ministers, independent of the civil service, migrated downwards from the Policy Unit until spads became the ubiquitous form of political personnel they are today. Donoghue comments: 'We had created a Policy Unit which, against all the odds and under five successive Prime Ministers from both main parties, and a medley of directors, has survived to this day' (ibid., p.134). Table 6.1 shows that the Policy Unit has continued under a succession of directors, several of whom stepped up to become MPs and later senior ministers.

Andrew Adonis

This extremely bright academic, journalist and later Cabinet minister and peer has claimed, significantly, that being a spad is the closest role to that of being an 'apprentice minister'. His comments made in the preface to the Institute for Government's (IfG) 'The Challenge of Being a Minister' is worth quoting from:

> I was lucky. I became a minister in 2005 after seven years as a special adviser (spad) in Tony Blair's Number 10, dealing constantly with ministers and civil servants. As a Spad I learned a huge amount about how Whitehall and Westminster work, and how they can be made to work. I

TABLE 6.1 List of Policy Unit directors

	Policy director	*Years*	*Prime Minister*	
1	Bernard Donoughue	1974–76	Harold Wilson	Labour
		1976–79	James Callaghan	Labour
2	John Hoskyns	1979–82	Margaret Thatcher	Conservative
3	Ferdinand Mount	1982–83		
4	John Redwood	1983–85		
5	Brian Griffiths	1985–90		
6	Sarah Hogg	1990–95	John Major	Conservative
7	Norman Blackwell	1995–97		
8	David Miliband	1997–2001	Tony Blair	Labour
9	Andrew Adonis	2001–03		
10	Geoff Mulgan	2003–04		
11	Matthew Taylor	2005–05		
12	David Bennett	2005–07		
13	Dan Corry	2007–08	Gordon Brown	Labour
14	Nick Pearce	2008–10		
15	Paul Kirby	2011–13	David Cameron	Conservative
16	Jo Johnson	2013–15		
17	Camilla Cavendish	2015–16		
18	John Godfrey	2016–17	Theresa May	Conservative
19	James Marshall	2017–19		
20	Munira Mirza	2019–22	Boris Johnson	Conservative
21	Andrew Griffith	2022–22		

Source: Wikipedia (n.d.).

> worked closely with the Prime Minister and other ministers, observed their contrasting styles, their rise and (all too often) their fall, their successes and failures, and advised on successive reshuffles. However maligned the office of Spad may be, it is an excellent preparation – in many ways an apprenticeship – for ministerial office [I would say this is maybe more true of spads even than the role of the PPS]. Apprenticeships are a good thing; we need more of them in all fields of employment. Far from decrying the reign of ex-Spads – David Cameron, George Osborne, Ed Miliband, Ed Balls et al – we should welcome the fact that at least some ministers come to office with an apprenticeship worth the name, beyond years of mere service in the House of Commons. In the case of key members of the present Cabinet, it was their only apprenticeship; their 1997 counterparts, from the Prime Minister downwards, lacked even this preparation.
>
> *(Riddell et al., 2011)*

Spads have had a considerable influence on British politics: entering the political world when relatively young, they become immersed in the political side of a department's work and, as such, often enter politics as MPs for their respective parties and, having served a ministerial 'apprenticeship', shin quickly up the promotion ladder to hold high office. Examples include Andy Burnham who served as a spad for Culture Secretary Chris Smith and went on to become Secretary of State for Health, David Cameron who went on to serve as PM for six years, David and Ed Miliband who both served in Labour Cabinets and Simon Stephens who worked as a spad for Tony Blair as his health adviser being deemed so effective he went on to direct the NHS as a whole under Conservative governments. One spad provided Michael Hesletine, indirectly, with one of his best party conference jokes. He informed conference, 18 October 2011, that the recent Labour Leader's speech on 'neo-classical endogenous growth theory' was not actually written by Gordon Brown but by his 27-year-old special adviser, Ed Balls (Higgins, 2010). 'So it wasn't Brown's ... pause .... it was Balls!': much (deserved) laughter ensued.

Jack Straw, an early spad

The MP for Blackburn, later Home Secretary and Foreign Secretary, first entered the world of politics via the political adviser route and as such was arguably the first spad as we know them in the modern era. Having qualified brilliantly in the bar exams, Straw was looking forward to a career as a barrister but was already a highly 'political' person having served as president of the Leeds University Union, then as president of the National Union of Students 1969–71 plus as an elected member of Islington Council. Shortly after the 1974 election when Labour returned to power with a very slim majority Straw was telephoned by Ted, the husband of Barbara Castle. As an Islington Alderman, Castle knew Straw and when he met up with them Barbara explained that whilst Brian Abel Smith was to be her policy adviser, she wanted Jack to become her 'political adviser' (Straw, 2012, pp.93–94). Straw established a route that so many have subsequently followed. There was a hurdle to be crossed initially as at that time advisers paid out of public funds were not allowed to be councillors. However, after an exchange of letters with Wilson and some Cabinet discussion, it was decided Straw could continue as a councillor and did so until 1978. Castle's biographer, Anne Perkins, comments on Straw's time at Barbara's side in a way that anticipates the roles spads have come to play in assisting their overworked ministers to function effectively:

> Nearly two years into the job, the student activist turned local councillor had carved out for himself a vital role as special adviser / linkman with the trade unions, with disaffected doctors, with backbenchers as well as press and policy adviser. He plied her with lines to take and arguments to use in

Cabinet; he had a keen eye for trouble ahead and a quick appreciation of defensive strategies.

(Perkins, 2003, p.407)

Jonathan McClory of the IfG echoes Adonis in commenting that:

While an increasing number of MPs boast politics-heavy CVs having worked as local councillors, parliamentary researchers, union officials or journalists, only former Spads have the advantage of having worked hand-in-glove with a minister. This gives them an insider's knowledge of the Whitehall machine, as well as the benefit of having observed where and why their minister succeeded or failed.

(McClory, 2011)

Figure 6.1, which emerged from interviews underpinning the IfG's 'The Challenge of Being a Minister', reveals that 'using special advisers effectively ranks fourth as the most frequently identified factor in ministerial effectiveness' (McClory, 2011).

Clearly, time spent as a spad gives politicians a flying start in the competitive world of British politics. Spads have also played major roles in helping governments to sustain their periods in power. Alistair Campbell was one of several spads who (mostly) successfully managed the crucial area of media relations for Tony Blair's New Labour governments. Theresa May was so dependent on her Home Office spads, Nick Timothy and Fiona Hill,

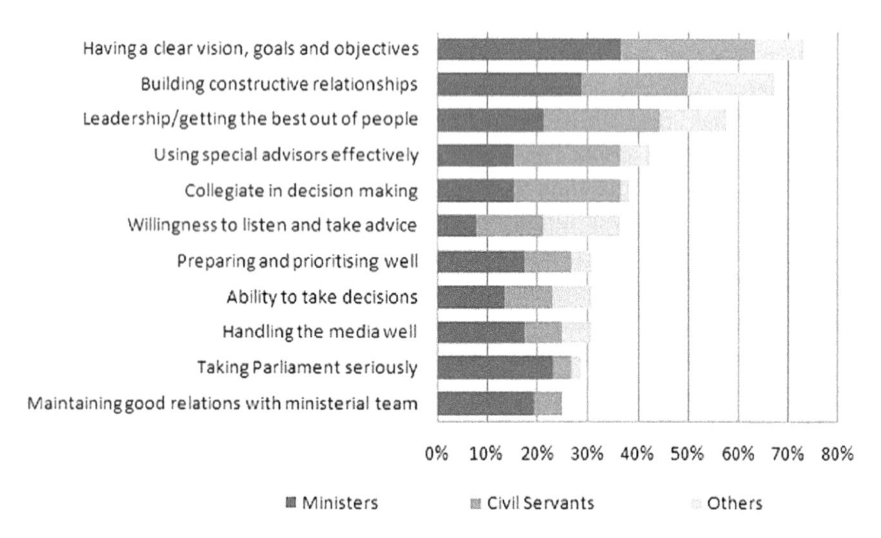

FIGURE 6.1 What makes an effective minister?

Source: McClory (2011). © 2023 Institute for Government.

that she installed them both as Joint Chiefs of Staff once she moved into Number 10. It was rumoured that Mrs May, not a natural policy wonk, relied on Timothy for many of her policy ideas. (Timothy's (2020) grasp of contemporary political ideas are manifested in his *Remaking One Nation: The Future of Conservatism.*) Unfortunately their time in office did not end happily; they exemplified a tendency seen elsewhere when spads have clearly exerted too much power over their boss and via her over ministers and civil servants: their allegedly imperious manner made them extremely unpopular – they were nicknamed by critics as the 'Gruesome Twosome'. In the wake of her disastrous 2017 election when, far from delivering an expected huge majority, May lost what little majority had been won by Cameron in the 2015 election, her Joint Chiefs of Staff took a fair amount of the blame from Tory MPs. Mrs May was told that unless she sacked them both she would face a leadership challenge (Asthana and Mason, 2017). Accordingly, they were both stood down while Theresa May stayed in office courtesy of a deal with Ulster's Democratic Unionist Party.

Whilst spads can assist and enable the advancement of ministerial careers, they can also advance themselves through four pay bands, beginning at £40,500 and rising to £145,000, a salary close to that of the PM. Being at the centre of the decision-making process offers its own obvious rewards but the downside is that a special adviser's appointment terminates with the government which appoints it and new employment has to be sought. Spads usually subscribe to the political platforms of their government employers and are appointed for their special skills: political strategy like Dominic Cummings, economic policy expertise like Alan Walters or media expertise like Alistair Campbell, guru to Tony Blair.

Spads are not only central to ministerial promotion, their efficacy has been such that they have in a sense promoted *themselves* to the highest forums of influence. They spend a great deal of their time in close company with their ministers and share advice inputs with the most senior civil servants, pressure group leaders and a wide range of other ministers. In other words spads have constant access to ministers and are key elements of the 'core executive' who lead the big departments as well as the staff of Number 10. They are usually on call 24/7 and help their ministers run their departments, deal with crises as well as feed in policy ideas. They assiduously seek to promote the careers of their ministers and brief the media with every scrap of positive news they possibly can. At the same time they have been known to brief against ministerial rivals and leak embarrassing items against rivals in policy conflicts and certainly for promotion (see section on Damian McBride below). No doubt they do this because, like Peter Cardwell, spad to James Brokenshire, Secretary of State for Northern Ireland, they admired and supported their minister's career, or their own careers would be enhanced if their boss were to be promoted and, perhaps most important, they lose their jobs should their minister be reshuffled to the backbenches (see Cardwell, 2020).

Spads overstepping: Jo Moore and 'burying bad news'

This example of a spad's misstep led to the resignation of herself, a colleague and her Secretary of State. On 11 September 2001, when the two World Trade Center towers were destroyed by terrorist attacks costing 3,000 lives, Jo Moore, a special adviser in the Department for the Environment, Transport and the Regions emailed her press office as follows, 'It's now a very good day to get out anything we want to bury. Councillors' expenses?' (Harper, 2001). This hyper-cynical suggestion led the Secretary of State, Stephen Byers to ask his permanent secretary, Richard Mottram, if Moore should be subject to disciplinary action. When this email became public, Mottram famously (and hilariously) remarked, expletively, to a colleague: 'We're all f****d. I'm f****d. You're f****d. The whole department is f****d. It's the biggest cock-up ever. We're all completely f****d' (Rawnsley, 2002). The repercussions of Jo Moore's naïve and unforgivably callous comment did not lead to her immediate resignation, possibly because of her close relations with Number 10 aides Alistair Campbell and Anji Hunter but when the row reignited in February 2002, she, her boss Martin Sixsmith and later her Secretary of State Byers all had to resign. Close relations with Number 10 are clearly vital for ministers and for spads but within that pressured decision-making space, spad–PM relationships can be problematic.

Harold and Marcia: a too 'intimate and dominating' a relationship?

Before the case of the Johnson–Cummings relationship, perhaps the most astonishing and in some senses worrying relationship between a PM and an 'outsider' political adviser – before the notion of spads had even emerged – was that of Harold Wilson and his 'personal and political secretary', Marcia Williams. I found the facts of their partnership so unusual and surprising that I provide an analysis culled from the biographies of those who worked closely with both advisers.

Marcia was educated at the independent Northamptonshire High School and then Queen Mary College London. She became secretary to the Labour Party's General Secretary and claims her first contact with Wilson was when he gave her a lift when she was waiting for a bus. Joe Haines's more colourful version is that they both met at an official dinner with Khrushchev at which George Brown engaged in a drunken argument with the Soviet leader, which the efficient Marcia took down in shorthand; Wilson, again on hand with his car, gave her a lift home afterwards.

According to his biographer, Andrew Roth, she explained to him during this journey that she was the person who had been sending him anonymous warnings of a 'Gaitskellites' plot to damage him. Joe Haines speculates in his memoirs that 'something of significance must have happened that night'; it is easy to surmise what this might have been – and many rumours of an affair have circulated – but there is no real proof (Haines, 2003, p.14). The one piece of evidence often quoted is that Marcia once told Mary Wilson: 'I slept with your husband six times in 1956 and it wasn't very satisfactory' (Wilson, 2023); Mary Wilson denied Harold had such an affair but there is no definite proof either way. Marcia went on to become his close aide and head of his political office and, from biographical evidence, developed a powerful hold over the PM that is certainly unprecedented. Haines describes her revealingly as:

> more than his secretary. ... She was his manager and his 'political wife' ... But she also identified a weakness which was not apparent to others in those days: that he was a man whose private insecurity was huge, as was her own. Perhaps it takes one to know one. She fed that weakness. She encouraged him to believe in conspiracies against him because she believed in them herself.
>
> *(Haines, 2003, p.12)*

Their relationship was clearly very close and from all accounts she wielded some kind of power over him, claiming that she had evidence which could destroy him and bring down his government. Haines relates an incident when Marcia had accepted an invitation to a reception at the House of Lords – she had been awarded, controversially, a peerage at Wilson's recommendation in 1974. She insisted Wilson accompany her which, reluctantly, he did but after a short while the PM left and returned to his desk. According to Haines she later blazed into his office and called him 'A little c***. What did you think you are doing? You come back with me at once' (ibid., pp.94–95).

If it was only Haines claiming such behaviour by Williams, it might be thought that an ex-tabloid hack is not to be believed but the memoirs of Bernard Donoughue, highly respected academic and founder of the Policy Unit, seem to confirm the mysteriously dark hold Marcia Williams had over the Labour PM.

> Her behaviour towards him and others who worked for him was often unusual, even intolerable, but he always tolerated it. He was at time clearly afraid of her ... and quickly realised that for some reason he dare not correct or rebuke her. He certainly did not dare get rid of her. When she refused to go through the process of security clearance required for employment in government, he took the risk of signing her PV [Positive

> Vetting] clearance even though she would not allow the security forces to interview her.
>
> *(Donoughue, 2003, pp.199–200)*

Donoughue recalls a telephone conversation with Marcia in which she said that whenever Wilson visited her, 'I give it to him with both barrels'. As 'punishment' for not taking her phone calls, according to Donoughue's memoirs, 'I'm getting him worried. He knows that I am up to all his tricks. I will keep playing with him and he will come out here soon. He knows I've got his number' (ibid., pp.199–200).

He explains the extent of her power over the PM:

> Those who have access [to the PM] have influence on the levers of power. Marcia controlled access to and from the whole personal and political side of Wilson's life, including all aspects of the Labour Party, much of his finances and his patronage. Any one of the team who inadvertently trespassed on her broad territory did so at considerable personal and professional peril. … With the exception of civil servants, his governmental colleagues, the press and a few acquaintances, anybody wishing to see or talk to the Prime Minister was advised to make contact with and through her. Her disapproval meant exclusion.
>
> *(ibid., p.200)*

One extraordinary suggestion made in both the Haines and Donoughue memoirs is that Wilson's doctor, Joe Stone, thought Marcia was 'not always properly balanced' and even talked of 'putting her down', i.e. *killing* her, in a secret fashion so that nobody would know (ibid., p.212). Elsewhere it has been suggested Stone had become obsessed 'by a disturbing notion: murdering Marcia might just be "in the national interest … it may be desirable to dispose of her. We've got to get this woman off his back"' (Andrews, 2021). The veracity of this murky account has never been fully investigated and resolved but, given the contemporary murderous intentions Jeremy Thorpe had towards his former lover Norman Scott, it cannot be easily dismissed (Bloch, 2014, p.305).

It would be wrong however to assume both Haines's and Donoughue's assessment of Marcia was totally negative. They allowed she was highly intelligent, hard-working and able to provide excellent, incisive advice to Wilson, but both underline that such benefits were paid for in the coin of the dominating hold she exercised over the most powerful man in the country. Anything she wanted from him he seemed willing to give, were it being picked up personally at the airport or being awarded that controversial peerage. It is worth pointing out, however, that Lady Falkender never spoke in the House of Lords despite becoming its oldest member.

Finally, by far the most notorious of the gifts Harold gave to Marcia was accepting her suggestions for his Resignation Honours list, written on pink paper: the so-called *Lavender List*. Donoughue points out that such honours differ from the normal run of honours in that they were usually bestowed upon those who had rendered *personal service* to the PM: most of the Lavender List people were friends of Marcia – an unelected personal adviser had hijacked the PM's power of patronage to serve her own 'promotional' ends. Joseph Kagan became a peer apparently because he had helped finance Marcia's Political Office and provided her with her first house in Wyndham Mews. He was later jailed for 'serious currency offences' (Donoughue, 2003, p.194). Marcia was dazzled by the world of showbiz and included on her list were the brothers Lew Grade and Bernard Delfont.

Donoughue points out that another of Marcia's friends, the economist John Vaizey, was in 'total opposition to Harold Wilson and all he stood for'. Also very hostile to Wilson were two ennobled businessmen, James Hanson and James Goldsmith; another close friend was property dealer Eric Miller with whom Marcia had some romantic involvement – he shot himself before a highly critical Department of Trade and Industry report on his management of his property company. Clearly this was a travesty of the honours system and brought it into substantial disrepute. The story of Marcia and Harold certainly stands as a unique yet salutary warning how someone allowed such close, even intimate, access to the PM, can traduce government privileges for their own very personal ends.

Marcia slurs refuted?

Shortly after the above section was written about Wilson and Marcia Williams a well- researched and persuasive book appeared by Linda McDougall, former television journalist and wife of the late Grimsby MP, Austin Mitchell. As a self-described 'insider' she is therefore someone well acquainted with the inner workings of the Labour Party. Where some see a 'baleful influence', she sees a 'loyal' and productive 40-year relationship (McDougal, 2023, p.x). She offers her well-researched book as seeking to:

> Rescue Marcia – a simply brilliant tactician and politician – from the patronising, misogynistic and dismissive verdicts of various male enemies and to suggest a more nuanced context to and understanding of her actions and reactions. ... There is a strong argument that Harold Wilson's political successes were a direct result of his recognition and acceptance that he needed the support of Marcia's practical and organisational skills and active and acute political antennae. It was a genuine and enduring partnership between a man and a woman at the top of the political ladder, never seen before or since in British politics.
>
> *(ibid., p.xi)*

McDougal presents a strong case – backed up by the likes of the BBC's political editor, John Cole – that Marcia was a very skilful and effective aide to Wilson and possibly the second most powerful woman in British politics in the twentieth century, after Margaret Thatcher. However, she also quotes Robin Butler as saying, 'Marcia was a bloody nuisance and such a bloody nuisance I could hardly believe.' Marcia was clearly a difficult woman but, to the extent that she helped Wilson promote himself up the political ladder and then its very top, she was perhaps the foremost example of how political advisers can turbocharge the career prospects of the ministers for whom they work (McDougal, 2023, pp.1–13).

Alistair Campbell, 'super-spin doctor'?

When he became Labour Leader, Tony Blair reflected the importance of the tabloid press by appointing one its leading journalists as his Press Secretary. The Yorkshire-born son of a Scottish vet, Campbell attended two grammar schools before studying modern languages at Cambridge. He then led a colourful life travelling and working in various jobs before becoming a tabloid journalist, working for the *Daily Mirror* and the *Today* newspapers. Alcohol is the classic indulgence of journalists and Campbell proved no exception but his depressive tendencies and the pressures of work led him to seek treatment for alcoholism – an addiction that he remedied through abstinence. Working for Blair, he acquired a reputation for an aggressive approach to his fellow hacks when conducting press conferences but, given his Labour sympathies, probably more to those on the right than the left. The public presentation of political news has an umbilical relationship with the choice of direction policies take: it is highly likely that someone who advises on presentation will also have a role in influencing the policies he or she is asked to feed into the hungry maw of the British media. Campbell's incisive judgement and force of personality turbocharged his role from mere spin doctor to Blair's right-hand man. Some even began to call him 'Deputy Prime Minister': anyone doubting this should dip into his wonderfully explicit diaries where they can see how his days were filled with advising on high policy, appointments (promotions and sackings), defusing media crises, relations with foreign heads of government and their leading officials. Campbell soon became a national figure and some of his passionate defences of his boss dominated the headlines. Especially prominent was the 2002 case of Dr David Kelly, who committed suicide after his involvement in the 'dodgy dossier' affair predicting that some of Iraq's chemical and biological weapons could be deployed within 45 minutes, an estimate that he claimed was included at the insistence of Campbell, at that time Downing Street Director of Communications. After being involved in such a high-profile way – in effect becoming the story, not merely the agent of its dissemination – Campbell took a back seat in New Labour's media management. But he continued to make hugely energetic interventions in national politics after Labour lost power in 2010 and Tory rule was installed for over a decade. Along with Marcia Williams, and Dominic Cummings, he is among the most consequential political advisers since 1945.

Damian McBride: the spad from hell?

McBride was a most unusual kind of aide, a bright Cambridge graduate of Irish descent who initially worked as a civil servant communications director at the Treasury, when Gordon Brown was Chancellor, and was shifted into Number 10 when Brown succeeded Blair. When at the Treasury he had overseen the campaign to replace Blair with his boss. In other words, McBride became the leading defender and promoter of Gordon Brown and was clearly someone none too scrupulous about the methods available to him.

One of his first transgressions occurred on the eve of the 2004 Labour conference when a leaked story revealed 'senior' Whitehall communications directors had 'savaged No 10 during a private meeting for media manipulation'; this compounded an ongoing concern about 'spin' and collapse of public trust in government. An inquiry focused on Damian McBride as the source of the leak: a former Whitehall permanent secretary told the *Guardian*: 'The idea that Gordon Brown did not know Damian McBride was a wrong 'un is absurd. He was warned' (Wintour, 2009). This testimony and other examples suggest Brown, and indeed previous PMs and senior ministers, chose some of their aides for their ruthless 'enforcer' abilities ignoring their activities as long as they were not personally involved. According to Nick Watt in the *Guardian*, McBride 'was known simply as the Dog, short for his nickname Mad Dog. To his enemies he was McPoison.' Watt allowed that 'of all the characters who have worked for Gordon Brown over the years he [McBride] was one of the sharpest, most intelligent and wittiest' (Watt, 2009).

In a section of his memoirs titled 'Going to the Dark Side', McBride wrote the following confessional few paragraphs:

> People tell you things when you do the job I did, in a way that you become some diabolical inversion of a priest in the confessional box; told about other people's sins precisely in the hope that you'll expose them to the world.
>
> Labour, Conservative or Liberal Democrat; ministers, MPs or advisers; if they'd ever shared their secrets with colleagues in Westminster, the chances were I ended up being told about them by someone they'd confided in, who was not the friend they thought.
>
> Drug use, spousal abuse, secret alcoholics, extramarital affair, clandestine visits to seedy saunas and brothel, a bizarre range of what the newspapers

> would call 'unnatural sex acts'. And then dozens of instances of individuals, almost always men, deemed not to be safe to be left alone with junior officials late in the evening: the bullies, harassers and gropers.
>
> *(McBride, 2013, p.385)*

McBride reckons he 'did nothing with 95% of the stories I was told – except write them down for potential future reference' (ibid., p.385). In other words, he was the equivalent to a *News of the World* 'sleaze meister' at the heart of government, working to defend and advance the career interests of the Labour PM. 'Politics', he writes:

> isn't 'showbusiness for ugly people'. They're *exactly the same* [my italics]. Showbusiness – like politics, business and the media – is mostly full of ordinary people whose position or fame gives them the ability to play out of their league when it comes to sexual relationships, often with much more junior colleagues.
>
> *(ibid., p.385)*

The power relationships within Westminster, McBride reckons, makes it 'as seedy and sex driven as Hollywood, and often more so, especially for those MPs who use the demands of spending weekdays in London away from their family as an excuse to live a double life' (ibid., p.387).

His step too far was to plan, along with the blogger Derek Draper, a new gossip blog to rival the Guido Fawkes website – to be called *Red Rag*. He had already been removed from his day-to-day briefing of the press role but hoped this new venture would be an effective weapon of opposition. However the suggested smears about senior Conservatives, including the sex life of David Cameron's wife Samantha, were seen as crossing any number of red lines. Gordon Brown was quick to distance himself from his close aide: 'there is no place in politics for the dissemination or publication of material of this kind' (Hinsliff, 2009a). In his memoir, McBride details how he spoke to Gordon Brown on the phone and offered his resignation; Jeremy Heywood later texted that 'it is to your great credit that you helped Gordon reach the only possible decision in the circumstances' (McBride, 2013, p.402).

Dominic Cummings: rise and fall of a 'superspad'?

If Bernard Donoughue and Jack Straw were the two earliest examples of the modern spad and Alistair Campbell the most powerful, then Dominic Cummings has been arguably the most controversial. He had an astonishing rise and fall career, which illustrated not only both the extent and the limits of how powerful this modern form of political life can be but also some of the more traditional verities of survival in the volatile world of politics. 'Dominic

Cummings made Johnson's premiership', write Seldon and Newell, 'and he destroyed Johnson's premiership. No aide to a British Prime Minister in British history was quite like him. None were so influential, nor so destructive once they left office' (Seldon and Newell, 2023, p.243).

Cummings was born into a middle-class family and was privately educated before entering Exeter College Oxford where, studying under historian Norman Stone, he was awarded a first in Ancient and Modern History. One of his former tutors has described him to the *New Statesman* as 'fizzing with ideas, unconvinced by any received set of views about anything'. He was 'something like a Robespierre – someone determined to bring down things that don't work' (Lambert, 2023). After Oxford, Cummings lived 1994–97 in Russia, pursuing an entrepreneurial airline dream that never materialised. Back in the UK he became a professional campaigner, being employed by Business for Sterling working against the prospect of the euro being introduced: having immersed himself in the media he developed ideas about its reform, including a hostile attitude towards the BBC. His leading role opposing Labour's devolution plan for the northeast of England brought him to wider attention and he was engaged, not being a Conservative member, as a spad to Michael Gove. Two signal aspects of his working practice were soon made manifest: he got things done. He was successful in helping Gove introduce 'free schools' and restructuring the Department of Education but, second, treated everyone with such abrasive contempt that he became much hated: Cameron described him as a 'career psychopath' (Gillespie, 2020).

In 2013, Cummings and another Department of Education spad were accused of bullying a senior civil servant involving the use of intimidatory bad language. The case was settled out of court via a payment of £25,000. But this event, in part, prompted Cameron to *demote* Gove out of Education into the office of Chief Whip, leaving Cummings without a job. These CV negatives, however, proved no impediment to him becoming campaign director of Vote Leave in 2016. It was he who coined the dynamic slogan Take Back Control and succeeded substantially in effecting an historic victory to persuade the country to vote for severing UK membership of the European Union. When Johnson took over the nation's helm in 2019 he asked his comrade in arms to join him as his chief adviser in Number 10: he was trusted to 'exercise enormous control over other advisers, cabinet ministers and policy decisions' (Oulton, 2020). Seldon and Newell's well-researched book on Johnson's reign records the iron grip Cummings exerted on the government's mission to 'get Brexit done'.

> 'From now on No.10 will be run like NASA' was the leitmotif, with Cummings in charge at mission control. He was totally in his element: here he was ruling the roost in No.10, as if 'all his past life had been but a

> preparation for this hour and for this trial', as Churchill had said. Those present were intimidated, intrigued and riveted.
>
> *(Seldon and Newell, 2023, p.74)*

During his first six months, there was much praise for Cummings among both political and civil service staff. 'A total force of nature in that period, he put us on a war footing. The whole system changed around him in No.10 and he gave the machine what it had lacked before' (ibid., p.75). In the autumn of 2019, Cummings' fingerprints could be detected in the idea of proroguing Parliament and the expulsion of 21 One Nation Tory MPs who had the temerity to vote against the possibility of a no-deal Brexit outcome. Later on, Cummings led the election campaign chipping in with another simple but effective slogan – Get Brexit Done – and helping to smash Labour's Red Wall strongholds thus delivering to Johnson a huge majority. Such a slogan seems not especially clever, perhaps, but in practice it proved spectacularly effective. It also provides yet another reason why spads are useful to politicians seeking promotion, especially to reaffirm control of the ultimate prize of Number 10. Civil servant aides might boast brilliant Oxbridge credentials but their professional ethic of non-partisanship, would preclude them from coming up with anything like an effective party-political slogan.

However, Cummings's personal agenda did not stop at enabling the ambition of Boris Johnson: he also espoused wider aims of transforming the status quo-loving civil service mindset and dragging it into the twenty-first century. His modus operandi in realising his vision was a kind of public administration 'terrorism', which certainly worried a fair number of senior mandarins. In a 3,000-word blogpost he outlined what kind of person he would like to see in government service: 'super-talented weirdos' with 'genuine cognitive diversity' rather than Oxbridge applicants with degrees in English. He continued:

> We need some true wild cards, artists, people who never went to university and fought their way out of an appalling hell hole, weirdos from William Gibson novels like that girl hired by Bigend as a brand 'diviner' who feels sick at the sight of Tommy Hilfiger or that Chinese-Cuban free runner from a crime family hired by the KGB. If you want to figure out what characters around Putin might do, or how international criminal gangs might exploit holes in our border security, you don't want more Oxbridge English graduates who chat about [French psychoanalyst Jacques] Lacan at dinner parties with TV producers and spread fake news about fake news.
>
> *(Syal, 2020)*

Rounding off his extended blog post he summarised his requirements:

> We want to hire an unusual set of people with different skills and backgrounds to work in Downing Street … The categories are roughly: data scientists and software developers; economists; policy experts; project managers; communication experts; junior researchers, one of whom will also be my personal assistant; weirdos and misfits with odd skills.
>
> *(Syal, 2020)*

His personal assistant, he indicated, would be someone who was prepared to 'sacrifice' weekday evenings and 'many weekends. It will be exhausting but interesting and if you cut it you will be involved in things at the age of 21 that most people never see' (Syal, 2020).

But, rather like his boss in the end, Cummings was undone by the Covid-19 pandemic. During the mandatory lockdown, Cummings took a 264-mile journey north to his family home in County Durham when suffering Covid-like symptoms.

Despite his claim that his relocation was in the interests of child care for his son should both parents fall ill, there was a tsunami of public criticism: it seemed there was one rule for the people in charge and another for the rest of us. His many enemies called for his resignation but Johnson stood by him and endorsed the public explanations offered by his aide in a bizarre public statement on 25 May in the Rose garden of Number 10. Cummings's star never really rose again after this scandal but the killer blow was delivered by his involvement in the politics of Downing Street's Kitchen Cabinet when it was suggested his Vote Leave ally Lee Cain might be promoted to Chief of Staff. Allegedly tensions were so high Cummings had 'taken to miming throwing a hand grenade over his shoulder every time he left a room'. His many enemies (generated by his personal manner) howled for his dismissal, this time successfully: on 13 November 2020, he hurried out of Downing Street, cardboard box in hand (Oulton, 2020, p.5).

Like his boss, he had found governing rather more problematic than campaigning where, like Johnson, his true talent probably lay. His record as a campaigner was impressive – Brexit, then the 2019 election – but his 'obnoxious and arrogant manner were ultimately his downfall' (ibid.), together with his ill-thought-through ideas regarding 'weirdos and misfits' in January 2020.

Seldon and Newell describe how Cummings choreographed the dismissal of Sajid Javid as Chancellor and then Mark Sedwill as Cabinet Secretary. 'He's got to go mate' was Lynton Crosby's typically blunt advice to Johnson about his chief adviser in the wake of the Rose Garden press conference (Seldon and Newell, 2023, p.299), but Johnson's response was 'I am with him shoulder to shoulder. We can't lose Dom. He's integral to us' (ibid., p.301).

His partnership with Boris Johnson helped promote the maverick Etonian to establish for a while a vice-like grip on UK politics, and to promote his own standing as the most powerful spad, perhaps ever and certainly since Marcia Williams and Alistair Campbell.

Boris Johnson and the battle of the spads

A consequence of his dealings with Cummings was that Johnson's relationship with his aides became a national talking point. Manchester-born Murina Mirza, originally a Marxist who became a Tory supporting Brexiter, was hugely important to Johnson. He described her as 'extraordinary', 'ruthless' and 'among a small number of women who have shaped my life' (Parke, 2022). It's worth noting here that a major important influence on Johnson's years in Downing Street was another powerful political player: his wife Carrie, who once headed up the Tory party's communications. Mirza resigned in February 2022 over what she said was his 'scurrilous' claim that, when Director of Public Prosecutions, Keir Starmer failed to prosecute Jimmy Savile. Michael Ashcroft wrote a book focusing on Carrie's influence (Ashcroft, 2022), which was reviewed by Gaby Hinsliff in the *Guardian*:

> There is an extraordinary bitterness to the extensive verbatim quotes, from heavily disguised anonymous sources, that follow. Carrie is portrayed as something of a spoiled princess, insecure and vengeful and lacking in 'intellectual depth'. Worse, she has entrapped Boris in such an 'emotionally disruptive relationship' that he seems actively scared of her. Similar claims have been aired before, not least by Cummings, but the charge here that there's 'something not right' about Carrie is a serious one. Yet it goes virtually unquestioned. Whoever his source is, Ashcroft apparently considers them beyond reproach.
>
> *(Hinsliff, 2022)*

Lee Cain, a former Johnson comrade in the Leave campaign, had been drawn into Downing Street as Johnson's Director of Communications but clashed with other aides over proposed daily televised briefings of journalists; when he was offered a compromise role as Chief of Staff, Tory MPs objected to what appeared to be the iron grip of Brexiters' power at the centre of government. Cain resigned in November 2020 after Mirza opposed his promotion (Wearmouth, 2020). A symbol of the importance of spads to British political life was Boris Jonson's plan to ennoble two of his aides, making them the youngest ever members of the Lords: Ross Kempsell, 30 years old, and Charlotte Owen, a former assistant to Johnson believed to be in her late 20s. Ben Gascoigne, a former Deputy Chief of Staff, was also on the list: all three became life peers.

Liz Truss and her slaughter of Number 10 spads

Liz Truss, who became PM on 6 September 2022, appeared to worship at the shrine of Margaret Thatcher and did her best to emulate her style of rule. That formidable premier was famous for knowing what she wanted doing and allegedly tended to decline advice unless it reflected her own values and beliefs. But at least she kept on trusting the Policy Unit to provide useful advice as a check and counter to the civil servants who daily submitted ideas and policy advice. Liz Truss, however, virtually abolished the Policy Unit and laid waste to the 40 or so spads who worked in Number 10.

Times Policy Editor, Oliver Wright, reported 5 September that Truss 'has made clear she wants a much slimmed down No 10 in the mould of Thatcher'; another source predicted a 'bonfire of special advisers and officials in Downing St. She thinks the current operation is too bloated and heavy. ... She wants a total break from the Boris era' (Wright et al., 2022). Kit Malthouse reckoned Truss wanted to 'abolish the prime minister's department set up by Johnson' and shift responsibility for driving change back to the Cabinet Secretariats, 'After an intensive summer with a firm grip on events, revamped risk management and a newly configured vigorous delivery engine, we are primed and ready' (ibid.).

Truss appointed Mark Fullbrook in the crucial role as Chief of Staff; a former colleague of Australian political strategist Lynton Crosby, he brought in some senior colleagues from his own firm Fullbrook Strategies. She also brought in a number of people who worked for right-wing think tanks. Her senior economic adviser, Mathew Sinclair, was a former chief executive of the Tax Payers Alliance, a group that campaigned for lower taxes. Sophie Jarvis was brought in from the Adam Smith Institute, a pro-neoliberal free-market think tank.

Matt Hancock

The most spectacular example of a spad who not only failed to advance the promotion of their political master but achieved their ruin instead involved a female aide to Matt Hancock, Gina Coledangelo. Matt Hancock – who ironically started his career as an economic adviser and then Chief of Staff to George Osborne, Chancellor of the Exchequer – was caught on camera enjoying Covid-rule-breaking close embraces with his aide and mistress. He was forced to resign his office in shame and lost the Tory whip but took an unusual route to rehabilitate himself: he accepted an invitation, and the promise of £400,000, to join the reality show, *I'm a Celebrity, Get Me Out of Here* in an attempt to transform his then disastrous public image. The initial reaction was one of derision and even his MP colleagues used the programme's app to urge that he suffered even more of the infamous and bizarre 'bush-tucker trials' where contestants have to undergo torturous experiences like eating a kangaroo's penis or anus and negotiate underwater hazards involving snakes, eels and plentiful excrement. Contrary to expectations, Hancock took to the tests with typical enthusiasm, if not some unexpected courage, and emerged third in the final rankings. Poll surveys showed his performance had indeed improved his public image. However, Cabinet Minister, Grant Shapps, was unsympathetic, producing this wonderful quote: 'It's often said that politics is show business for ugly people. I think Matt Hancock should be back in Parliament with the rest of us uglies, representing his constituents, rather than in a jungle down under' (Rigley, 2022).

Reflecting on the relatively career abandonment of Michael Portillo, after his failed attempt at becoming Tory Leader and Ed Balls after Labour's 2015 defeat, it might seem that some really talented politicians, following a big reverse, can suddenly decide that any continuing struggle to obtain high office is not worth the effort. Matt Hancock was not the only ex-spad to trouble Sunak's government in December 2022. Reflecting on his six weeks in office as PM he described with self-effacing wit that it was a 'relief' that 'now he was just the shortest prime minister and not the shortest serving one as well' (Wright et al., 2022). In an example of how a resignation of a spad can win headlines, on 9 December 9 a special adviser to Suella Braverman, Nimco Ali, a close friend of Carrie Johnson resigned. She was hired to advise on violence against women and girls in 2020, but now claimed that 'Suella and I are on completely different planets when it comes to the rights of women and girls – and also the way we talk about ethnic minorities and specifically people like me who are from a refugee background' (Zeffman, 2022).

References and further reading

Ashcroft, M. (2022) *First Lady Intrigue at the Court of Carrie and Boris Johnson*. Biteback.

Asthana, A. and Mason, R. (2017) 'Conservatives say May must sack "monsters who sunk our party"'. *Guardian*, 10 June.

BBC News (2013) 'Damian McBride reveals smears against Brown's rivals'. 20 September.

Blick, A. (2004) *People Who Live in the Dark*. Methuen.

Bloch, M. (2014) *Jeremy Thorpe*. Little, Brown.

Cabinet Office (2022) 'Publication of special advisers interests 2023–2023'. 20 July. www.gov.uk/government/publications/cabinet-office-publication-of-special-adviser-interests-2022-2023.

Cardwell, P. (2020) *The Secret Life of Special Advisers*. Politico's.

Cardwell, P. (2023) 'The Spads are in charge: I know, I was one'. *The Times*, 9 March.

Constitution Society (2010) 'Looking for that special someone: The enduring relationship between politicians and special advisers'. 29 July. https://consoc.org.uk/publications/archive-looking-for-that-special-someone-the-enduring-relationship-between-politicians-and-special-advisers/.

Donoughue, B. (2003) *The Heat of the Kitchen*. Politico's.

Fowler, N. (1991) *Ministers Decide*. Chapman.

Gillespie, T. (2020) 'Who is Dominic Cummings: A former PM branded him a "career psychopath" – here's what you need to know about Boris Johnson's top aide'. Sky News, 15 November.

Guardian (2005) 'Special adviser row threatened Straw's job'. 4 January.

Haines, J. (2003) *Glimmers of Twilight*. Politico's.

Harper, K. (2001) 'Bury bad news now in crisis, memo urged: Email sent just after attacks on US'. *Guardian*, 9 October.

Higgins, C. (2010).'Gordon Brown's ode to post neo-classical endogenous growth theory'. *Guardian*, 10 May.

Hinsliff, G. (2009a) 'Damian McBride forced to quit over "sex smear scandal"'. *Guardian*, 11 April.

Hinsliff, G. (2009b) 'Key Brown aide quits over labour sex smear scandal'. *Observer*, 12 April.

Hinsliff, G. (2022) 'First Lady intrigue at the court of Carrie and Boris Johnson: Thinly veiled and thinly drawn'. *Guardian*, 20 March.

Lambert, H. (2023) 'Dominic Cummings, the Machiavel in Downing Street'. *New Statesman*, 3 June.

Leadsom, A. (2023) *Snakes and Ladders: Navigating the Ups and Downs of Politics*. Biteback.

McBride, D. (2013) Power Trip: A Decade of Policy, Plots and Spin. Biteback.

McClory, J. (2011) 'Why special advisers are more than cabinet apprentices'. 27 May. www.instituteforgovernment.org.uk/article/comment/why-special-advisers-are-more-cabinet-apprentices.

McDougal, L. (2023) *Marcia Williams: The Life and Times of Baroness Falkender*. Biteback.

Oulton, M. (2020) 'The rise and fall of Dominic Cummings'. *Boar*, 21 December.

Parke, P. (2022) 'From Munira Mizra to Malala: The five women who have shaped Boris Johnson's life'. *Grazia*, 3 February.

Perkins, A. (2003) *Red Queen*. Macmillan.

Rawnsley, A. (2002) 'Why nothing sticks to New Labour'. Observer, 3 March.

Riddell, P., Gruhn, Z. and Carolan, L. (2011) 'The challenge of being a minister: Defining and developing ministerial effectiveness'. Institute for Government, 24 May. www.instituteforgovernment.org.uk/publication/challenge-being-minister.

Rigley, S. (2022) 'Matt Hancock should be "back in Parliament with us uglies"'. LBC News, 28 November.

Smith, S. (2021) 'Murdering Marcia: Harold Wilson and the plot to kill his secretary'. *Independent*, 25 March.

Seldon, A. and Newell, R. (2023) *Johnson at 10: The Inside Story*. Atlantic.

Spirit, L. (2022) 'Young aides included on Boris Johnson's lords list'. *The Times*, 7 November.

Stanley, M. (2022) 'Special advisers: History and comment'. www.civilservant.org.uk/spads-history_and_comment.html.

Straw, J. (2012) *Last Man Standing*. Macmillan.

Syal, R. (2020) 'Dominic Cummings calls for "weirdos and misfits for no 10 jobs"'. *Guardian*, 2 January.

Timothy, N. (2020) *Remaking One* Nation*: The Future of Conservatism*. Polity.

Watt, N. (2009) ‘Damian McBride’s departure marks the end of a bumpy Whitehall career’. *Guardian*, 13 April.
Wearmouth, R. (2020) ‘Who’s inside no 10? These are the key figures in Downing Street’s power struggle’. *HuffPost*, 12 November.
Wikipedia via Wikiwand (n.d.) ‘Number 10 Policy Unit’. www.wikiwand.com/en/Number_10_Policy_Unit
Wilson, F. (2023) ‘“I went to bed with Harold Wilson six times – it wasn’t satisfactory”: Why Lady Falkender terrified Westminster’. *Daily Telegraph*, 30 October.
Wintour, P. (2009) ‘Damian McBride affair: The spin doctor, the secret inquiry and a trip to the races’. *Guardian*, 21 April
Wright, O., Swinford, S., Zeffman, H. and Smyth, C. (2023) ‘Sunak has restored stability but there’s trouble down the line’. *The Times*, 10 December.
Yong, B. and Hazell, R. (2014) *Special Advisers: Who They Are, What They Do and Why They Matter*. Hart.
Zeffman, H. (2022) ‘Nimco Ali: Adviser to Home Office quits with Suella Braverman attack’. *The Times*, 10 December.

7

OPPOSITION PARTIES AND PROMOTION

> Lots of people do not think it is a very good idea to go and be an MP and sit on the opposition benches for 18 years.
>
> (Jonathan Powell, in PASC, 2009, p.10)

> One day in government is better than one year in opposition.
>
> (David Cameron, in Swinford et al., 2023)

> Tory MPs should be aware before they vote on Tuesday evening that the abyss of opposition is deep. Fall into it and very few will ever make it back to the top.
>
> (William Hague warns Tory MPs of possible consequences of not voting for Sunak's 'Rwanda Plan' Immigration bill; Maidment, 2023)

Those of us who follow the ins and outs of politics, including journalists and other parts of the media, tend to focus on the government – its MPs and ministers clambering up the hierarchy, hoping to make it big – but very often the equally important struggles for preferment occur when parties are in opposition; indeed leaders of the opposition often walk into Number 10 after winning an election with precious little executive experience: both Blair and Cameron are good examples, plus Nick Clegg who became Deputy PM after the 2010 election.

DOI: 10.4324/9781003405085-8

The Conservatives' 1922 Committee

This body formed originally, not, as is often believed, out of the Carlton Club meeting in October 1922 during which Tory MPs demanded ending the coalition government with Lloyd George's Liberal Party. Rather its origins emerged from that very parliamentary practice, a dining club of Tory MPs elected in 1922; it soon assumed a role of representing the interests of back-bench MPs separate from any government ministers. It might seem an inappropriate metaphor for a Conservative body but it acts as a kind of trade union for Tory back benchers. The current chair at the time of writing is Sir Graham Brady, MP for Altrincham West since 1997 and chair of the '22' since 2010. Serving on the committee is a sign of one's fellow MPs' trust and a way of catching the eye of the party leadership. The party leader has the sole right of appointment in opposition to the Shadow Cabinet from the MPs available. Incoming Tory MPs seek to become part of its membership, in the expectation that shadow portfolios will transform into the real thing come the election victories, which during the twentieth century enabled the party to dominate government office for two-thirds of the time.

Labour's Shadow Cabinet elections

For many years Labour's practice when in opposition, reflecting, in contrast to the Tories, its self-consciously democratic traditions, was to appoint its Shadow Cabinet via a system of annual elections. This facilitated the progression of Labour MPs up the party's hierarchy in opposition usually at the beginning of a parliamentary session. The top five positions 1951–2010 reflecting the changing rosters of 'old favourites' and 'rising stars' as the extracted results show (Wikipedia, n.d.c):

1951:

1. Jim Griffiths (Llanelli)
2. Glenvil Hall (Colne Valley)
3. Hugh Gaitskell (Leeds South)
4. Alfred Robens (Blyth)
5. James Chuter Ede (South Shields)

1961 (adding votes received):

1. Harold Wilson (Huyton) 175
2. Frank Soskice (Newport) 174
3. Douglas Houghton (Sowerby) 169
4. Denis Healey (Leeds East) 161
5. Michael Stewart, (Fulham) 160

1991:

1. Gordon Brown (Dunfermline East) 150
2. Robin Cook (Livingston) 149
3. John Smith (Monklands East) 141
4. Ann Clwyd (Cynon Valley) 137
5. Bryan Gould (Dagenham) 136

In 1996, the year before the Blair landslide, the top five positions were:

1. Margaret Beckett (Derby South) 251
2. Ann Taylor (Dewsbury) 250
3. Clare Short (Birmingham Ladywood) 218
4. Gavin Strang (Edinburgh East) 217
5. Robin Cook (Livingston) 215

The final shadow election took place in 2010 and the top five on that occasion were:

1. Yvette Cooper (Normanton, Pontefract and Castleford) 232
2. John Healey (Wentworth and Dearne) 192
3. Ed Balls (Morley and Outwood) 179
4. Andy Burnham (Leigh) 165
5. Angela Eagle (Wallasey) 165

Fairly naturally, given the context, these league tables became the focus of much intense inner-party rivalrous ambition. MPs would eagerly lobby their colleagues to gain their support for these regular popularity polls. The 2011 'Refounding Labour' report was an attempt to rebuild and modernise the party (Labour Party, 2011). Electing one's fellow party members to shadow positions was impeccably democratic but sometimes Labour leaderships conclude that certain practices are too democratic to be functional. Ed Miliband was opposed to the elections, which he believed were a 'distraction' from the 'job of holding the government to account'; he believed too much time was spent on internal campaigning, which detracted from the perception of a party 'ready for government' (Channel 4 News, 2011). In 2010 Labour MPs voted against scrapping the annual ballots when in opposition but, in July 2011, they backed the abolition by a large majority: 196 out of 257. The decision was later approved by the party's National Executive Committee and by the autumn conference too. Miliband called the decision 'excellent' and said, 'we need to spend our time talking to the public and not ourselves' (Neild, 2011). However John McDonnell, on the left of the party and a future Shadow Chancellor, was 'really disappointed' by the abandonment of a 50-year tradition of internal democracy. The result obtained for the Labour Leader the same appointment powers enjoyed by the Conservative Leader. Perhaps the decisive factor in Labour's abandonment of the elected Shadow Cabinet was because the Leader's choice as PM would be restricted. Seldon quotes Wilson as complaining the system meant he had to appoint Cabinets comprising his 'enemies' (Seldon, 2024, p.232).

Factions

One feature of the now-abandoned elections was the role played by internal groupings within the Parliamentary Labour Party (PLP). New MPs can sign up to them for a variety of career-related reasons: ideological agreement, social life opportunities (lots of dinners and drinks meetings) or maybe adherence to a particular 'big beast' MP as patron. These groups met regularly and submitted lists of recommended members for fellow MPs to support in the annual elections. This 'factionalism' was common on both sides of the House and in Labour was evident in the post-war *Keep Left* group. The leading members of this group included Richard Crossman, Michael Foot and Ian Mikardo plus 12 more, linked by profession – mostly middle class – and shared a common criticism of Labour's foreign policy reflected in its eponymous 1947 pamphlet. By the early 1950s this group had become 'Bevanites' – around the charismatic Welsh MP. The group emerged following Bevan's 1951 resignation from the Cabinet (over charging for NHS prescriptions), joined by John Freeman and Harold Wilson; quite possibly Wilson's resignation was a calculated ploy to establish his left-wing credentials for a future leadership bid. The group went on to comprise some three dozen MPs, the core of the party's future centre-left Tribune Group. Opposed to them were the 'Gaitskellites', not an organised group but led by intellectual heavyweights: Gaitskell himself (Chancellor 1950–51 and then Leader of the opposition 1955–63); Anthony Crosland (author of the hugely influential *The Future of Socialism* and future Foreign Secretary); Roy Jenkins (very talented pro-Europe biographer and future Chancellor and Home Secretary); plus Douglas Jay (leading Keynesian and future Treasury minister and President of the Board of Trade). This faction represented the so-called revisionist socialists of the centre-left, arguing against more nationalisation and for the acceptance that the post-war 'mixed economy' had been transforming. Ambitious MPs could decide whether to throw in their lot with the rebellious left with some organised support in the constituencies or support the majority Gaitskellite movement. Most of the above faction members went on to sit in Labour Cabinets, with the exception of Mikardo who experienced no difficulties avoiding the seductions of office and remained on the back benches (Mikardo, 1988).

Moving ahead into the twenty-first century, Labour's factions still exist and MPs can choose to offer their support to any of the following: *Labour First* (seen as the voice of the traditional right of the party); *Labour for the Common Good* or *Blue Labour* (aims to combine the soft left, old right, plus Blair and Brownites to resist the Corbynite left); *Progress* (dedicated to New Labour values); *Compass* (soft left think tank and pressure group that helped Chukka Umunna rise through the party's ranks); *Left Futures* (left-wing blog edited by Bennite Jon Lansman); *Labour Together* (aims to unite New Labour with other elements of the party); *Momentum* (established to promote the ideas of Jeremy Corbyn when he was Leader but has lost much influence since the accession of Keir Starmer in 2020); Corbyn had the Labour whip removed when he refused to accept the findings of the Equality and Human Rights Commission's critical report on how Labour had handled the problem of anti-Semitism within its ranks; he was later prevented standing for Labour in his Islington constituency. However, he and his brand of socialism still command support within the Labour Party, both in the Commons and the country.

Conservative groupings

Traditionally the Conservatives have not embraced so many inner groups. In the 1950s there were a number of pressure groups that influenced party members and MPs: the *Bow Group*, established in 1954, emerged as a forum of debate on Conservative policies, perhaps originally favouring One Nation ideas but going on to embrace the support of John Major, Michael Howard, Michael Heseltine and even Norman Tebbit. The *League of Empire Loyalists* banged the drum for retaining the British Empire while it was mostly being dismantled; the *Monday Club*, founded in 1961, urged a blend of high Toryism and anti-immigration policies. Also wielding some small influence was the *Racial Preservation Society* founded in 1965. The *Bruges Group* was established in 1989 to advance Margaret Thatcher's sceptical view of the European Union. Moving ahead to the 2020s Peter Walker's analysis revealed a quarter of Tory MPs belonged to one or more internal groupings: the *Covid Recovery Group* was formed to resist the restrictions imposed to curb the spread of the Covid-19 pandemic restrictions; the *Net Zero Scrutiny Group* is sceptical about the harmful effects on the poor of strict emissions targets; the *Common Sense Group* is mainly concerned with countering 'subversive' bodies like Black Lives Matter; the *Northern Research Group* seeks to boost spending and investment in the north of Britain; and the *European Research Group* is the hugely influential group of Brexit-supporting Tory MPs, which, during its time of peak influence 2018–20, enhanced the political careers of the likes of Boris Johnson, Suella Braverman, Jacob Rees Mogg, Iain Duncan Smith and Steve Baker (Walker, 2023). Finally, the *New Conservatives* comprising mostly MPs elected in 2019 and from Red Wall seats aimed to influence party policies in preparation for the 2024 election. At the time of writing it has 254 members with Miriam Cates and Danny Kruger seen as leading lights.

Labour and Conservative share of power

Labour MPs are more used to seeking promotion when out of government as they have been the traditional party of opposition with only occasional periods in power: 1945–51, 1964–70, 1974–79 and 1997–2010. Conservative MPs, by contrast, have seen their party dominate two-thirds of the twentieth century and, so far, the larger part of the twenty-first. The Tory opposition 1997–2005 saw the prominence of a new breed of ambitious MPs who dominated the Tory–Lib Dem coalition government 2010–15. They both provide evidence supporting the assertion by Katy Balls that:

> In many ways the year of defeat is an ideal time for ambitious to enter politics. Cameron, Johnson and George Osborne were all in the 2001 intake (Labour majority 167) and found that a party depleted, demoralised and in opposition offers ample opportunity for promotion.
>
> *(Balls, 2023)*

'It's like buying a blue chip firm at the bottom of the market', one MP told Balls. 'It's an enticing thing to rebuild the party. It does need to renew and you can be part of that.' 'It's far better to be a new MP in opposition than in government', an 'old hand' tells Balls, 'You have an opportunity for a much more rapid rise' (Balls, 2023).

Ideology

Often ambitious MPs look to advance their cause by embracing a new variation on their party's central ideas. This certainly was the case with Margaret Thatcher who was first inspired by neoliberal ideas through her colleague, Sir Keith Joseph, who had become convinced that the post-war consensus, initiated by Labour but then also supported by his own party, had become a dead weight on economic success. He argued that genuine Conservativism had lost its way and should return to its respect for standing back from economic intervention. In a speech at Upminster, 22 June 1974, Sir Keith declared:

> The post-war consensus had been a failure, its inherent contradictions are intractable... the only way forward was a market economy within a framework of humane laws and institutions. Rather than moderating,

compromising and endlessly searching for the middle ground, it fell to Conservatives to bring about conditions in which free enterprise can carry forward. to levels others nearby are enjoying.

(Lacey, forthcoming 2025, p.105)

Edward Heath angrily dismissed Joseph's ideas as 'this usual nonsense' in response to one of his colleague's Cabinet papers but others, led by the MP for Finchley and influenced by Joseph's (rather heretical) think tank, the Centre for Policy Studies (CPS) absorbed and promoted the new ideology soon to be sanctified as 'Thatcherism'. In his *Forging the Iron Lady*, Terry Lacey comments that to Heath, 'the whole enterprise seemed rather harmless, which only served to stoke ill feelings later as it became clear the CPS would serve as the intellectual challenge to his leadership' (Lacey, forthcoming 2025, p.101). William Keegan later described the CPS as 'the Joseph/Thatcher powerbase for attacking everything Ted stood for' (ibid., p.103).

New Labour showdown: Brown versus Blair

This clash of Labour's two 'big beasts' in opposition occurred after a period of very low fortunes for Britain's party of the left. After dominating a chaotic 1970s, Margaret Thatcher had made the 1980s her own with a landslide post-Falklands victory in 1983 and a comfortable follow up in 1987. Meanwhile the SDP (Social Democratic Party) breakaway came close to removing Labour as the second party of opposition in 1983, though by 1987 that danger had receded and morphed into a new party, the Liberal Democrats.

Neil Kinnock's hopes of winning at least a hung Parliament in 1992 were ended when John Major emerged with a small but workable overall majority. In the wake of Kinnock's resignation, the able, reliable, but arguably less than dynamic John Smith took over. He appointed Gordon Brown as Shadow Chancellor and made Tony Blair Shadow Home Secretary. Brown's history as a 'Son of the Manse' from Kirkaldy, Renfrewshire, was that of a wunderkind, outstanding intellectually and also very good at sport. Sadly this latter skill at rugby led to his losing the sight of an eye via a detached retina – he also narrowly avoided losing his other eye – but his academic ability ushered him into Edinburgh University when he was too young even to buy drinks at the Union bar. By throwing himself into student politics he managed to be elected Rector whilst still a student, sharing the administration of the ancient Scottish seat of learning with senior academics more than twice his age. He went on to write a doctoral thesis on Scottish Labour during the interwar years, later followed up by a biography of the Independent Labour Party politician, James Maxton. He was elected for Dunfermline East at his second attempt in 1983 and was soon climbing Labour's shadow hierarchy.

For his first years in the Commons, Brown shared a room with Tony Blair and both became firm friends until, that is, the leadership came up for contest in the wake of John Smith's sudden death from a massive heart attack in May 1994. Almost instantly, Brown and Blair became rivals. Tony Blair could not have been more different from Brown in terms of his background and personality: the second son of Leo and Hazel Blair, the former being the illegitimate son of two entertainers who was adopted as a baby by Glasgow shipyard workers, James and Mary Blair. Leo worked as a junior tax inspector but studied for an external law degree at Edinburgh University. He then emigrated to lecture at Adelaide University before returning in 1958 to a similar role at Durham University. Leo had ambitions to be a Tory MP and provided Tony with a typical upper-middle-class education: prep school, Fettes (where he was unhappy as a boarder) and then the posh St John's College Oxford. His early years at Oxford were dominated by his involvement with his band, Ugly Rumours, but by the end of his time there, he was ready to accept politics as an integral part of his life: he joined the Labour Party. His relationship with his wife-to-be, Cherie Booth, also an accomplished lawyer and later QC and a passionate, lifelong Labour Party adherent, greatly strengthened his identity as a Labour supporter.

In 1983 his search for a candidacy bore no fruit until he learned the Trimdon branch of the Sedgefield constituency had not yet decided on its shortlist nominee. Its secretary, John Burton, in one of those moments that can determine the future course of a politician's life, took a shine to him and the constituency, which had been on the cusp of adopting left-winger Les Huckfield, chose the smart young lawyer instead. Blair is very clear that when he shared that room, Brown provided an excellent 'apprentice's master course' on how to be a politician: managing the media outlets, framing speeches and delivering them, understanding the arcane procedures of the Commons. Brown's 'accidental' substitution for a hospitalised Smith in 1988 enabled him to tear strips off a 'complacent and growingly indolent' Nigel Lawson (Brown, 2017, p.79). Brown, in his memoirs, noted that as Shadow Chancellor he came top in the Shadow Cabinet annual election. There could be no doubt that post-1992 Brown was seen as the dominant possibility as Smith's successor. But Blair was making inroads. His use of 'tough on crime, tough on the causes of crime' – a line ironically bestowed upon him by Brown – was the perfect marriage of Labour ideology and Tory toughness, which he deployed to good effect in his daily speeches and interviews.

It's helpful at this point in the story of the two soon-to-be rivals to bring in the involvement of Peter Mandelson, the hugely well-connected, subtly skilled 'original' spin doctor. With Herbert Morrison as his grandfather he was, oddly enough, Labour 'aristocracy', who had moved from television to be appointed by Neil Kinnock as Labour's Director of Communications in 1985. Before long, his legendary skills had won him the soubriquet 'The Prince of Darkness' – bestowed upon him by the media he so expertly manipulated. He became a close confidant of Gordon Brown as well as friendly with Blair but as a 'moderniser' who wanted to reform the party and make it attractive to middle-class voters he also shared a vital common cause with both men. Increasingly his input migrated from 'media' issues to central political issues as well. It is inevitable that someone responsible for presentation should take a keen interest in what he was being asked to present (personal interview).

When an important leading politician dies suddenly close friends and family are naturally devastated but very quickly, led by a media keen to establish the 'runners and riders' for the resultant contest, those same close friends are found positioning themselves and carefully counting their potential allies and supporters. John Smith's heart attack on 12 May 1994 was such an event. Mandelson describes how he 'had expected him [Brown] to be the default modernising choice' (Mandelson, 2010, p.161), yet journalists were asking equally about Blair's intentions: a chat with Derry Irvine, Blair's head of chambers, elicited the view that 'It has to be Tony' (ibid., p.163). Soon afterwards Mandelson's close friend, Alistair Campbell, when asked on *Newsnight* who should be the next Leader had answered 'without hesitation, Tony Blair': senior back bencher Gerald Kaufman also reckoned Blair had the stronger appeal, 'He's a game changer' (ibid., p.165). Paul McKinney, a former aide to Gordon weighed in with the view that 'Tony is better equipped. Gordon just isn't right for it' (ibid., p.166). Mandelson's assistant, Derek Draper, told him Gordon 'simply didn't sway people the same way' as Tony (ibid., p.166). Mandelson soon met Blair in the Commons, who boldly declared he was ready to stand and wouldn't withdraw in Gordon's favour (see Chapter 3). The Prince of Darkness agreed 'to do nothing, in talking up Gordon to damage his own prospects': he reflected in his memoirs that 'Gordon had been the senior member of our trio [with Gordon and John] that it simply didn't occur to him that his claim would not take precedence, or that Tony would be anything but supportive' (Mandelson, 2010, pp.159–163). If Brown believed this about his friend, he was wrong.

Blair's attitude towards the leadership

Tony Blair claims he initially assumed and wanted Brown to be Leader. 'I actually rejoiced in it. I didn't want the job. I was high enough to espy its responsibility and its pain. No, if someone else could do it, I would be the loyal and supportive lieutenant' (Blair, 2010, pp.58–59). Blair's memoir displays his ambition for the top job beyond doubt:

> In my view we needed a complete top to bottom reorientation of our programme and policies. In particular we needed to separate conceptually a commitment to our values (time less) from their application (time bound).

> So, of course we should always fight for social justice; but in today's world that didn't mean more state control.
>
> *(ibid., p.49)*

The party had lost in 1992 he maintained, 'because we had failed to modernise sufficiently and we now had to do so, not by shades but by bursts of vivid colour' (Blair, 2010, p.49).

As for Brown, Blair was by degrees becoming a little disillusioned with his talented colleague. Smith had accepted, in the wake of the 1992 defeat, that the Deputy's position should be either Brown or Blair. Blair felt that two Scots at the helm would be 'a problem, especially as it was precisely in the south of England that our support was thinnest' (ibid., p.53). Chief Whip Nick Brown – a close ally of Gordon – took 'soundings' and reported 'the strong consensus it should be Gordon' (ibid., p.54). Blair's response?

> I knew this was not true. It couldn't be. Not even the PLP at its daftest was that daft. ... from that moment I think I detached a little from Gordon; just a fraction, imperceptible to the eye ... unaccompanied by any diminishing of affection. The seed was sown of my future insistence that I should be leader, not him.
>
> *(ibid., p.54)*

He adds, revealingly:

> I was out in front taking risks, and this was the time for risk takers. I spotted that; he didn't. He was brilliant, had far more knowledge of the party than me, with an acute and, even then, well-honed brain; but it operated within familiar and conventional parameters. Within the box he was tremendous but he didn't venture outside it.
>
> *(ibid., p.59)*

Clearly Brown, so immersed in his own roles, had not realised how Blair's media-friendly profile had risen so rapidly. Mandelson suggests it was Brown's failure to stand against Smith in 1992 after Kinnock resigned, and his 'effectively pressurising him out of entering the race for deputy leader', which 'determined' Tony 'not to be dissuaded this time'. Mandelson noted 'Gordon was furious with Alastair and seething about the press which increasingly was coming out for Blair'. He persuaded Mandelson to inform the press that the 'two modernising contenders' would 'not stand against each other' (Mandelson, 2010, pp.159–163). Brown was aware that his 'moderniser' profile in increasing Labour's national appeal was weakened by Tony's greater attractiveness to voters in the south of England. Mandelson sensed Brown's frustration: 'The leadership was the prize he had most coveted. Now

I sensed it was slipping away' (ibid., p.165). Given he was close to both aspirant leaders, Mandelson faced a dilemma, but finally he opted for Blair. When Blair asked him to 'help him do it' his later account read like a scene out the film of his life:

> For a moment we stood looking at each other by the green leather topped table at the north end of the Aye Lobby. 'Peter' I said, putting a hand on each shoulder 'don't cross me on this. This is mine. I know it and will take it.'
>
> *(Blair, 2010, p.63)*

Both candidates managed to meet and discuss the coming election and Blair sensed Brown, having understood the way things had moved, was ready to step aside though not yet ready to say this out loud. Before the famous Granita dinner, Brown had dined with Nick Brown and Charlie Whelan where it had been agreed:

> Brown would bow out – but on the best terms which could be secured. The view was that he could still win, despite the polls – a BBC one showed Blair enjoyed 47% of the party and Brown only 11% – but only by summoning up those very dark forces which Brown had agreed with Mandelson might sabotage the whole cause of modernisation.
>
> *(Macintyre, 2000, p.305)*

A dinner at the Granita restaurant near Blair's Islington home was arranged. At this meeting it was agreed Brown would not stand against Blair 'putting party unity and teamwork above personal ambition' (ibid., p.172). According to Mandelson, it was *not* agreed that Blair would stand down from the premiership at some agreed time. This version is, crucially, at odds with Brown's own memoirs, which make clear that in exchange for standing down, Blair would give Brown 'control of economic and social policy and would stand down during a second term' (Brown, 2017, p.100). Bitterly Brown complained, 'When I offered to chair Tony's leadership campaign, he demurred. And while I helped to write his leadership speeches, I was frozen out of the campaign' (ibid., p.101). This misunderstanding/disagreement is now clear in retrospect and helps explain the bitter feud Brown waged against Blair for much of his premiership. The leadership election took place in 1994 involving not Gordon Brown but Margaret Beckett and John Prescott. Blair won easily with 57 per cent of the votes (see Table 7.1).

Brown of course did not abandon his ambition to become PM: Donald Macintyre advised him to be 'patient' – he 'could still reach' his Downing Street destination (Macintyre, 2001). According to James Naughtie's book, *The Rivals*, specific departmental responsibilities for the two were

TABLE 7.1 Labour Party leadership election, 1994

Candidate	*Affiliated (33.3%)*		*Constituencies (33.3%)*		*PLP (33.3%)*		*Overall result*
	Votes	*%*	*Votes*	*%*	*Votes*	*%*	*%*
Tony Blair	**407,637**	**52.3**	**100,313**	**58.2**	**198**	**60.5**	**57.0**
John Prescott	221,367	28.4	42,053	24.4	64	19.6	24.1
Margaret Beckett	150,422	19.3	29,990	17.4	65	19.9	18.9

Source: Wikipedia (n.d.b).

delineated: Environment, Transport, Trade and Industry for Brown; Education, Health and Home Office for Blair. Interestingly, in his review of the book, Macintyre interprets Naughtie as suggesting that, given Blair's well-known penchant for making people 'feel he has told them what they want to hear, it would be understandable if Mr Brown inferred that Mr Blair expected not to stay in office for more than two full terms' (Macintyre, 2001).

The Liberal Democrats: Fragile hopes of ministerial glory

The Liberal Democrats are often overlooked as a near irrelevant appendage of our party system: sometimes referred to, before the rise of the Scottish National Party (SNP), as the 'half' part of our two-and-a-half party system. However, only a brief survey of the party's political history in the twentieth century reveals a historical wealth of comings together with Labour followed by widening schisms that consistently frustrated Liberal and later Lib Dem ambitions to occupy or at least share those governing front benches. The Liberal Party's decline from the great days in government under Gladstone and Lloyd George seems almost too steep to believe, the damage being done by rifts between supporters of Asquith versus Lloyd George, the Samuelites and Lloyd George, plus the gradual emergence of Labour as a rival for working-class votes, gained at the expense of the Liberals as the more preferred radical voice (see Dangerfield [1935] for an influential analysis of the decline). It is interesting to gather from the Adonis biography of Ernie Bevin that his political hero was not the expected Keir Hardie but the Liberal PM, Henry Campbell Bannerman – under whom Liberals won a landslide 400 seats in 1906. Under a half century later in 1955 the party won a mere six under Welshman Clement Davies. (Incidental note of interest: my father was a distant cousin to the man elected Liberal Leader in 1945 of this band of then only 12 MPs.)

The problem for all politicians is that, rather like other 'chancy' professions – popular music, the media, acting, artistic creation, where luck can play such a decisive role in one's success – a long period of obsessive energy, hope and physical effort can end up in relative or even total failure. This is especially true for Liberal and Liberal Democrat candidates aspiring to enter Parliament and, in that famous phrase, 'make a difference'. Reduced to a tiny rump the party faced extinction but under the inspired leadership of first Jo Grimond, then Jeremy Thorpe (until his politically fatal misjudgement), David Steel, Charles Kennedy and Paddy Ashdown, the party carved out for itself a role as a kind of 'protest party' available for those who wished a plague on the other two main houses. The problem with such a position is that it is unlikely to ever result in a Commons majority and, accordingly, provide ministerial office for its MPs, their ambition forever frustrated.

In 1974, a hung Parliament quickened the blood of Liberals but a fair number opposed any deal: crowds outside the Downing Street meetings between the PM and Thorpe were 'mostly hostile to Heath' (Bloch, 2014, p.388). Thorpe says he was offered a coalition – Heath denied this – in which he would become Home Secretary. Robert Armstrong, Heath's PPS, warned that 'aspects of Thorpe's private life' not yet known to the public, might make the Home Office, 'highly unsuitable for Thorpe' (ibid., p.389). Predictably Heath squashed Liberal requests for proportional representation. Jeremy's high hopes of a coalition are evidenced by reports of him ringing around friends 'bearing them in mind' for 'a peerage and junior office'. But 14 Liberal MPs were furious Thorpe was not consulting them and Chief Whip David Steel's advice finally killed the idea so this 'sliding doors' moment in Liberal history came and went, leaving ambitions unfulfilled. 'The huge Liberal vote was largely a protest against Heath's incapacity to deal with the worsening industrial crisis' and that Liberals could not risk 'propping up a defeated Prime Minister' unless they were offered 'a cast iron commitment to change the electoral system' (Bloch, 2014, pp.373–393).

The Social Democratic Party

Labour MPs on the moderate or right of the party, led by the so-called Gang of Four (Roy Jenkins, David Owen, Shirley Williams and Bill Rodgers), appalled by the swing of support to Tony Benn's brand of left-wing socialism, caused headline news in 1981 by setting up their own rival political party. Later the new SDP teamed up with David Steel's Liberals to fight the 1983 election: the 'Alliance' polled 25.4 per cent of the vote to Michael Foot's Labour 27.6 per cent, perilously close to second place. The Tories won a landslide with 42.4 per cent, convincing a generation of Labour voters – including this author – that any party perceived as too left-wing or 'extreme' by British voters is unlikely ever to win a general election. When the Alliance did little better in the 1987 election the lesson of 1983 seemed to be underlined but the fact that the sum of Labour and SDP–Liberal Alliance votes, 53.4 per cent, would have trounced Thatcher's

42.4 per cent, set the scene for Labour's eventual embrace of a New Labour policy portfolio much closer to that of the SDP than Labour under Michael Foot: Brown and Blair's New Labour.

Ashdown and Blair

As the 1990s progressed, Labour candidates contrived to forget some of their hostility to Thatcher's economic policies and to ramp down their use of the word 'socialism'. The Liberals under Paddy Ashdown also felt New Labour offered a possible elevator to a place in government. On polling day in 1997, he told Blair:

> I want to speak to John Prescott and Robin Cook first. Then I will come back to you later. I am sorry I cannot speak to you in more detail now, but I do want you to know that I am absolutely determined to mend the schism that occurred in the progressive forces in British politics at the start of this century.
>
> *(Ashdown, 2009, pp.296–297)*

Ashdown was keen to retire as Leader but, convinced he could do a deal with Blair, decided to stay on, seeing 'great potential to deliver things which I had stood for all my political life' (ibid., p.300). When the election delivered a landslide to Labour and 46 MPs for the Lib Dems he believed 'Labour had delivered huge dividends for us' (ibid., p.300). Alas for those ambitious 46 Lib Dem MPs, their hopes for office would not be fulfilled on this occasion. The very next day Ashdown discerned a change of tone from Blair, despite Cherie Blair having urged him to 'really go ahead with Paddy'. Both Prescott and Brown had shown visceral opposition to any close cooperation with the Lib Dems. Instead Blair offered a joint Cabinet Committee 'overseeing constitutional changes' with Blair adding, 'I am absolutely determined to change politics with you and heal the schism' (ibid., pp.296–297). Certainly devolution, the Human Rights Act and Freedom of Information Acts were passed but proportional representation, the Lib Dems' Holy Grail, proved eventually not to be a priority and the Jenkins Report on it was destined merely to gather dust. Ashdown's dream of a coalition was slowly buried under a welter of other issues and finally fizzled out, the victim of Labour's huge majority and sense of obligation to its own MPs before anything like largesse towards Ashdown could be considered; moreover, the Tories' massive defeat in 1997 and then 2001 exposed the once insuperable Tories as easily beatable. As Prescott, admitted, 'I am a tribalist, pure and simple. ... I want to preserve the Labour Party for my children' (Ashdown, 2009, p.312). 'The Project of reshaping the British political landscape has been ditched – even the joint committee, where Lib

Dems would sit as partners with Labour Cabinet members, has withered into non-existence' (Adonis, 2013).

The 2010 'Coalition' election

The result of this election was: Tories, 306, Labour 258 and Lib Dems a record 62: a coalition was needed to govern the country. There followed five days of pretty desperate negotiation, which have been well covered elsewhere (Adonis, 2013; Jones, 2013; Laws, 2016). Nevertheless, as Clegg's biographer notes, how remarkable it is that a dedicated group of people can campaign for decades, tell the world they are 'on the verge of a breakthrough and then be utterly gobsmacked, if not traumatised, when they actually get what they want' (Bowers, 2011, p.221). The 'love in' which took place on a beautiful sunny day in Number 10's Rose Garden dominated the news for weeks and overshadowed the sense of betrayal felt by so many voters who had voted Lib Dem to *prevent*, not facilitate, a Tory government

Cameron's most important Cabinet decisions had already been made: Nick Clegg as Deputy PM (with special responsibility for constitutional reform), a role often more titular and little regarded in the past, but within the context of the Coalition absolutely crucial.

Other Cabinet jobs went to:

- Vince Cable: Business, Innovation and Skills, President of Board of Trade.
- Danny Alexander: Secretary of State for Scotland, 12 May 2010 (followed by Michael Moore, 29 May 2010, and then Alistair Carmichael, 7 October 2013).
- David Laws: Chief Secretary to the Treasury, 12 May 2010 (followed by Danny Alexander, 29 May 2014). Laws was well liked by the Tories: Cameron and Osborne had even tried to 'head hunt him back in 2006: he had retorted "I am a Liberal, not a Conservative" '; ibid., p.223).
- Chris Huhne: Energy and Climate Change. He was forced to resign in 2012 and replaced by fellow Lib Dem, Ed Davey. Davey reflected in 2023 that 'We didn't tell people how much we were fighting the Tories, that was by design from Nick Clegg. He wanted to show that coalitions work. I argued that we should show a bit of Liberals that's anti-establishment, that's internationalist. But he was the leader. We served at his pleasure' (Williams, 2023).

Jo Swinson, Andrew Stunnel and Lyn Featherstone became junior ministers; Charles Kennedy (who sadly died in 2015) and John Leech refused to serve. Whilst the appointments must have slaked the thirst for office of Lib Dems for some hands, at long last, on the levers of power, they also took leading members out of the forum of debate and neutered their ability to criticise policies with which they disagreed. Cameron and Osborne also proved very effective at convincing voters that the early unpopular Coalition measures were the fault of their Lib Dem partners.

> [A]fter several months of the coalition, the Lib Dems began rapidly sinking in the polls. ... Since they had campaigned for certain things which were now not happening and against things that were, what the public saw was the Lib-Dems smoothing the way for unpopular measures and getting nothing in return.
>
> *(Bowers, p.256)*

When it came to the key issue of electoral reform the Tory duo were equally and arguably mendaciously effective. For many years a fairer voting system had been a pot of gold at the end of a political rainbow. In February 1974, the Liberals had polled 19.3 per cent of the votes and received a miserable 2.2 per cent of the seats. That May 2011 referendum – an important concession won by the Lib Dems out of the Coalition bargaining – therefore was the key to unlock and deliver the ambitions that drove so many Liberal Democrats to support, vote and stand for their party in parliamentary elections. It had been expected that Cameron would not be high profile in the campaign but Nick Watt's article mentions 'Senior figures in the 1922 Committee ... believe they forced the Prime Minister to play an active role' (Watt, 2011).

If the Lib Dems hoped for any public thanks for their share in government 2010–15, they were sorely disappointed by the results of the 2015 election where Cameron won with a small but overall majority: an impressive victory. The Lib Dems, having enjoyed their sniff of power had to pay the price of having their 57 seats reduced to a mere eight – even Nick Clegg lost his seat.

Scrolling forward to 2015, here's another analysis of another major Labour leadership contest in opposition.

Jeremy Corbyn elected Leader of the Labour Party, September 2015

Dramatic leadership contests are usually the product of several converging forces. Following Blair's blitzkrieg landslide win in 1997, he more or less repeated this victory in 2001 but then, understandably, struggled to win his third election so easily in the post-Iraq War world of 2005. Throughout this final period of Blairite rule he was assailed by Gordon Brown and his allies in a fratricidal fight for the succession. Finally this happened after something approaching a peaceful 'coup' in 2007; given that Brown had been plotting his premiership for several years Blair's Chancellor's accession to power was relatively uneventful. Labour immediately surged in the polls and preparations were made for an election, which would provide Brown with a personal mandate. However a conference speech by George Osborne proposing a cut in inheritance tax proved so popular it was the Conservatives' turn to experience a spike in the polls. Although he denied any causal link, Brown halted any move towards a general election.

There then followed a period in which Labour seemed to be jinxed by gaffes, embarrassments and policy disasters. Even worse, Brown seemed to lose his ability to communicate, arouse or persuade voters. Brown's period in office was a big disappointment to Labour supporters and was only rescued in terms of achievement by the calm way he and his Chancellor, Alistair Darling, handled the devastating 2007–09 financial meltdown, saving the British banking industry and providing a model for other countries worldwide. By the time the 2010 election came around the polls were suggesting Brown's incumbency, after over a decade of Labour in Number 10, was no guarantee of his tenancy being extended. Far from it. The 2010 election produced the first hung Parliament since 1974. The two parties most favoured by electoral arithmetic and careful preparation created the Lib Dem–Tory coalition government led by David Cameron with Nick Clegg as Deputy PM. Despite its initial apparent fragility it achieved five years of what turned out to be a very resilient period of government, featuring a false but effective blaming of Labour for the UK recession suffered in the wake of the 2008 financial collapse, the application of 'austerity' policies in the form of severe public spending cuts and a 2014 referendum on Scottish independence, narrowly lost by the SNP.

Throughout this period, Labour had been heartened by leads in the opinion polls but, as the 2015 election approached, they narrowed and the opposition, plus most of the pundits, became fairly sure the result would be another hung Parliament. As it turned out the result was a huge disappointment for Labour (even more so for the Lib Dems). After a truly surprising exit poll correctly predicted the Conservatives would become the biggest party, Labour had to accept the galling fact that Cameron would win a small but workable majority. These events provided the background for the astonishing revival of Bevanite socialism as *Corbynism* was soon to be called.

Richard Seymour, the Irish Marxist author, suggests some of the Corbynism phenomenon can be further explained by the:

> Secession of large parts of the electorate from the political system, as made evident in plummeting party membership and identification, and voter turnout. On the other side, politicians increasingly withdrew into the state, becoming less and less interested in the electorate except as a diminishing pool of participants to manipulate with good messaging.
>
> *(Seymour, 2017, p.xvii)*

Stepping into the political vacuum created by this concatenation of influences was a rather shy middle-aged man with no initial ambition ever to become PM. Corbyn's own upbringing many would see as idyllic: private education, spacious country houses with lots of room for children to run around and play. Despite their Labour Party membership and socialist principles Jeremy's parents saw no contradiction in paying for their four sons to attend private prep schools where they would be educated with fellow members of the middle classes. All passed the 11-plus exams, after which the Corbyns saw no reason to remain outside the state system. Perhaps surprisingly for a politician who was once feared on the right as a far left, wild man, Corbyn did not, like so many radical 'lefties', shine academically.

At the Adams Grammar School, Newport, Shropshire, his two Es at A level enabled him to study at North London Polytechnic but he left without a degree following long disagreements with his tutors. As a teenager he joined many worthy left-wing causes and spent two years on Voluntary Service Overseas in Latin America including time in Salvador Allende's Chile. Returning home he worked for a while as a local journalist before becoming a trade union organiser for the National Union of Public Employees and the Amalgamated Engineering and Electrical Union. Aged 24 years, he was elected to Haringey Council, 1974–83. In 1981 he worked on Tony Benn's attempt to become Labour's Deputy Leader, remaining a staunch disciple of Benn thereafter. He was selected as a candidate for Islington North in February 1982 and became an MP in the 1983 landslide election victory for Thatcher. Corbyn's mindset was probably more focused on foreign rather than domestic policy, perceiving the USA as a fundamentally malign force in the world: it perhaps followed that he tended to view America's enemies, including some terrorist groupings, as his 'friends'; this included members of Hamas and the IRA – he supported a united Ireland and once invited Jerry Adams to a meeting in the House of Commons. During New Labour's period in power he defied the whip 428 times and was probably the most rebellious Labour MP in the Commons.

An exhausted, traumatised-by-defeat Labour Party in 2015 reluctantly turned its attention to electing a new Leader. Corbyn's biographer, Rosa Prince, explains how in April 2015 David Lammy asked Jeremy to launch his (Lammy's) campaign in Tottenham; he happily agreed, delivering his stump anti-austerity speech. Lammy commented subsequently that 'I am absolutely clear that Jeremy had no clue at all at that point that he would be running to be leader a few weeks later' (Prince, 2016, p.178). Corbyn mourned the death of his hero, Tony Benn, in March 2014 and was likely unknown to newer Labour MPs. His closest political soulmate of 20 years was fellow Campaign Group member John McDonnell but, more widely, he was admired and well liked within the PLP. 'I love Jeremy', said Margaret Hodge, 'I've never seen him lose his temper' (ibid., p.179; she was to lose her temper with *him* in July 2018 when she accused him of being a 'racist and a f***ing antisemite'). Emily Thornberry's assessment could not have been warmer: 'I love Jeremy, he's a personal friend. I have a lot of time for him and a great deal of respect for him. ... He takes stands on things and fights his corner' (ibid., p.179). In his leisure time he famously relished his allotment, making jam, watching cricket, supporting Arsenal, reading (Wilde, Yeats, Achebe) and going to the cinema (*Casablanca*, *The Great Gatsby*). Colleagues testify to his kindness – sharing his sandwiches on long railway journeys Chris Mullin recalls – and was known to take leftovers from dinner parties to give to the homeless. The citation on his 2013 Ghandhi Peace Award read:

> Besides being a popular and hardworking MP, he has made time to speak and write extensively in support of human rights at home and worldwide. His committed opposition to modest truth in the arguments of those who have opposed him.
>
> *(ibid., p.178)*

Labour's leadership contest soon began to warm up. On 13 May 2015, Andy Burnham declared his candidacy 'to rediscover the beating heart of Labour' and became the bookies' favourite (Wikipedia, n.d.a). A bright working-class boy from Aintree, Burnham had a degree from Cambridge and had worked as a (spad) researcher for Tessa Jowell before serving in Cabinet as Culture and then Health Secretary. On the same day, Yvette Cooper announced she would also run; after her husband Ed Balls had lost his seat in the 2015 election, they both agreed this would be her turn to contest the leadership. A formidably well-educated politician (Oxford, Harvard, LSE) she had also served in Gordon Brown's Cabinet. The verbally fluent and charismatic Chukka Umunna was briefly in the contest but withdrew, perhaps wisely, when he found the 'pressure' too much to bear (Eaton, 2015). Tristram Hunt, the Shadow Education Secretary considered running for a while but withdrew, as did Mary Creagh and Dan Jarvis, leaving Liz Kendal as the only other and (at least openly) 'Blairite' candidate.

To be honest all the candidates at that stage bore the ideological imprint of their former Leader. Corbyn's biographer quotes a letter signed by ten first-time Labour MPs elected eight days earlier, which articulated an emergent political view within the party:

> As we seek a new Leader of the Labour Party, we are needing one who looks forward and will challenge an agenda of cuts, take on the powerful vested interests of big business and will set out an alternative to austerity – not one who will draw back to the New Labour creed of the past.
>
> *(Prince, 2016, p.223)*

The letter proved prescient once a straightforwardly left candidate stepped up to confront the uniformly and arguably quite bland Blairite opposition. Rosa Prince details how a 45-year-old carer, Michelle Ryan, having read the above letter, joined up with trade unionist Rebecca Barnes to launch an online petition campaign to install a 'left-leaning anti-austerity candidate', their petition ending with: 'Whilst the leadership contest is under way, we still wait in anticipation for a suitable candidate ready to take on these challenges and bring the much needed anti-austerity ideas to the forefront of the campaign' (ibid., p.227).

At this point Labour's left-wing MPs, looking for someone to champion their cause, resembled those right-wing neoliberal Tories in 1975, desperate to challenge the complacent corporatism of the Heath establishment. The petition was aired on *Red Labour*, a 2011 Labour pressure group promoting socialist ideas in the party. It attracted 5,000 signatures and won the attention of Corbyn, who later claimed the petition inspired his decision to run. The Bennite Campaign for Labour Party Democracy provided a nudge on 23 May when there was pressure on John Trickett to run, not to win but merely to show the left-wing's flag. John Lansman, on the group's executive, discovered Trickett had no desire to run but when Burnham's speech to City leaders on 29 May tacked to the right, left-wingers became even more determined that a left candidate should be found and persuaded to run. A group of left Labour MPs met to discuss the situation when Corbyn himself suggested 'What if I stand?' There followed a silence, Prince suggesting that it was felt that: 'With his record of more than thirty years of trouble-making, a number of Corbyn's colleagues feared he would be too much of an easy target for his rivals and the media' (ibid., p.233). Subsequent events proved this warning to be more than prescient.

However, after another few days of desperation it seemed there was nobody else willing to take up and drink what seemed to be a poisoned chalice: a project doomed to failure. At the next meeting, Corbyn announced he was willing to stand. This was met with reluctance from some but genuine support from more – Ronnie Campbell MP, who enthused 'Jeremy, have a go, get on the hustings, your turn' (Prince, 2016, p.236). Corbyn's slightly hang-dog explanation to the *Guardian* was that:

> We decided somebody should put their hat in the ring in order to promote … debate. And unfortunately, it's my hat in the ring. Diane (Abbott) and John (McDonnell) have done it before so it was my turn. I have never held any appointed office, so in that sense it's unusual, but if I can promote some causes and debate by doing this then good. That's why I'm doing it.
>
> *(ibid., p.237)*

Len McCluskey, head of the Unite union would have agreed:

> I was listening to Liz, Yvette and Andy and I reached for the nearest, sharpest object so that I could slit my wrists because the blandness and the sameness of that was something that was depressing. … And then Jeremy Corbyn arrived and electrified everybody.
>
> *(ibid., p.238)*

The bookies were not so impressed by a candidate described by Mathew Norman as 'a politician of breath-taking obscurity' and offered odds on Corbyn of 100–1 (Prince, 2016, p.241). Kat Fletcher, his election agent in Islington, was one of the few to exploit such early generosity, winning £2,000, which she promptly contributed to the cause. Assembling the necessary 35 nominations proved difficult. Diane Abbott, who represented the 'hard left' in 2010 had solved her problem by arguing with the likes of David Lammy that he 'had a responsibility to ensure that an ethnic minority candidate was on the ballot' (ibid., p.243). She suggested David Miliband 'lend' some of his supporters' votes to her; about a dozen Labour MPs who did not intend to vote for her, agreed, in consequence, to nominate her – she qualified and 'a precedent of "lending nominations" had been established' (ibid., p.243). Corbyn certainly needed help too as a number of those likely to 'lend' their votes to him were already being snapped up by Burnham and Cooper.

As Rosa Prince explains, a new left-leaning member of the party, one Stuart Wheeler, set up a Change.org petition urging MPs to elevate Corbyn into the ballot. The campaign soon took fire and when the PLP held hustings on 8 June someone there, who was not a Corbyn fan, reckoned:

> He was the most fluent, he was comfortable in his own skin, he was jovial, he knew what he was talking about, he had an argument, he knows what he believes in obviously. The others were all over the place. They were just weak, they didn't sound like they believed in anything. They sounded like slightly gradated versions of one another.
>
> *(Prince, 2016, p.249)*

Why should this be? How come a dropout from the North London Polytechnic proved a more effective communicator than a field including two former Cabinet ministers with Oxbridge educations? It could be that Corbyn was less ambitious than his opponents? Whilst they edited their words with such professional care to avoid alienating potential support, Corbyn was able to relax into his 35-year experience of honing his arguments. Moreover, whilst the variations of cautious Blairism failed to cut through, Corbyn's enhanced 1980s Bennite socialism came over as fresh and attractively optimistic. Tony Blair and his team had tried to expunge the notion of socialism from Labour's vocabulary. For a while it seemed to have worked but the 'religion' of socialism, born in the nineteenth century, promoted by books like *The Ragged Trousered Philanthropist*, and turbocharged post-war by Nye Bevan's proselytising, still had converts who had never abandoned their creed and had been waiting for someone brave and confident enough to breathe new life into these well- tried concepts and arguments.

Quite quickly, aided by online support and some leading back benchers – Jo Cox, Emily Thornberry, Clive Lewis, David Lammy, Sadiq Khan and John Trickett – who acknowledged:

> A huge amount of pressure was put on MPs on social media to endorse Jeremy even if they did not agree with his ideas, on the principle of 'Let's have a proper debate'. That did have a big effect. The social media movement is probably what got him on.
>
> *(Prince, 2016, p.252)*

Maybe so, but the decision of Margaret Becket and fellow candidate Liz Kendal to also nominate the ardent left-winger must have been a big boost at the time; Beckett later described herself as a 'moron' for doing so (ibid., p.252). Corbyn finally made the cut of 35 with only hours to spare – half of those who nominated Corbyn, went on to vote for a different candidate.

To moderates, the damage had been done. To adherents of the left and fans of Corbyn this was an opportunity of historic proportions: a genuine socialist Leader of Labour for the first time in maybe 70 years. Perhaps most important was the mobilisation of youth: suddenly a creed born of the needs of working people in the nineteenth century was being exhumed, restated and given new life by its born-again maverick secular priest. One of my former students enthused about the force of the ideas unleashed by Corbyn. The bookies responded by cutting his odds to 20–1 yet, even for his closest supporters, the idea of victory was still an absurd dream: Prince suggests their adjusted ambition now he was an approved candidate was merely 'to not finish last' (ibid., p.262). To this end Corbyn suggested a 'nationwide tour, speaking in towns and cities the length of the UK'. 'In fact', writes Prince, 'The national tour would become a dazzling procession, gathering pace, fans and momentum as it turned Corbyn from a slightly bumbling left-wing, middle-aged politician into something resembling a rock god in the eyes of his adoring supporters' (ibid., p.262). The confluence of an uninspiring group of electoral opponents, a recent history of Labour's political impotence and a government intent on cutting expenditure aimed at those most in need created an extraordinary phenomenon: a national party leadership contest conducted in the form of a raucous, vibrant popular national movement. The movement soon swelled the party's size by half a million new members.

Probably the largest percentage would be classed as young but some older former members, disgusted with New Labour's disastrous Iraq intervention, now gleefully rejoined, together with several members of hard-left groupings like the Socialist Workers Party. From these eclectic sources, Prince argues, 'the Corbyn camp began to assemble the most ruthlessly effective campaign machines ever put together for a leadership bid' (Prince, 2016, p.263). John McDonnel became campaign manager; unlike Corbyn he had been chief executive of the Association of London Authorities as well as Ken Livingstone's deputy at the Greater London Council. A gifted political administrator, Simon Fletcher, became a driving force behind the flourishing campaign. Fletcher was joined in Corbyn's press office by Carmel Nolan, centrally involved in a group close to Corbyn's heart, the Stop the War movement. Finally, in charge of his father's badly organised, frequently tardy lifestyle, was Sebastian Corbyn.

Despite the dramatic success of his campaign Martha Kearney had no affirmative reply on *The World at One* to her question whether he 'actually wanted to be Prime Minister'. This did not stop the *Daily Telegraph* stating this judgement on the BBC *Newsnight*'s live hustings on 17 June: 'The veteran socialist won repeated cheers from the audience as he called for an anti-austerity economic policy and railed against Tony Blair and the "illegal war" as more centrist candidates struggled to connect' (ibid., p.271). Prince quotes a Corbyn supporter: 'He was different. The other three looked as though they were using the same language and demeanour. They were trying to protect a decaying political culture' (ibid., p.272). Even now, in mid-June, Corbyn retained doubts and seriously considered withdrawing from the contest. Prince suggests this lack of commitment actually served his cause well in that 'Many found his almost relaxed manner refreshing in an age when most politicians weigh every word so carefully they often lose sight of their beliefs' (ibid., p.274). Prince also suggests that both Burnham and Cooper were struggling to find their voices during these early weeks. She quotes a senior Labour staffer as saying that Corbyn 'came up with a much more inspiring campaign than Yvette and Andy did. Andy was just all over the place; he flipflopped left, right and centre, blowing whichever way the wind was going' (ibid., p.275). As the chorus for revived Bennite socialism soared and swelled, the rival candidatures were dismayed and then seriously worried as nominations from constituency parties showed Corbyn taking the lead. After a rally in Birkenhead in early July, an astonishing 16,000 signed up as volunteers. George Osborne's Welfare Reform Bill was being introduced at this time and Labour, keen to occupy some of the zeitgeist occupied by the Tories, decided not to oppose it. Harriet Harman, who had not consulted the campaign teams, told Andrew Neil, 'We've got to recognise why the Tories are in government and not us, not because voters love the Tories but because they didn't trust us on the economy and benefits' (ibid., p.284).

Burnham's campaign manager's view was that this ten-minute interview 'handed the leadership to Jeremy Corbyn': 'It was the Welfare Bill that changed the race. Absolutely. It was the one moment in the race we can point to when suddenly we thought "this is now going to start slipping"' (Prince, 2016, p.286). Fears must have compounded when Burnham's attempt to persuade the Shadow Cabinet to move a reasoned critical amendment to Osborne's Bill ended in a fudge, which was in any case rejected in the Commons. Corbyn, plus 46 other Labour MPs, voted against the Bill – Burnham and Cooper had misjudged a crucial issue: Corbyn's cause, already in full flood, was now powerfully strengthened. On 22 July a YouGov opinion members poll revealed the astonishing way in which the contest had swung: Corbyn 43 per cent, Burnham 26 per cent, Cooper 20 per cent and Kendal 11 per cent.

Corbyn now seemed to acquire the self-belief he was lacking earlier on in the contest. His rallies continued across the country, audiences listening with rapt attention as the veteran left-winger delivered a different speech for every one of the 99 meetings and all without notes: support the NHS, ban Trident, reverse the austerity measures and expenditure cuts. His opponents who found it hard to fill village halls were dismayed to see Corbyn drawing huge crowds overflowing big venues: 'Corbynmania' had arrived and, unsurprisingly perhaps, after decades hiding in the political shadows, Corbyn found he was loving it. However he did not allow his celebrity to erode his own essential modesty, returning home on the night bus, travelling by cycle or public transport, often wearing sandals, even when an opposition car was available. His social media reach on Twitter and Facebook became vast and individual subscriptions – many of them courtesy of the '£3 registered supporters' scheme – ran in to the hundreds of thousands; so many people tried to sign up for £3 before the 12 August deadline that the party's computer crashed. Over 600,000 would be participating in the leadership election.

If Corbyn's four rivals had not given up all hope of winning, *The Times* poll of 10 August must have delivered a final hammer blow: Corbyn had a 32 per cent lead over his nearest rival – the ever-vigilant bookies now made him 2–1. Burnham's team leader, John Lehal, admitted 'we were in absolute denial about it, just looking at the numbers going, "This cannot be true"' (Prince, 2016, p.321). Corbyn's rivals now became more than a little desperate and floated a variety of last minute anti-Corbyn ploys. First was the idea that Cooper should allow Burnham to stand as a single 'unity' candidate but she refused and, in any case, in a preferential voting system such manoeuvres were irrelevant. Second was a joint statement by Kinnock, Blair and Brown warning of the dangers Corbyn posed to Labour's electability. This fizzled out too when it was remembered that Blair's earlier interventions along these lines had proved counterproductive. Burnham finally resorted to quasi-legal challenges, which Labour HQ eventually opted to ignore.

The result, announced in the Queen Elizabeth II Conference Centre 12 September 2015, more than confirmed the YouGov polls. Corbyn won by gaining over half of the votes cast – 59.5 per cent – with Burnham on 19 per cent, Cooper on 17 per cent and Kendal on 4.5 per cent. Corbyn's clear victory, however, marked only the beginnings of another bitter struggle against Labour's majority of moderate MPs who did not think he was the person to defeat the Conservatives. Unlike Thatcher, who had won a very surprising victory over the establishment within her own party, his fate was not to be catapulted into Downing Street but, after a heartening narrow loss to Mrs May in 2017, a catastrophic loss in 2019 to Boris Johnson. In the subsequent Labour leadership contest, his 'continuity candidate' Rebecca Long-Bailey lost to the moderate's champion Keir Starmer.

A note on nationalist parties

As explained in my preface, I have not included the SNP and Plaid Cymru in my ministerial analysis as neither of them has so far seemed likely to be relevant to such a study. While Plaid have only three members at Westminster – Leader is Liz Saville Roberts – the SNP returned 56 in 2015, 35 in 2017 and 44 in 2019. Naturally SNP Westminster MPs have leadership contests, beginning with Donald Stewart 1974–87, through Alex Salmond 2001–07, Angus Robertson 2007–17, Ian Blackford, 2017–22 and currently Stephen Flynn since 2022. His 'coup' – a term that he rejects – caused turbulence between the Westminster band of SNP representatives and their MSPs in Holyrood. It is unlikely the SNP would create a coalition government with either Labour or Conservatives as its prime objective of independence is wholly opposed by both parties. Nevertheless the possibility Labour might have done some kind of a deal with the SNP in 2010 was used by David Cameron as an argument against voting for Labour. At the time of writing such a possibility exists again should the election expected in 2024–25 prove to be a hung Parliament as in 2010. A coalition on 2010 lines would not be likely, though something along the lines of a 'confidence and supply' arrangement whereby the SNP would support Labour on confidence or budget issues but would not expect to have their members holding ministerial office.

References and further reading

Adonis, A. (2013) 5 Days in May: The Coalition and Beyond. Biteback.

Adonis, A. (2010) 22 Days in May: The Birth of the Lib Dem–Conservative Coalition. Biteback.

Ahmed, K. (2000) 'Revealed: Bitter truth of Blair-Brown feud'. *Observer*, 10 September.

Ashdown, P. (2009) *The Autobiography of Paddy Ashdown*. Aurum.

Balls, E. (2023) 'Who wants to be a Tory MP? Many it seems'. *The Times*, 24 February.

Blair, A. (2010) *A Journey*. Hutchinson.
Bloch, M. (2014) *Jeremy Thorpe*. Little, Brown.
Bowers, C. (2011) *Nick Clegg: The Biography*. Biteback.
Brown, G. (2017) *My Life, Our Times*. Bodley Head.
Cameron, D. (2019) *For the Record*. William Collins.
Chakelian, A. (2021) 'Labour's warring factions: who do they include and what are they fighting over?' *New Statesman*, 26 July.
Channel 4 News (2011) 'Miliband to abolish shadow cabinet elections'. 24 June.
Dalton, H. (1953) *Memoirs: Call Back Yesterday*. Muller.
Dangerfield, G. (1935) *The Strange Death of Liberal England*. Routledge.
Eaton, G. (2015) 'Why Chukka Umunna withdrew from the Labour leadership race'. *New Statesman*, 15 May.
Freedland, J. (2015) 'The Corbyn tribe cares more about identity not power'. *Guardian*, 24 July.
Hague, W. (2023) 'Tory rebels should be careful what they wish for'. *The Times*, 11 December.
Haseler, S. (1969) *The Gaitskellites*. Palgrave.
Howell, D. (2005) 'Keep left'. Oxford Dictionary of National Biography, 22 September. www.oxforddnb.com/display/10.1093/ref:odnb/9780198614128.001.0001/odnb-9780198614128-e-92511.
Jones, B. (2013) 'The road not taken and the "bad faith" thesis: Why a Liberal Democrat–Labour coalition never happened in May 2010'. *Political Quarterly*, Vol. 84, Issue 4, 460–469.
Jones, O. (2020) *This Land: The Struggle for the Left*. Penguin.
Labour Party (2011) 'Refounding Labour: A party for the new generation'. https://debatsocialista.files.wordpress.com/2011/03/refoundinglabour.pdf.
Lacey, T. (forthcoming 2025) ISBN: 978-1-032-66085-1.
Laws, D. (2016) *The Coalition: The Inside Story of the LD–Conservative Government*. Biteback.
Macintyre, D. (2000) *Mandelson and the Making of New Labour*. HarperCollins.
Macintyre, D. (2001) 'Donald Macintyre: Mr Brown could still reach no 10 – if he is patient'. *Independent*, 11 September.
Maidment, J. (2023) 'Lord Hague warns Conservatives could be "permanently" ousted from power'. *Telegraph*, 12 December.
Mandelson, P. (2010) *The Third Man: Life at the Heart of New Labour*. Harper.
Mason, R. (2015) 'Labour leadership: Jeremy Corbyn elected with huge majority'. *Guardian*, 12 September.
Mikardo, I. (1988) *Back Bencher*. Weidenfeld & Nicolson.
Neild, B. (2011) 'Labour MPs to abolish shadow cabinet elections'. *Guardian*, 6 July.
Norman, M. (2015) 'Corbyn's success is down to one man: Now what's his name?' *Independent*, 11 August.
Pimlott, B. (1985) *Hugh Dalton*. Cape.
Pogrund, G. and Maguire, P. (2020) *Left Out: The Inside Story of Labour Under Corbyn*. Vintage.
Prince, R. (2016) *Comrade Corbyn: A Very Unlikely Coup*. Biteback.
Public Administration Select Committee (PASC) (2009) 'Good government: Government and other responses to the Committee's eighth report of session 2008-09'. 28

October. https://publications.parliament.uk/pa/cm200809/cmselect/cmpubadm/1045/1045.pdf.

Rawnsley, A. (2001) *Servants of the People*. Penguin.

Seldon, A. (2007) *Blair Unbound*. Simon & Schuster.

Seldon, A. (2024) *The Impossible Office? The History of the British Prime Minister*. 2nd edn. Cambridge University Press.

Seldon, A. and Lodge, G. (2010) *Brown at 10*. Biteback.

Seymour, R. (2017) *Corbyn: The Strange Rebirth of Radical Politics*. Verso.

Swinford, S. (2023) 'Sunak in a lonely place as his Tory critics look to the future'. *The Times*, 9 December.

Swinford, S., Wright, O. and Allegretti, A. (2023) 'Sunak battles to unite Tories as Rwanda crisis exposes cracks'. *The Times*, 9 December.

Theakston, K. (2023) *British Political Prime Ministers*. Theakston.

Walker, P. (2023) 'What are the different conservative factions?' *Guardian*, 8 January.

Watt, N. (2011) 'No to AV campaign wins David Cameron plaudits from backbench MPs'. *Guardian*, 5 May.

Wikipedia (n.d.a) '2015 Andy Burnham Labour Party leadership campaign'. https://en.wikipedia.org/wiki/2015_Andy_Burnham_Labour_Party_leadership_campaign.

Wikipedia (n.d.b) 'Labour Party leadership election'. https://en.wikipedia.org/wiki/1994_Labour_Party_leadership_election.

Wikipedia (n.d.c) 'Labour Party Shadow Cabinet elections'. https://en.wikipedia.org/wiki/Labour_Party_Shadow_Cabinet_elections.

Williams, Z. (2023) 'We didn't show we cared enough: We won't make that mistake twice – Ed Davey on love, loss and the Lib Dems'. *Guardian*, 16 May.

8

HOW TO BE AN EFFECTIVE MINISTER

> In all my years of experience, I have never heard anyone recommended for appointment to be a minister on the grounds he would be a good minister. Nobody ever said that he would be jolly good at running a department, that he had the qualities of management and so forth. The qualities required, quite frankly, are loyalty and brilliance at performing in the House.
>
> (Lord (Charles) Powell, private interview)

> Cabinet itself has long ceased to be an efficient body: it is too large, too untrustworthy and too prone to grandstanding. It begs revivifying.
>
> (Anthony Seldon, 2024a, on the conclusions of the Institute for Government's 'Power for Purpose')

The job of being a minister

Before trying to analyse the skills required to achieve competence as a minister and advance upwards through the ministerial hierarchy, it is perhaps necessary to explain what the job entails: indeed, most people outside the political world have a very hazy idea of what these mysterious figures actually do once appointed by PMs to any junior or even senior posts in the Cabinet office.

Often an MP is allocated to a departmental job without really knowing much about it. Lib Dem minister Jeremy Browne confessed to his private office on his first day: 'I don't wish to be rude, lovely you're all here, but I haven't really got the faintest idea of what all of you do.' This quotation is drawn from the Institute for Government's (IfG) excellent 2017 report, by Nicola Hughes, 'How to Be an Effective Minister: What Ministers Do and

DOI: 10.4324/9781003405085-9

How to Do It Well' (Hughes, 2017, p.6) and which goes on to explain these features and some related problems about the job of being a minister:

- *Long hours*: Vince Cable (Business Secretary 2010–15) reckoned his job 'by far the most difficult job I've ever had to do, intellectually and physically. I'd normally do 15 hours a day' (ibid., p.7).
- *(Junior) ministers*: They have no one to delegate to: 'junior ministers have very little control over their workload' (ibid., p. 8).
- *Minutiae*: Ministers find much time is spent reading and responding to enquiries, ploughing through paperwork and, in many cases, keeping up with their constituency work.
- *'On call 24/7'*: Ministers have to work through their red boxes even during periods when Parliament is not sitting. They often have to work in their official cars to and from home and find their evenings taken up with visits and speaking engagements.
- *Competition for one's time*: Non-governmental organisations, domestic pressure groups, business leaders and the media, all queue up for the minister's time – he or she has to prioritise: 'A programme like the *Today* programme, probably more than any other programme, really matters because it sets the tone for the day – if you screw up on a programme like that, you are absolutely stuffed' (the late Alistair Darling, Labour Chancellor 2007–10; ibid., p.9).
- *Ministerial responsibility extends beyond the department*: Ministers are bound by the doctrine that they must defend and promote the whole range of government policy, even if they privately oppose it. After being interviewed on their own responsibilities, interviewers will often pop in a question on an issue concerning another department or on whether a particular minister is going to be sacked: convincing replies are essential to avert potential media storms. This means ministers must be prepared at all times to be more or less across all the major current issues.
- *Ministers are accountable for all aspects of their departments*: Ministers are blamed if things go wrong in the areas within their department's remit. They are on permanent alert for 'firefighting' measures.
- *Travel*: Ministers are constantly on the go, domestically, or abroad when their department has international connections.
- *Parliamentary duties paramount*: Ministers are constantly on alert for parliamentary votes and, to protect their majorities, they need to keep their constituency role well serviced. The successful piloting of bills through the legislative process is a role they must perform well if they have ambitions to move up the ladder. Oliver Letwin, an experienced former Tory minister explains the extent of the challenge: 'Ministers have to be very good performers in Parliament, on the box and the radio, they have to find ways to deal with lobby groups and they have to run a department;

it's impossible for anyone to be expert in all of these in every respect' (ibid., p.11).

- *Reform*: Ministers not only have to handle their departmental responsibilities but also consider how performance can be improved.
- *Working with civil servants*: Ministers constantly work with civil servants who arrange and service all the many ministerial meetings during each day. Alan Johnson (Cabinet Minister 2006–10) says they 'will work with you to deliver what you want' (ibid., p.13). Civil servants, indeed, are crucial to a minister's promotion prospects: he or she cannot achieve the success needed without civil servant cooperation producing it.
- *Team building among ministers*: Secretaries of state often talk about building their 'team' of ministers but the IfG interviews with ministers revealed their unsurprising lack of feeling they were part of such a team. 'Junior ministers tend to work on their own portfolios and can have very little interaction with their fellow ministers' writes Hughes in her IfG report. Her additional comment recognises the weight of their individual ambition: 'There can be rivalry and negative briefing between ministers and special advisers from the same team as was reported during divisions between Blairite and Brownite factions of Labour' (ibid., p.16). Margaret Becket believed greatly in teamwork and 'tried to build trusting relationships with whichever minister she was given' (ibid., p.16). Most Cabinet-level ministers hold regular meetings with junior minsters usually including the unpaid PPSs who, similar to those spads hoping to become MPs, are a little like 'apprentice ministers', learning through observing and helping.

'Promotable skills' for ministers

Much is spoken and written about the qualities for which the PM looks in his colleagues when appointing them to ministerial office. However, most taxpaying voters would also hope that when choosing or further promoting their ministers, PMs also consider how competent they are: do they have sufficient amounts of the requisite skills to do the job? This chapter draws on several books including: Peter Riddell's *15 Minutes of Power*, Gerald Kaufman's *How to be a Minister* and Hutton and Lewis's (2014) book of the same title. Several reports by the influential IfG have also been drawn upon. However my emphasis in this chapter is not so much 'how to' negotiate the labyrinthine thickets of Whitehall and the mysterious unwritten constitution but more on the inherent skills ministers require to perform these specialised tasks. Below I consider a number of qualities and, more importantly, skills that have been mooted as of key importance for political success in, mostly, democratic systems of government. I leave until last the most important quality of all – mastery of the spoken word – because without a high level of verbal skills, politics in the UK can never provide any kind of career for its ambitious participants.

Loyalty

Loyalty is stressed as a key – with some PMs, maybe, wrongly, *the* key quality: one thinks of Johnson and Truss who were prepared to appoint only people they felt were completely loyal. Arguably this is a sign of insecurity by a PM – strong leaders should admire competence as much as loyalty.

Inclusivity

An aspirant to office might well have other desirable characteristics, like having a regional or 'Celtic Fringe' provenance, being female or of non-British ethnicity when inclusivity is thought a necessary political virtue.

Strong constitution

Certainly an oft-forgotten requisite key quality for anyone aspiring to be in the Cabinet is an extremely robust constitution and willingness to work long days stretching into the night. Pitt the Younger (1759–1806) suffered from gout throughout his life, made worse by medical advice that a bottle of port a day would improve the condition, which of course was the opposite of the case. His exhausting 18-year stint as PM weakened his constitution considerably and he died far too young. George Canning also died before his time, having served for only 199 days before succumbing to illness. The Liberal Henry Campbell-Bannerman became PM just as his health waned and is the only PM to have died in Number 10 Downing Street. Randolph Churchill, Winston's father, was hailed as a future PM after serving as Chancellor but his poor health denied him the even higher office for which he seemed destined. Thought to have been infected with syphilis in his youth it eventually wore him down and during a world tour intended to help cure him he returned home before Christmas 1894 and died the following month. Iain McLeod, probably the most able Tory of his generation, was denied his proper stint as Chancellor by ill health. A wartime injury plus habitual smoking and regular overwork combined to cause him being rushed to hospital on 7 July 1970; on 22 July he died of a heart attack: another victim of a heart attack was Labour Leader, John Smith in May 1994.

Mental health

This is a further underappreciated aspect. Viscount Castlereagh in the early nineteenth century was a case in point: he carried a very heavy workload when he served as Foreign Secretary during very turbulent times and began to manifest the dangers such intense political activity can inflict upon mental health. By 1822 he began to show fairly obvious signs of a nervous breakdown: speeches in the Commons were often incoherent and, weirdly, offering confessions for illegal homosexual activities. Entering his bedroom 12 August 1822, his doctor discovered Castlereagh had cut his own throat and died. More recently Charles Walker MP (chair of the All-Party Parliamentary Group on Mental Health) informed the Commons in 2012 that he was a 'practising fruit cake' suffering all his life from a ritual-based obsessive compulsive disorder requiring him to do things in multiples of four (Mulholland, 2012). Walker's admirable honesty, to be fair, helped to make politicians' mental health something that can now be discussed without too much embarrassment or shame. Some of this problem might be systemic. In his podcast *The Rest Is Politics*, former Cabinet minister Rory Stewart reckoned 'politics is a very strange and challenging profession which had negatively affected his own mental health' (Stewart and Campbell, 2022).

Academic ability

Being very clever is often or even usually considered the sine qua non of political success and there is a fair bit of evidence that this is the case. Previous PMs have often been precociously able intellectually: perhaps the most outstanding example is the aforementioned (William) Pitt the Younger, usually considered to be one of the greatest two or three of Britain's PMs. Born into an intensely political family his father – the much-revered former PM, Lord Chatham or Pitt the Elder – was a major influence upon his life. His father had hated Eton and, given his son's fragile health, William was educated at home by a tutor (Edward Wilson), supplemented by his father's constant constructive attentions. He became something of a political prodigy – as Mozart was to music, William Pitt was perhaps to politics – he was able at a very young age to instantly translate from Latin and Greek to a high standard. 'By the time he arrived at Cambridge (sent there because his father had hated Oxford) Pitt could translate several pages of Thucydides without any previous study and barely a mistake' (Hague, 2004, p.18). Maintaining his precocity he became Chancellor aged 23 years and, extraordinarily, PM aged only 24 years. His counterproductive prescription, mentioned above, of quantities of port to treat his gout severely shortened his life and, matching his early precocity perhaps, he died at the very young age for a PM, of 46 years old.

During the nineteenth century, academically outstanding PMs included Robert Peel (PM 1834–35 and 1841–46) who became the first Oxford student (Christchurch College) to take a double first in Classics and mathematics. William Gladstone (1809–98) was another academically brilliant PM, considered by his biographer, Roy Jenkins, to be the cleverest of all our PMs. Yorkshireman Herbert Asquith was one of the first intellectually brilliant pre-First World War politicians who graced the twentieth century Conservative Party. From a middle-class social background, he was educated at home and at the City of London School and then, via a scholarship, on to Balliol College Oxford. His biographer Roy Jenkins quotes his official biographers that: 'What his tutors discerned was the application of an extraordinarily muscular intelligence to a subject [Classics] for which he had a marked sympathy rather than an uncanny specialised aptitude of a Jebb or a Murray' (Jenkins, 1964, p.17).

Arthur Balfour, who served in Cabinet in many offices including PM, was first known as a well-regarded philosopher, publishing in 1879, *A Defence of Philosophic Doubt*, *The Foundations of Belief* and *Theism and Humanism*. Harold Macmillan, yet another Eton and Balliol man, was also very scholarly: famously, when fighting in the First World War, seriously wounded, lay for over 12 hours in a shell hole, distracting himself by reading the classical playwright *Aeschylus* in the original Greek. Macmillan's consensual 1938 *Middle Way* influenced the direction of his party for the next three decades. Hugely influential also, was RAB Butler who graduated from Pembroke College Oxford in 1925, with one of the highest first-class degrees in history ever awarded by the university. He was elected a fellow of Corpus Christi College and gave lectures on the politics of the French Third Republic. It is sometimes suggested Macmillan's resentment of RAB's intellectual brilliance explained why he prevented his elevation to the top job in the early 1960s. Rab became president of the Cambridge Union, entering the Commons in 1929 and was almost instantly given junior office. His strategic error was to support Chamberlain's appeasement policy but, whilst he never became PM, he is probably most Conservatives' favourite choice for the title of 'The best PM we never had'. When I asked the podcast *The Rest Is Politics* whether PMs needed to be very clever, the answer was that such a quality is highly desirable.

So it would seem being very academically clever can be an asset to a successful political career but it is not an essential one. Indeed being very clever was sometimes seen as a disadvantage for Tories: published philosopher Balfour was given the derisive nickname 'Pretty Fanny'. Paul Waugh of the *i* newspaper observed furthermore that:

> The Victorian philosopher John Stuart Mill famously described the Conservatives as 'the stupid party'. When challenged on it, Mill's fuller quote was just as waspish: 'I never meant to say that the Conservatives are generally stupid. I meant to say that stupid people are generally Conservative.'
>
> *(Waugh, 2022)*

Macmillan once quipped in an interview that it was Labour who were supposed to be the clever ones and it was true that Labour, probably at that time, attracted more well-known intellectuals than the Conservatives. Indeed Harold Wilson (Labour PM 1964–70 and 74–76) was once accused (and not just by Tories) of being, in fact, 'too clever by half to be trusted with power' (Earl, 1966). At Oxford his tutor confirmed that Wilson was 'far and away the ablest man I have taught' (Earl, 1966). James Callaghan was clearly a very bright schoolboy but his family could not afford to send him to university so he became a senior tax inspector then a prominent trade union official. Professor Harold Laski thought highly of his intellect and, indeed, his political career quickly progressed once in the Commons. He served as Chancellor, Home Secretary and Foreign Secretary and then, in 1976, against a phalanx of Oxbridge graduates, won the leadership of his party to become PM: some achievement for a boy whose formal education ceased with secondary school. Kwasi Kwarteng, a noted historian, is perhaps a good example of how academic brilliance – he even captained Trinity College's winning University Challenge team – does not necessarily amount to political wisdom or sound judgement (Fry, 2022).

Within an essentially pragmatic party like the Conservatives it might seem predictable that 'intellectuals' are distrusted but the fact that a Labour PM was criticised in the same way suggests that maybe this distrust of clever politicians is something more widely shared within our political culture. It was also echoed by Michael Gove's infamous Brexit campaign comment that we had 'heard enough from experts' (Mance, 2016): I've often felt that British voters – in any case mostly indifferent to politics – are resistant to 'isms' and 'cleverness' generally. Additional reinforcement of this argument is evidenced by Britain rather shunning the kind of 'public intellectuals' one finds given so much attention in France and Germany.

After 1945, Labour too saw something of a similar influx into its own ranks of a number of war-hardened MPs who desperately wanted to halt similar disasters in the future, including the hugely influential Tony Crosland (1918–77), the brilliant 'Renaissance man', multilingual, Dennis Healey (1917–2015) and others like Douglas Jay (1907–96), Roy Jenkins (1920–2003) and Tony Benn (1925–2014) who all contributed ideas and government achievements powerfully influencing the future direction of their party. Perhaps a distinction has to be made between the brilliant 'prodigies' and the 'grafters' who advanced through ambition and hard work. Harold Wilson was certainly unusually clever but, like Margaret Thatcher with whom Pimlott compares him, was no *prodigy* in school and university. He notes both future PMs attended a council primary school and both won places at grant-aided grammar schools. 'Both passed into Oxford (a glittering prize for any grammar school pupil), but each did so by a narrow margin. Neither was regarded as brilliant at school' (Pimlott, 1992, p.34).

Another category of cleverness includes those who were academically average to poor but politically were highly effective. In this grouping one might place old Harrovian, Stanley Baldwin (PM 1923–24, 1924–29 and 1935–37) who shone not at all at Cambridge – he managed only a third-class honours degree – but proved a superbly wily and successful politician. Another inter-war premier might also occupy this category: Neville Chamberlain, who never really took to study yet served as Chancellor and PM 1937–40. In the modern era, John Major who, from humble beginnings – he famously passed only three O levels – proved his qualities first as a banker and then as a local councillor, a minister and then PM 1992–97: it would seem a demanding occupation in some cases, for example Callaghan's inland revenue career, can nourish the intellect as effectively as any elite education. Demanding maybe a category of their own are two titans of the political world neither of whom experienced higher education but were among the most brilliant politicians in British history: Lloyd George (PM 1916–22) and Winston Churchill (PM 1940–45 and 1951–56).

Seldon notes that of the 50 or so PMs, 'Forty-four went to Oxbridge (thirty to Oxford, fourteen to Cambridge), but only one completed a doctorate, Gordon Brown, one of the most intellectual of all.' He continues, 'Politics is strewn with brilliant figures who never made it to the top, including Charles James Fox in the eighteenth century, Lord Randolph Churchill in the nineteenth, and Roy Jenkins in the twentieth' (Seldon, 2024b, p.201). But we still haven't addressed the question posed by the less clever leading politicians: how come some of them have succeeded so well? Ronald Reagan was never rated as an intellectual but is now judged as one of the best recent US presidents. Despite his lack of brain power and even assiduity – he was said to take 'two hours downtime' every afternoon while our PMs find 18 hours a day is still not enough – he is credited with ending the Cold War amongst other achievements. The answer, I think, lies in the difference between mere cleverness and the crucially important *good judgement*. Tony Blair was/is a brilliant politician but his determination that Saddam Hussein harboured weapons of mass destruction in defiance of all evidence, revealed a surprising and fatal lack of judgement. A sporting analogy is perhaps appropriate here. Like politicians, cricket captains have to assess how they can achieve their goals. Both face situations involving a multiplicity of factors: the cricketer, for example, having to be aware of the state of the pitch and the speed of the outfield, the quality of his bowlers and batters, the state of the game and the psychological make-up of the opposition, plus the time available and, playing in the UK, the ever-uncertain weather. Politicians have to consider an even more impenetrable blizzard of imponderables plus the possibility of unexpected events. Liz Truss, for example, Oxford educated and reckoned to be very bright, offered in her ill-advised 'mini budget' (September 2022) a series of unfunded tax cuts, which spooked the international money markets and hastened the crisis which ended her brief 49-day stay in Number 10.

Both 'players' of their games have to be aware of *all* the factors present in a situation; it would seem that experience and calm consideration are key elements in success in both areas of activity: Harold Macmillan was rumoured to have a sign on his desk reading 'Calm contemplation unravels all problems'. An England cricket captain does not require an Oxbridge degree to make the right calls, nor do PMs or indeed ministers with hearts set on their advancement, but the latter do need to be able to understand the complex problems that inevitably will confront them and, here, intellectual acuity is a requisite. Perhaps an additional quality for both is a degree of intuition as to the right course to take: risks are involved and *have* to be taken but all factors involved in a political problem cannot *always* be perceived. If their judgement proves correct, for instance Boris Johnson's belief in December 2019 that voters were desperate to end the ferocious squabbling and political gridlock by 'getting Brexit done', then great political benefits follow – i.e. Johnson's majority of 80 after that 2019 election. But if they are proved wrong – like Lib Dem Leader, Jo Swinson, who invested wholly in that election in the idea that a majority of Remainers would elevate her into Number 10 – then promising political careers can be destroyed: Swinson even lost her own Dunbarton East seat in 2019 and seems since to have abandoned politics altogether. Academic brilliance then, does not seem to provide a huge advantage for political careerists. Politics is a trade that is advanced best through learning its intricacies via experience plus generous helpings of guile, cunning and the ability, perhaps, to massage the truth.

Listening and memory skills

Harold Wilson famously had an astonishing memory; able to extract key points from a speech, article or report quickly and accurately. Labour's Chancellor, Sir Stafford Cripps, a KC, could absorb information immensely rapidly as a result of his legal training – top civil servants also develop this impressive skill. But perhaps the key intellectual skill is being able to make decisions. Another analysis suggests politicians under pressure, as they frequently are, have to demonstrate the following additional executive skills: 'impulse control, emotional regulation, organization, planning, prioritization skills, problem-solving, time awareness, and overall mental flexibility' (Lensch and Witter, 2020).

Decision-making

Some people are good at identifying the relevant factors inherent in a problem but take too long making up their mind – evidence to the Covid

Inquiry in 2023 suggested remedial action to counter Covid-19 was too late in being delivered. Former Labour Cabinet member, Jack Straw, expresses the problem thus:

> The thing that I believe that no one can know until they are faced with it is whether they can make decisions. And not just one decision, with the luxury of a day to think about it, but a box full of decisions and another box full. Inevitably some decisions take longer than others to make, and properly so given the need for evidence to be assembled, but time is often tight in politics and emergencies not infrequent so ministers have to make their decisions knowing that the future might prove their decisions misguided with much obloquy coming their way.
>
> *(Hughes, 2017, p.1)*

Jim Murphy, former Blairite Cabinet minister reinforces this point:

> The thing you've got to get used to as a minister is that you know least about the given subject of anyone in the room and yet *you've* got to make decisions. But you realise very quickly that what you're there for is to hear the best possible advice, apply your political judgement across it and make a decision.
>
> *(Murphy, 2022, p.4)*

Given the number of internal and external departmental meetings with colleagues to agree on policy plus those with outside lobbying bodies or those concerned with finance during strikes, another important skill is that of *negotiating*. Former Home Secretary, Alan Johnson, declared in an IfG interview that his trade union experience was a 'very good grounding' for being a minister (Hughes, 2017, p.7).

These abilities are essential and can exist in someone even when academic evidence of excellence is not present. Nigel Farage, for example, was educated at the private Dulwich College where he was good at sport and provocative debate – an English teacher once accused him of holding 'fascist' views; he never went on to study at university, yet turned out to be one of the, perhaps the single most, effective politicians of his generation, being more responsible for Brexit than any other person, including Boris Johnson and, yet, while achieving election to the European Parliament, never made it into the House of Commons. He was truly gifted at appearing as a beer swilling, fag smoking, 'ordinary' guy. His provocative style was especially effective on television – he appeared dozens of times on the BBC's *Question Time* – and his extraordinary rudeness to European Union (EU) officials – he told Herman von Rompuy, the EU President that he 'had the charisma of damp rag and the appearance of a low-grade bank clerk' – was much applauded and enjoyed by those voters antagonistic to membership of the EU. His appearance as a contestant in *I'm a Celebrity, Get Me Out of Here* in 2023, however, was met with a mixed reception: Richard Osman, in his podcast, *The Rest Is Entertainment*, suggested Nigel's political messages were sinking like a stone with the programme's 'light entertainment' audience.

A good example of how the intellect informs political skills was reflected in columnist Robert Colville's comments on Rishi Sunak's 'Five Pledges' speech on 4 January 2023. While describing the speech as a 'polished professional performance' he thought Sunak's true ability shone in the subsequent Q and A.

> Challenged on the state of the NHS, the PM fired back fact after fact about how much the government had already spent and done. His voice was lower, his gaze was sharper. He was completely on top of his brief. It is often forgotten how rapid Sunak's rise was and how much he has had to learn on the job. He became PM only five years since he first became a junior minister. ... He is so young that one of his own ministers, John Glenn, sat on the panel that approved him as a parliamentary candidate. He was, says Glen, 'the most impressive he ever saw'.
>
> *(Colville, 2023)*

It's also worth adding that an additional skill, the ability to speak foreign languages, is a useful tool to have available and one of which Mrs Thatcher admitted she rued the lack. Very few British politicians speak any language other than English – Ted Heath's schoolboy French was much ridiculed – though there are exceptions: Tony Blair spoke good French and even dared to address the French National Assembly in its own tongue, with a high degree of success; Dennis McShane, former Labour minister for Europe, speaks several European languages, as does former Deputy PM, Nick Clegg.

The written word

During my brief time as a civil servant I noticed how effective, cogent and forceful written memos could be; my Assistant Secretary, a man called David West, was regarded as someone with one of the 'best pens in Whitehall' albeit in the rather formal style of Whitehall. I also noticed how often senior officials and ministers hardly ever wrote anything themselves but signed memos drafted by more junior staff. This is not to say that mastery of the written word is an unimportant skill for ministers. Approving or amending drafts requires skills equal to those of the draftees, and politicians, unlike their officials, need good writing skills to get to their ministerial position in the first place. Many also seek to pursue and advance their careers through newspaper articles or, often, books. Journalists, of course to some extent play the same persuasive game as politicians and very often swap careers to become full-time politicians; for example, Nigel Lawson, Michael Foot, Norman Fowler and, of course, Boris Johnson. Churchill, also contributed regularly to journalism to disseminate his views and earn the large amounts of money he deemed necessary to finance his extravagant lifestyle; the same could be said of Johnson who also wrote an admiring and widely selling biography of Churchill – many reckon he sees himself as a modern Winston.

Tony Blair was famed for the spoken word and, like so many PMs and senior ministers, he employed 'speech writers' but his Press Secretary, Alistair Campbell, confided on his podcast with Rory Stewart (*The Rest Is Politics*) that, apart from a short period at the beginning of his time as PM, he wrote all his own speeches. In another podcast, the BBC's *Newscast* (2023), a former Number 10 speech writer recalled that David Cameron was very much 'hands on', explaining his ideas and then editing and amending as the speech developed. It is also the case that sometimes ministers or even sympathisers will make suggestions to the PM in the form of a speech they might deliver should they agree with the policy proposal: a kind of 'oven ready' policy to borrow a phrase from the former PM. Finally on this skill, some ministers could be unhappy with the drafting skills of civil servants: Oliver Letwin complained in an IfG interview of 'a huge amount of terrible guff, at huge, colossal length' (Hughes, 2017, p.14).

Humour

The British are famed for their sense of humour and there is no doubt that politicians who develop a well-formed sense of humour can use it to advance their careers. We forgive people who make us laugh a great deal and it might be argued that Boris Johnson based his political style to a large extent on his ability to amuse voters: in amusing them he avoided making politics as deadly boring as a majority seem to think it is. His carefully curated image as an entertaining 'non-politician' cut through even to those who don't normally vote and proved a winning characteristic in 2019 when his opponent was the rather dour Jeremy Corbyn.

Harold Wilson also had a gift for the witty epigram: 'The Tories never actually talk about getting rid of their leader, then suddenly there is a flash of steel between the shoulder blades and rigor mortis sets in' (AZ Quotes, n.d.a). At a meeting in the 1960s he was heckled over immigration:

Heckler: Why does your party support letting savages into the country?

Wilson (instantly): Sir, we do not support letting savages into our country. But we occasionally let them into our meetings.

(Richard Harris, tweet, 7 August 2018)

Tony Blair was also adept at deploying humour. Towards the end of his time as PM, when his enemies in his party had unsheathed their knives, he visited a school along with Alan Johnson. He began his speech with 'I'd like to introduce Alan Johnson, my friend', raising a laugh when he added 'sometimes I think he's the only friend I've got left' (Kalif, 2007). David Cameron also earned an admiring laugh at his first PMQs when he told Blair that, 'He was the future once' (BBC News, 2016). Ted Heath was certainly not known for his wit but when Harold Wilson was hit by an egg in the 1970 election campaign he quipped to a question about it that: 'It means that men – and perhaps women – are walking the streets with eggs in their pockets, just on the off-chance of meeting the Leader of the Opposition' (BBC Home, 1970).

David Lloyd George, the *Welsh Wizard*, was especially good at skewering his opponents with witty barbs: on being asked what place Arthur Balfour would have in history he replied, 'He will be just like the scent on a pocket handkerchief' (Ratcliffe, 2016); and of Neville Chamberlain, 'He might make an adequate Lord Mayor of Birmingham in a lean year' and 'he saw foreign policy through the wrong end of a municipal drainpipe' (ibid.). Perhaps his most notorious quip – for which he would be vilified in the modern day was: 'when they circumcised Herbert Samuel they threw away the wrong bit' (AZ Quotes, n.d.b). Winston Churchill proved a fount of witty comments about politics, three of his most famous being: (about Clement Attlee) 'A modest man, who has much to be modest about' (Ratcliffe, 2018); (about Stanley Baldwin) 'He occasionally stumbled over the truth, but hastily picked himself up and hurried on as if nothing had happened' (International Churchill Society, 2009); and, finally, 'An appeaser is one who feeds a crocodile – hoping it will eat him last' (Ratcliffe, 2018). Perhaps it is easier to produce such epigrammatic witticisms when writing or when one has time to create them rather, one of William Hague's skills, than deliver witticisms live in debate.

Charm

'Those who have charm don't need brains', quips Evelyn Waugh in *Brideshead Revisited*. This may have some truth but the concept is a rather fluid one as one person's spikey belligerence can be perceived by others as an element of a politician's charm, yet given that persuasiveness is the key spoken word skill, a speaker with charm is likely to be more persuasive than a politician lacking this quality. Dennis Healey, for example, had a larger-than-life charm, very witty in speech – he described debating with Geoffrey Howe, for example, 'like being savaged by a dead sheep'. However, Healey could be a tad too forthright, used abusive expletives in his opinions and ruffled the feathers of several of his MPs as well as leading trade unionists. Harold Wilson worked hard at confecting a reassuring image with a working-class charm: (despite his middle-class Oxbridge education) he retained his Yorkshire accent (interestingly Roy Jenkins replaced any Welsh accent he might have had with a rather forced received pronunciation one), took pleasure in pipe smoking (he preferred cigars), beer (he preferred brandy) and liking for HP Sauce (probably genuine). Tony Blair had large quantities of charm, which helped explain the extent of his persuasiveness, though towards the end of his time as PM some perceived this as a disguise for his mendacity. Among my interviewees for this book I found Lords Carrington and Parkinson extremely charming and Kenneth Baker equally so (despite his foul-smelling cigarillo smoking). Cameron too displayed a patrician species of superior charm but it was not enough to prevent him losing his bid to keep Britain within the EU.

Edward Heath was perhaps too socially insecure and stiff in speech-making to earn the adjective of charming and many of his MPs complained he seemed as PM to have jettisoned the quality he deployed so successfully as Chief Whip. His successor, Margaret Thatcher's image was not at all characterised by charm but her staff always attested to an extremely kind and empathetic boss. She also worked hard at showing interest in people she had met, spending extra hours of her precious time handwriting hundreds of Christmas cards. Boris Johnson seemed to offer a kind of paradox. He was something of a loner in his private life though his much publicised 'success' rate with women suggests a charm hidden from much of the public, not to mention (before Carrie) his long-suffering wife. However when campaigning and indulging in his frequent publicity-winning stunts, he clearly possessed a charm that reached – according to the Heineken cliché of the time – parts of the electorate that other politicians could not reach' and was prized by Cameron as the party's 'star player', though perhaps more as a campaigner rather an administrator.

Kaufman encourages ministers to deploy charm when dealing with their officials: 'Any minister can occasionally lose his temper, and no one will mind. But Systematic rudeness is remembered and resented' (Kaufman, 1980, p.33). When Johnson was PM his Secretary of State at the Home Office, Priti Patel, was found guilty by the Standards Officer, Alex Allan, of bullying her staff but Johnson ignored the verdict and, absurdly, it was Allan who resigned in protest. In the autumn of 2022, Deputy PM Dominic Raab, seemed to have flagrantly ignored Kaufman's advice as several complaints of his bullying were made by officials who had served under him in previous ministries; he was forced to resign on 21 April 2023.

Optimism

I add this quality having read an article by Danny Finkelstein in *The Times* where he quotes Martin Seligman's book, *Learned Optimism*:

> The defining characteristic of pessimists is that they believe bad events will last a long time, will undermine everything they do, and are their

> own fault. The optimists, who are confronted with the same hard knocks, think about misfortune in the opposite way. They tend to believe defeat is a temporary setback, that its causes are confined to this one case. The optimists believe defeat is not their fault: circumstances, bad luck or other people brought it about. Confronted by a bad situation, they perceive it as a challenge and try harder.

Seligman (2006) shows that Boris Johnson's 'boosterism', though intensely irritating to his critics, was 'almost certainly an electoral advantage'. Finkelstein concludes Johnson's 'relentlessly upbeat rhetoric had something to say for it. I still do' (Finkelstein, 2022).

Teaching skills

In his excellent study, *The Prime Ministers*, Steve Richards emphasises that top politicians have, in their leadership skills set, major roles as political educators, noting that:

> At their peak they [Wilson, Thatcher, Blair] were all political teachers. They sought to make sense of what they were doing or what was happening around them. This was especially true of Thatcher and Blair. Thatcher was an instinctive teacher, making complex ideas and contentious policies become reassuringly accessible. Her ability to teach was helped by the fact she did not delve too deeply into the complexities herself. ... Blair could frame an argument more effectively than any modern leader and would advance the arguments across all media outlets most days of the year.
>
> *(Richards, 2019, p.17)*

Reading the zeitgeist

Along with speaking skills, covered below, perhaps a politician's most important skill, especially PMs, is understanding correctly what voters are thinking and wanting. So Thatcher was able to read the nation's mood accurately in 1979 that most people wanted an end to the inflationary uncertainty of the 1970s; Blair intuited voters' desire for the refunding of public services; and Johnson in 2019 that most voters wanted to 'get Brexit done'.

Speaking skills

Norman Tebbit once said that Neil Kinnock's muddled arguments reflected his muddled mind and whether one agreed with him or not – I don't – it has to be true that clarity of speech mirrors clarity of thinking. The ability to persuade in public has its origins deep in the history of mankind but came to the fore, perhaps during the time of the Ancient Greeks, for use in legal disputes and the developing form of democratic political participation. Great orators emerged like Demosthenes and Lysias as well as teachers like Isocrates and Gorgias. During the Middle Ages, rhetoric was taught in universities but that faded as the modern era approached. In the modern day the ability to persuade is probably still the key political skill deployed in public but, more importantly in the current age, not face to face but via the visual and audio and, of course, social media. Inevitably the method of verbal communication has evolved with the technology of dissemination. In the nineteenth century people were employed in large crowds to shout out the messages delivered by speakers to those standing further back. The invention of electricity saw the advent of the microphone and radio made dissemination of the spoken word worldwide.

For the first masters of the political speech in the democratic age we go back again to Pitt the Younger who learnt much sitting at the knee of his father, former PM, Pitt the Elder, who had displayed a devastating mastery of political speaking. His son's biographer notes that, 'Each time he (Pitt the Elder) was appointed to government it was because his speeches were too effective or his support too great to keep him out' (Hague, 2004, p.8). His father:

> particularly enjoyed passing on to William examples of eloquence from contemporary or classical writers and speakers and asking him to study them. He taught him to speak in a clear and melodious voice by making him recite each day passages from the best English poets, particularly Shakespeare and Milton.
>
> *(ibid., p.17)*

The younger Pitt took a special interest in the speeches of famous people and was keen to teach himself the secrets of oratory. Asquith also shared this interest and it served him well. His former headmaster 'testified that his speeches in the school debating society exhibited all the gravitas and massive precision which were later recognised as the most notable Asquithian oratorical characteristics' (Jenkins, 1964, 17). Baldwin, as noted above, was not especially academically clever but was sharp enough to recognise the importance of radio, introducing the homely voice of the PM to every home in the country via his famous 'fireside chats' and, in the USA, Roosevelt was doing the very same thing to great effect on his efficacy as President. Churchill, of course, contributed immensely to the war effort with his eloquent, morale-rousing broadcasts.

Later, Richard Nixon demonstrated how democratic politicians could harness the new medium of television in 1952 when he gambled successfully on buying television time to make his famous 'Checkers' broadcast. In 1960 he was eclipsed in this same arena when John F. Kennedy bested him in a presidential debate before the 1960 election though, arguably, this was the result of Kennedy's Hollywood good looks rather than the content of his arguments. British politicians took a little longer to adapt their skills to the new technology. Eden proved stiff and awkward in front of the camera, though Macmillan was a substantial improvement. Wilson's capacity for persuasive argument was spotted by his contemporary at Jesus College Oxford, Professor Robert Steel, who thought that in debate 'He spoke with clarity and force. He could put a case in a very persuasive manner and unless you felt strongly you accepted what he said.' This skill was put to some effect as PM when he smoothly mastered the art of performing on television (Pimlott, 1992, p.41) while Ted Heath never did, appearing tense and ill at ease with the medium. Perhaps Margaret Thatcher was one of the first politicians to seek voice training via elocution lessons to make her voice less shrill and lower in tone in debate and on the media. After initially appearing stiff she soon improved and became competent if not expert in most forms of media appearance. Michael Foot was less successful, a brilliant public speaker he tended – fatal error – to address the television as if he was at a public meeting.

As soon as Tony Blair broke on to the political scene it was obvious he was a supreme political communicator. His early acting prowess when a Fettes schoolboy was clearly channelled into his media appearances, none more so than his brilliant, apparently spontaneous, 'Peoples' Princess' speech after the death of Diana, Princess of Wales. He was able to be relaxed and engaging in interview and also excel in Commons debates and at PMQs, despite the discombobulating nerves from which he confesses he always suffered before and during them.

Blair's communication skills are a difficult benchmark for Labour Leaders. Compared to him, his successor Gordon Brown seemed plodding and boring, bereft of the aggression that made him so dangerous when debating with Nigel Lawson as Shadow Chancellor. More recently, supporters of Jeremy Corbyn, like Andrew Fisher in the *Guardian* lament, 'Where's Labour's Fervour? Can you imagine hundreds of thousands of young people chanting "Oh, Keir Starmer"?' (Fisher, 2022; a reference to when Corbyn addressed the Glastonbury audience in 2017). Clearly the defeat of Corbyn's candidate (Rebecca Long-Bailey) at the hands of Starmer had not diminished the zeal of Jeremy's former aide for his left-wing leadership of the party. The next day the letters page in *The Times* made short work of this argument:

> Fisher is right that Labour's current poll lead may shrink and the result at the next election is far from assured. But possibly two years away from

> that moment, given a choice between a crowd chanting 'Oh Keir Starmer' and a sizeable and sustained poll lead, I know which I would opt for.
>
> (*Skues, 2022*)

> Politics is not essentially about entertainment or excitement and big membership figures do not correlate to election results. I know those who supported Corbyn are disappointed, but this is nothing like the disappointment felt by many Labour Party members when Corbyn became leader. We had to watch the disaster unfold in slow motion.
>
> (*Skues, 2022*)

Gordon Brown was less accomplished as a speaker and especially so, for some reason, when he became PM. Cameron, however, was also very skilled as a debater and media performer: May was way down the list by comparison and Johnson a strange case. He took the celebrity route to prominence, becoming a star comic turn on *Have I Got News for You* and using constant stunts to keep himself in the public eye as a 'character' and lovable rogue. However, he proved a poor communicator in other contexts, never having made, in my opinion, a memorable Commons speech, often waffling and losing his thread of thought in debate and at PMQs. Liz Truss was also challenged by such occasions, delivering flat, stone-faced contributions in Parliament and elsewhere. Addressing her annual party conference having become PM, she promised, as the climax of her underwhelming speech in a flat and limply bored tone: 'we will deliver, we will deliver, we will deliver' (Reuters, 2022): the usually totally biddable Tory conference audience had difficulty in producing any fervency of applause.

Bringing this list up to date, Sunak is a decent communicator in most situations but, unlike Blair for example, lacks the gift of making the words sing. On 4 January 2023, he delivered his 'five priorities' speech, which continued to register his shift away from Johnsonian confrontation towards an attempt at almost Blairite cooperation. It earned the following assessment by the witty Quentin Letts in *The Times*: 'Rishi Sunak skipped in with a maddeningly antiseptic air of purpose … what a wonderfully terrible speech it was, shimmering with disinfectant, its piety levels almost Californian. He was as wide-eyed as a girl guide talking about badges' (Letts, 2023a). Letts allowed, however, that during the later Q and A, 'a sparkier and more commanding Sunak was seen'. The next day Letts reported on Starmer's similar 'vision' speech and, while less critical of the Labour Leader, summoned up enough venom to say 'He did his best to look animated. You cannot fault him for effort but he remains, for all his oratory lessons, a stodgy performer' (Letts, 2023b). Sunak certainly seems happier when answering questions – and knowing how to deal with difficult questions is definitely a key ministerial skill – but even he sounded shifty when refusing to tell Laura Kuenssberg on her 8 January 2023 discussion show whether or not he subscribed to private health insurance.

A greater and better rewarded skill for any aspiring minister is the ability to strike someone down with witty remarks when in debate or at the Despatch Box, should they climb the full height of that greasy pole, for PMQs. These weekly events are just that: 'events'. Back benchers gather to cheer their respective Leaders on and the exchanges are designed to maintain or improve their morale; the public at large is indifferent. PMs are not obliged to actually answer questions at PMQs so we saw Boris Johnson seeking to undermine the confidence of Labour Leader Keir Starmer by calling him 'Captain Hindsight', suggesting that he 'flip flopped', could not make up his mind, and was a boring lawyer who couldn't understand how ordinary people lived. Starmer, who is indeed a trained lawyer, found Johnson's waffling and playing to his own party gallery difficult to accept, but eventually joined in the exchange of what often sounded like schoolboy insults in the playground.

Yet being quick and agile on one's feet with insulting, crushing wordplay is an important skill in British politics – see above on 'humour' – and indeed, other democratic polities too. One has only to give the example of Donald Trump in his 2016 contests, where he aimed his poisoned verbal darts at one leading rival after another, eventually eliminating all of them: 'Lyin Ted' Cruz, 'Crooked Hillary' (Clinton) and 'Pocahontas' (Elizabeth Warren who claimed, wrongly, it turned out, to be descended from American Indian stock). Once President, he also mocked North Korea's Kim Jong Un as 'Little Rocket Man'.

As covered in Chapter 5 on the media, politicians have to survive and thrive within this challenging world if they want to advance their careers. Those MPs who have a flair for performing on the media are often seen first on programmes such as the lunch time discussion show, *Politics Live*, when their performances will be monitored and, if good at defending and advocating the government line, their promotion chances will be enhanced. Politicians like Grant Shapps proved wonderfully effective on camera when defending the governments in which he served and was frequently sent out to do the morning round of breakfast chat shows to deliver, what for many was calm and healing balm.

The primacy of the spoken word in UK politics

Some would argue – as Lords Carrington and Baker did to me – that the Commons was devalued by Blair's apparent indifference to it. But, whatever its status, diminished no doubt by MPs' preference for speaking to cameras on St Stephen's Green outside Parliament, rather to colleagues inside, it remains the stage on which the nation's business is acted out. Anyone who has served in government or has studied the process with care will tend to argue that performance in the House is the sine qua non of future ministerial success (in this case 'performance' means the floor of the House, though assiduous work on select committees can also win attention and preferment). So Kenneth Baker told me: 'If a minister ... doesn't take his brief through the House of Commons competently and gets into trouble, he is a casualty, because the system will itself say so.'

That wise old commentator Peter Riddell of *The Times* reinforced the point: 'You have shown that you are in charge both in relation to Opposition MPs and your own backbenchers. Ministers who have obviously failed in the House and in handling a bill have been sacked' (private email). Former PPS to Tony Blair and Chief Labour Whip in the Lords, Bruce Grocott, puts it more emphatically:

> If someone clearly could not command the Commons from the dispatch box, I mean if you can't operate in the House of Commons in a Parliamentary system to the admiration or at least the respect of your colleagues, then you would not get far past first base and neither should you.
>
> *(private interview)*

But perhaps the most revealing comments were by Charles Powell on the appropriateness of such Commons-related expertise:

> Given how political careers are made in this country, i.e. by performance in the House of Commons, self-advertisement, self-confidence and so on are the great qualities. Other countries are very different. France is through bureaucracy; Germany through provincial politics. For us, the only way is through performance in the House of Commons. That to me doesn't seem to nourish the best qualities for being a good minister.
>
> *(private interview)*

He went on to provide the title quotation for this chapter:

> In all my years of experience, I have never heard anyone recommended for appointment to be a minister on the grounds he would be a good minister. Nobody ever said that he would be jolly good at running a department, that he had the qualities of management and so forth. The qualities required, quite frankly, are loyalty and brilliance at performing in the House.
>
> *(Lord (Charles) Powell, private interview)*

Powell, then, regretted the primacy of mere spoken performance as the basis of promotion.

Andrew Adonis, on the other hand, thought such 'training' by no means inappropriate:

> It is fashionable to say the House of Commons as a training ground is largely irrelevant to the job of being a minister, but I don't think that is the case at all. To be an effective minister you have to be effective at explaining – a large part of the job is acting as a spokesman for the government. The single most important forum of explanation of government policy … is the Commons. … The capacity to explain and develop a winning argument … are well cultivated by the House and the wider processes of politics – local politics and activities that an MP has to engage in.
>
> *(private interview)*

Moving up the ministerial ladder, requires a politician to show he or she can do the job. A large part of this will still be in the House, as junior ministers are often given the task of piloting new legislation through to completion. Completely different skills, however, are required to: take advice from but not merely be led by civil servants; chair inter-departmental meetings – often involving outside experts; negotiate with other colleagues, particularly in the Treasury; absorb a huge amount of information and keep it in perspective; to work very long hours; and to show skill and aplomb with the media.

Many people will think of promotion in business terms but politics offers a totally different environment in which to operate: John Hoskyns's jibe about the House not containing enough talent to staff a medium-sized multinational company is certainly debatable, but there are many differences between the requirements of politics and business. Peter Riddell though thinks Hoskyns was basically right: 'It is certainly true that ministers are promoted using criteria not prevalent in any other organisation and the processes which other organisations use are totally absent in Whitehall' (Riddell, 2020, p.173).

Bernard Ingham (Mrs Thatcher's former Press Secretary) for his part did not think the comparison relevant:

> I think business experience is rather overstated. It takes guts to stand on the floor of the House of Commons. It takes a certain ability to perform well there. We aren't comparing apples with apples. This is the point that Hoskyns never got. Politicians have to secure elections. Senior businessmen do not. All they have to do is keep the shareholders happy.
>
> *(private interview)*

Nevertheless a key point lies herein regarding ministerial skills. In business a new recruit spends years at lower grades acquiring knowledge of the company before being promoted to a level of substantial responsibility. By comparison, a junior minister is often thrown into the deep end, with huge responsibilities, with no knowledge or relevant skills within an organisation employing hundreds and serving millions. Lynne Featherstone reflected on her initiation as a minister thus: 'I literally didn't have a clue. I didn't even know what a submission was. Literally nothing' (Hughes, 2017, p.1). Tony Blair often complained that he lacked sufficient talent among his back benchers and in August 1998 appointed Scottish media executive Gus MacDonald, via a peerage, as Minister for Business and Industry at the Scottish Office. Scottish Secretary Donald Dewar commented: 'He has the right qualification, he has the track record, and he is someone I'm very happy to have on board' (BBC News, 1998). To those Scottish Labour MPs who might have thought this a snub to their abilities, Dewar pointed out, 'none of them has been the chief executive of a major public company' (ibid.; see Chapter 4 for more discussion of recruitment from outside Parliament).

Easy on the ear an advantage

Writing in *The Times*, columnist James Marriott regrets the fact that neither Rishi Sunak nor Keir Starmer has a pleasant speaking voice. The latter, he commented, might look like a PM but did not 'sound like one', going on to observe:

> A politician's voice is his or her most distinctive attribute – it ranks above clothes and above physiognomy. Churchill's most identifiable feature was not his bald infant's head but his indistinct patrician's growl. Margaret Thatcher's husky commanding purr was more crucial to her 'image' than the pearls or pussy brows. Likewise Tony Blair with his halting, earnest, slightly camp diction.
>
> *(Marriott, 2023)*

The ideal minister: Heseltine?

Senior civil servants, frustrated by advising ministers who lack the necessary clear aims for the future, or the skills to deliver them, regularly praised Michael Heseltine in the interviews conducted by the IfG's excellent report: 'The Challenge of Being a Minister', by Peter Riddell et al. 'One, far from starry-eyed, senior official described Heseltine as a "dream minister"', going on to express a definitive summary of the ideal kind of minister: one 'with a clear vision, who was not distracted by day to day trivia, and able to translate a set of priorities into plans and to punch his weight in cabinet'. Another official who had worked with him closely was equally lyrical: he was a 'magic combination – managed to do the job without being very high maintenance and having a sense of where he wanted to go. He had a magic wand' (Riddell et al., 2011, p.23). The authors comment that 'The civil servants who worked with him saw Heseltine as an exceptional motivator with an unusual ability to inspire and enthuse' (ibid., p.23). He was also a minister who appeared to cross, successfully, the border between 'policy' and 'administration'. Civil servants tend to see themselves, a little jealously perhaps, under the departmental directions of PUSs, as controlling the administration side of things. Heseltine swept away such distinctions: as a successful businessman he was aware that creating a policy is one thing, implementation demands a careful management of the process. He devised his Management Information System for Ministers (MINIS) in the Department of the Environment in 1979 and applied it wherever he was appointed. This entailed requiring heads of divisions to cost what each member of their staff were doing to the nearest £1,000; according to Heseltine's biographer, Michael Crick, this was anathema to PUSs. This new information flow was a kind of revolution and bestowed benefits, especially when repeated annually; however MINIS was not adopted by other ministers and the media had no interest in highlighting such an esoteric aspect of government.

Riddell et al. (2011), mention Nigel Lawson and Kenneth Clarke as highly effective ministers with clear vision and sets of priorities, delegating clear spheres of responsibility to junior ministers. Effective ministers gain promotion, become 'big beasts' and leave lasting legacies: in the case of Heseltine including:

> regenerating Merseyside (notably after the 1981 riots in Liverpool) and the docklands of East London; by playing a leading role in replacing the poll tax with the council tax; by constructing High Speed One, and, more controversially, in pushing through the construction of the Millennium Dome.
>
> *(ibid., p.25)*

At the time of writing, a senior Labour ex-Chancellor, Alistair Darling, passed away and the testimonials in his wake suggests he too should be added to the above list of ministerial honour. His greatest moment arrived in 2007 when his preternatural calm under immense and sustained pressure, saw his country, and perhaps the West as a whole, survive the biggest economic crisis since 1929. David Cameron's tribute was to a 'thoroughly kind and decent man. Despite us representing opposing parties, I valued his immense contribution and enjoyed working with him … we owe him a huge debt of gratitude' (Horne, 2023). His PM at the time, Gordon Brown, remembered a 'statesman of unimpeachable integrity whose life was defined by a strong sense of social justice' (ibid.).

Heseltine was possibly the ideal minister but, the worst possible? I'd select John Stonehouse who initially so impressed Harold Wilson with his working-class background, (apparent) steady marital status and his unusual confidence and effectiveness as a junior minister. This favourable perception began to fade after rumours circulated regarding his dodgy business dealings, his extra-marital philandering and possible spying for an Eastern European communist country.

When all these negative factors reached a climax in November 1974 he faked his own death by drowning after disappearing from a Miami beach and then was unmasked as living under a false identity in Australia. His defence of mental illness, brought on by the strains of ministerial life, was disbelieved: it was obvious to most that he was an opportunistic charlatan totally lacking in principle. He ended up serving time in prison before dying of a heart attack in March 1988. A three-part drama in 2023 alleged several of these accusations, denied by his family (Griffith, 2023). Would it have been possible to detect Stonehouse's unsuitability before given ministerial office? Not really, given his conman's ability to persuade and dissemble, but his career stands as a warning to PMs everywhere that bad apples – or politicians who become so – do sometimes target a political career for reasons purely of personal gratification (Express & Star, 2023).

How to do it well

Finally in this chapter I wish to address and summarise the advice given to ministers by the already oft-quoted and authoritative IfG's 2017 report on 'What Ministers Do and How to Do It Well' (Hughes, 2017).

- *Clear sense of purpose*: The consensus among interviewees was that a minister needs to have clear objectives that can be communicated to officials: 'You are there to drive a political agenda, not just to respond efficiently to submissions in your box.' 'Ministers who were seen as successful were those who communicated and maintained focus on achieving a clear objective' (ibid., p.21).
- *Prioritise*: Chris Huhne (Secretary of State for Energy 2010–12) advised to 'prioritise down to really a very limited number of priorities', this being the best way to extract the best of their own and the department's time and effort. Liam Byrne (Chief Secretary to the Treasury, 2008–10) advised 'to set a target of doing a keynote speech one month into the job to lay down a strategic agenda for my time in office' (ibid., p.20).
- *Good, timely decisions*: PMs don't appoint for their detailed policy knowledge 'but more often because they know them and trust their judgement'. Alan Johnson says, 'It's no good waiting a week's time because

you'll have another whole set of problems come up that you have to make a decision on. And the civil service want you to be decisive'. Jack Straw comments that often, in response to a crisis, decisions are taken hastily and 'inevitably, on inadequate information. ... [You have] to make the best decisions and then to move on, and accept that some of the decisions will not be correct in retrospect' (ibid., p.21).

- *Team work and challenge*: 'Effective ministers are willing to be challenged, to listen and work constructively with their officials, fellow ministers and external stakeholders.' 'You just make better decisions ... if you expose yourself to a broader range of voices' (David Willetts, Minister of State for Universities and Science 2010–14) (ibid., p.22).
- *Win public support*: Ambitious ministers must minimise public opposition and try to cite public support for their ideas: 'You've got to go out to the outside world and make them part of your mission.' (Ed Balls, Secretary of State for Children, Schools and Families 2007–10) (ibid., p.23).
- *Earn respect of Parliament*: The IfG report warns that: 'Ministers who perform badly in Parliament can lose the confidence of the whips, their backbench colleagues and eventually the Prime Minister' (ibid., p.23). Sir Bob Neill MP says, 'never take the House of Commons for granted' (ibid., p.23). Mark Hoban (Minister of State, Work and Pensions 2012–13) 'if you can command the respect of your opponents ... [and] you handle it well and sensitively and carefully and are solid and robust in your defence ... you get a lot of brownie points for that' (ibid., p.23). David Howell (Secretary of State for Energy and then Transport under Thatcher) noted that Willie Whitelaw used his 'charm, humour and agility in the House' so that it mattered less that 'his grasp of policy detail was not strong ... if you can keep ... the party on your side, that is a great relief, enabling you to get on with the main jobs of the minister' (ibid., p.24).

The advice of David Davies, Secretary of State for exiting the EU 2016–18, to incoming ministers

- The first thing that I did for my four junior ministers on meeting them was to *encourage debate*: 'make sure your officials know they can disagree with you' (Davies, 2022).
- *Stop them overwhelming you*. 'For example, the first day you get into office, call your predecessor and read them the contents' of your first box – 'because officials will bring you all the things that your predecessor turned down'. 'Two reasons, it stops Whitehall pulling a fast one, but it also teaches Whitehall a lesson when the new minister says, "No, you can't do that"' (ibid.).

- Clear your diary: 'They'll fill it with things that they want to do, not what you want to do. When I went into the Cabinet Office, my diary was full of all that' (ibid.).
- Boxes:'The last thing was in many ways the most important thing, although you can't always manage it: do your box in the office. Require the box at 5pm and then do it. Now, your first night you'll be there for four hours. But by the time you've done it a few times, you'll be there for two hours. Because, in those days at least, if you were still in the building, then the person who wrote the papers had to be there too. There's a nice discipline on officials if, in order to give you a policy paper, they've got to sit in the office until seven o'clock at night. It will stop them giving you frivolous papers' (ibid.).

Preparing for ministerial office

It is hardly surprising that, when first appointed, ministers complain they know too little about the job they have been given. Peter Riddell's book, 15 Minutes of Power notes that, 'Few new ministers have much idea of what doing the job involves – or have received sufficient, if any, preparation – apart from the still small, though prominent and influential, group of former special/political advisers' (Riddell, 2020, p.xxi). It seems weird to those of us outside looking in on the political world to discover there is no real preparation for the job of minister in a department, despite it possibly handling a budget of billions of taxpayers' money and affecting the daily lives of everyone. Baroness Shepherd recalls that she felt she 'needed an induction course' on being first appointed. This proved to be a short talk from the then Cabinet Secretary, Robin Butler with two other newbie ministers, John Redwood and David Maclean in attendance. He reckoned Edwina Currie was 'impressive' for setting herself objectives once becoming a minister; Shepherd wondered 'where it could be considered exceptional to set objectives when starting a new job' (Shepherd, 2000, p.98). Margaret Beckett was dubious about the need for 'training' as nothing 'could prepare you for the pressure of ministerial life, only experience helps' (Riddell et al., 2011, p.43). Norman Baker also expressed scepticism:

> Part of the skills of being a politician, insofar as you have them, you learn before you get to office: how to communicate with people, I hope; how to prioritise your time; and how to absorb information quickly. These are the skills that a member of parliament has to have, so in that sense a minister has the same skills.
>
> *(ibid., p.43)*

However, as the Public Administration Select Committee 2011 report 'What Do Ministers Do'? concluded, apart from those usual MP capabilities, 'other skills, notably those required to oversee a large and complex organisation are unlikely to be developed during a member's career in the House' (PASC, 2011). Clearly some politicians view such training as threatening as it might suggest they were ill prepared for the job. Ministers with spad experience, of course, will be familiar with ministerial life and won't suffer the culture shock of those lacking such preparation. Politicians, however, are resistant to the idea of 'in service professional training', believing that, as politicians, they have an automatic, perhaps intuitive, understanding of the job's requirements.

This point was eloquently expressed by Patricia Hewitt, who organised briefing sessions for incoming Labour ministers in 1997: 'What was really depressing was that the Shadow Cabinet didn't really feel they needed any training or development' (Hughes, 2016). They thought that as ministers they would be making decisions and implementation would be someone else's problem. Parliamentary, and political skills are important but are not sufficient to make for an effective minister. Riddell's IfG research led him and his colleagues to conclude from their well-attended programme for junior ministers towards the end of the 1997–2010 Labour government – focusing on 'leadership and ministerial team development, budget and resource management, working with the centre past and future' plus working and managing relations with civil servants – that 'there was overwhelming support for the value of such a programme that should be offered sooner for junior ministers' (Riddell et al., 2011, p.46). The IfG report also quotes Nick Raynsford's evidence to the 2006–07 PASC inquiry that he was impressed by the technical expertise of ministers he met in international gatherings. It seems they were appointed on the basis of their knowledge and skills and not their political status as in the UK. This means that British ministers are often ill-informed on the areas for which they are responsible.

Jacqui Smith, former Home Secretary, admitted to IfG researchers, 'I think there should have been more induction. When I became Home Secretary, I'd never run a major organisation. I hope I did a good job, but if I did it was more by luck than by any kind of development of those skills' (ibid., p.48). The report offers an appraisal system for individual ministers whereby Cabinet ministers would have a review conversation with the PM 'annually with inputs in advance from the Cabinet Secretary taking advice from the ... permanent secretary and others as appropriate'. Junior ministers would have 'review conversations' twice a year with the Secretary of State, also with inputs from officials, plus a short annual review with the PM 'on a rolling basis, throughout the year' taking up no more than 40–50 hours of valuable time (ibid., p.51).

Concluding comment

The job of being a minister, especially a junior one in a democratic system of government, is exhausting, insecure and only rarely very successful. In many biographies of Cabinet members or denizens of Number 10, the 'junior minister' years are not given much prominence but indicated more as stepping stones to the higher offices later achieved. But to negotiate that journey, from candidate to MP, and then to junior minister and upwards, a combination of the relevant skills covered in this chapter will have been necessary. The key attribute remains, in UK politics, the gift of speaking well, especially in the Commons. Since 1945 all our PMs have owned a selection of the requisite key skills but the major one still has to be speaking skills. Some ministers have proved lacklustre verbally, their periods in power proving short. Almost certainly the career of Gavin Williamson, twice a Cabinet member, was characterised by criticism of his very poor speaking skills in the Commons, not to mention his cringe-making injunction to Vladimir Putin to 'Go way and shut up' (Walker, 2021). Liz Truss was another whose speaking style was flat, colourless and frankly embarrassing. What happens if an ambitious politician lacks some of the essential political skills enumerated in this chapter? Some manage to survive despite a record of failure – for example Chris Grayling and the above-mentioned Williamson who, like Grayling, survived in the Cabinet for some time partly through having backed the right horse in leadership contests. Others departed at lower levels, perhaps the most famous being Edwina Currie, a talented and very ambitious junior health minister who was sufficiently unwise to state in December 1988 that: 'Most of the egg production in this country, sadly, is now affected with salmonella' (Hickman, 2006). A storm of protest exploded from the egg industry when consumption fell by 60 per cent. Currie's dreams of a becoming a senior minister collapsed in tatters and she became famous only for her very readable diaries, which revealed her four-year affair with John Major (Currie, 2003).

References and further reading

Note

Highly recommended extra material is accessible from the high-quality, six-part podcast series from the Institute for Government, *Becoming a Minister*, drawing on recollections from a variety of former ministers.

AZ Quotes (n.d.a) www.azquotes.com/quote/1433184.

AZ Quotes (n.d.b) www.azquotes.com/quote/1140365.

BBC Home (1970) On this day: '1970: British prime minister hit by flying egg'. 1 June.

BBC News (1998) 'Broadcaster appointed to Scottish Office'. 3 August.

BBC News (2016) 'David Cameron's first PMQs: "He was the future once"'. 13 July.

Colville, R. (2023) 'Sunak "the anti-Boris" wants his party to eat its vegetables, but MPs still yearn for red meat'. *Sunday Times*, 8 January.

Currie, E. (2003) *Diaries 1987–92*. Little Brown.
Davies, D. (2022) 'Ministers reflect archive'. Institute for Government. Transcript, 22 September. www.instituteforgovernment.org.uk/ministers-reflect/david-davis.
Earl, L. (1966) 'Harold Wilson: "My how he's changed!"'. *Guardian*, 26 December. archive.macleans.ca/article/1966/6/18/harold-wilson-my-how-he's-changed.
Express & Star (2023) 'The incredible life of John Stonehouse: A once high-flying MP who faked his own death'. 2 January.
Finkelstein, D. (2022) 'Don't fall for gloomy tales of British decline'. *The Times*, 21 December.
Fisher, A. (2022) 'Where's Labour's fervour? Can you imagine a crowd chanting "Oh, Keir Starmer"?' *Guardian*, 14 December
Flynn, P. (2012) *How to Be an MP*. Biteback.
Fry, E. (2022) 'Kwasi Kwarteng's awkward moment on University Challenge where he swore twice'. *Daily Mirror*, 23 September.
Griffith, B. (2023) 'EXCLUSIVE: Horrified wife of Stonehouse drama MP says show a "vicious attack" on her family'. *Daily Mirror*, 7 January.
Hague, W. (2004) *William Pitt the Younger*. HarperCollins.
Hickman, M. (2006) 'The big question: Was Edwina Currie right about salmonella in eggs, after all?' *Independent*, 17 November.
Horne, M. (2023) 'Starmer leads tributes to "calm and honest former chancellor"'. *The Times*, 1 December.
Hughes, N. (2016) 'Ministers reflect: The Labour years, 1997–2010'. Institute for Government, 26 September. www.instituteforgovernment.org.uk/article/comment/ministers-reflect-labour-years-1997-2010.
Hughes, N. (2017) 'How to be an effective minister: What ministers do and how to do it well'. Institute for Government, March. www.instituteforgovernment.org.uk/sites/default/files/publications/Ministers_Reflect_WEB.pdf.
International Churchill Society (2009) 'Finest hour 101, winter 1998–99'. 6 June. https://winstonchurchill.org/publications/finest-hour/finest-hour-101/how-churchill-saw-others-stanley-baldwin/.
ITVX (2023) *Stonehouse*, January.
ITVX (2023) *The Real Stonehouse*, documentary on his career made to accompany the drama, giving a more accurate account of his life and misdeeds.
Jenkins, R. (1964) *Asquith*. Collins.
Kalif, R. (2007) 'Blair to step down June 27'. *Financial Times*, 10 May.
Kaufman, G. (1980) *How to Be a Minister*. Faber.
Lensch, J. and Witter, L. (2020) *10 Things Politicians Should Be Thinking of Right Now*. Innovation in Politics Institute.
Letts, Q. (2023a) 'Californian-style piety doused in disinfectant'. *The Times*, 5 January.
Letts, Q. (2023b) 'A vision of the future pixelates and freezes'. *The Times*, 6 January.
Mance, H. (2016) 'Britain has had enough of experts, says Gove'. *Financial Times*, 3 June.
Marriott, J. (2023) 'If only Rishi and Keir were easier on the ear'. *The Times*, 12 October.
Mulholland, H. (2012) 'Charles Walker MP: I've made peace with myself. I've got it off my chest'. *Guardian*, 26 December.
Murphy, J. (2022) 'A minister reflects'. Institute for Government, 7 October.

Newscast BBC (2023) 'Interview with No 10 speech writer'. 6 December.
Pimlott, B. (1992) *Harold Wilson*. HarperCollins.
Public Administration Select Committee (PASC) (2007) 'Skills for government'. Institute for Government. https://publications.parliament.uk/pa/cm200607/cmselect/cmpubadm/93/93i.pdf.
Public Administration Select Committee (PASC) (2011) 'Smaller government: What do ministers do?' 77th Report of Session 2010–11. www.parliament.uk/globalassets/documents/commons-committees/public-administration/Ministersmemosforweb.pdf.
Ratcliffe, S. (2016) *Oxford Essential Quotations*, 4th edn. Oxford University Press.
Ratcliffe, S. (2018) *Oxford Essential Quotations*, 6th edn. Oxford University Press.
Reuters (2022) 'Deliver, deliver, deliver: Truss vows change and thanks'. *Guardian*, 5 September.
Richards, S. (2019) *The Prime Ministers*. Atlantic.
Riddell, P. (2020) *15 Minutes of Power*. Profile.
Riddell, P., Gruhn, Z. and Carolan, L. (2011) 'The challenge of being a minister: Defining and developing ministerial effectiveness'. Institute for Government, 24 May. www.instituteforgovernment.org.uk/publication/challenge-being-minister.
Seldon, A. (2024a) 'Let 2024 be the year our hotchpotch bureaucracy is consigned to history'. *Sunday Times*, 17 March.
Seldon, A. (2024b) *The Impossible Office? The History of the British Prime Minister*, 2nd edn. Cambridge University Press.
Seligman, M. (2006) *Learned Optimism*. Vintage.
Shepherd, G. (2000) *Shephard's Watch: Illusions of Power in British Politics*. Politico's.
Skues, R. (2022) 'Starmer doesn't need a personality cult to win'. Letter to *Guardian*, 21 December.
Stewart, R. (2022) Freezing bills, mental health in politics, and Rory's new job'. *The Rest Is Politics*, 31 August.
Walker, P. (2021) '"Russia should go away and shut up": Gavin Williamson's biggest blunders'. *Guardian*, 15 September.
Waugh, P. (2022) 'We'll all suffer if the Tories become the stupid party on Net Zero'. *i*, 11 July.

9

DREAMING OF DOWNING STREET

Churchill, Lord Home and Liz Truss

> Who'd want to be prime minster? But you know, people do. It's quite extraordinary.
>
> (Deborah, Duchess of Devonshire to Mathew Parris; Parris, 2022)

> I didn't want it enough. I didn't want the cost that came with it.
>
> (Ben Wallace on why he decided not to contest the premiership; Allegretti, 2024)

> I don't have many friends in politics.
>
> (Boris Johnson to Gavin Williamson; *The Rise and Fall of Boris Johnson*, Channel 4, 2024)

> Why on earth would anyone – especially those seeking to lead the Conservative Party – want to be prime minister? Well, you get a fancy Georgian house in central London, hundreds of staff, private travel and a chat with the King every week. You even get the chance to do some good and improve people's lives. And whatever happens you'll have a place in history. But why, right now, would anyone in their right mind put themselves through a leadership election so they can get the top job? When I asked this question of an experienced former Downing Street staffer the answer comes: "I honestly could not answer it."
>
> (Kuenssberg, 2022)

As previous chapters have illustrated, sometimes graphically, political ambition creates conflict when several rivals compete for the same post. Competition for the lowest ranking ministerial posts, PPS, is at times almost non-existent – in 1997 New Labour sought to award every MP with at least something

DOI: 10.4324/9781003405085-10

equivalent. But as the ladder ascends then so does the degree of rivalrous desire, right up to the post at the tip of that famous greasy pole: residing in Number 10 Downing Street. Here dwell, according to Harold Wilson's Press Secretary, Joe Haines, 'the navigators of history' (Haines, 1977, p.1). Chapter 7 analysed two leadership contests by Labour in opposition; this chapter will examine three of the key prime ministerial/party leadership contests. The first reaches back a decade before this book's approximate 1950 starting point to the most consequential of all such contests, which occurred in May 1940, at the outbreak of the Second World War.

Winston Churchill becomes PM, May 1940

This contest for the top job in a country that at the time seemed to be en route to possible or even probable military disaster has been much analysed, even mythologised. Perhaps the best historical analysis of this intense period in British political history is Nicholas Shakespeare's masterful, *Six Minutes in May*. Another of my reasons for starting with this example is the major, relatively unsung, role played in it by a (very) distant relative of mine, the Liberal MP, Clement Davies (1884–1962).

As was noted in Chapter 1, Churchill was a very unusual man, a view that he certainly held of himself, but to become this imagined 'man of destiny', Winston Churchill had to transform himself from being a wayward political maverick with a past marred by several major failures: Home Secretary in 1910 who ordered the army to quell the Tonypandy Riots; architect of the failed Gallipoli landings in 1916; when Chancellor he returned Britain to the Gold Standard, triggering inflation and unemployment; not to mention his fervent (possibly racist) opposition to Indian independence. Moreover, his outspoken attacks on the rise of Nazism, whilst vindicated by history, occurred within and against the dominant pro-appeasement consensus. In the late 1930s he was viewed, along with David Lloyd George – after being PM in 1922 Lloyd George never held another government post – as someone in the twilight of his career and certainly highly unlikely to become a legendary wartime PM.

War began on 1 September 1939 and an extended 'phoney war' then ensued until the attempt to frustrate the German invasion of Norway, which turned out to be a serious failure of equipment, leadership and tactics. Despite British naval superiority, seven destroyers were lost and a sense of failure attended Britain's first attempt at coming to grips with the German enemy. The Norway Debate on the conduct of the war, 7–9 May 1940, was the gateway to Churchill's great opportunity. This debate was probably the most intense and passionate in British parliamentary history: its ironic outcome that the person officially responsible for the failure – the First Sea Lord, Churchill – shortly afterwards replaced Chamberlain as

PM. Nicholas Shakespeare's brilliant account reads like a political thriller: I summarise below.

Chamberlain spoke first, trying hard to put a persuasive gloss on the widely perceived military disaster. His problem, though, as Shakespeare notes, was that he 'tended to speak like the chairman of a Chamber of Commerce'; in Duff Cooper's words the PM:

> has no charm of manner or command of rhetoric. The unexpected epithet, the telling metaphor, the burst of eloquence – all those qualities that render the speeches of Winston Churchill an unending source of delight are utterly foreign to the oratory and character of Chamberlain … his voice was thin, his prose unimaginative, his delivery uninspiring.
>
> *(Shakespeare, 2017, p.262)*

His assertion that 'the balance of advantage lay on our side' promoted the Liberal Dingle Foot to disbelieve his ears: 'No one listening to his speech would have supposed that Britain had suffered a major defeat.' Clement Attlee's speech came next: 'Quiet, prim schoolmasterly, bald headed' he objected that the government had made 'no provision for the inevitable German counter stroke and had not appreciated the vital importance of protection from the air' (ibid, p.264).

It is a little strange that this historic debate was opened up by politicians who were all rated as poor speakers. Liberal Leader Archie Sinclair, another such, itemised some of the shocking weaknesses of the Norway campaign: 'The men … had no snowshoes or white coats. The anti-aircraft guns were utterly useless' (ibid., p.265). After a few more speakers stepped up, Sir Roger Keyes, dressed, astonishingly, in the full-dress uniform of a First Sea Lord, determined to defend the navy's reputation against 'the cowardice of Whitehall'. Usually a dull speaker (yes, him too), Keyes's delivery was catalysed by his evident rage. The watching Russian Ambassador, Ivan Maisky, reckoned 'Keyes' words had the effect of shells fired from a 16-inch gun'. According to another listener in the Stranger's Gallery, the old admiral 'had the rivetted interest of a packed house and obviously a lot of sympathy'. Duff Cooper thought Keyes's uniform had a big impact:

> The sincerity that lay behind his words gave them life. Those who listened knew that here was no scheming politician, no seeker after office, no captious critic, no party hack. The loyalest of men, he could no longer offer his loyalty to the Prime Minister.
>
> *(ibid., p.268)*

Keyes, however, like several other speakers, did not point the finger of blame at his friend Winston Churchill but longed 'to see a proper use made of his great ability'.

Leo Amery came next, a contemporary and rival of Churchill's at Harrow – Winston had bullied the smaller boy – and a distinguished former Cabinet member, he had a carefully prepared speech but, in an example of the randomness of Parliament's processes, his earlier attempts to catch the Speaker's eye over a period of four hours had failed and MPs began to drift out once the 8.00 p.m. dinner hour had been reached. He later explained that 'the whole effect of what I had to say depended on the response of a live House and not on those who might care to read it in Hansard' (ibid., p.270). Amery, an extremely able politician was another one who found it hard to make his words 'sing'; he was a 'lamentable orator'. Faced with an almost empty House, Amery now received some vital assistance from a back-bench Independent Liberal MP from mid-Wales, Clement Davies.

Tall, with thin sandy hair, Davies had been close to a child prodigy in his Llanfyllin school, winning a scholarship to Cambridge where he set new highs for first class honours in law. He went on to qualify for the bar and, with the help of his near total recall memory, quickly became one of London's most successful silks. He later deplored his failure to keep a diary, helping to explain why his role in the defenestration of Chamberlain is so little acknowledged; an additional explanation, as Shakespeare notes, is that he was not a 'self-promoting' politician. He also notes 'Davies's gift was for friendship and not subversion', attributing his transformation from a National Liberal 'loyal supporter of the government' to the sudden death of his son from an epileptic seizure: tragically two more of his four children also died aged 24 years. Rather than retreat into alcoholic binges, to which, some claim, he was allegedly prone (his family contest this suggestion), he turned his 'fighting spirit and fury against the government' (ibid., p.246). On 13 September 1940, Davies chaired the first meeting of the All-Party Action Group, also known as the *Vigilantes*, committed to improving government conduct of the war. Meeting in the Reform Club, with Robert Boothby as its secretary, its membership included Attlee and Greenwood, by the end of the year it numbered about 60 MPs. J.M. Keynes and Ernest Bevin also turned up to address the group, all part of Davies's dedication to remove the PM from office and replace him with a national government (Roberts, 1976).

'The Welsh speaking radical supplied something Amery outstandingly lacked: the ability to befriend and cajole MPs, irrespective of their political make up' (ibid.). This quality came to the fore during the Norway Debate. While Amery stressed that so few were present to hear his speech, Clement Davies set about making this his 'finest hour'. 'In the lead up to the debate', writes his grandson, Christopher Clement-Davies, his grandfather 'had no sleep for three days as he rallied MPs by phone and in person and took part in a whirl of critical discussions' (Clement-Davies, 2020). He slipped out of the Chamber to comb up a decent audience from the Tea Room, Library, Strangers bar and various other watering holes. Slowly MPs, including an initially reluctant Lloyd George, persuaded by his daughter Megan and his (briefly) dining companion, Davies, began to fill the chamber to listen to an Amery who was now 'very doubtful I could make the whole speech I had prepared … I did not feel like talking for more than a few minutes' (Shakespeare, 2017, p.271). However, from a slow start, he gathered strength to deliver 'one of the most famous speeches in parliamentary history'. Ronald Blythe describes the transformation as, 'a squashed little man with the minimum of presence suddenly seemed, to the hallucinated eyes and strung up nerves of the House, to loom over Parliament like a monolith' (ibid., p.272). Amery laid into the Norway disaster, its botched planning and execution plus the appalling complacency of an inadequate (and, on the night, absent) premier. Having captured the attention of the House, Amery now found himself 'going on to a crescendo of applause' (ibid., p.274). He had been unsure whether to use his final flourish, fearing it was possibly too strong for the audience, but now swept along by being at one with his fellow MPs, he unleashed the magnificently brutal injunction of Oliver Cromwell to the Long Parliament in 1553: 'You have sat too long here for any good you have been doing. Depart, I say, and let us have done with you. In the name of God, go!' (Sherrin, 2022). The irony of all this is that nobody can confirm that Chamberlain was actually present in the House to hear Amery's final lines. According to Harold Nicolson, who was present, 'The Opposition broke out into violent cheering', a rare enough event when such histrionics were almost never heard in the Chamber (Shakespeare, 2017, p.276). Another irony is that Amery had been seeking to persuade Parliament: Cromwell had been dismissing it to replace it with effectively a military dictatorship. Even worse developments for the PM were in store for the next day. It had been assumed by most MPs in the House that the debate was just a debate with no vote at the end of it, but, persuaded by Davies, yet again a crucial intervention, Attlee and his senior colleagues agreed to force a division: Herbert Morrison made this decision public at the end of his contribution.

Finally came the worst cut of all: Lloyd George's speech.

> In his flexible, melodious tenor, Lloyd George talked of how the disaster in Norway, despite all the warnings, had left us in 'the worst strategic position in which this country has ever been placed'. With a scathing rebuke to the Conservative back bench, he said that Hitler did not hold himself answerable to the Whips or to [Chief Whip] David Margesson.
>
> *(Shakespeare, 2017, p.287)*

Separating Churchill from any blame, he caused Winston to jump up and claim 'complete responsibility'. Lloyd George provoked laughter by suggesting that he should not allow a 'misplaced loyalty' to allow himself to be converted into an 'air raid shelter to keep the splinters from hitting his colleagues' (ibid., p.288). Many laughed but Chamberlain was furious; he could not prevent the famous war leader's damning peroration: 'I say solemnly that the Prime Minister should give an example of sacrifice, because there is nothing which can contribute more to victory in this war than that he should sacrifice the seals of office' (ibid., p.289).

Poor Chamberlain was distraught at the fierceness of these attacks but how much more when the division result was served up by the tellers? Parliament contained 615 MPs (originally elected back in 1935) but only about 550 were present in the debate. Margesson had annoyed not a few MPs by insisting on a three-line whip for the vote: the instruction to support the PM could not have been more emphatic. After the division, some 60 abstained; 481 voted with the balance divided 281 to 200. In normal times such a vote would have been seen as a comfortable victory but after such a titanic debate with the country desperately losing the war, a rebellion of 41 Tory MPs was deemed a fatal judgement on the war's leadership, as it soon proved to be for Neville Chamberlain.

Hindsight seems to inform us that Churchill – outspoken anti-Nazi, gifted orator, experienced Cabinet member – was the natural successor to Chamberlain; but at the time this was certainly not the case. Labour MPs tended to see the grim figure who had condemned them as 'unfit to govern' and had fought them during the General Strike: 'many of them were frightened of Winston', Stafford Cripps told Lloyd George. 'The Conservative Party', writes Shakespeare, 'regarded him with equal fear, distaste and mistrust'. Baldwin opined that 'for leadership, Conservatives would turn him down every time'; Samuel Hoare estimated 'four out of every five Tory backbenchers would vote against a Churchill premiership'. Further, the Speaker, allegedly neutral, confided his lack of confidence in such an 'unreliable' character. Even the King felt that Churchill heading a coalition would be 'very undesirable' (ibid., p.319).

The preferred person for PM was, undeniably, Edward Wood, Lord Halifax, supported by a fair proportion of Tory MPs, by Hugh Dalton ('no other choice'), not to mention Attlee and Morrison too (at Dalton's request, RAB Butler passed on this intelligence by letter to Halifax). As if this consensus were not enough, Lloyd George weighed in with the view that 'Winston could not be PM – it would have to be Halifax' (Shakespeare, 2017, p.324).

At this vital stage of the war a crucial issue was, what was to be Britain's next step? Given the disastrous start to the war and a growing awareness that Hitler's war machine was about to invade the Low Countries and France, Halifax was firmly not keen on becoming PM. Churchill's memoirs, according to his biographer Roy Jenkins, confuse the historical record by describing a dramatic meeting with Chamberlain and Halifax, Friday 10 May, in which the former tried to install Halifax as his successor. 'As I remained silent, a very long pause ensued. It certainly seemed longer than the two minutes which one observes on Armistice Day' (Jenkins, p.583). Jenkins dismisses this version as inaccurate: no long silence was required 'to get Halifax to exclude himself [and] he stressed the great disadvantage he would suffer as a PM who was a peer' (ibid., p.583). Halifax's Permanent Secretary in the Foreign Office, Alexander Cadogan, was relieved ('I think he is not the stuff of which a PM is made in such a crisis' adding 'But I'm not *at all* sure of WSC'; ibid., p.584).

So at the end of this very intense episode the person arguably most responsible for the Norway debacle, emerged as the new PM. The outcome of the Norway Debate made Chamberlain's resignation inevitable but the ultimate reason for Churchill's enthronement had more to do with Halifax's disinclination to assume such onerous responsibilities during such a tumultuous time. Yet, emerging from this historical account, and those of others including Bob Boothby, is the mostly unrecognised contribution of Clement Davies.

> Clement Davies and I wanted Churchill. The King, the Prime Minister, and a great majority of the Conservative Party wanted Halifax and I think that, but for Davies, Attlee and Greenwood, the leaders of the Parliamentary Labour Party would have settled for Halifax.
>
> *(Boothby, 1978, p.144)*

Davies's successor as MP for Montgomeryshire, Emlyn Hooson, describes his predecessor as 'the principal architect of the replacement of Chamberlain by Churchill' (Hooson, 1998). By 6.00 p.m. 10 May, just as the phoney war ended and Hitler invaded France, Winston Churchill became PM. 'Thank God', said a colleague of Lord Beaverbrook's. 'Do not thank God he replied, thank Clement Davies' (Shakespeare, 2017, p.245).

Supermac's 'events' and the ensuing succession

Harold Macmillan was PM 1957–63, arguably the first modern post-war premier but, born in 1894, he still manged to retain a slight whiff of the Victorian era and quite a bit more of the Edwardian. Born into the prosperous publishing family of Scottish origin, he was educated at a prep school where he learnt classical Latin and Greek. He went on to study at Eton though a near fatal attack of pneumonia required the services of a home tutor, the high Anglican Ronald Knox, who enabled him to win a scholarship to Balliol College Oxford. Badly injured in the First World War he later served as Aide-de-Camp to the Duke of Cavendish, the Governor General of Canada whose daughter, Dorothy, he married. In 1924 he was elected for Stockton-on-Tees where the economic depression and social poverty of his constituency affected him greatly and placed him firmly on the 'One Nation' wing of the party and something of a 'radical' (Lloyd George's word) within it. His book *The Middle Way* was a plea for a pragmatic, centrist governing philosophy. During the Second World War he served at a junior level under Churchill and then was promoted to Cabinet status to work closely with General Eisenhower. In 1951, he was made Minister of Housing and Local Government by Churchill and his subsequent success marked him out as a rising star, serving as Secretary of State for Defence, Foreign Secretary and then Chancellor 1955–57 before emerging from the Suez debacle as PM.

Macmillan's era in Downing Street is still regarded by some as a major achievement though his success in escaping the shadow of Suez was seriously marred by Charles de Gaulle's humiliating rejection of his European Economic Community (EEC) application and then by the Vassal and Profumo scandals. Nevertheless, he managed to increase his party's majority in the 1959 election, preside over a growing economy, be dubbed 'Supermac' by the press and be respected by John F. Kennedy for his wise advice on international affairs. However, by 1962 much of this gloss had worn away. A major scandal emerged in 1961 when a spy ring was discovered at the Underwater Detection Establishment at Portland, involving 'Gordon Lonsdale' (in reality a Soviet agent), followed shortly afterwards by the unveiling of the Secret Intelligence Service officer, George Blake, as a spy; then in September 1961 John Vassall, an Admiralty clerk – under threat that his homosexuality would be revealed – was discovered to be spying for the Soviets. Before any of this scandal had cooled down another, even more toxic, hit Macmillan's government: the discovery of Defence Secretary Profumo's affair with Christine Keeler, a girl who allegedly was also having an affair with Captain Ivanov of the Soviet Embassy; no novelist could have even made up such an unlikely plot.

After the Defence Secretary denied the affair in the Commons, the event brought forth this memorable and furious televised response from Lord (Quintin) Hailsham: 'A great party is not to be brought down because of a squalid affair between a woman of easy virtue and a proven liar' (Wikipedia, n.d.). Biographer D.R. Thorpe suggests that Macmillan's Victorian sense of decency caused him to be very distressed by these sexual scandals, not to mention his aversion to adultery related to his own wife, Lady Dorothy's, long affair with Tory MP Robert Boothby.

These scandals both deflated any of the air left in the Supermac bubble; he consequently decided on a 'super' reshuffle to inject new life into what he had himself come to view as his faltering administration. Doubtless his own mordant perception reflected a sequence of by-election losses – the most serious of which was Orpington in March 1962 when Eric Lubbock, the Liberal candidate sensationally overturned a 24,000 majority on a 20 per cent swing. Shortly afterwards Stockton-on-Tees (his former seat) was retained by Labour in April, Montgomery by the Liberals in May and Leicester

North-East by Labour 12 July: some diagnosed a fading administration. His infamous night of the long knives taking place on the fateful Friday 13 July (see Chapter 4), entailed the sacking of one third of his Cabinet, according to his foremost biographer, 'one of the most damaging errors of Macmillan's entire premiership' from which 'he was never to recover the initiative' (Thorpe, 2011a, p.522; and see Chapter 4).

Meanwhile overseas policy proved alarmingly problematic. In October 1962, the discovery of Soviet missiles in Cuba held UK politics and the rest of the world in a state of existential crisis. Macmillan's advice to Kennedy was allegedly wise and appreciated but it must have taken its toll on someone close to his seventieth birthday. And then, in January 1963, General De Gaulle vetoed Macmillan's plan for Britain to join the EEC. No wonder after all these happenings in the early years of the decade, he answered an interviewer about what kept him awake at night of 'Events, dear boy, events' (Quote Investigator, 2020). Thorpe comments that Macmillan had bet everything on Europe: it was to be 'our deus ex machina ... dish the Liberals ... give us something new after 12–13 years; act as a catalyst of modernisation ... a new place in the international sun. It was Macmillan's ace, and De Gaulle trumped it' (Thorpe, 2011a, p.537).

The wounded PM began to ask himself if he should, or even wanted to, lead his party into the upcoming general election scheduled for 1964. Thorpe notes that not only the succession was at issue in 1963 but also the rules of how it should take place. Humphrey Berkely, the MP for Lancaster, had suggested instead of the 'soundings' within the party and the 'emergence' of a new Leader (ibid. p.538), some sort of an electoral process should be introduced. Thorpe's comments enable us to glimpse inside Tory thinking at that time on democratic reform:

> The reaction of the party hierarchy was not dissimilar to Ernest Bevin's mangled comment on the Council of Europe in 1949 – 'If you open that Pandora's Box, you never know what Trojan horses will jump out'. Lord Aldington, the deputy party chairman was horrified. 'Humphrey, he asked in disbelief, surely you are not advocating one man one vote are you?' Berkely was made to feel as if he had 'suggested the leader of the party should be elected by the entire adult population of the African continent'.
>
> *(ibid., 538)*

Macmillan's thoughts of standing down, according to his memoirs, before the 1964 election were shared with Douglas-Home, the Foreign Secretary who, 'was very distressed to think that I had any idea of retiring but could well understand my reasons and thought they were sound. [He] fears there will be complete disunity in the party and that great troubles will follow' (Macmillan, 1973, p.494). The PM met the Queen on 20 September and explained that he would not lead his party at the next election. Macmillan thought that despite her expression of 'full understanding', she was 'very distressed' (ibid., p.495). Macmillan was fully aware that his intended departure would create a raft of potential and real problems for the party and for his Queen. The problem was that, unlike with the case of Churchill in 1955, the succession was by no means clear; Macmillan feared, with some prescience, there would be 'continual dissension and intrigue' (ibid., p.494).

It was true that there were several candidates who fancied their chances. The most obvious was Butler, a hugely able, creative, highly experienced politician and minister but somehow desperately unattractive to the party as a whole. John Morrison, Chair of the 1922 Committee of back-bench Tory MPs had, remarkably, told Butler to his face that 'the chaps won't have you', a judgement confirmed by those other members of the '22' Butler had consulted (Thorpe, 2011a, p.548). Why was this so? In his biography of Butler, Michael Jago attests to Butler's intellectual ability. Having failed to win a scholarship to Eton, he won a scholarship from Marlborough School to Pembroke College Cambridge (Jago, 2015, pp.30–41). His eventual grade in his Cambridge Tripos was one of the highest firsts in the history of the university and procured for him a fellowship at Corpus Christi College. Joining the Diplomatic Service and becoming an MP in 1929, he became PPS to the Foreign Secretary and proceeded up the promotion ladder, becoming the main Commons spokesman in the Commons in 1938. During the war, he became Education Secretary and, in 1951, Chancellor in Churchill's second administration. Having served as a stand-in PM once for Churchill and then for Anthony Eden, it was widely expected he was next in line for the top job. However, against this, was: his own view of himself was that he 'was neither an Etonian nor a blue blooded landowner, and he had seemed vieux jeu (old fashioned) to younger members' (ibid., p.326); his association with the 1930s policy of appeasement; his lacklustre speaking style, which failed to stir his fellow MPs in the Commons; Macmillan's disdain for colleagues who had no wartime experience; not to mention 'unprepossessing in his dress appeared pedestrian beside the elegant Edwardian figure of the PM (ibid., p.327). Finally it is often suggested that being very clever as a Conservative MP was not at that time necessarily an advantage: Butler, of course, was not just clever academically, but brilliantly so.

Macmillan, who tended not to respect those who had not borne arms – to a degree a pervasive view of non-combatants by those who had fought during the war – certainly shared the undeservedly low opinion of Butler but could not initially decide between Hailsham and the younger, but widely admired, Iain Macleod. Ted Heath, former highly regarded Chief Whip and in charge of the foiled EEC negotiations, might well have assumed the leadership in 1963 had the application proved successful. Enoch Powell was another 'Young Turk' but, while clearly brilliant intellectually, his often maverick judgements were viewed as suspect. Another of the younger generation, Reggie Maudling, was also extremely able and a fancied 'runner' in any future leadership contest but viewed by some (probably unfairly) as too casual and lacking in charisma and presentational skills in particular.

The availability of so many putative leaders was another reason why Macmillan felt he had to stay on to avoid appearing to 'cut and run' in the face of so much instability within the party. As autumn 1963 approached, Macmillan confided to his son Maurice that he now thought he'd stay on as PM for another two or three years. On 7 October, the PM was on the eve of telling the Cabinet that he would carry on in office: 'On the night of 7th October I reached the firm decision to continue and fight the Election' (Macmillan, 1973, p.500). However, it was on this very night that an 'event' occurred which changed everything: 'In the middle of the night ... I found it impossible to pass water and an excruciating pain when I attempted to do so. I was seized with terrible spasms' (ibid., p.501). The PM ended up in hospital just when the party conference was taking place in Blackpool.

Macmillan wrote a letter to Alec Douglas-Home that he read out to the gathering in which he stated age and current health meant he would not be able to lead the party into the next general election. The letter was the starting gun for the somewhat frenzied succession struggle that then ensued. The Conservative Party's procedures for such replacement seem, from a modern standpoint, to be weird and badly organised. There was no formal way of declaring one's candidacy: 'people merely came to be perceived as a "prospective prime minister"', as Anthony Howard noted in the *New Statesman*, in an article entitled 'Mr Home or Mr Hogg?' Both being members of the Lords, he wryly observed, 'sheltered them throughout the crucial years [of establishing their worth] and then put them down safe and sound within a few yards of the winning post' (Howard, 1962); thanks to Anthony Wedgwood Benn's successful campaign to enable peers to give up their titles, both Douglas-Home and Hailsham now had a route available to Number 10. Hailsham was not shy of advertising his candidacy and was assisted by Randolph Churchill's distribution, USA style, of 'Q' buttons and of Hailsham's own appearance in his hotel lobby with his infant daughter Kate and her feeding bottle. Quite probably this unabashed pursuit of the prize backfired within the then Tory culture, which rather flinched at such obvious self-advertisement. How things changed later on with Boris Johnson's 'celebrity politician' antics! But Hailsham offered a candidacy that fell between Butler and Macmillan's senior generation and the emergent younger talent like Heath, Maudling and Joseph.

Even before the Blackpool conference, leadership issues had been discussed by senior Tory figures. Thorpe reports on the July 1963 meeting in the west coast home of John Morrison, chairman of the 1922 Committee, with former Chief Whip, Ted Heath. Morrison informed him that senior colleagues on the '22' had concluded Alec Douglas-Home should run for Leader. Morrison spoke to Home who arranged for a medical to confirm his physical ability to take on the role. Heath left Morrison's home on the island of Islay, determined to throw his support behind Alec Home, whose name had certainly *not* been bruited as a contender outside these rather characteristic 'under the radar' manoeuvrings. Once Home's name had entered at this senior level, more influential back benchers and former ministers like Nigel Birch rallied to his cause. His most influential backer, however, according to Thorpe, was Selwyn Lloyd, the ex-Home Secretary and Chancellor who was widely respected within the party: 'in a manner quite dissimilar to Randolph Churchill's advocacy of Hailsham, quietly spread the claims of the Foreign Secretary' (Thorpe, 2011a, p.564). Thorpe adds a revealing anecdote that Lloyd, the Lord Chancellor, and the Chief Whip:

> went for a walk along the seafront at Blackpool to discuss options. Here they were accosted by a Labour-voting old age pensioner who told them that his socialist household recognised in Home the qualities to lead the nation. Selwyn Lloyd later recalled that this pensioner represented the 'gnarled voice of truth'.
>
> *(Thorpe, 2011a, p.564)*

At the Blackpool conference, 11 October 1963, Home delivered his foreign affairs speech: it was received with rapture. The newspapers next day echoed this assessment while the speeches of Maudling and Butler were seen as lacklustre. Home's failure to deny he was challenging for the top job, Robin Day concluded, meant he was definitely putting himself forward. When Butler learned that Home was leaving shortly to have a medical, he asked him why and was told the reason was Alec had been approached to become party Leader. This apparently astonished and upset Butler who had maybe assumed that as the virtual deputy to Macmillan, he would become automatically the go-to replacement. However when he delivered his speech to close the conference, it was obvious, despite the massive political interest, that, never an inspiring, extrovert speaker, Butler had again not risen to the occasion.

At this stage the bookies were offering Butler and Hailsham at a joint 5–4 and Alec Home 4–1, though shortening. The problem for the two front runners was that while both had their blocks of supporters, they both also had significant amounts of opposition. Home came to be seen as the candidate around whom the party could unite and win the next election in 1964. Some saw this as a compromise solution but others were solid in their support of the somewhat diffident but charming and much liked Scottish aristocrat. He appealed perhaps to a traditional deference within the party but also to a belief that the aristocracy were motivated not by personal honour but by a genuine non-partisan desire to serve the nation. Macmillan, who by this time was solidly for Alec, insisted that the widest possible soundings should be taken of opinion within the party, and the Chief Whip, Martin Redmayne, reported to Macmillan on the results of his soundings based on 300 Tory MPs. Six names had been mentioned – Heath, Hailsham, Macleod, Maudling, Butler and Home (though with some doubt at the time, as to whether the last named was standing). Hailsham was third in first preferences but had many opponents. The most often first choice was Alec Home about whom there was genuine enthusiasm. Macmillan then consulted Cabinet members who varied in their support of Hailsham or Butler but all seemed to agree that if the deadlock had to be broken, Alec was the man.

On 17 October a series of visitors consulted with Macmillan in his hospital room on the succession. Cabinet preferences were reported by the Lord Chancellor, Lord Dilhorne, as ten for Home, four for Maudling, three for Butler and two for Hailsham. Soundings in the Lords according to Lord St Aldwyn also revealed a majority for Home though, according to Lord Poole, Joint Party Chairman, young Conservatives were reported to be 80–90 per cent for Hailsham; he also claimed that party members would choose Hailsham and that it would be 'disastrous to go for Home: he was not widely known and would lead to a disunited Cabinet' (Thorpe, 2011a, p.308). Macmillan was concerned that the new PM should be able to 'dominate the House of Commons. ... The advantage of a 14th Earl ... was that he could spread out and become a Palmerston figure. The advantage of Hailsham was that he was a Parliamentary performer, though his manner was a little arrogant' (ibid., pp.308–309). Hailsham, having heard Alec Home was to be the choice, said the idea was 'a disaster' and threatened to 'denounce him publicly' (ibid., pp.561–563). Nevertheless, when the Queen visited Macmillan (resplendent in a silk shirt) in the hospital he read out to her a prepared memorandum. The Queen agreed Home was the candidate most likely to command general support. A short time later, at the Palace, she invited him to form a government. Having consulted with colleagues, including, crucially, those rival candidates, especially Butler, he returned to the Palace to confirm he was able to form an administration; he quickly set about forming his Cabinet. Hailsham, meanwhile, no doubt fumed that his chance had gone.

The magic circle issue

Assessing the way Tory Leaders were appointed, the 'emergence' method now seems bizarre and undemocratically antique. But to be fair, in the case of Alec Home, a fair amount of democratic consultation and polling within the party – even if not in public – did indeed take place. However, the impression remains that the crucial consultations occurred within the senior elite figures of the party. The 'magic circle' debate, following Alec Home's accession, resonated widely in the Conservative Party and catalysed the move away from the traditional 'emergence' of Leaders following 'party soundings' towards a democratic election system. It all began with an article by Iain Macleod in the *Spectator* on 17 January 1964, which included the following claim that when he discussed the future leadership of the party with Reginald Maudling and his wife:

> Home [was] never mentioned in any connection. Neither of us thought he was a contender, although for a brief moment his star seemed to have flared at Blackpool. It is some measure of the tightness of the magic circle on this occasion that neither the Chancellor of the Exchequer nor the Leader of the House of Commons had any inkling of what was happening.
> *(Bogdanor, 2014)*

Macmillan's biographer, D.R. Thorpe, published an online article analysis of the issue, concluding that 'the article ... did immense damage to the Conservative Party' (Thorpe, 2011a, p.1).

Masquerading as a review on Randolph Churchill's book on the leadership contest, the article was not in the review section but appeared as the magazine's lead editorial. In essence it was an attack by the party's Joint Chairman and Leader of the Commons on the selection of Home rather than Macleod's choice, RAB Butler. Though not explicitly stated, Macleod's 'magic circle' was widely understood to be 'the nine men from the party's elite whom he thought responsible for the selection' (Thorpe, 2011b, p.4). The fact that all but one of this group were Old Etonians, added a partisan slant to the controversy. Thorpe points out that while some Tory MPs favoured a generation 'jump' to consider the likes of Heath, Maudling or Macleod himself, the passage of the Peerage Act on 31 July 1963 opened the chance for ambitious peers to also measure up themselves for the top job. Given that the Palace strongly wished not to be involved in the process it asked for a single recommendation from the Conservative Party. Macmillan accordingly set in train a 'comprehensive consultation of the entire Conservative Party, both in parliament and outside' (ibid., p.4) entailing the services, as we have noted, of Lord Dilhorne (Cabinet), Martin Redmayne (other ministers and MPs) and Earl St Aldwyn (Lords) plus Lord Poole (party members). As Thorpe comments, 'If there was a magic circle, it was a very large one' (ibid., p.4).

Macmillan's resignation letter to the party conference referred to the need for the 'customary processes of consultation to be carried on within the party about its future leadership' (ibid., p.4). The problem was that in previous leadership changes – 1911, 1923, 1940 and 1957 – there were no 'customary processes'. Thorpe stresses, however, that Macmillan's consultations leading to his so-called Thursday Memorandum, which included mention of 'aggrieved Butler supporters' (Macleod and Powell refused to serve in Home's Cabinet), had been wide and the Memorandum was a fair reflection of opinion throughout the party. Thorpe makes the important point that:

> in Conservative leadership contests, opponents of a candidate prove more important in the final outcome than supporters. Home became leader because his support was not confined to one specific wing of the party. In addition, Home was several people's second choice, and few people's last choice.
>
> *(ibid., pp.2 and 5)*

The importance of the magic circle article, however, cannot be underestimated: Thorpe calls it a 'political earthquake', which 'firmly established in the political consciousness the idea of Eton providing a privileged caucus of backstairs fixers' (ibid., p.1).

I thought it might be useful at this point in the chapter to inform/remind readers of the rules regarding the election of an MP to the leadership of their party – rules especially important when such 'promotions' in the governing party constitute the creation of a new PM, as happened in 2019 for Boris Johnson and in 2022 for first Liz Truss and then Rishi Sunak.

Rules of the game: How do the main parties elect their Leaders?

Here, the current leadership contest rules for the Tory, Labour and Lib Dem parties are explained. See also the excellent book by Leonard P. Stark on leadership contests during the last three decades of the twentieth century (Stark, 1996).

Conservatives leadership contests

Only two years later in 1965, Conservatives adopted elections as a means of choosing its future Leaders. Further tweaks were made in succeeding years producing the following set of current rules:

Stage 1: Nominations

Candidates have to gain the support of at least eight of their fellow MPs. This requirement used to entail two MPs but the new rule was designed by the 1922 Committee to winnow out no-hopers in a crowded field.

Stage 2: First secret ballot

The process is to reduce candidates: those winning less than 5 per cent, or 17 Tory MPs, to be eliminated.

Further ballots

The process continues until only two candidates remain: this has the advantage of producing 'finalists' chosen by an electorate that has had opportunity to judge their strengths and weaknesses.

Throughout this period candidates can participate in the media, most importantly TV debates.

Members choose

After a month's nationwide hustings, members (around 160,000 in 2019) vote make the final decision. Critics point out that such contests between elections empowers a tiny unrepresentative fraction of registered voters to select the PM.

Labour leadership contests

1. Candidates have to be nominated by 20 per cent of their fellow Labour MPs, 5 per cent of Constituency Labour Parties or at least three affiliates of the party, two of which have to be trade unions.
2. Ballot: party members and affiliates vote via a preferential system, 1, 3, 4 etc. (membership in July 2023 just under 400,000).
3. The candidate with the lowest vote is eliminated and their preferences redistributed. Ballots continue until a candidate receives 50 per cent of the vote.
4. A similar procedure is followed for the deputy leadership.

Liberal Democrat election rules

1. Candidates need the support of 10 per cent of MPs plus 200 party members (90,000 in 2023) drawn from at least 20 local parties.
2. Balloting is via a postal vote of all party members.

Liz Truss

My next leadership contest to be analysed was relatively recent to the time of writing. The year 2022 was a year of intense political drama at the top of the Tory Party caused by the gradual though dramatic implosion of Boris Johnson's government.

Events leading to Liz Truss becoming PM for 49 days

On the heels of the Partygate scandal, which had revealed Boris Johnson had attended social gatherings that breached the legal restrictions imposed to control the spread of Covid-19, Conservative support for their maverick Leader had experienced a steep decline. The most visible sign of this was the confidence vote of 6 June 2022, made after the requisite 54 letters had been sent into the chairman of the 1922 Committee, Sir Graham Brady. Johnson celebrated that he had *won* the vote – 211 votes for him – but avoided mention of the 148 who had voted against, a galling 41 per cent of the overall vote. The PM's supporters cited the case of Theresa May who won a similar vote in December 2018, 200–117, but continued in office; his critics pointed out that she only survived for another year. In 1940 a vote of confidence after the Norway debacle was won by Chamberlain but his potential majority of 213 was reduced to 81 – he resigned shortly afterwards. To lose 41 per cent of your party's MPs' support was a crushing blow and shortly afterwards Cabinet member Oliver Dowden resigned: the ship was beginning to lower in the water but Johnson still stubbornly insisted on clinging to the wheel. His grip was further loosened after the loss of two crucial by-elections on 24 June, Honiton and Tiverton to the Lib Dems, and Wakefield regained by Labour after a scandal concerning the Tory incumbent. Sebastian Payne's wonderful account of Johnson's fall relates how his desperate Number 10 aides were trying every possible ploy to prevent what seemed to be an inevitable exit by their boss (Payne, 2022, pp.123–149). But the coup de grace was eventually delivered by an evening at the Carlton Club, 29 June 2022.

Chris Pincher had been elected in 2010 for Tamworth and, given his love of Parliament and the world of politics, he was an obvious pick for the Whips' Office: made junior whip in July 2016 and later promoted to Assistant Chief Whip. However his sexual incontinence combined with a heavy drinking habit led to complaints from those he had harassed. The party spent several months looking into these complaints and eventually cleared him of breaking the party's code of conduct. Theresa May promoted him to Deputy Chief Whip in 2018 and he won applause for his effective management of MPs during those difficult times that May experienced without a majority.

After Johnson became PM, Pincher served as Europe minister and then at Housing. In early 2022, there was talk of a leadership challenge and Pincher, disappointed not to get the Chief's job, returned to the Whips' Office as Deputy. Payne quotes a Cabinet minister saying Pincher was 'obviously unsuited' to his role but 'desperate to get it … I went to a lot of meetings where Pincher had to shore up Boris's support. He had poor manners and was really quite rude to some of the supporters' (Payne, 2022, p.153; and see also an equally gripping account in Seldon and Newell, 2023, chs 9 and 10). Rumours of Pincher's tendencies were legion at the time of this appointment, including allegations of inappropriate behaviour towards two Tory MPs at the 2017 party conference. Johnson was initially 'reluctant' to appoint him but given, according to one aide, 'that he was the best man for the job', his appointment went through. Payne comments, 'Johnson and his team seemed unaware of rumours, or had a partial grasp of the issues, but were not aware of the full facts and did not seek to find them out' (Payne, 2022, p.154).

This omission came back to haunt Number 10 on the night of 19 June when a clearly inebriated Pincher allegedly groped two men and was asked by a fellow MP to leave the club. Sarah Dines, also a whip, passed on her account of the evening to Chief Whip Chris Heaton-Harris who initially took no action. But the story was out and when the *Sun* contacted Downing Street, Pincher was told he had to resign, which he did, citing in his letter that 'last night I drank far too much. and embarrassed myself and other people' (Lee and Nevett, 2022). It seemed at first the government, keen to avoid another by-election loss after the two the previous week, told the press that Pincher, having resigned and apologised, would remain as an MP. But the press wasn't going to let Johnson off so lightly: they asked, given the rumours about the man, why did he get high office in the first place? He answered he had no knowledge of these claims but, after a few days in which government replies were none too convincing, Lord Simon MacDonald's magisterial contribution was transforming. He was former PUS and passionate Remainer, at the Foreign Office when Boris had been Foreign Secretary, who disliked Johnson because he had retired him out of the FCO. He tweeted a damning letter, 5 July, to the Parliamentary Standards Commissioner stating that Johnson had been informed personally all about Pincher's behaviour back in 2019: a complaint had been made in the summer of 2019 about Pincher, regarding actions similar to what happened at the Carlton Club. Crucially the letter stated that Johnson 'was briefed in person about the investigation and the outcome of the investigation' (ibid., p.169). Shortly afterwards Health Secretary Sajid Javid resigned, followed by Rishi Sunak the Chancellor. Payne tells how Johnson 'exploded' when he heard Sunak had resigned as he had made his career and tried hard to involve him in every major decision: he saw it as a 'personal betrayal' and 'very bad manners' to inform the PM via a tweet rather than personally. The 'great betrayal thesis … was thereupon pumped out every day' by Dorries, Rees-Mogg and the *Daily Mail* (Seldon and Newell, 2023, p.552).

Differences between Johnson and Sunak, however, ran deep on policy as well as the former's suspicions his Chancellor was on 'manoeuvres' to replace him. Sunak could not abide Johnson's tendency to announce unfunded big plans, for example £250m for a new 'national' yacht. 'Nothing did more damage to their relationship than Sunak's perception of Johnson's financial incontinence and flip-flopping of decisions'. Suspicions grew throughout 2021 as the party conference approached, 'Boris felt Rishi was trying to bamboozle him with data and find ways to get around him according to an aide' (Seldon and Newell, 2023, pp.527–528).

After Johnson's vote of confidence on 6 June, it seemed to most that the government was about to collapse but Johnson was not going without a last ditch fight; he set about reshuffling his diminished pack. The most significant replacement was then Education Secretary, Nadhim Zahawi, a conspicuously loyal politician, it seemed to many, to whoever had the power to advance his career. He became Chancellor, Steve Barclay became Health Secretary. Zahawi was replaced by Michelle Donelan: Payne records,

> The thirty eight year old arrived at Number 10 a quarter of an hour after Zahawi and was desperate for a Cabinet role: while in a waiting room she texted Nigel Adams (close aide to Johnson) almost directly asking for Education Secretary. She went into the Cabinet Room, where the PM was appointing ministers, begging for a Cabinet job. She was jumping up and down like a pogo stick with excitement, one person present said.
>
> *(Payne, 2022, p.187)*

While seeking to renew his damaged administration, a deluge of resignations was taking place with letters blaming Johnson's lack of transparency and truthfulness and much else. This wholesale exodus of 62 ministers plus a bevy of PPSs, trade envoys and party vice chairs truly marked that the end was nigh and, on 7 July, Johnson finally faced reality and resigned, his fingers prised at last off that famous black Number 10 door. At his last PMQs he defiantly quoted Arnold Schwarzenegger's line – Hasta La Vista Baby! – about coming back to his Commons audience suggesting he'd soon be back in Number 10. What is interesting from this analysis is that, even though those being reshuffled in this last gasp attempt to cling on to power must have known Johnson's political life was surely severely limited, they were mostly both happy and excited to accept the compliment of office being offered. As in the classic *The Last Days of Hitler*, by Hugh Trevor Roper, those politicians surrounding their doomed Leader were still intent upon receiving honours and positions of authority.

The brief and tragic rise and fall of Elizabeth Truss

Like so many top politicians, Liz Truss has never been short of self-confidence: 'I think I would be a very good Prime Minister' she opined to a visitor when Foreign Secretary, going on, however, to indulge an extraordinary piece of self-analysis, 'there are just two problems: I am weird and I don't have any friends. How can you help me fix that?' (Cole and Heale, 2022, p.229). Born to left-wing academic parents she spent six early years in Paisley, joining CND (Campaign for Nuclear Disarmament) and anti-Thatcher marches. Her mathematician father then became a lecturer at Leeds University, to where they moved in 1985. A year living in Canada prompted unfavourable comparisons with the education she received in Roundhay Comprehensive, Leeds. One of her brothers commenting on her competitiveness 'she was someone who had to win' added that if she was losing at a board game 'she might disappear rather than lose' (ibid., p.13). Her school clearly wasn't all that bad: she won a place from it to Merton College Oxford in 1993 to read PPE.

Already an active Liberal Democrat she threw herself into campus politics, joining the pro-EU Reform Club, becoming known for her rebel views on many issues. One of her tutors, Marc Sears, recalls a 'memorable student' whose essays always surprised as 'creative, self-consciously unconventional and when pressed in debate, she almost never backed down' (ibid., p.22). Her views evinced fierce libertarian beliefs – some criticised her, however, for 'attention seeking'; her debates with fellow students were often lubricated by a fair amount of alcohol. Her advocacy of a referendum on abolishing the monarchy at the 1994 Lib Dem Brighton conference was well delivered but, to the relief of Paddy Ashdown, aware of its toxicity, voted down. While regarding Conservatives as 'really homophobic and old fashioned, spending a lifetime in opposition did not appeal', and she 'became a Tory in her final months at Oxford' (ibid., pp.30–31). After spells working for Shell and the think-tank Reform, and after two unsuccessful electoral attempts, was voted into the Commons for South West Norfolk. After two years as a junior Education minister, she rocketed into the Cabinet as Secretary of State for Environment. The *Guardian* attributed this to Cameron's need to 'target gender imbalance' but allowed Truss was 'one of the most articulate and sure footed of the new intake' (Watt and Wintour, 2014).

Despite initially supporting Remain in 2016, her progress from hereon was spectacular: a not altogether successful stint as Lord Chancellor under Theresa May 2016–17, followed by Chief Secretary to the Treasury 2017–19; then Secretary of State for International Trade under Johnson (2019–21) who then promoted her to Foreign Secretary in 2021. When Johnson imploded in July 2022, she now qualified as a relative Cabinet 'big beast' to pitch for his job. Cole and Heale's *Out of the Blue* title of their book on Truss is well chosen in that Truss seemed to have 'ghosted' her way into contention, yet having served so widely in senior positions, surely she had been justified in believing she could be a 'very good prime minister'? She certainly hit the ground running after Johnson's departure, despite never resigning from Johnson's Cabinet she declared her candidacy on 10 July. According to one of her aides:

> Rishi was already trying to talk to people that were never going to vote Conservative in his video, we went straight for the membership and gave them what they wanted to hear. As PM I will lead a government committed to core Conservative principles. Low taxes, a firm grip on spending and driving growth in the economy.
>
> *(Cole and Heale, 2022, pp.240–241)*

Tory MPs vote for new Leader in July 2023

Truss had earlier complained that 'I don't have any friends' (ibid., p.229) but she must have realised that should the leadership contest reach the point of a membership vote, she had more than a few thousand 'friends' among this disproportionately right-wing grouping and suddenly, when her prospects brightened, she found a bevy of new MPs – not without ulterior motives perhaps – pitching to be the closest of friends. An interesting exchange when Johnson's career was dipping low but still in place, is related by Cole and Heale when Alister Jack was in his car with Mark Spencer and a call came through from Kwasi Kwarteng on the phone, to ask 'Are you a Liz guy?' Jack replied no he wasn't. '[S]o you are a Rishi guy?' continued Kwasi. 'No. Let's be clear Kwasi, I'm a Boris guy and furthermore I have the Chief Whip in the car with me' (Cole and Heale, 2022, p.228).

There were eight candidates for the leadership and hence the top job of PM: Penny Mordaunt, Kemi Badenoch, Suella Braverman, Jeremy Hunt, Rishi Sunak, Liz Truss, Tom Tugendhat and Nadhim Zahawi. Sunak was clearly the favourite to top the poll of MPs but the rules required the top two candidates to be chosen in a run-off vote by the 160,000 party members, known to be generally older, whiter and more right-wing than the majority of voters and MPs as well. This was the gallery to which the candidates were required to play and the tone was set in the televised public hustings. Debate was quite robust, for some too much so, and party voices were raised that excessive 'blue on blue' verbal conflict was bad for the party. At first Truss performed badly but she soon picked up the pace assisted by her spads and several others. After the initial rounds of voting the leaders were Sunak, Mordaunt and Truss but in the final round Truss leap-frogged Mordaunt to make it into the crucial second place: Sunak 137, Truss 113, Mordaunt 105.

Clearly Tory MPs favoured the former Chancellor but analyses of the membership suggested either Truss or Mordaunt would quite easily defeat Sunak. Then began a series of debates before members between these two colleagues and rivals. The first polling of the two aspirant PMs put Truss ahead by 62 per cent to Sunak's 38 per cent: a mountain for even this able and optimistic politician to climb.

Meanwhile a brutal game of beneath the radar briefing was ongoing – Truss was accused of being 'economically illiterate': her team aimed at Rishi's wealth and expensive wardrobe. 'In the battle for the Tory Party's souls, there was no love lost between the pair' (Cole and Heale, 2022, p.255). This became evident during the first debate in Stoke, 25 July 2022. Sunak charged at the Foreign Secretary (interrupting '22 times in the first 12 minutes', Truss's team claimed), condemning her short-term 'sugar rush' of 'unfunded and irresponsible' tax cuts:

> Can you imagine what it is going to do for everyone here, everyone watching? That's thousands of pounds on their mortgage bill, that is going to tip millions into misery and it means we have no chance of winning the next election.
>
> *(ibid.)*

Truss calmly replied, in an echo of Leave's 'project fear' jibe, that she did not believe 'this negative, declinist language' (ibid., p.255).

The backlash for Sunak was instant: he was accused of being rude and 'aggressive' and, that dread word, 'mansplaining' (Elgot, 2022). The next day, Truss told *The Times* that 'Rishi Sunak has tonight proven that he is not fit for office. His aggressive mansplaining and shouty private school behaviour is desperate, unbecoming and is a gift to Labour' (Cole and Heale, 2022, p.256). The tone of the contest had plummeted but in the eyes of the older, richer, middle-class electorate, Sunak had probably let his cause down badly. Things were not about to improve: at the first meeting of party members in Leeds the following day, Truss was able to exploit being on her home turf while Sunak was accused from the floor of 'stabbing Boris in the back'. Truss had clearly overcome any nerves and now had the confidence to increase the volume of her tax cutting agenda; she was well on the way to win the extended contest for the leadership. Seeing the way the wind was blowing, Penny Mordaunt, against whom Truss's team had only recently launched 'some of the most brutal political attacks of modern times', came out publicly on 2 August in favour of Truss. Cole and Heale comment that 'with the promise of a Cabinet job, all it seems was forgiven' (ibid., p.260).

On 13 August, Robert Buckland, the Welsh Secretary, who had previously backed Sunak, changed his mind and also declared for Truss. Despite a misstep over proposing varying pay rates for public servants in accordance with differing regional costs of living, Liz Truss's bandwagon, led by Mark Fullbrook (previously a supporter of Zahawi and Mordaunt) kept on rolling until on 5 September 2022 when she was announced the winner with 57.4 per cent of the votes to Sunak's 42.6 per cent. Sunak's share of the vote was surprisingly large, given earlier polling indications of a 24-point gap but the Tory membership had shown that the Truss campaign had successfully massaged their predilections and preferences, while the shadow of betrayal surrounding Sunak's allegedly (malevolently) choreographed resignation, possibly proved fatal. There were no handshakes or smiles when the two candidates were given the result ten minutes before the announcement – the bad blood remained. Thus ended a year of unprecedented political turmoil in the Conservative Party and with a new and even more economically right-wing PM in Downing Street, ensured the turmoil had another, catastrophic lap to run.

Truss had met with advisers at Chevening on 13 August to discuss who should occupy her Cabinet. Some of the big jobs had already been allocated: Kwarteng as Chancellor, for example, but her attempt to move Suella Braverman down from Home Secretary to Justice was rejected as was her attempt to make Iain Duncan Smith Chief Whip. Her close friend Therese Coffey became Health Secretary with the added bonus of becoming Deputy PM. Penny Mordaunt, whose support had been so welcomed, was not made a departmental head but was finally persuaded to accept continuation of her role as Leader of the House; the expression on her face when she left Number 10 suggested she was not best pleased with the arrangement. A former minister in Johnson's Cabinet is quoted as saying, 'She's made the choice to have people completely aligned with her: so much for her campaign pledge that she would be happy to work with Rishi Sunak should she win the contest' (Cole and Heale, 2022, p.278). Once in Number 10, Truss sacked over two dozen spads and civil servants who had worked for Johnson: the Number 10 Policy Unit was all but disbanded. On 7 September, she announced a popular £187 billion subsidy of energy costs, though the attendant plan to re-examine fracking was not so well received.

The next mega announcement was Kwarteng's mini budget on 23 September. Many had expected something reflecting what Truss had been promising throughout her campaign: a bold attempt to encourage economic growth via massive tax cuts. Such expectations were not disappointed. Kwarteng proposed to cut the basic rate of income tax to 19 per cent from April 2023, saving 31 million people £170 a year; the 45 per cent rate for those on incomes over £150,000 was to be abolished leaving one higher tax rate of 40 per cent; the planned increase in corporation tax from 19 per cent to 25 per cent by April 2023 was cancelled; the freezing of alcohol duty was scrapped; and VAT-free shopping for overseas visitors was also to be scrapped at a cost of £2 billion. The total cost to the Exchequer was to be around £45 billion a year and, worryingly, an accompanying Office for Budget Responsibility's estimated impact was not published. The Office for Budget Responsibility's chief executive said, 'We were not asked to produce an updated forecast for him. And we were not asked to publish any forecasts alongside that [mini-budget]' (Islam, 2023).

The tax cuts were virtually uncosted and were presumably to be the result of borrowing; at PMQs Truss answered Kier Starmer with the assurance there would be *no* reductions in public spending.

Thomas Pope for the Institute for Government called it a 'huge gamble, all the more worrying given the lack of scrutiny applied to a package hurriedly put together' (Pope, 2022). The *Daily Mail* headlined the budget with 'At Last! A *True* Tory Budget' (Groves, 2022) but elsewhere alarm signals were screeching disastrously around the international markets. The cost of borrowing for the UK surged from 3.5 per cent to 4.3 per cent; inflation rose to 10.6 per cent; the FTSE 100 slumped by 232 points as confidence took flight; the pound fell to a record low against the dollar of 1.03 after Kwarteng compounded his ill-advised measures with a promise to make yet further cuts; mortgage lenders, aware interest rates had increased, withdrew 1,621 mortgage products from the market. Economic experts calculated his budget would benefit only the rich.

Truss attempted to counter the bad news by giving interviews on eight BBC local radio stations, hoping for a less hostile response: she was almost totally savaged, leading the comedy duo Exploding Heads to tweet: 'By choosing to do a round of interviews across local radio stations rather than nationally, Liz Truss has ended up proving her policies are toxic across the whole of the UK. Absolutely genius' (Twitter, 29 September 2022). In apparent desperation Truss sacked Kwarteng – wholly unfairly given he was implementing a jointly agreed policy – appointed Jeremy Hunt in his place and had to watch him on 16 October reversing most of those problem unfunded tax cuts. Four days later, to no one's surprise, she resigned, explaining:

> We set out a vision for a low tax, high growth economy that would take advantage of the freedoms of Brexit. I recognise though, given the situation, I cannot deliver the mandate on which I was elected by the Conservative Party. I have therefore spoken to His Majesty the king to notify him that I am resigning as leader of the Conservative Party.
>
> *(Prime Minister's Office, 2022)*

Election of Rishi Sunak

The Tory party braced itself for another possible traumatic leadership contest for the third PM within a matter of months. The 1922 Committee set a requirement of 100 nominations for candidates to qualify, seeking to reduce the number competing. Sunak and Mordaunt met the requirement, with an expected throw of his hat in the ring by Boris Johnson. He eventually claimed he had the support of 100 MPs – though doubts were raised when could not provide their names – but then decided to withdraw from the contest, claiming that it was 'not the right time' for him to attempt a comeback without 'a unity party in parliament' (Andersson, 2022). On 24 October, only two breathless minutes before the deadline, Mordaunt too withdrew leaving the premiership open for Rishi. Her withdrawal meant the party membership could not overrule MPs as they had done so disastrously, given the outcome, with Truss. On 24 October, Rishi Sunak became party Leader and appointed PM the following day without a ballot of MPs or party members.

It has to be said that there was a certain justice in this outcome: Sunak had presciently informed Truss: 'Borrowing your way out of inflation isn't a plan, it's a fairy tale' (Landler, 2022). What even now seems hard to believe is that a small number of MPs and a large percentage of party members believed Truss's plans were the obvious route to prosperity: a simple answer to a very complex problem. Possibly, Truss, who often behaved as if she was impersonating Margaret Thatcher, thought she was occupying a moment similar to the Iron Lady when she was being roundly criticised by the 'wets' in the early 1980s yet stuck to her guns and proved, as Conservatives and many others believed, her remedies actually worked when applied.

Finally, a brief insight into what actually being PM is like.

A typical day in the life of a PM

> Every day began at 5.30 am., or shortly afterwards, when the alarm would go off and I would try to get out of bed to be at the kitchen table going through my paperwork by 5.45. I have always been a morning person, but I would still need to kick start my system with a strong cup of instant black coffee. This was the time of day I could focus and get things done.
>
> It all centred around the big red box – often more than one – which would be stuffed with papers submitted by my staff overnight. I would get through reams of them, and shocked them with my continued enthusiasm for this task, and also my eagle eye for detail. An average box would contain thirty-two notes or briefings – each one of which might be dozens of pages long – as well as four intelligence reports and nine letters to read and sign. I'd also read some of the letters I'd been sent by members of the public, of which there were about 300,000 in my first six months as PM. That was before all the papers in my 'day file', which would contain the relevant information for each meeting, debate or event. A typical 'PMQ pack' alone would be two ring binders.
>
> After that work and some breakfast with the family, I would head down to my office and plonk the heavy box on the desk of Ed Llewellyn or Chris Martin, who replaced James Bowler as my principal private secretary.
>
> When people asked if I enjoyed the job, I was never quite sure how to answer. It was hard, and I had to make decisions that I knew would have a huge impact on people's lives. But I never got over the feeling of it being an immense privilege to have such an opportunity. And I liked it – I liked the intellectual and physical challenge of being a political decathlete, switching from one discipline to the next and trying to give every single one of them your best.
>
> *(Extracted from Cameron's For the Record, 2019, pp.198–200)*

References and further reading

'Sadly Steve Richards' excellent 2021 'The Prime Ministers We Never Had' (Atlantic) with its superb opening chapter on RAB Butler, came out too late for me to draw upon its wisdom.'

Allegretti, A. (2024) 'Ben Wallace: Toxic addition to politics wrecks marriages and families'. *The Times*, 1 March.

Andersson, J. (2022) 'Boris Johnson: Standing in the leadership race not the right thing to do'. BBC News, 24 October.

BBC News (2022) 'What was in the mini-budget and what is the government's new plan?' 17 October.

Bogdanor, V. (2014) 'The Spectator book review that brought down Macmillan's government'. *Spectator*, 18 January.

Boothby, R. (1978) *Recollections of a Rebel.* Hutchinson.

Cameron, D. (2019) *For the Record.* William Collins.

Channel 4 (2024) *The Rise and Fall of Boris Johnson*, 13 March.

Clement-Davies, C. (2020) 'Clement Davies: Triumph and tragedy. A personal portrait of the former liberal leader'. Lecture on Davies by his grandson. Lloyd-George Society, February.

Cole, H. and Heale, J. (2022) *Out of the Blue: The Inside Story of the Unexpected Rise and Rapid Fall of Liz Truss.* HarperCollins.

Courea, E. (2022) 'Rishi Sunak to be crowned after winning Tory leadership contest'. *Politico*, 24 October.

Culbertson, A. (2022) 'Jeremy Hunt reverses "almost all" tax cuts in mini-budget and says energy support scheme to be scaled back'. Sky News, 17 October.

Elgot, J. (2022) 'Rishi Sunak "aggressive" in Tory leadership debate, say Tory supporters'. *Guardian*, 26 July.

Grierson, J. (2022) 'How Kwai Kwarteng's mini budget hit UK economy in numbers'. *Guardian*, 30 September.

Groves, J. (2022) 'At last! A true Tory budget'. *Daily Mail*, 24 September.

Haines, J. (1977) *The Politics of Power.* Cape.

Hooson, E. (1998) *Clement Davies: An Underestimated Welshman and Politician.* Transactions of the Honourable Society of Cymmrodorion.

Howard, A. (1962) 'Mr Home or Mr Hogg?' *New Statesman*, 4 December.

Islam, F. (2023) 'The inside story of the mini-budget disaster'. BBC News, 25 September.

Jago, M. (2015) *RAB Butler: The Best Prime Minister We Never Had?* Biteback.

Jenkins, R. (2001) Churchill: A Biography. Pan.

Kuenssberg, L. (2022) 'Tory leadership: Why would anyone want to be prime minister now anyway?' BBC News, 22 October.

Landler, M. (2022) 'For Truss and the Tories, a "fairy tale" unravels'. *New York Times*, 14 October.

Lee, J. and Nevett, J. (2022) 'Chris Pincher: Tory whip resigns saying he "embarrassed himself"'. BBC News, 11 July.

Macmillan, H. (1973) *At the End of the Day 1961–63.* Macmillan.

Parris, M. (2022) 'Sunak would be a breath of fresh air as PM'. *The Times*, 7 May.

Payne, S. (2022) *The Fall of Boris Johnson: The Full Story.* Macmillan.

Pope, T. (2022) 'Kwasi Kwarteng's new era of economic policy is a major gamble'. Institute for Government, 23 September. www.instituteforgovernment.org.uk/comment/kwasi-kwarteng-economic-policy-gamble#:~:text=On%20tax%20in%20particular%2C%20the,nettle%20on%20big%20tax%20reform.&text=Kwasi%20Kwarteng%20leaving%20No.,carrying%20his%20Plan%20for%20Growth.

Prime Minister's Office (2022) 'Prime Minister Liz Truss's statement in Downing Street: 20 October 2022'. www.gov.uk/government/speeches/prime-minister-liz-trusss-statement-in-downing-street-20-october-2022#:~:text=Prime%20Minister%20Liz%20Truss%20gave%20a%20statement%20in%20Downing%20Street.&text=I%20came%20into%20office%20at,security%20of%20our%20whole%20continent.

Quote Investigator (2020) 'Events, my dear boy, events'. 31 August. https://quoteinvestigator.com/2020/08/31/events/.

Roberts, D.M. (1976) 'Clement Davies and the fall of Neville Chamberlain 1939–40'. *Welsh History Review*, 1 January, Vol. 8, 188.

Seldon, A. and Newell, R. (2023) *Johnson at 10: The Inside Story*. Atlantic.

Shakespeare, N. (2017) *Six Minutes in May: How Churchill Unexpectedly Became Prime Minister*. Vintage.

Sherhan, Y. (2022) 'Liz Truss has resigned: Here's how she lost control'. *Time Magazine*, 20 October.

Sherrin, H. (2022) ' "In the name of God, go": The enduring significance of Cromwell's 1653 quote'. History Hit, 21 June. www.historyhit.com/in-the-name-of-god-go-significance/#:~:text=%E2%80%9CYou%20have%20sat%20too%20long,critiques%20of%20the%20country's%20powerholders.

Stark, L. (1996) *Choosing a Leader: Party Leadership Contests in Britain from Macmillan to Blair*. Macmillan.

Thompson, J. (2004) 'Revealed: Why Churchill considered negotiating with Germany in 1940'. *Independent*, 24 October.

Thorpe, D.R. (2011a) Supermac: The Life of Harold Macmillan. Pimlico.

Thorpe, D.R. (2011b) 'Magic circle'. Oxford Dictionary of National Biography, 19 May.

Trevor-Roper, H.(1947) The Last days of Hitler, Macmillan.

Watt, N. and Wintour, P. (2014) 'Liz Truss enters cabinet as David Cameron targets gender imbalance'. *Guardian*, 15 July.

Wikipedia (n.d.) 'Quintin Hogg, Baron Hailsham of St Marylebone'. https://en.wikiquote.org/wiki/Quintin_Hogg,_Baron_Hailsham_of_St_Marylebone.

Wyburn-Powell, A. (2003) *Clement Davies: Liberal Leader*. Politico's.

10

PROMOTION OF GENDER, LGBTQ+ AND ETHNICITY MINISTERS IN BRITISH GOVERNMENT

> I believe that every woman in the country has had her own life affected in some way by the women in Parliament. I also believe that the effect has been profoundly positive and empowering.
>
> (Rachel Reeves on women and promotion; Reeves, 2019, p.4)

To become a minister in the UK political system it is necessary for an aspirant to be a member of Parliament, most relevantly, the House of Commons; the promotion of women to ministerial rank therefore has been dependent upon those who have won seats in that Chamber. Given that women, as late as 1928, were not entitled to stand for Parliament or even to vote (with no age or property ownership limitations) until after a famously long and bitter struggle, it is hardly surprising, therefore, that, despite tremendous strides since that date, they still lag behind their male counterparts in the ministerial promotion stakes. As Rachel Reeves in her excellent study, *Women of Westminster*, records:

> In 1918 there were no facilities for women in Parliament. A gallery for 'ladies' to watch the proceedings of Parliament was shielded by a metal grille so the men in the Commons couldn't see the women watching them. … Women were not expected to be parliamentarians – they were wives, mothers, home makers, society hostesses, shop and mill workers. Not in positions of authority, certainly not in their clubs.
>
> *(Reeves, 2019, p.4)*

DOI: 10.4324/9781003405085-11

Women in Parliament

If we ignore the imprisoned Sinn Fein's Constance Markievicz who never took up her place won in December 1918, the first woman to enter the Commons was Nancy Astor, elected in 1919 for the Conservatives after her wealthy American-born husband Waldorf Astor acceded to the House of Lords. She recalls that Winston Churchill told her that her arrival in Parliament made him feel 'like a woman had entered my bathroom and I had nothing to protect myself with except a sponge' (Beaumont, 2020). With her beauty and ready wit, she soon became well known and a leading political society hostess, hosting events at Cliveden and their London home, St James's Square. Her role was something of a compromise with the prevailing view that politics was not a proper career for women in that, while Astor was highly political, her role was more similar to that of politician's wife than someone formally in charge of decision-making; that development was still a few years away.

Female membership of the Commons was slow to rise and it was a hostile environment for the few women – Astor claimed some men refused even to speak to her and deliberately shouted when she asked questions from the Commons' floor. Yet times were changing, if only at a funereal pace. Part of this is explained initially by the UK's first past the post voting system, which is thought less likely to elect women than the party list proportional systems used in most European countries. Second, combined with first past the post voting, widespread sexist attitudes: constituency party selection committees have tended to favour men over women, thinking women are less likely to win elections; this has meant that half of the population suffered discrimination and were denied the political promotion chances available to men. By 1931 only 15 women were MPs by 1979 only 3 per cent of MPs were women, rising to 9.2 per cent in 1992 but their visible roles at least provided the foundation on which women could build and win success in their campaigns to benefit women and children.

Several of these early pioneers were made of stern stuff: ('Red') Ellen Wilkinson, elected for Labour in 1924 for Middlesborough East, rose to national prominence as a co-organiser of the Jarrow March against unemployment in 1936. She later served during the Second World War as a junior Home Office minister under Herbert Morrison – with whom it was rumoured she had an affair – and was Education Secretary in Attlee's first government before ill health sadly removed her. Nancy Astor and Margaret Wintringham, the Liberal MP for Louth (elected 1921), were mainly responsible for the 1925 Equal Guardianship of Children Act giving mothers the right to be joint guardians of their children. The 1945 Family Allowances Act was the result of a long campaign waged by the Independent MP, Eleanor Rathbone, supported by Labour's Edith Summerskill and Nancy Astor. In 1975 another woman, Barbara Castle, ensured payments would be made

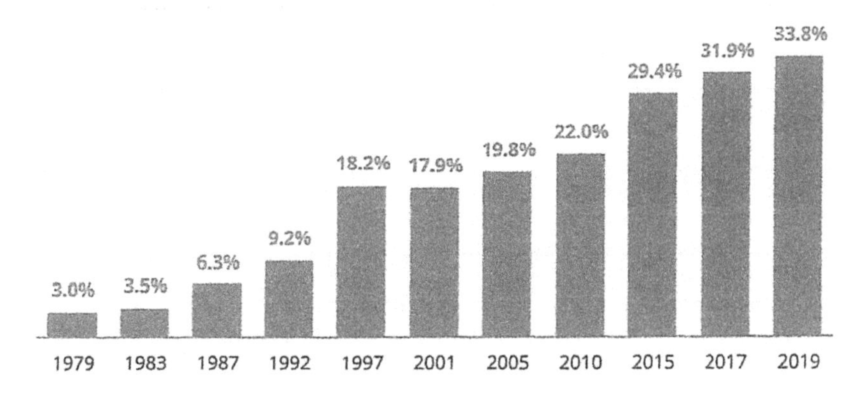

FIGURE 10.1 Women in politics and public life

Source: Buchanan (2024), © House of Commons Library, 2024.

Sources: Rallings and Thrasher, British Electoral Facts 1832-2006, 2012. House of Commons Library Briefing Papers (10/36) General Elections 2010, 2015, 2017, 2019.

directly to mothers. Castle was also responsible for the 1970 Equal Pay Act. Pressure grew in the Labour Party to skew selection towards women via 'all women shortlists'.

As Figure 10.1 shows, a big leap in female representation occurred in 1997, repeated in 2001 when it increased from less than 10 per cent to 18 per cent. From this point a steady growth proceeded until another spike upwards in 2015 and a score of 32 per cent in 2019. Overall 491 women have been elected as MPs since 1918: 58 per cent elected as Labour MPs, 29 per cent as Conservative. However pleasing these increases in percentages might appear, it compares poorly internationally with three countries with over 50 per cent women, Sweden with 47.3 per cent, Spain with 41.1 per cent and Norway 40.8 per cent, leaving the UK as low as thirty-ninth position worldwide. Despite the increased female presence in the Commons, some women, echoing the complaints of the likes of Nancy Astor and Margaret Wintringham, still view it as more 'male than female-friendly': firebrand former Labour MP, Laura Pidcock, excoriated the 'intimidating' atmosphere:

> It reeks of the establishment and of power; its systems are confusing – some may say archaic – and it was built at a time when my class and my sex would have been denied a place within because we were deemed unworthy. I believe that the intimidating nature of this place is not accidental. The clothes, the language and the obsession with hierarchies, control and domination are symbolic of the system at large.
>
> *(Reeves, 2019, p.231)*

Angela Rayner was a woman from an even more disadvantaged background than Pidcock, who rose up through the union movement to become a Labour candidate and explains her initial thinking: 'People like me can't be MPs. And so I stood to prove that people like me can be elected' (ibid., p.235). Tales abound of Neanderthal male attitudes like the Conservative MP who once told Dawn Butler, of Afro-Caribbean descent, that 'it was inappropriate for a cleaner to be in the lift with them. She replied, "Number one it's rude. It doesn't matter who uses the lift ... and number two, I'm not a cleaner, I'm an MP." '

Party leaderships

Conservatives have been slowly catching up with Labour but are at least able to boast that all three women PMs have been Conservative (Thatcher, 1979–90, May, 2016–19 and Truss, September to October 2022). Viable Labour female politicians like Barbara Castle and Shirley Williams were often tipped as possible Leaders but never made it. Why so? Some point to the traditions of male-dominated trade union influence in the British labour movement, but nobody has really been able to explain why the more progressive and liberal parties, Labour and the Lib Dems – remember the Lib Dems did flag-up the short-lived Jo Swinson as their Leader in 2019 and the Greens have had the excellent Caroline Lucas, not to mention Nicola Surgeon leading the SNP for a decade – have not yet found a woman MP who has been able to enter Number 10. This is even more surprising when in 2017 only 30 per cent of Conservative members were female while 48 per cent of Labour members were. Labour women have been elected in large numbers to the Commons yet have never risen to take the Leader's position. A *Spectator* article suggests that it might be a product of how the media treats women:

> Perhaps Labour hasn't had a female leader because of the lacklustre coverage any female politician receives. It's a focus that rarely strays beyond red-carpet territory of 'Who are you wearing?', when lists of High-Street labels outweigh those on policies, and one that thinks it's appropriate to ask Liz Kendall how much she weighs.
>
> *(Pearse, 2015)*

In May 2019, Harriet Harmon – who herself acted as an interim Leader in 2010 and 2015 – found it 'embarrassing that the party that regards itself as the party of equality, the party that has more women MPs than all the other parties put together, has nevertheless never had a woman leader and the Conservative party has had two':

> If you argue for positive action, which the women's movement in the Labour Party has, then that will be and has been resisted. If you are always pushing at barriers, you're a productive force, but not necessarily

a popular one. Those leading that charge can come to be considered too unpopular for the top job. That is an explanation, but it's not an excuse. There's no justification for not having a woman leader. We've had a party for 100 years, we regard ourselves as the party of equality – next time it's got to be a woman.

(Harmon, 2019)

Current candidates, in my view, would include Angela Raynor, the Deputy Leader, Rachel Reeves, the Shadow Chancellor, Lisa Nandy, Shadow International Development Secretary and Brigid Philipson the Shadow Education Secretary. Whilst Labour itself still wonders why it's never had a female Leader, the *Daily Mail* on 7 September led with the headline: 'Female PMs ....It's Tories 3 Labour 0'.

The House of Lords

It is often forgotten that women were frozen out of entering the Lords until the Life Peerages Act 1958: 'four decades after women were granted the right to stand as an MP' (Hertner, 2022, p.249). Baroness Wootton was the first woman to take up her life peerage through the Peerage Act 1963, allowing women to sit in the House of Lords; women also became eligible for hereditary peerages (a privilege destined, of course, to be ended for both men and women in 1999). Primogeniture, the right of succession since feudal times, had been bestowed, and remains the case, upon the eldest son, thus severely disadvantaging women (see House of Lords Library, 2022). However, the impact of the House of Lords Act was to increase female presence in the Lords from 8.8 per cent to 15.8 per cent. Hertner notes that the establishment in 2000 of the House of Lords Appointments Commission led to increased numbers of women peers: by 2020 the percentage was 28 per cent, just over one fifth of total membership. An additional male preserve barrier was surmounted in 2014 when the Church of England allowed women to be ordained as bishops. The following year, the difficulties of women bishops gaining membership of the upper chamber was facilitated by the Lords Spiritual (Women) Act 2015; the first woman bishop to join the Lords was Rachel Treweek in September 2015. Small victories, maybe, but important symbols that the principle has been established that the former blanket male privilege is slowly but surely being reduced. It is certainly encouraging to campaigners that the first two Lord Speakers were women: Baroness Hayman (2006–11) and Baroness d'Souza (2011–16) (Hertner 2022, pp.249–240).

Women in government

Isabelle Hertner cites Kenny's view on the (then) two women PMs that, 'women often come to power when the job is least desirable and are left to clear up for someone else's mess: Thatcher became Leader after two lost elections and May followed Cameron's Brexit debacle.' Hertner notes that Andrea Leadsom was also a candidate in that election and made the mistake of suggesting gauchely, that as she had children she 'had a real stake in the future of our country, a tangible stake' (Hertner, 2022, p.253). As May and her husband had been unable to have children, this ploy was much criticised in the media as offensive and unfair: Leadsom quickly stood down from the contest, thus allowing May to become PM unopposed.

Junior ministers

Junior ministers, of course, provide something like a talent pool for Cabinet and PM appointments. Theakston points out that after 1964 every Cabinet contained at least one woman but at the junior levels:

> Of the 24 female junior ministers serving between 1945–83 four were peeresses and one served part of her career in the Lords. Those from the Commons were recruited after an average of 6.8 years on the backbenches and at an average age of 46 (the same as men). Fifteen of the 24 were Labour appointments and nine Conservatives, reflecting the greater number of women Labour MPs and the willingness of Labour prime ministers to appoint women to their governments.

He also noted that the women were 'assigned to a narrow range of departments. Two thirds of women's assignments have been to domestic social departments; 40% of all postings were to Education, Pensions/Social Security or Health departments' (Theakston, 1987, pp.49–50).

Women Cabinet members

Nancy Astor, as mentioned above, was a glittering society hostess but she could only provide the physical and social context for political decisions, not make any herself. As women members of the House of Commons became an established feature, more were drawn into government at the highest level. The first was Margaret Bondfield, Minister of Labour in Ramsey MacDonald's second administration 1929–31. The next woman was also Labour, Ellen Wilkinson, Education Secretary 1945–47 and, in 1953, Florence Horsbrugh became the first Conservative to achieve Cabinet-level membership. Barbara Castle was prominent in Harold Wilson's government 1964–70 and again 1974–76 but was not seen as one of Jim Callaghan's people, when he took over from Wilson. The Tories' talisman, Margaret Thatcher, was Education Secretary in Edward Heath's government 1970–74, then Leader of the opposition before serving 1979–90 as the first ever British woman PM. She, however – 'I owe nothing to Women's Lib' (Green, 1982, p.180) – only appointed one other woman to Cabinet level: Janet Young, as the less than major role as Leader of the House of Lords.

Virginia Bottomley served under John Major 1992–97 but after her a cohort of Labour women featured in Cabinet membership including Valerie Amos, Hilary Armstrong, Catherine Ashton, Margaret Beckett, Hazel Blears, Yvette Cooper, Harriet Harmon, Pat Hewitt, Margaret Jay, Tessa Jowell, Ruth Kelly, Helen Liddell, Estelle Morris, Mo Mowlam, Clare Short, Jacqui Smith and Ann Taylor ; that made 28 members 1918–2010. Since then, Conservative women have featured strongly: Theresa May (including PM 2016–19), Justine Greening, Nicky Morgan, Theresa Villiers, Liz Truss (as Foreign Secretary 2021–22), Andrea Leadsom and Amber Rudd. Then under Boris Johnson we had Priti Patel and Penny Mordaunt before Liz Truss's brief sojourn as PM where her principal women appointments were Therese Coffey, Suella Braverman and Penny Mordaunt with Wendy Morton appointed as the first female Tory Chief Whip. David Cameron was keenly aware of the need to promote more women, especially the talented MPs who entered the Commons in 2010. In September 2012, Cameron sacked his Health Secretary, Andrew Lansley, and awarded junior roles to Anna Soubry, Helen Grant and Liz Truss. 'The appointments', write Truss's biographers, 'were clinically designed to neuter claims Downing Street had a "women problem"' (Cole and Heale, 2022, p.86).

Furthermore, at the time of writing, Rishi Sunak's Cabinet includes eight women, including Therese Coffey, Suella Braverman, Kemi Badenock and Chloe Smith. From this list it is obvious women have made huge strides at the highest levels of British government, having moved away from that narrow range of domestic departments to include the highest offices in the land, for instance the Home and Foreign Offices, though no woman has yet served as Chancellor of the Exchequer – at the time of writing, late 2023. Rachel Reeves no doubt hopes shortly to claim that honour.

The story of the improving representation of women in Parliament and government stretches back into the nineteenth and early twentieth centuries and progress was very slow until catalysed by war and a tendency for a reluctant patriarchal culture to lag behind legal reforms. It has also to be recognised that feminism has faced and still faces ideological barriers. Thatcher was female but, as already mentioned, did little to advance her gender's interests; in the USA, Phyllis Schlafly led a counter-feminist crusade in favour of the traditional family – this is ongoing and finds an echo in British Conservativism (see Hertner, 2022, p.257). Interestingly the UK lags behind several other countries not just in women MPs but in ministerial offices held. In March 2021, Sweden had 57.14 per cent of women ministers, Austria 57.14 per cent, Belgium 57.14 per cent and Canada 51.43 per cent (Inter-Parliamentary Union, 2021). The 'long march' of gender equality in Britain needs to continue and penetrate more deeply into the UK establishment before campaigners can judge their objectives are anywhere near being achieved.

Raynor's ascent

Finally, this section would not be complete without a mention of the extraordinary progress of Labour's Angela Raynor, a striking example of victory over circumstance. Her provenance from a desperately poverty stricken background – father on benefits who soon left and mother with bipolar disorder who was sectioned for attempted suicide – where she and her siblings were dependent on nearby grandparents for a once a week bath; all this compounded by leaving school at 16 years old without qualifications and pregnant with her first child, Ryan. She supported herself and son by working shifts in a care home. She believes supporting her child was a turning point, 'all of a sudden I had a little being that I had to care for. I wanted to prove that I could provide for him' (Chan, 2018). Another turning point was joining the union Unison and soon became a fiery rising star activist, 'That kind of encouragement and support turn people's lives around' (O'Hagan, 2023). A friend and ally, Mags Hindle, who knew Raynor at this time, recalled, 'She wasn't afraid of getting the job done; you couldn't ask for a better ally ... she wants to get up to the top and hopefully stay there' (ibid.). Her abundant energy and fast-maturing intellect has enabled her to become Deputy Leader of the party – confidently handling PMQs in Starmer's absences – and in pole position for a big job if Labour makes it into government.

LGBTQ+ politicians and promotion

The percentage of LGBTQ+ people in the UK population clearly has a role to play in their number reflected in the Commons and also in ministerial posts. According to Penelope McClure in the Office of National Statistics (ONS):

> An estimated 1.4 million people aged 16 and over in the UK identified as lesbian, gay or bisexual (LGB) in 2019 – a statistically significant increase from 1.2 million in 2018 – continuing the self-identification trend we have seen over recent years. People aged 16–24 continue to be the most likely to identify as LGB, however the proportion of older adults identifying as LGB, while much smaller, is increasing.
>
> *(McClure, 2019)*

This minority is perhaps surprisingly well represented in British politics both among MPs and in ministerial ranks. Surprise reflects the long-ingrained homophobia in British society, especially in elite circles. Homosexual acts were deemed illegal for many years and the trial and imprisonment of Oscar

Wilde in 1985 for 'gross indecency with men' revealed how intense this prejudice was at all levels of society (Bertram, 2020). The prejudice persisted into the twentieth century even though homosexuality flourished in certain circles, such as the highly intellectual and aesthetic Bloomsbury Group, which ignored homophobia and contained several bisexual men and women among its members. During the 1940s and 1950s a number of politicians maintained secret gay relationships, discovery avoided because if caught such acts would lead to shame and possible incarceration. Both main parties contained such in-the-closet members, including Labour's Tom Driberg who somehow lived his gay life openly and was never exposed in public though many knew of his sexual orientation. It is said the Conservative Party held back from publicising Driberg's then scandalous activities in case Labour retaliated by outing Lord (Bob) Boothby who not only carried out a long-standing affair with Harold Macmillan's wife Dorothy, but also attended homosexual parties and shared a lover with gay gangster Ronnie Kray. The trial of Liberal Leader Jeremy Thorpe for the attempted murder of his gay lover, Norman Scott, electrified the nation but probably in a fashion that reinforced homophobia rather than diminishing it. In 1973, Labour MP Maureen Colhoun left her husband and children and came out as a lesbian; she was subsequently shamed and deselected by her local constituency.

Margaret Thatcher was fairly tolerant of the sexual peccadillos of her colleagues but regarded homosexuality as a threat to the traditional family. She was also opposed to adverts in the 1980s warning of the dangers of AIDS if they mentioned any acts of gay sex. She was certainly hostile to gay culture, writing, 'Homosexual activists have moved from seeking a right to privacy to demanding social approval for the "gay" lifestyle, equal status with the heterosexual family and even the legal right to exploit the adolescent uncertainty of adolescents' (Hertner, 2022, p.257).

But Thatcher was trying to reverse a movement already well under way, with the popularity of gay pop singers like Boy George and androgenous ones like David Bowie reducing hostility to gay life. The AIDS 'plague' engendered perhaps more sympathy than disgust, especially the film *Philadelphia*, which featured Tom Hanks as a tragic AIDS fatality. In 1997, Steven Twigg sensationally defeated Michael Portillo in Labour's landslide victory. But there was a further symbolism to the victory: Twigg was openly homosexual whereas the defeated Portillo was someone with gay experience who insisted on remaining in the closet. The very next day Chris Smith came out as the first openly gay Secretary of State. The barriers were falling in one of the most rapid and complete U-turns in British cultural attitudes. In 1998, in a *Newsnight* interview with Jeremy Paxman, Mathew Parris, himself gay, outed Peter Mandelson, whose homosexuality was already fairly well known; it seems those who had survived the years when their sexuality was illegal still found it difficult to come out publicly when this had ceased to be. New Labour emphasised its liberal attitudes to LGBTQ+ people by repealing, in 2003, Section 28 of the Local Government Act, which had banned schools from 'promoting homosexuality' – in practice, mentioning homosexuality existed at all. At this time the Conservatives were hanging on to very illiberal social attitudes – being dubbed in 2002 'the nasty party' by Theresa May – and David Cameron set about modernising the party he led after 2005. Not only did he open the door widely to more woman candidates but also softened attitudes towards LGBTQ+ people. He continued this liberal approach when in government after 2010 and enabled gay marriage in 2013 with the Marriage (Same Sex) Couples Act, though less half of his MPs voted for it.

Guardian journalist, David Shariatmadari, calls this cultural transformation by 2015, 'the quiet revolution' and notes that 'Gay MPs were tolerated as long as discretion ruled.' But other MPs had joined the crusade – Edwina Currie tabled an amendment to reduce the age of consent for gay men down from 21 to 16 years – there was no such law applying to lesbians. The amendment failed but John Major and Michael Howard supported it and the former later met Ian McKellen in Downing Street for discussions. 'By the time Labour were in power, it was clear that society had changed dramatically' (Shariatmadari, 2015). In 2017, 45 LGBTQ+ MPs were elected to the Commons: 7 per cent of the whole membership. In the USA, only seven members of Congress are openly gay but, in Ireland, which decriminalised same sex relations as recently as 1993, Leo Varadkar, has been Ireland's Taoisoch. Additionally, Elio Di Rupo became Belgium's PM, Johanna Sigurdoardottir was elected PM in Iceland, as was Xavier Bettle in Luxembourg. Leading Labour MPs who are gay, are Chris Bryant, Ben Bradshaw, Wes Streeting and Angela Eagle; finally, in 2019 (Lord) Andrew Adonis came out as gay.

Chris Smith, that first openly gay Cabinet minister, accused Boris Johnson of having a 'blind spot' when it came to appointing LGBTQ+ people to his Cabinet and said that it was 'a matter of great regret' that there were no such 'out' members in his 'top team' in February 2021 (Parker, 2021). This is not to say no Conservative LGBTQ+ MPs have served as ministers in recent Conservative governments: Justine Greening (Secretary of State for Education 2016–18), David Mundell (Secretary of State for Scotland 2015–19), Nick Boles (Minister for Skills 2014–16), Conor Burns (Minister of State for Northern Ireland 2019–20 and Trade September to October 2022) and Chris Pincher (Deputy Chief Whip February to June 2022). Chris Smith's criticism was correct up to a point: Boles was appointed by Cameron, Greening and Mundell by Theresa May but Burns was a Johnson appointee as was Pincher, though the row over his alleged drunken harassment of young men – Boris is said to have commented 'Pincher by name pincher by nature' – led directly to the former PM's defenestration. It is now commonplace for LGBTQ+ people to become MPs in either Labour, Conservatives or Lib Dem (David Laws, Chief Secretary Treasury 10–29 May 2010 and Simon Hughes Minister of State for Justice and Civil Liberties, 2013–15, plus Layla Moran MP) and it proves no impediment to promotion from the back benches into ministerial office.

Promotion of ethnic minorities in British government

Given that our country was invaded and imperially took over so many countries from Elizabethan times onwards, there is something appropriate, maybe tinged with justice, that on 24 October 2022 someone of Indian heritage should have arisen to the highest political office in the land. The journey to this appointment represents is a long one and involves the gradual erosion of discriminatory attitudes that have caused so much social dislocation at various times in the past century. As with women, increasing ethnic diversity in UK politics begins with the number elected to Parliament, given the British system of limiting its ministerial recruitment pool to those in the legislature. Inevitably immigration, especially from once-colonial dependencies since the end of the Second World War, has vastly increased the number of ethnic groupings in the UK. Of course the British Isles were originally populated two millennia ago by early tribes like the Celts and Picts then by the Romans; their kingdoms being overwhelmed by waves of incoming tribes including the Anglo-Saxons, then the Vikings from Scandinavia and the conquering Normans – descended from Vikings – from France. At various stages there were influxes of immigrants: Jewish people with William the Conqueror but then expelled by Edward I only to be allowed back in by Cromwell; Huguenots from France; Irish people during the nineteenth century, plus Jews fleeing pogroms in Russia and Poland, and smaller numbers, of imperial provenance, from Africa via the slave trade, China and other parts of Asia plus the Middle East.

It's fair to say this earlier immigration was absorbed slowly over centuries but then things began to speed up rapidly. After 1945, there was the Windrush generation entering from the Caribbean – invited to help rebuild Britain – and in later decades substantial immigration from India and Pakistan; and finally an influx of Eastern European immigrants during the first two decades of the present century. In 1950, only 0.1 per cent of the population differed from the majority white population: by 1961 the figure was 0.8 per cent; by 1981, 3.9 per cent; and by 2021, 14.4 per cent of the UK population was from a minority varying from 2.2 per cent for Northern Ireland and 16.1 per cent for England (ONS figures see Jones, 2021, and Figure 10.2).

Not all immigrants have looked so very different from the dominant white population but those with brown or black skins have had to endure substantial hostile prejudice. This has meant that it has taken quite a long

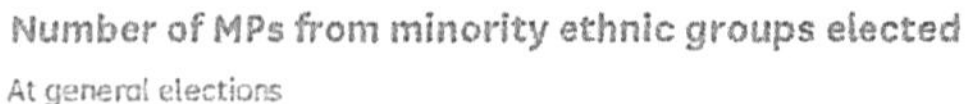

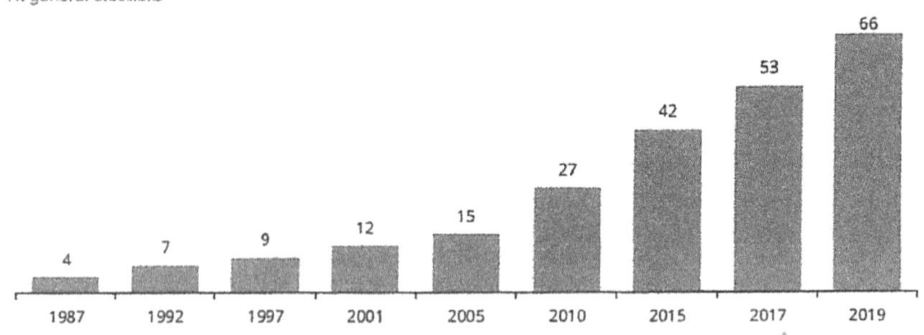

Source: British Future (2019), House of Commons Library Briefing Paper CBP7529, UK Election Statistics: 1918-2019

FIGURE 10.2 Ethnic diversity in politics and public life

Source: Uberoi and Carthew (2022), © House of Commons Library, 2023.

time for this latter group of ethnic minorities to become integrated and represented in the political system.

Ethnic minorities in the legislature

The modern increase in ethnic minority MPs since the latter twentieth century has been dramatic, as Figure 10.2 illustrated. Numbers increased from only four in 1987 – Diane Abbott, Paul Boateng, Bernie Grant and Keith Vaz – to 12 in 2001, then 27 in 2010, 47 in 2015 and then 66 in 2019. Of those, 41 were Labour (62 per cent) and 23 Conservative (35 per cent); two Lib Dem MPs were of the same provenance; 37 out of the 66, women. Nobody can deny that racist attitudes towards black and brown people have at governmental level disappeared but among voters majorities for such candidates have increasingly been registered all over the country.

Ethnic minorities in executive office

Many would cite the earliest example of an ethnic minority in the Commons was Benjamin Disraeli, someone of Sephardic Jewish background who converted to Christianity to advance his political career. He became a famous PM, of course, though he was not the first Jewish MP. Samson Gideon, son of a Jewish City of London banker served as an MP 1770–1802; Lionel Rothschild was the first practising Jew to take his seat in 1858. The first example of an ethnic minority MP who came close to becoming a minister was Sir Ernest Soares (1864–1926) who was of Portuguese/Brazilian origin.

Son of a Liverpool merchant, he attended St John's College Cambridge from where he managed to leave with a third-class degree in law, becoming a Manchester solicitor in 1888. He was active in the Liberal Party and elected for Barnstable in 1905, becoming PPS (unpaid – the lowest rung of the ministerial ladder) to the Home Secretary Herbert Gladstone. Baron Sinha of Raipur, a hereditary peer, was the first peer from an ethnic minority background to be elevated in 1919 to the House of Lords and in the same year he also became a PUS for India.

Ethnic minority groups had to wait another 77 years for the next person to be listed from their ranks as a government minister and that was someone who seemed to most people as quintessentially English: Sebastian Coe. According to the House of Commons paper 'Ethnic Diversity in Politics and Public Life' (Uberoi and Burton, 2022), the famous athlete was elected as a Conservative MP in 1992 for Falmouth and Cambourne and was made an Assistant Whip in 1996; such a classification of someone appearing so quintessentially English might seem odd but is made because his mother was half Indian. He lost his seat in Labour's 1997 landslide but was elevated to the peerage in May 2000. Next on the list was Paul Boateng who in 1997 was elected for Brent 1987–2005 and was the first ethnic minority politician to become a member of the Cabinet (as Chief Secretary to the Treasury). Next came a clutch of Labour ministers: Keith Vaz, David Lammy, Parmjit Dhanda, Sadiq Khan, Shahid Malik and Dawn Butler. Of these last named, Keith Vaz and Sadiq Khan rose to the position of Minister of State and went on to become Mayor of London but the others achieved only PUS-level appointments.

It might seem counter-intuitive for the Conservatives as the less 'progressive' or liberal party to, first, have placed three women in Number 10 and, second, to have placed so many ethnic minority Tory MPs in their Cabinets: Priti Patel, Kwasi Kwarteng, Nadhim Zahawi, Alok Sharma, James Cleverly, Kemi Badenoch and Ranil Jayawardena. Of course the most important promotion has been that of Rishi Sunak to the topmost job in British politics – PM. Born in Southampton to Hindu parents of Punjabi descent, he followed the traditional upper-middle-class route to success – prep school and Winchester College, where he became head boy, before going on to Oxford and gaining a first in PPE: in other words he followed the classic background for a British elite member with which to enter the world of politics. He also studied in America at Stanford University where he met his future wife, Akshata Murty, the daughter of Indian billionaire R.N. Narayana, founder of Infosys.

After a spell working for Goldman Sachs, a hedge fund in the USA and for his father-in-law, he entered Parliament in 2017 via William Hague's old seat of Richmond in Yorkshire. He was soon given office, serving as PUS for local government under May and then Chief Secretary to the Treasury under Johnson 2019–20. This was followed by a meteoric promotion, replacing

Sajid Javid as Chancellor in February 2020. He was feted by the press and the public for issuing generous assistance to those suffering from the Covid-19 pandemic and became that rare thing: a very popular politician.

However his popularity took a knock when it was revealed his heiress wife had not being paying UK tax on her income from shares in her father's company through her privileged non-dom status. As Johnson's star began to fall Sunak was (perhaps unfairly?) fined by police for also attending a Partygate event, but when the Johnson ship began to sink it seemed clear he was interested in taking his former boss's place. His first contest against Liz Truss was bruising. He attacked Truss's planned tax cuts as completely mad and became quite animated in some of the debates, probably appearing too aggressive. Tory members, who had the power to elect the new PM, were not so impressed by Sunak, some of them resentful at what they thought was his strategic resignation in order to bring down Johnson and then take his place. Whether they had doubts about a Hindu of Indian descent becoming the country's top-elected official is not at all clear but it was obvious senior Tories did not want their members to vote again after the debacle of Liz Truss. Sunak was elected by his MP colleagues, infuriating many party members who felt disenfranchised. The BBC reported a lifelong Tory voter, a Mr Mathews, ripping up his membership card and claiming that 'by selecting someone only six weeks after he lost to Ms Truss, Tory MPs had gone against the "express wishes of the grassroots" ' (Nevett, 2022). But Sunak had won an astonishing victory, coming back from the dead against Truss: all his criticisms of Truss's policies had seemed to have been proved right and he was expected to calm down the tempers and get the government back on some kind of sensible trajectory.

Was his rise to the top job so remarkable? Indian media sources reported great surprise and satisfaction at one of their own becoming the PM of their former colonial master. Labour mostly applauded the diversity aspect of Sunak's elevation but commentators on the left were quick to add qualifications. Nesrine Malik in the *Guardian*'s welcome was cautious indeed:

> If having the first brown prime minister whose household is richer than the king, whose politics penalise asylum seekers and the poorest members of society, was what was required to unlock this realisation then I'll take it. A win is a win.
>
> *(Malik 2022)*

The *New York Times* took something of the same approach, pointing out that Sunak took his oath of office on the *Gita*, a book of Hindu scripture. It also stressed his elite education, employment in banking and hedge funds plus his marriage to the 'daughter of one of India's wealthiest men' (Specia and Kwai, 2022).

Concluding comment

Liz Truss was only in post for a record short six weeks but she might still treasure one feature of her brief sojourn at the 'top of the pole': 'the most diverse cabinet ever' (Bland, 2022). As Bland points out: 'In 2001 91% of Conservative MPs were male and every single one of them was white.' But with Kwasi Kwarteng as Chancellor, James Cleverly as Foreign Secretary and Suella Braverman as Home Secretary, none of the four most senior jobs in British government was held by a white man. Cameron's priority A list, drawn up in 2005, encouraged local associations to consider good candidates from different ethnic backgrounds. In Johnson's last Cabinet one in five members was from a minority background. Ethnic minorities in relation to all MPs was a ratio of 1 in 15, and of party members one of 1 in 33. This contrasts with Labour, which in 2019 won 64 per cent of ethnic minority voters compared with the Conservatives' 20 per cent. Bland, however, points out that such facts do not mean Tories will necessarily have liberal views on immigrants: Braverman supported Patel's Rwanda deportation policy and Sajid Javid's decision to revoke the citizenship of Shamina Begum (Bland, 2022).

References and further reading

Beaumont, C. (2020) 'Women in parliament from 1918–2020'. British Library, 23 October.

Bertram, C. (2020) 'How Oscar Wilde's libel trial backfired and ruined his life'. Biography, 15 July. www.biography.com/authors-writers/oscar-wilde-trials-downfall-gross-indecency.

Bland, A. (2022) 'Wednesday briefing: Liz Truss has appointed the most diverse cabinet ever. What does that mean?' *Guardian*, 7 September.

Browning, S. (2019) 'Women in politics and public life'. House of Commons Library, 4 March. https://commonslibrary.parliament.uk/research-briefings/sn01250/.

Buchanan, I. (2024) 'Women in politics and public life'. Research Briefing no. 01250, House of Commons Library, 6 March. https://researchbriefings.files.parliament.uk/documents/SN01250/SN01250.pdf.

Chan, E. (2018) '"I curled up in a ball and thought that's it": Labour MP Angela Rayner reveals the heart-wrenching moment she was told her son Charlie "wouldn't survive" after he was born at just 23 weeks'. *Mail Online*, 18 January.

Cole, H. and Heale, J. (2022) *Out of the Blue: The Inside Story of the Unexpected Rise and Rapid Fall of Liz Truss*. HarperCollins.

Cowley, P. (2005) *The Rebels: How Blair Lost His Majority*. Politico's.

Evennett, H. (2022) 'Women, hereditary peerages and gender inequality in the line of succession'. House of Lords Library, 3 October. https://lordslibrary.parliament.uk/women-hereditary-peerages-and-gender-inequality-in-the-line-of-succession/.

Green, J. (1982) *The Book of Political Quotes*. Angus & Robertson.

Harmon, H. (2019) 'Why there has never been a female Labour leader: And why the time is now'. *Harper's Bazaar*, 8 March.

Hertner, I. (2022) 'Gender and British politics', in B. Jones, P. Norton and I. Herner (eds), pp. 245–261. *Politics UK*. Routledge.
Inter-Parliamentary Union (2021) 'Women in politics: New data shows growth but also setbacks'. 10 March. www.ipu.org/news/women-in-politics-2021.
Jones, I. (2021) 'Latest figures on ethnic diversity in the UK'. Yahoo! News, 31 March.
Kenny, M. (2018) 'From Thatcher to May and beyond: Women in British politics', in N. Allan and J. Battle (eds), *None Past the Post: Britain at the Polls 2017*, pp. 121–140. Manchester University Press.
McClure, P. (2019) 'Sexual orientation, UK: 2019'. Office for National Statistics. www.ons.gov.uk/peoplepopulationandcommunity/culturalidentity/sexuality/bulletins/sexualidentityuk/2019.
Malik, N. (2022) 'Yes, Sunak at No 10 is a "win": In exposing the emptiness of elite diversity rhetoric'. *Guardian*, 31 October.
Merelli, A. (2018) 'The LGBT political glass ceiling is cracking wide open'. Quartz, 20 June.
Morgan, T. and Whithead, T. (2015) 'The spy files: Lord Boothby's sordid sex parties with Ronnie Kray revealed in MI5 files'. *Daily Telegraph*, 23 October.
Nevett, J. (2022) 'Tory members vent fury at Rishi Sunak's coronation by MPs'. BBC News, 25 October.
O'Hagan, S. (2023) 'Eyes on the prize'. *The Times*, 16 July.
Parker, J. (2021) 'Johnson has LGBT "blind spot", says first openly gay cabinet minister'. BBC News, 24 February.
Pearse, A. (2015) 'Here's an important reason why Labour has never chosen a female leader'. *Spectator*, 25 August.
Reeves, R. (2019) *Women of Westminster*. Bloomsbury.
Shariatmadari, D. (2015) 'The quiet revolution: Why Britain has more gay MPs than anywhere else'. *Guardian*, 13 May.
Specia, M. and Kwai, I. (2022) 'Sunak's ascent is a breakthrough for diversity with privilege attached'. *New York Times*, 24 October.
Theakston, K. (1987) *Junior Ministers*. Blackwell.
Uberoi, E. and Carthew, H. (2022) 'Ethnic diversity in politics and public life'. Research Briefing no. 01156. House of Commons Library, 30 September. https://researchbriefings.files.parliament.uk/documents/SN01156/SN01156.pdf.

11

'PROMOTION VELOCITY' AND THE 'BORIS PROBLEM'

> I have climbed to the top of the greasy pole.
>
> (Benjamin Disraeli on becoming PM; Gov.uk, n.d.)

> Nicholas Soames says Boris Johnson is 'no Churchill' and his 'dismal' Cabinet is 'the worst in 36 years'.
>
> (Tapsfield, 2020)

> I want Boris to become Tory leader because he will make politics fun!
>
> (BBC interviewee quoted by Max Hastings; Hastings, 2023)

Cabinets, 1945–2023

This section is a short note of the social provenance and composition of selected recent Cabinets and the number of years it took their members to gain promotion to this level; I'm calling this their comparative 'promotion velocities' (thanks to my brother Pete for suggesting this concept).

Attlee's Cabinet, 1945–50

This group reflects the wide social range of those recruited for Labour's first post-war Cabinet and the great achievements represented by some of its members. They included Labour's first woman in the Cabinet since Margaret Bondfield (1929–31) – Ellen Wilkinson was appointed in 1945, and survived two years as Education Secretary before her death in 1947. Working-class membership was, perhaps surprisingly, similar to Ramsey MacDonald's two short ministries at 11 (1924) and 12 (1929–31; see Table 11.1, below) and

DOI: 10.4324/9781003405085-12

it is easy to forget contained Jack Lawson, a miner, with ten siblings who left school for the mines aged 12, Tom Williams who also went down the mines aged 12 and Nye Bevan aged 14. George Isaacs, Arthur Greenwood, Manny Shinwell, A.V. Alexander and Joseph Westwood were also working class and received very little formal education. 'Red' Ellen Wilkinson was also from the poor working class but was able to win a scholarship to Manchester University. Similarly James Chuter Ede was working class and won a scholarship to Cambridge but had to drop out after a year as his living expenses were not covered. Working-class Greenwood attended Leeds University while Shinwell was virtually self-educated.

At the other end of the social scale came the so-called middle-class intellectuals who attended public schools. There were three old Etonians – Dalton, Lord Listowel and Lord Pakenham – who, inevitably perhaps, attended Oxbridge (where the future Mary Whitehouse supporter, Lord Longford, astonishingly was once a member of the Bullingdon Club). Others were Sir Stafford Cripps (Winchester and UCL), Viscount Stansgate (Tony Benn's father) originally elected a Liberal MP in 1906 and then joined Labour in 1928, Pethick Lawrence (Eton and Cambridge), Viscount Jowitt (Marlborough and Oxford) and Attlee himself (Haileybury and Oxford). Three of Attlee's Cabinet members preceded their parliamentary membership with service in local government. An interesting insight on the political side of promotion is seen in Attlee's treatment of George Brown, a fierce young MP and close to Ernest Bevin who, in 1947, had plotted to replace Attlee with his mentor. The plot failed but Attlee, maybe to keep him busy and bound by ministerial loyalty, made him a PUS in Agriculture and Fisheries where he soon showed his ability. Noting his talent, Attlee promoted him to Minister of Works – a non-Cabinet role – in 1951 in the wake of Bevin's death.

Churchill and Eden Cabinets, 1951–57

These two Cabinets were significant for their high number of public school members including 11 Etonians, 3 Harrovians and 2 Wykehamists; 12 went to Oxford, 5 to Cambridge and 4 to Sandhurst. Seven members were peers of the realm, one of whom, remarkably perhaps, was Lord Leathers. This former businessman had been born in Stepney, a poor part of London, and had no elite education of any kind but was deemed 'a very remarkable man' by Winston Churchill who spotted his talent when a director of a subsidiary of Peninsular and Oriental shipping lines in 1930 (Churchill, 1966, p.132). He was elevated to the peerage in 1941 and made Minister of War Transport – accompanying the PM to the Yalta and Potsdam conferences: he later served in Cabinet 1951–53 as Minister for Coordination of Transport, Fuel and Power. He is significant, of course, because he sat among all these old Etonians and aristocratic types only because of that chance meeting.

How many other talented men and women, one reflects, were never even detected, let alone considered, and even if they had been, would anyone but Churchill have been able to parachute them into the British Cabinet? Both the immediate post-war administrations included only one woman each: Ellen Wilkinson and Florence Horsburgh; however, from this slow beginning, as shown in Chapter 10 the pace of female promotion to the Cabinet gradually gathered force.

These two sets of Cabinet memberships reflect an age when British social mobility, catalysed by the war, was at an important cusp. Attlee's landslide victory had ushered in a new era where working men with scant formal education could become part of a new elite. Churchill's Cabinets on the other hand manifested the last gasp of an era when Eton- and Oxbridge-educated men – with one exception no women as yet – smoothly slotted into the highest positions of national control. Eden's short administration foreshortened by the Suez fiasco, appointed a Cabinet including 11 old Etonians, 16 university educated men (14 of whom attended Oxbridge), no women and no working-class members.

Cabinets compared

It is interesting to compare the dramatic change in social composition between post-war Cabinets and those in the twenty-first century (see Table 11.1). The most striking difference between the Attlee–Churchill and the decades later Brown–Cameron Cabinets in terms of social background is reflected in the reduction of old Etonians from seven to one – Gordon Brown on zero, though the number of public school attendees remained roughly similar for the 1951 and Coalition Cabinets at 14 and 12 respectively: Brown's Cabinet had only four. The number of university-educated members increased from 11 to 20, with Brown's Cabinet on 22, reflecting the increasing percentage of university graduates over this half-century period: elite Oxbridge graduates increasing from 9 to 15 for Churchill and the Coalition and Brown's surprisingly close on 11. In 1951 there was only one female Cabinet member – in 2010 it was seven; Tony Blair had nine of his so-called babes in his first Cabinet; seven working-class members, eight public school-educated though none from Eton, only three Oxbridge graduates but 20 university-educated members. Gordon Brown had five women: if those attending Cabinet are included, the number was eight. Churchill had only one working-class member: David Cameron two. Churchill one woman: Cameron eight. Churchill and Brown chose no ethnic minority member at all but the Coalition contained just one of the many to come in future Tory administrations.

Cameron's 2015 Cabinet displayed a step change in Cabinets for both of the big parties in two respects containing, surprisingly, five working-class members, no less than eight women and two ethnic minority members.

TABLE 11.1 Social and educational composition of British Cabinets, 1895–2016

			Class				*Education*			
			No.	*Aris.*	*Mid.*	*Work.*	*PS*	*Eton*	*Univ.*	*O&C*
Aug.	1895 Con.	Salisbury	19	8	11	–	16	7	15	14
Jul.	1902 Con.	Balfour	19	9	10	–	16	9	14	13
Dec.	1905 Lib.	Campbell-Bannerman	19	7	11	1	11	3	14	12
Jul.	1914 Lib.	Asquith	19	6	12	1	11	3	15	13
Jan.	1919 Coal.	Lloyd George	21	3	17	1	12	2	13	8
Nov.	1922 Con.	Bonar Law	16	8	8	–	14	8	13	13
Jan.	1924 Lab.	MacDonald	19	3	5	11	8	–	6	6
Nov.	1924 Con.	Baldwin	21	9	12	–	21	7	16	16
Jan.	1929 Lab.	MacDonald	18	2	4	12	5	–	6	3
Aug.	1931 Nat.	MacDonald	20	8	10	2	13	6	11	10
Jun.	1935 Con.	Baldwin	22	9	11	2	14	9	11	10
May	1937 Con.	Chamberlain	21	8	13	–	17	8	16	13
May	1945 Con.	Churchill	16	6	9	1	14	7	11	9
Aug.	1945 Lab.	Attlee	20	–	8	12	5	2	10	5
Oct.	1951 Con.	Churchill	16	5	11	–	14	7	11	9
Apr.	1955 Con.	Eden	18	5	13	–	18	10	16	14
Jan.	1957 Con.	Macmillan	18	4	14	–	17	8	16	15
Oct.	1963 Con.	Home	24	5	19	–	21	11	17	17
Oct.	1964 Lab.	Wilson	23	1	14	8	8	1	13	11
Jun.	1970 Con.	Heath	18	4	14	–	15	4	15	15
Mar.	1974 Lab.	Wilson	21	1	16	4	7	–	16	11
Apr.	1976 Lab.	Callaghan	22	1	13	8	7	–	15	10
May	1979 Con.	Thatcher	22	3	19	–	20	6	18	17
Nov.	1990 Con.	Major	22	3	17	2	14	2	20	17

May	1997 Lab.	Blair	22	–	15	11	8	–	21	3
Jun.	2007 Lab.	Brown	23	–	22	1	4	–	22	11
May	2010 Coal.	Cameron	23	1	20	2	12	1	20	15
May	2015 Con.	Cameron	22	–	17	5	10	2	19	12
Jul.	2016 Con.	May	22	–	17	5	5	1	21	10
Average 29 Cabinets			20	4	13	3	12	4	15	11
		16 Con. Cabinets	20	5	13	1	15	7	16	13
		8 Lab. Cabinets	21	1	12	8	7	0.4	14	7
		2 Lib. Cabinets	19	6.5	11.5	1	11	3	14.5	12.5

Source: adapted from Mortimore and Blick (2018, p.101). The early part of this table is largely based on Guttsman (1963).

Aris.: *Aristocrats* are those who had among their grandparents the holder of a hereditary title.
Mid.: *Middle class*.
Work.: *Working class* are those whose parent(s) appear to have had a manual occupation when they were growing up.
PS: *Schools* are classified as public schools if members of the Headmasters' & Headmistresses' Conference or the Girls' Schools Association.
O&C: Oxford and Cambridge Universities.

Theresa May's Cabinet was similarly diverse with five public school members, five working class but only one ethnic minority, Sajid Javid.

Johnson's first Cabinet: some observations

This contained three working-class members and seven women, though 11 if those attending Cabinet are included. Johnson's Cabinet and, indeed, his Number 10 staff, contained a fair number of Leave supporters active in the Brexit campaign. The former included Dominic Raab, Priti Patel (once Head Press Officer, way back for Goldsmith's Referendum Party), Andrea Leadsom (who worked hard to obtain Commons approval of May's Brexit deal) and Theresa Villiers (a Brexiteer veteran). Number 10 Leave aides included: Dominic Cummings (head of Vote Leave with supervisory authority over all spads), Lee Cain (Head broadcasting Vote Leave) plus Ben Gascoigne, Nikka Da Costa, Robert Oxley, Lucia Hodgson, Chloe Westley, Oliver Lewis and Damon Poole (Wickham, 2019).

Interestingly three of Johnson's rivals in the 2019 leadership contest, Dominic Raab, Sajid Javid – not uncritical of Johnson – and Matt Hancock, once voted out, all conveniently switched their support to Johnson and were rewarded with Cabinet places. Javid's role as Chancellor, however, did not last long: Johnson and Cummings insisted he sack his senior aides and replace them with Number 10 nominees. 'I don't believe any self-respecting minister would accept those conditions', he said when resigning (Georgiadis et al., 2020). He was instantly replaced by Rishi Sunak, previously a Brexit-supporting Chief Secretary to the Treasury, continuing his meteoric rise through the ranks to become Chancellor. He was hugely popular during the pandemic for his furlough subsidy to mitigate salary losses – then a losing candidate to Liz Truss in the contest for Johnson's job when he resigned in July 2022 and finally PM, 25 October 2022, when Truss's 49-day passage through Downing Street came to an ignominious end.

Johnson's Cabinet was surprisingly diverse regarding class and gender: three members of ethnic minorities –Patel, Javid and Sunak. Interestingly, many Jewish people have risen high in British politics as they have in just about every area of society but as a 'white' social group they are often so well integrated their ethnicity is rarely mentioned – think of Sir Keith Joseph, Nigel Lawson and Leon Brittan – and in Johnson's Cabinet, Raab and Grant Shapps. This has not stopped some Jewish MPs, of course, being viciously targeted by online anti-Semitic trolls.

Cabinet university background is interesting under Johnson: 20 of the 27 Cabinet members (includes those with rights of attendance) were university educated with 12 attending Oxbridge. In his biography of Nigel Farage, Michael Crick alights on the United Kingdom Independence Party's (UKIP) member of the European Parliament candidate list for South West England, George Eustice, in bottom place, a 27-year-old fruit farmer who entered Parliament in 2010 and in 2020 became Secretary of State for Environment, Food and Rural Affairs (Crick, 2022, p.86). He is also the only graduate of Writtle University College, founded in 1893 and which attained university college status in 2016.

Johnson's 'caretaker' Cabinet, July 2022

Johnson's controversial 'caretaker' Cabinet was formed once he had resigned but allowed to continue in office until his successor was appointed. Priti Patel became Home Secretary, Liz Truss replaced Raab as Foreign Secretary from September 2021, Kit Malthouse, an old friend of Johnson from his mayoral days, was brought in as Chancellor of the Duchy of Lancaster, Steve Barclay replaced Javid as Health Secretary, Nadhim Zahawi, whose desire to support whoever was PM or about to become so had caused him some confusion, delightedly became Chancellor in place of Sunak, though this last was an appointment that struck some as a sign of desperation. Shailesh Vara added to the diversity of this briefly assembled team, becoming Northern Ireland Secretary, 7 July 2022, before being dismissed by Liz Truss on 6 September following her victory over Sunak in the leadership contest.

Truss's Cabinet

This Cabinet team survived for the historically shortest period of 49 days but was initially praised as being 'the most diverse ever' (Bland, 2022). Truss, of course, was the UK's third female PM and Kate Nicholson in the *HuffPost* noted that, in addition: Truss had 'a large majority [68 per cent] of privately educated ministers'; she had 'booted out almost everyone who supported Rishi Sunak' (in the contest she had recently won); 'while rewarding her most loyal supporters'. She also observed that Truss was 'the first in UK history not to have a white man holding one of the "great offices of state" '; these being James Cleverly as Foreign Secretary, Suella Braverman as Home Secretary and Kwasi Kwarteng as Chancellor (Nicholson, 2022). After their first debate both Truss and Sunak affirmed they would be happy working together: evidence of this rather false bonhomie was revealed by both PMs excluding their rivals from their first Cabinets. Those making Truss's Cabinet for the first time must look back ruefully on their farcically ephemeral elevations, just as Truss consoled herself revealingly with the thought that, 'at least I've been prime minister' (Owen and Pierce, 2022). It is from such ambitions that political careers, long or short, great or ignoble, are made.

Sunak's Cabinet

Sunak's Cabinet was created in the wake of possibly the period of greatest political turmoil since the fall of Thatcher. His reappointment of Jeremy Hunt as Chancellor – it was rumoured he personally favoured Oliver Dowden or Mel Stride – indicated a search for stability: denying Penny Mordaunt a promotion but keeping her as Leader of the Commons plus recalling the talented Michael Gove also reflected stability and continuity. Dominic Raab was brought back in as Deputy PM and Justice Secretary. Suella Braverman was rewarded for her key support – she was believed to have crucially softened the views of some right-wing opponents who thought Sunak had brought Johnson down. Braverman's appointment was controversial – not just because of her right-wing credentials but because she had been forced to resign only six days earlier for a security breach.

Therese Coffey was moved from being Liz Truss's Deputy PM and Health Minister to Environment. Sunak's sackings from the Truss Cabinet included the close supporter of the two previous PMs, Jacob Rees-Mogg, who pre-empted his exit with a hand-written resignation letter; Kit Malthouse, another Johnson intimate, was dumped as well as Robert Buckland who had originally backed Sunak but then switched to Liz Truss – presumably with an eye to a big job – but thereby ruled himself out of consideration. Such are the penalties for backing the wrong horse in prime ministerial contests. Sunak's top team included five women and five from non-white ethnic backgrounds. Despite the absence of any old Etonians, the social background of Sunak's team did nothing to offset the widespread awareness of his considerable wealth: according to the Sutton Trust, 19 of 31 Cabinet members were privately educated – 61 per cent – twice as much as Theresa May's Cabinet of 30 per cent and more than Cameron's 50 per cent (Tapper, 2023). Writing in the *Sunday Times*, Tom Newton Dunn compared 'Establishment' looking Keir Starmer and his working-class deputy with Sunak and his deputy, Dominic Raab, suggesting the PM needed to appoint a non-privately educated woman, possibly Gillian Keegan (Newton Dunn, 2023).

Promotion velocity

By this term I mean the number of years it took MPs to travel from their first entry into either Chamber of Parliament to their arriving into the Cabinet. This very general figure can include years spent out of politics after electoral defeat, absence through illness and those brought in via reshuffles. When an opposition finally wins an election after a long break, several MPs can enter Cabinet with little or no previous government experience: with the exceptional case of the great trade unionist, Ernest Bevin, who entered the War Cabinet in 1940 without any experience even as an MP, since his Commons membership was arranged via an unopposed election for Wandsworth Central. Some ministerial jobs were not always part of the Cabinet so, while John Strachey served as Secretary of State for War, he was, for this reason, not a Cabinet member. There is some evidence that MPs elected in the same year experience a sense of competition with each other as they rise through the ranks. However, in some cases, politicians are forced to sit out some parliamentary terms through loss of their seats – like Dalton and Manny Shinwell – or in earlier decades have changed parties: for example Churchill, Addison and Benn's father, William Stansgate.

The average time taken to reach Cabinet status in Attlee's two ministries was 16.6 years. Those waiting over 20 years to reach the Cabinet comprised six working class MPs – including Labour's first woman Cabinet member, Ellen Wilkinson – and two public schoolboys (Dalton and Pethick Lawrence). Lord Christopher Addison began his interesting political career as a Liberal MP where he became the first Minister of Health in 1919 but then switched to Labour in 1929 where, as a Cabinet member, he refused to join MacDonald's resultant National Government in 1931. Raised to the peerage in 1937 he became Labour Leader in that Chamber, serving briefly in Attlee's second Cabinet 1950–51: it had taken him 35 years to make Cabinet rank, the longest in my period of study. Some politicians were elevated to the Cabinet virtually along with their entry into Parliament – Ernest Bevin being one of the most striking examples but almost equalled by Oliver Littleton, who entered the Commons via a by-election in 1940 and two years later was in the Cabinet: a promotion velocity of only two years, but in untypical wartime conditions.

Churchill and Eden's stints in government reveal an average promotion velocity of 12.4 years, with Gwilym Lloyd George, originally a Liberal, elected in 1922 after which he served in the governments of MacDonald, Neville Chamberlain and Churchill's wartime coalition: after 1945 he drifted into the Conservative Party, becoming Churchill's Home Secretary in 1954, with gaps out of Parliament giving him a promotion velocity of 32 years.

Moving forward into the twenty-first century, the Coalition's promotion velocity average was 11.3 years, Cameron's 2015 Cabinet 11.2 years, Theresa May's 11.7 years, Johnson's 9.0 years, Truss's 7.8 years and Sunak's 9.8 years. So a general downward trajectory can be discerned from the post-war period. This might suggest that the phenomenon of the 'career politician', whereby very ambitious young politicians enter politics very young and proceed to be rapidly promoted and stay in post, might be at work here.

Harold Wilson's two years is the fastest peace-time ascent I can find. Hugh Gaitskell, another with a glowing record as a wartime civil servant, became Minister for Power in 1947 without a seat in the Cabinet though with the right to attend: he made it into Cabinet in 1950, as Chancellor. It is true that Transport and General Workers' Union leader Frank Cousins was parachuted into the Cabinet in 1964 without a Commons seat, something which was soon rectified in 1965. Patrick Gordon Walker, too, who had served in Attlee's government and in shadow positions, was appointed Foreign Secretary despite having lost his Smethwick Commons seat in a controversial 'racist' contest. Reg Sorenson obligingly took up a seat in the Lords but his erstwhile Leyton voters denied the new Foreign Secretary the success many thought would be automatic: he eventually won Leyton in 1966 and went on to serve in Cabinet positions. Perhaps the closest 'velocity' to Wilson's is Clare Coutinho who was promoted to the Cabinet 31st August as S of S for Energy, when Grant Shapps was made Defence Secretary, having been elected 12th December 2019: a promotion velocity time of just over 3.5 three years. Interestingly she too was once a special adviser, who, experience suggests, tend to make the most promotable junior ministers.

As a contrast to those jet propelled promotees mentioned above, it's worth looking at the opposite end of the promotion spectrum. Nick Gibb served as Schools Minister from July 2014 to November 2023 under three different PMs. All that time at the Minister of State level but there was no step up to the Cabinet table, despite having been described as 'the most influential schools minister in England's history' (Clarence-Smith, 2023). He told the *Daily Telegraph* that one of the reasons he didn't make that leap was because he was unable to attend social events and do the networking necessary to become a promotion candidate because he felt he had to keep his gay relationship secret; 'in politics in the 1980s and 1990s, it was absolutely impossible for such a thing to become known' (ibid.).

The Boris problem: democracy's porosity can promote the wrong type of politician

According to his sister Rachel, Boris Johnson wanted to be 'world king' as a child – unlimited dominion over everyone – a sentiment that most parents would recognise in progeny when emerging into their 'toddler' phase, but which in Johnson's case seemed to have persisted throughout his life, forming a foundation plank of his adult psyche. That he was very clever is beyond doubt, as his subsequent Eton and Oxford education amply demonstrated but, whilst many would have been satisfied with his early journalistic success, Boris observed, 'they don't put up statues to journalists' (Peck, 2023): he was after distinctions ranking with eternal greatness. Martin Hammond, Boris's Eton housemaster, famously wrote of him that, 'I think he honestly believes it is churlish of us not to regard him as an exception, one who should be free of the network of obligations which binds everyone else' (O'Toole, 2022).

From Eton he moved on, via a scholarship, to Balliol College Oxford where he read Classics, played (this not so widely known) tight head forward for his college rugby team and became a luminary of the notorious upper-class Bullingdon Club, a hugely well-known campus figure socially, mixing with a wealthy upper-middle-class/aristocratic set and, at his second attempt in 1986, President of the Oxford Union. He was furious to miss a 'first' in Classics – the product of too much socialising and not enough attention to his studies – and left Oxford with an amazing network of contacts but, academically, only a 2:1; a good enough degree for most graduates but not for someone as obsessively ambitious as Johnson. Indeed his apparent mindset invokes the famous Gore Vidal quotation, 'It is not enough that I succeed – others must fail.' He clearly desperately resented the success of others, even one of his own siblings: his sister Rachel it seems had to preface her phone call with a warning of 'bad news' when informing Boris that his younger brother Jo had achieved the glowing prize which had eluded him: an Oxford 'first'.

Seldon and Newell in their definitive study of Johnson's three-plus years in Downing Street define his 'core characteristics' in their first chapter covering their subject's development:

- The ability to 'communicate using charisma and humour with the public far and wide, to read the mood and currents of politics and to inject his inimitable energy into the system to change thinking about what could be achieved'.
- 'An all-consuming self-absorption and self-belief that impelled him to be the most important and visible person and to be impatient of any person, precedent or procedure getting in the way.'
- 'A lack of moral seriousness not mitigated by his razor-sharp intellect and beguiling rhetorical skill. Causes, commitments, colleagues as well as pledges, policies and partners were regarded as merely transitory and transactional' (Seldon and Newell, 2023a, p.11).

After a disastrous week as a management consultant, Johnson was made Brussels correspondent of the *Daily Telegraph* by its editor, Max Hastings, whom he had met whilst at Oxford. From here he delighted *Telegraph* readers with tales of the European Union's foolishness, many of them self-invented to the extent his editor finally had to sack him. Undaunted he next edited the *Spectator* and became an amusingly bumbling – surely self-confected? – star on the BBC's *Have I Got News for You*.

His recruitment of the celebrity culture to his cause has been a major factor in both the damage to others his scrapes have caused as well as his success. Johnson's long-standing affair while editor with a female *Spectator* columnist and the fact that he lied about it to Michael Howard, led to his sacking from his shadow opposition role. Yet he surprisingly defied predictions of his career demise in 2008 by winning the London mayoralty against Ken Livingstone in a Labour city, followed, even more impressively, by a second term in 2012. Within the Tory Party his ability to steal Labour votes earned him the reputation of possessing the so-called Heineken effect: the electoral ability, as in Heineken's famous advert, 'to reach parts' no one else could reach. From being 'form clown' he morphed into national 'lovable rogue', thereby charming millions of voters into placing their crosses alongside his name. His combination of a quirky British sense of humour and a classic education enables him to entertain his audiences with bohemian unorthodoxy while his plentiful use of Latin tags suggests to them – possibly falsely – a reservoir of hidden intellectual talent. Toby Young summed up his close friend's charm:

> Everything he did was laced with the same dry sardonic humour. No one ever gets the impression they are being talked down to by Boris – it's not like he's playing a role and expecting people to be taken in by it.
>
> *(Purnell, 2012, p.244)*

Once in the Commons in 2014 he continued his journalism and his *celebrity* style of politics. His vigorous and typically mendacious leadership of the Leave campaign – to the astonished despair of fellow Etonian David Cameron – in the 2016 referendum alongside Michael Gove and Leave's leader, Dominic Cummings, probably explains why Remain was narrowly defeated. In the chaotic aftermath many thought Johnson would inevitably become PM but Gove's sensational last-minute disavowal of his cause resulted in Theresa May becoming PM instead. Johnson assiduously set out to criticise May and, after she lost her slim majority in her 2017 election debacle, her attempts to pass her Brexit deal offered Johnson the 'rugby ball out of the scrum' for which he had been waiting (O'Flynn, 2022). A despairing May resigned in May 2019 and a contest for her replacement took place. His adoring followers in the wholly unrepresentative Conservative Party membership enabled him to defeat Jeremy Hunt with ease.

Once promoted to Number 10 Johnson appointed Dominic Cummings – a rebellious fellow maverick who, it seemed, also felt that widely accepted rules should not apply to him – as his chief adviser. His urgent political problem was that Nigel Farage's UKIP party was eating up right-flank Tory voters: he needed to reinvent the Conservatives as the *real* Brexit party. This he managed to do by brutally removing the whip from 21 of his MPs who had had the temerity to vote against the possibility of a 'No Deal' Brexit, including such respected 'centrist' figures as former Chancellors Ken Clarke and Philip Hammond, plus the highly able former ministers David Gauke, Greg Clark and Dominic Grieve. In so doing he seriously weakened the experienced and talented centrist One Nation element of his party.

In an attempt to pre-empt time-consuming criticisms while forcing Brexit through, he sought to prorogue Parliament but was foiled when the Supreme Court ruled such a step to be illegal; in his defence he claimed he had received legal advice it would not be so. From hereon Johnson, supported by Cummings, displayed his, at that fraught time, genuine gift for intuiting what voters wanted: priceless for any leading politician. His 'Get Brexit Done' emphasis drew back millions of Tory voters attracted by Nigel Farage's UKIP makeover 'Reform' Party as well as those sick to death of the squabbling over the 2016 referendum's verdict. His so falsely called 'oven-ready' Brexit deal served to effect formal approval but its settlement of the Northern Ireland border proved merely a problem passed on for a later PM to solve. When the general election arrived, courtesy of Jo Swinson's mistaken belief Remain voters would sweep her into Downing Street, he won a stonking great majority of 80 seats, some 40 contributed by a demolished Red Wall of Labour's former stronghold northern seats. In these constituencies, Labour voters decided to change the habits of a lifetime and vote for Boris rather than the left-wing Jeremy Corbyn. Much has been written about Boris Johnson's political magic and his 2019 majority of 80 seats. He had claimed he would 'Get Brexit Done', defeat the threat of the extreme-left Jeremy Corbyn and 'Put Farage back in his box' (Cockroft, 2019). He certainly achieved two of them – Farage had been already bested before the vote according to the pollsters, and on the day Labour was soundly trounced. Rafael Behr shrewdly points out that

> When Johnson replaced Theresa May, he cast his predecessors as a relic of the old politics. She was the last governor of *Remainia* – a country abolished by the Brexit revolution. May's time in office was written off, along with the previous six years when David Cameron had been prime minister.
>
> *(Behr, 2022)*

Johnson was able to take Britain out of the European Union on 31 January 2020 but, given the acute problems still being caused throughout this period by the nature of his Northern Ireland deal, it would be false to claim even by the end of 2022, that Brexit had been wholly achieved.

However, master of all he surveyed in January 2020, Johnson was destined to meet his nemesis in the form of the impossible to predict coronavirus pandemic, which, by February, had established a foothold in the UK. Slow to recognise the true national danger, and unsure at times of how strictly the country needed to be 'locked down', he ordered 'you must stay at home' on 23 March 2020. Johnson suppressed his own doubts about the lockdown but went on successfully to encourage the roll-out of Britain's own effective Covid-19 vaccine; his Chancellor Rishi Sunak also essayed a successful £70 billion furlough scheme to save the jobs that would otherwise have been lost. When Johnson himself caught Covid-19 – he had insisted in shaking hands when visiting hospitals – he was briefly in hospital and his life in danger but he eventually recovered, if visibly weakened. An insight into the limits of his governing skills is provided by Anthony Seldon and Raymond Newell's

Johnson at 10 study. Dominic Raab was drafted in to take the helm during his boss's absence.

> 'In advance we were told about his bullying and shouting', recalls one official. Despite Raab's overly brusque style, most political staff and senior civil servants praised his handling of the situation not least for the contrast with his boss.
>
> *(Seldon and Newell, 2023a, p.212)*

Once the PM was back:

> Officials soon found themselves pining for Raab's ability. "It's astonishing that we were grateful for Raab, because tasks like chairing meetings, being decisive and willing to let people down are so basic, but the prime minister we had just couldn't do them" says one.
>
> *(ibid., p.212)*

None of this was perfect – the limits of his stewardship of the pandemic are meticulously recorded by Arbuthnot et al. (2021) – but Johnson would have certainly survived had his conduct of the pandemic not suddenly blown up in his face over a year later in November 2021 when the *Daily Mirror* reported that illegal social gatherings had been held in Whitehall during Christmas 2020. Johnson denied any parties had taken place and assured the House that any gatherings had occurred well within the rules at the time. However Johnson's decline in satisfaction polls and widespread decline of public trust had perhaps already begun in October 2021 when Tory MP, Owen Paterson, was found by the Standards Commissioner to have made an 'egregious' breach of lobbying rules (Allegretti, 2021). Johnson led calls – prompted to a degree by sympathies regarding the recent suicide of Paterson's wife – to pause any suspension until the structure of such inquiries was reformed. Such blatant and incompetent bending of the rules to save one of their own was a huge own goal. Dominic Cummings, now sacked as Boris's right-hand man, accused his former boss of being like an out of control shopping trolley, veering all over the place.

Johnson's firm stand on supporting Ukraine after February 2022 won plaudits worldwide and added a major plus item but, simultaneously, too many items were also appearing on the debit side. Two such major events were the loss of two by-elections: at Wakefield and, especially, Tiverton and Honiton 24 June. They added to the impression among Tory back benchers that Johnson's magic had departed and that the general election in 2024–25 was now Labour's to lose.

However it was Partygate, as the scandal came to be called, which extended and deepened the crisis, with evidence emerging that Johnson had attended several of these rule-breaking events. Keir Starmer exploited these examples of the rule-makers as rule breakers in Downing Street: they were not following the rules everyone else had loyally obeyed. Labour polls soared and Tory back benchers became very worried until all that was required to topple the PM was the scandal initiated by Chris Pincher's attempts at harassing young men in the Carlton Club, 3 July 2022. On 7 July 2022, when it became clear Johnson had lied about not being told of Pincher's previous offences prior to his appointing him Deputy Chief Whip, mass resignations of half of all ministers from his government caused Johnson finally to resign. Typically, he did so with defiance rather than remorse and finished his resignation speech in the Commons with the suggestion he would soon be back in Number 10. Such a prediction looked less likely once the Privileges Committee's long-awaited report landed.

Looking back on his promotion to Cabinet and then to Number 10, it is extraordinary that Johnson lacked that one essential quality reckoned to be necessary for such progress by most commentators: a high reputation as a parliamentarian. His attendance was sketchy: during his first four years as an MP – 2001–05 – he came only 525th of 659 MPs in terms of just turning up to represent his constituents; he was even worse 2005–08. In any case his style of speaking did not suit the nation's key forum; as sketch writer Quentin Letts testified:

> He was terrible in the Commons, an echoing parody of himself. The Commons sees through you in a way institutions don't. ... You see, Boris isn't angry. You've got to be angry: you've got to feel things as an MP, but there's no soul, no church in him. No belief. Most people don't go into politics out of vanity but maybe he has. It's not a class thing, Jacob Rees Mogg, who's similar in some ways, holds the Commons. He's very clever, he's done his homework and he *feels* it. ... Boris can make very good conference speeches but the Commons is different. You're being challenged, you're quite often playing to an empty house, which is difficult, or you're looking straight at your opponents. Boris was good on HIGNFY but that was effectively as a show biz character. He's not very good when he's up against an audience of real people.
>
> *(Purnell, 2012, pp.232–233)*

In conclusion, Boris Johnson's career as 'anti-politician' politician is a warning that in an age of populism it is too easy for voters to believe that simple solutions, delivered with wit and charm maybe, but not based on reliable evidence, is the way to govern the country. Johnson was and still is a very talented politician but his flaws of minimal respect for the truth, lack of attention to detail and an inability to put in the necessary hours of hard preparatory graft should have ruled him out as a suitable occupant of

Number 10. Tory MPs and party members were deluded for too long that this establishment maverick could work political miracles both for himself, his party and the country as a whole. Seldon and Newell's excellent study, reinforces the fact that he was over-promoted to a job he could not perform to the right level.

> Prime Ministers are all inclined to speak hyperbolic words in their moment of victory, and perhaps we shouldn't hold them to the letter of what they said. But equally Johnson did utter the words and they bear repeating: 'Everything I do as Prime Minister will be devoted to repaying that trust.' Ultimately, it was because that trust to voters was not repaid, or honoured, that he could do nothing more as Prime Minister and had to resign.
>
> *(Seldon and Newell, 2023a, p.136)*

When departing from office Johnson showed no contrition at misdemeanours, more like defiance at being rejected: his claim that his defenestration was 'the biggest stitch-up since the Bayeux Tapestry' was straight out of the Trump playbook (Wilcock, 2022). Finally his Resignation Honours list contained the usual depressing mix of cronies and relatives; nothing, perhaps, so became his time in Downing Street as his manner of leaving it. Indeed, Johnson was soon back in the headlines again concerning his promised resignation honours and the report of the Privileges Committee on whether he lied to the House of Commons over Partygate.

His original list allegedly included a knighthood for his father and several peerages for colleagues who had been close to him during his premiership including some MPs – Nadine Dorries and Nigel Adams among them – who would have had to stand down from their seats in order to transfer to the Lords. Johnson met with Sunak on 2 June and claimed that Sunak had agreed to forward his list of preferments to the House of Lords Appointments Committee (HOLAC). Sunak denied any such promise had been made, merely that he had forwarded the list to HOLAC, which had sent it back refusing peerages for eight nominees. Nadine Dorries was so furious that her move up to the Lords was refused that she resigned her seat – as 'punishment' of the government? We'll never know and on 19 October her Mid-Bedfordshire seat was lost to Labour in a by-election.

The second aspect of the Boris-based furore at this time was the report of the Privileges Committee into whether he had lied to the Commons about those Whitehall 'parties' being within the legal guidelines he had himself set. Having been given an advance copy of the report in early June, he learnt that he would be suspended for over ten days, thereby triggering a recall procedure in his constituency whereby a by-election might be called. Rather than take this risk, plus faced a Commons vote on his fate, he chose to resign as an MP, calling the committee a 'kangaroo court' (Heron, 2023) intent upon a 'witch-hunt' (Macaskill and Bruce, 2023), which had decided to drive him out of the Commons. Dorries and Adams also resigned in solidarity – thus causing three by-elections – and it was rumoured six more MPs would follow suit, creating a mutiny within the party. However, even Johnson loyalist John Redwood advised against such action and the *Sunday Times* on 11 June was able to run the headline: 'Allies Abandon Johnson as Tory Mutiny Falls Flat'.

The report was damning. He was found to have deliberately misled the House and committed major contempts of Parliament. Had he not already resigned he would have been suspended from Parliament for 90 days. In the debate on the report there were powerful speeches criticising the former PM and only a few in his support, the most notable being that of the recently knighted Sir Jacob Rees-Mogg. The vote was 354 approving and only seven voting against (not including Rees-Mogg): supporters are said to have boycotted the vote fearing it would expose how fragile Johnson's support had become. Ironically his constituency, Uxbridge and South Ruislip, against most predictions, was held by the Tories at the resulting by-election in July 2023.

References and further reading

Adu, A., Elgot, J. and Allegretti, A. (2022) 'Who is in and who is out? Key figures in Rishi Sunak's cabinet'. *Guardian*, 25 October.

Allegretti, A. (2021) 'MP Owen Paterson faces suspension for breaking lobbying rules'. *Guardian*, 26 October.

Allegretti, A. (2023) 'Boris Johnson faces loss of Westminster pass as MPs back Partygate report'. *Guardian*, 19 June.

Arbuthnot, G., Calvert, J. and Johnson, A. (2021) *Failures of State*. Mudlark.

Balls, K. (2023) 'Who wants to be a Tory MP? Many it seems'. *The Times*, 24 February.

Bartlett, P. (2014) *Ellen Wilkinson: From Red Suffragist to Government Minister*. Pluto.

BBC News (2002) 'Major and Currie had four-year affair'. 28 September.

Behr, R. (2022) 'Boris Johnson's allergy to the truth could be a winning strategy for Liz Truss'. *Guardian*, 3 August.

Bland, A. (2022) 'Wednesday briefing: Liz Truss has appointed the most diverse cabinet ever. What does that mean?' *Guardian*, 7 September.

Blick, A. and Hennessy, P. (2022) *The Bonfire of Decencies: Repairing and Restoring the British Constitution*. Haus.

Churchill, W. (1966) *The Grand Alliance*. Cassell.

Clarence-Smith, L. (2023) 'Nick Gibb: I hid my sexuality – Politics was very different 20 years ago'. *Daily Telegraph*, 9 December.

Cockroft, S. (2019) 'Boris Johnson warns Tories face "extinction" unless they deliver Brexit and put Nigel Farage "back in his box"'. *Standard*, 5 June.

Comerford, C. (2023) 'Priti Patel blames Conservatives for poor local election results as she praises Boris Johnson'. *i*, 13 May.

Crick, M. (2022) *'One Party after Another': The Disruptive Life of Nigel Farage*. Simon & Schuster.

Currie, E. (2002) *Edwina Currie: Diaries 1987–1992*. Little Brown.

Duncan, E. (2023) 'The OK boomer: When privilege gets dangerous'. *The Times*, 15 April.
Eagleton, T. (2022) 'The Tories will never be united'. Unherd, 16 July.
Forsyth, J. (2022) 'The retiring type'. *Spectator*, 13 December.
Freedland, J. (2021) 'Never forget the Johnson government's disasters'. *Guardian*, 11 March.
Georgiadis, P., Provan, S. and McCormick, M. (2020) 'Rishi Sunak replaces Sajid Javid: As it happened'. *Financial Times*, 13 February.
Gov.uk (n.d.) 'Past prime ministers: Benjamin Disraeli, the Earl of Beaconsfield'. www.gov.uk/government/history/past-prime-ministers/benjamin-disraeli-the-earl-of-beaconsfield.
Guttsman, W.L. (1963) *The British Political Elite*. MacGibbon & Kee.
Guy, J., McGee, L. and Kottsasova, I. (2022) 'Boris resigns after mutiny in his party'. CNN, 7 July.
Hastings, M. (2019) 'I was Boris Johnson's boss: He is utterly unfit to be prime minister'. *Guardian*, 24 June.
Hastings, M. (2023) 'To move on, consign Boris Johnson and his vanity to spam'. *The Times*, 11 June.
Heron, K. (2023) 'Boris Johnson quits as MP and claims "kangaroo court" privileges committee tried to "drive him out"'. LBC News, 9 June.
Heseltine, M. (2000) *'Life in the Jungle': My Autobiography*. Coronet.
Ivers, C. (2022) 'Nadine Dorries, "I owe Boris Johnson undying loyalty"'. *Sunday Times*, 19 February.
Kettle, M. (2022) 'Boris's next move could be even more alarming'. *Guardian*, 5 August.
Knapper, D. (2022) 'Boris Johnson cheerleader, Jonathan Gullis quits role as Cabinet crumbles'. Stoke on Trent Live, 5 July.
Kuenssberg, L. (2021) 'Owen Paterson: Tories may regret rule change move'. BBC News, 3 November.
Lawrence, F., Pegg, D. and Evans, R. (2021) 'Lobbying for "naked bacon": How the Owen Paterson scandal began'. *Guardian*, 5 November.
Le Conte, M. (2019) *Haven't You Heard? Gossip, Politics and Power*. Bonnier.
Littleton, O. (1962) *The Memoirs of Lord Chandos*. Bodley Head.
Macaskill, A. (2023) 'UK privileges committee's findings about Boris Johnson'. Reuters, 15 June.
Macaskill, A. and Bruce, A. (2023) 'Decrying "witch hunt", Boris Johnson resigns from UK parliament'. Reuters, 9 June.
May, J. (1973) 'Opinion structure of political parties: The special law of curvilinear disparity'. *Political Studies*, Vol. 21, Issue 2, 135–151.
Mortimore, R. and Blick, A. (eds) (2018) *Butler's British Political Facts*. Palgrave Macmillan.
Newton Dunn, T. (2023) 'Sunak has a wealth problem: That's why he needs a Tory version of Angela Raynor'. *Sunday Times*, 8 April.
Nicholson, K. (2022) 'Liz Truss' Cabinet is the most diverse ever: But there's still one under-represented group'. *HuffPost*, 7 September.
Nugent, C. (2016) 'David Cameron's resignation honours list: Who is in his court?' *Guardian*, 6 August.
O'Flynn, P. (2022) 'Booting Boris was a catastrophic error'. *Spectator*, 20 October.

O'Toole, E. (2022) 'Boris Johnson school letter: Eton teacher despairs about PM's "effortless superiority"'. *National*, 19 January.
Owen, G. and Pierce, A. (2022) 'I'm relieved it's all over ... but at least I've been prime minister': What Liz Truss told tearful Downing street staff as she prepared her resignation'. *MailOnline*, 27 October.
Peck, T. (2023) 'RIP Boris Johnson's political career: we hardly knew ye'. *Independent*, 26 March.
Purnell, S. (2012) *Just Boris: A Tale of Blond Ambition*. Aurum.
Riddell, P., Gruhn, Z. and Carolan, L. (2011) 'The challenge of being a minister: Defining and developing ministerial effectiveness'. Institute for Government, 24 May. www.instituteforgovernment.org.uk/publication/challenge-being-minister.
Rousseau, S. (2022) 'Who's in UK prime minister's cabinet?' Reuters, 26 October.
Sabljak, E. (2022) 'All the Tory resignations from Boris's government'. *Glasgow Times*, 6 July.
Seldon, A. and Newell, R. (2023a) Johnson at 10: The Inside Story. Atlantic.
Seldon, A. and Newell, R. (2023b) 'Trapped in the Covid bunker'. *Sunday Times*, 23 April.
Shipman, T. (2022) 'Neutered: Minute by minute account of the PM's downfall, shows how belief in his own invincibility led to the unkindest cut of all'. *Sunday Times*, 10 July.
Stewart, H., Mason, R., Elgot, E. and Walker, P. (2019) 'Who's who in Boris Johnson's first cabinet'. *Guardian*, 24 July.
Stewart, R. (2022) *The Rest Is Politics*, Podcast, 18 July.
Sumption, J. (2022) 'Our system of conventions won out this time: But if Johnson had been mad as well as bad, the whole edifice could have fallen'. *Sunday Times*, 10 July.
Tan, R. (2019) 'Nicolas Soames, Churchill's grandson to be expelled from Tory Party for voting against Boris Johnson'. *Independent*, 4 September.
Tapper, J. (2023) 'Going to private school makes you twice as likely to vote Tory, study finds'. *Observer*, 8 April.
Tapsfield, J. (2020) 'Winston Churchill's grandson Tory MP Nicholas Soames says Boris Johnson is "no Churchill" and his Cabinet is "the worst in 36 years"'. MailOnline, 10 August.
Wheeler, C., Yorke, H. and Pogrund, G. (2023) 'Allies abandon Johnson as Tory Mutiny falls flat'. *Sunday Times*, 11 June.
Wickham, A. (2019) 'The definitive guide to who's who in Boris Johnson's number 10 team'. Buzzfeed, 30 July.
Wilcock, W. (2022) 'The greatest stitch-up since the Bayeux Tapestry'. *MailOnline*, 1 August.
Wolf, M. (2023) *The Crisis of Democratic Capitalism*. Allen Lane.
Yorke, H. (2023) 'Combative Kemi, the "rottweiler" loved by the party but snapping at Sunak's heels'. *Sunday Times*, 23 April.

12

CONCLUDING COMMENTS

> We give it everything until we can't any more.
>
> (Leo Varadkar on retiring as Taoiseach; McDaid, 2024)

> It is the highest and most legitimate pride of an Englishman to have the letters MP written after his name. No selection from the alphabet, no doctorship, no fellowship be it ever so learned or royal a society, no knightship – not though be it of the Garter – confers so fair an honour.
>
> (Anthony Trollope [who once tried, unsuccessfully, to get elected for my home town of Beverley in 1868]; AZ Quotes, n.d.)

> It helps to be a character to scramble into power, but you need to have character to stay there.
>
> (Terry Eagleton; Eagleton, 2022)

This final chapter attempts to pull together some of the disparate foregoing themes and to make some concluding observations about promotion and our body politic, particularly its health and efficacy. Estelle Morris's quoted 'Just Like Us' observation, as readers might have gathered, is only partly correct: to be sure, when we meet politicians, they might resemble 'us' in many ways but, as I have sought to point out, in certain important ways they are very different. They often seem to be addicted to or infected by a 'politics bug', which drives them to compete against fellow addicts for the limited places available at the very top of the nation's political elite. Trollope's quote above gives an insight into how the politically inclined perceive the honour of entering the legislature. People like Harold Wilson, Michael Heseltine,

DOI: 10.4324/9781003405085-13

William Hague and Margaret Thatcher seem to set their sights on glittering political prizes very early in life and become expert in the complex games involved in their upward journey.

Enoch Powell famously said that 'all political careers end in failure' (Lekbo, 2020) but it overlooks the lifelong satisfactions derived from the obsessive desire to prove wrong that mordant observation about the outcomes of pursuing power. So often, for such people, it is a lifetime's condition comparable, perhaps, to those committed to creative professions like acting, art or the writing of fiction. History has shown that sometimes the pursuit of power can become so visceral that it threatens to damage the fragile tendons of democracies. Examples of this tendency – responsible for all those checks and balances in the US constitution – are rare in British history but I would argue that such a dangerous excess of ambition in the person of Boris Johnson just about fits this category.

Lesser known routes to promotion

I have already referred in this book to the argument adduced by former Deputy Chief Whip, Tristan Garel Jones, that there *is* a promotion system and that it comprises basically the whips' intelligence-gathering operation plus government reshuffles. Alternatively, Geoffrey Howe argued there was no such system: promotion was delivered courtesy purely and only of the PM. I hope my chapters on the Whips' Office, reshuffles and the media (Chapters 3, 4 and 5) prove that while Howe is correct in that the PM is the ultimate arbiter of who gets the leg up the promotion ladder, there are more decentralised processes whereby the MPs gain promotion via something approaching a system. There are, however, other influences determining this upward progression that are less obviously acknowledged.

Crossing the floor

One small group of politicians who changed their parties and managed to achieve ministerial jobs is worth noting. The majority of defectors, if they did so with promotion in mind, were disappointed – but history provides evidence of at least six, three of whom made Cabinet rank, who did manage to achieve ministerial office having 'crossed the floor'.

Winston Churchill

Winston Churchill's career stretches back beyond the main focus of this book but, as the most famous and celebrated defector, cannot be ignored. He left the Conservatives for the Liberals in 1904 and, close to Lloyd George, went on to serve as President of the Board of Trade, 1908, then Home Secretary, 1910–11, before several positions during the First World War when he also, astonishingly, fought in the trenches. He defected back to the Tories in 1922, becoming Chancellor 1924–29. His long stint on the back benches, warning of Hitler's menace, ended in 1940 when he became PM until 1945 and PM again in the May to July of that year's 'caretaker' administration. In 1951 he served until PM for his third and last time until 1955.

Gwillym Lloyd George

Gwillym Lloyd George, second son of the 'Welsh Wizard' David, migrated towards the Conservatives during the war after serving as a Liberal MP, gaining office in 1951 and then serving as Home Secretary, 1954–57.

Reg Prentice

Reg Prentice, Secretary of State for Education, 1974–75, was deselected in 1977 and when he defected to the Tories he was made a PUS in Social Security. His final post – something of an anti-climax – was as President of Devizes Conservative Association.

Shaun Woodward

A Tory MP, Woodward was a one-time media executive who fell out with his party over its hostility to gay people and defected to Labour in 1999. William Hague wrote him a letter condemning his 'careerist ambitions' (BBC News, 1999) and, indeed, after serving in junior office he was made Secretary of State for Northern Ireland by Gordon Brown, 2007–10. His marriage to a daughter of the Sainsbury's empire enabled him to become the only MP who employed a butler.

Alan Howarth

This Tory MP was elected in 1983 for Stratford upon Avon. He defected to Labour in 1995 and, after a safe seat was found for him in Newport East, he became PUS in Education in 1997 and a year later PUS in the Department of Culture, Media and Sport. In 2005 he stood down from the House and was made a member of the Lords shortly afterwards.

Quentin Davies

Another Tory MP who disliked Cameron's leadership and, having earlier attacked Brown, then claimed to admire him greatly after he defected to Labour in 2007, serving as a junior Defence minister, 2007–10.

Nepotism and cronyism

Whilst this means of progressing oneself is not as rife now as it was during more formative periods of our representative democracy, a few more recent examples can be identified. Lord Salisbury appointed his nephew, Arthur Balfour, Secretary of State for Ireland in 1887, thus giving rise to the affirmative saying, 'Bob's yer uncle'. Macmillan appointed his nephew, Andrew Cavendish (11th Duke Devonshire), as a junior minister in the Commonwealth Office in 1960, promoting him to Minister of State in 1962, something Cavendish described (probably exaggeratedly) as 'the greatest act of nepotism ever' (Stewart, 2008). Then, moving to cronyism, there was Tony Blair appointing his former flatmate Charles Falconer to a succession of legal posts in his government. David Cameron's Resignation Honours list, according to Tim Farron 'contained so many cronies, it would have embarrassed a medieval court' (ibid.). The *Guardian* listed the honours given to party donors including, Andrew Cook (knighthood) who gave £1 million to the party over the previous decade, Jitesh Gadhia (peerage) a member of the Tory Party's exclusive donors, the Leaders Group and a peerage to Ed Llewellyn, his Chief of Staff and fellow Old Etonian (Nugent, 2016).

Comebacks

Making his departure speech in July 2022, Boris Johnson invoked the name of Cincinnatus, a Roman politician who stood down from politics and 'returned to his plough' but who then returned to lead his city when it faced a crisis. Some interpreted this as a promised comeback, though critics pointed out that the result of this Roman's comeback was to become a dictator in order to crush a rebellion by the common people. There is a tendency to conclude that once politicians have been sacked or resigned their careers are over. This is not necessarily the case; some manage to re-enter the fray and get repromoted to the same or even a higher level than before. Disraeli's extravagant but disastrous Commons debut in 1837 was thought at the time to be his political funeral but he soon shrugged off this failure, made his name by criticising Robert Peel, forming the Young England group of MPs and making it to Chancellor by 1866, becoming PM in 1874.

The already mentioned Winston Churchill, too, suffered a number of failures in his early career, including the bloody failed Gallipoli campaign, plus a stint as Chancellor that made the economy worse: indeed, he seemed during the 1930s to be, like his erstwhile ally Lloyd George, an exhausted figure, beached on the shoreline of political has-beens. But when the crisis beckoned in 1940 it was he who rose to the occasion, fought five years of desperate but successful conflict, adding a less distinguished period as PM 1950–55. More recently Michael Heseltine effected a dramatic comeback. 'Hezza' did not defect from his party but he did from Thatcher's leadership of it having walked out of Thatcher's Cabinet in 1986 after which it seemed his career might be over. However, his determination to fulfil his ambition of becoming PM did not fade away and he became a fervent agitator for his own alternative view to that of Margaret Thatcher. When his big chance arrived in 1990 he failed to achieve the top job but managed to make a comeback to Cabinet rank when John Major appointed him Environment Secretary and a very cooperative Deputy PM. 'Hezza' has earned his place as a major figure in British political history.

Harriet Harmon became Secretary of State for Social Security in 1997 but was sacked in 1998 for perceived failure. However she kept quiet and assiduously supported the party, becoming Solicitor General in 2001 and in 2007 narrowly winning the post of Deputy Leader over Alan Johnson.

And, of course, there is Peter Mandelson, twice drummed out of high office under Tony Blair who remarkably was called back into the Cabinet, becoming virtually Deputy PM under Gordon Brown in June 2009.

At the time of writing, Boris Johnson's departing 'hasta la vista' promise has not been fulfilled, but the founding by Lord Peter Cruddas of the right-wing Conservative Democratic Organisation in December 2022 has possibly set its sights on a return of the blond-haired maverick and its May 2023 Bournemouth conference saw Priti Patel lamenting the rejection of the party's most successful PM since Thatcher (www.youtube.com/watch?v=BQCRPCNJ83g).

There are also at least two politicians from the major parties who are young enough and occasionally hint at the desire to return to front line politics: George Osborne and David Miliband.

David Cameron, of course, was reshuffled back into front-line politics on 13 November 2023, when Rishi Sunak moved (an apparently reluctant) James Cleverley from Foreign Secretary to Home Office and then, sensationally, called back Cameron from 'civilian' life to serve in his government. Reappointing a former PM into the Cabinet had not occurred since Alec Home was moved into the same office by Ted Heath. The last time a peer was called to serve in the Cabinet as Foreign Secretary was Lord Carrington in 1979.

Direct appeals to the PM

It was not unknown for MPs to write memos to the PM recommending their own services as ministers. Attlee used to call them job applications. Plentiful evidence of them exist in the Prem 5 files of the National Archives but the best one I've heard was a shamefaced admission by Rory Stewart on his podcast with Alistair Campbell, *The Rest Is Politics*, confessed that he had, to his shame, sent creepy little notes to David Cameron, congratulating him on recent speeches and the like, in the hope he'd recognise him by giving him a job and extracting him from the 'horror' of the back benches. An alternative route was influencing PM advisers to put in a good word for them as evidenced by the diaries of Alan Clarke (2000).

Select Committees as alternative route to ministerial office

Select Committees are part of the legislature, not the executive but membership of these committees, which help call all the major departments to account, can become a highly detailed introduction to issues across the whole of government policy. Becoming the chair of such a committee can be a position of substantial influence on government policy and the door to future ministerial appointments. Tony Wright was briefly PPS to Lord Irvine but left after a year to spend 11 years as chair of the Public Administration Committee, which he turned into a kind of super-professorial-level seminar into the efficacy of UK government. He has, thereby, exercised far-reaching influence on our national political institutions. Chris Mullin, former MP for Sunderland, in conversation with Dr John Neugebauer declared: 'Anyone who is on a major select committee – such as Treasury or Home Affairs – may find they have more influence from being on that committee than being a junior minister – that was certainly my experience' (Neugebauer, n.d., p.4).

Mayoral route

It might be worth mentioning that a new route to power might evolve out of the growing number of elected mayors. Trevor Phillips has noted that, 'five out of the past six French presidents entered politics as powerful local mayors' (Phillips, 2023). Elected mayors have taken on much more importance in recent months and while only Boris Johnson has progressed into Downing Street, it would be no surprise to see another: Andy Burnham, ex-Labour Cabinet member, has so developed his role as Mayor of Greater Manchester, that he has attracted the nickname of 'king of the north'.

The casting couch route to promotion?

Given that women were not allowed within the British legislature until after the First World War, the opportunity for female politicians to be the beneficiaries of an approach more often associated with Hollywood producers has been very limited. There is a paucity of such examples of this in modern UK politics. Ellen Wilkinson probably had an affair with Herbert Morrison during the Second World War when she worked closely with him as a junior minister but her elevation to Attlee's 1945 Cabinet as Education Secretary was surely on the basis of her already formidable reputation as a very active Labour MP (Reeves, 2019, pp.83–84; Barlett, 2014). A better, though failing example, is probably that of Edwina Currie who famously had an extended affair (1984–88) with John Major before he became PM. After much breathless anticipation as he ascended the promotion ladder and became a candidate in 1990 'If John wins, oh whoopee', she confides to her (admirably honest and well-written) diary after chatting to Major in the wake of Thatcher's demise: 'and if God is listening, I would like a place in the Cabinet please, asap' (Currie, 2002, pp.216–217). Poor Edwina had an anguished time waiting for the call but it never came; Major never elevated her in the manner she imagined and for which she had hoped. She 'appeared to be forgotten' she complained, 'it felt like I'd been pushed off in a boat adrift at sea' (BBC News, 2002). Major let it be known later that 'it is the one event in my life of which I am ashamed'. Currie, who had been genuinely in love with Major, was upset not to even receive an index mention in his autobiography.

Role of gossip

To some extent most people enjoy gossip: at worst it can be unfairly damaging of someone's character, at best it merely expresses a natural interest in people. Politicians are greatly into gossip and the Tea Room of the House of the Commons, not to mention its numerous bars, are buzzing hives of 'who is up' and 'who is down'. This is hardly surprising. Politics, as has been mentioned, resembles a game and, like soccer fans who spend hours in the pub discussing their players, so politicians do something similar. But is this merely tittle-tattle of no more significance than people chatting in pubs or in coffee shops about their holidays? Tim Bale suggests that Westminster gossip is important: 'you can't really understand how parties tick, you can't get under a party's skin, unless you have a sense of what people are talking about on a day-to-day level and the way that they're doing it' (Le Conte, 2019, p.20). Another author points out that, 'In Westminster, as in life, those day-to-day conversations can be about the professional but a healthy chunk of those will be about the personal' (ibid., p.20). MPs love to gossip about who is manoeuvring for higher things and who is abjectly failing in ministerial posts. Such gossip won't necessarily decide promotions or sackings but it will likely provide a context in which whips channel information back to their Chiefs and therefore be a factor in appointments or sackings.

The case of Norman Lamont's political demise is a good example of how gossip arising from a tabloid story about a sex therapist – labelled Miss Whiplash by the press – to whom Lamont had, quite innocently, rented out the basement of his house. 'The recession had bitten deeply', wrote John Major, 'and the press needed a target. they waged a relentless campaign to ridicule him. Norman's credibility plummeted. The satirists piled in and speculation about whether he could survive was constant ... he became a bird with a wing down.' Almost certainly these fabricated gossip-based stories contributed to Lamont's fate in the May 1993 reshuffle when he was replaced by Ken Clarke (Major, 1999, p.678).

Another thread of this point relates to civil servants. Claims of bullying by Priti Parel and Dominic Raab in more than one department in which they worked suggests officials discussed their political masters regularly and, in these cases negatively. But it follows that 'positive' gossip by officials about ministers – I've already mentioned my recollection of comments on David Owen as a junior minister – will also make its way up the whips' information channels; the 'private office' network is a well-known communications circuit within Whitehall and is bound to bear witness to those ministers who are cutting the mustard and getting things done. I'm fairly sure Westminster gossip plays a significant role in appointments as well as policy decisions but the phenomenon, as yet, is too elusive to merit further study.

Attempted coup

Fortunately Britain has mercifully been spared any history of a coup taking the place of the democratic promotion route to the top political job in the country, but evidence exists that in the late 1960s there was at least the glimmer of such a plot. It is explained and analysed in several places but a short and clear account is found in Andrew Lownie's highly readable *The Mountbattens: Their Lives and Loves*.

On 8 May 1967, Mountbatten hosted a meeting at his Kinnerton Street home with press mogul Cecil King, *Daily Mirror* editor Hugh Cudlipp and Chief Scientific Adviser Solly Zuckerman. All four – possibly influenced by Central Intelligence Agency-inspired rumours that Harold Wilson was a Soviet agent – were disenchanted with his government.

> According to Cudlipp, King, after outlining his concerns about the Wilson government and the need for action, asked Mountbatten if he would agree to be the titular head of a new administration in such circumstances? Mountbatten turned to his friend: 'Solly, you haven't said a word so far. What do you think of all this?' Sir Solly rose, walked to the door, opened it and then made this statement: 'This is rank treachery. All this talk about machine guns at street corners is appalling. I am a public servant and will have nothing to do with it. Nor should you, Dickie. Mountbatten expressed his agreement and Sir Solly departed.
>
> *(Lownie, 2020, p.319)*

Lownie goes on to conjecture that 'Dickie' was not uninterested in being PM but at 67 years old, thought that together with his royal connections he was too old to seriously consider such an idea.

Changes in the politics of promotion

There have been four major changes to the politics of promotion in my view. First, the recruitable pool has been affected by the rise of the career politicians who have tended to enter Parliament when young – Cameron, Osborne, David and Ed Miliband – and rise to the top jobs thus excluding the cohorts of middle-aged and older lawyers, farmers, soldiers and businessmen who used to be a feature of Parliaments a few decades ago. While career politicians are in many ways a good thing – they learn the ropes early on and tend to become effective ministers – they do deny British government much needed expertise in many areas of our national life. Kevin Theakston makes an interesting comparison between these career politicians and an earlier era:

> Of course, there was once a class of young political careerists who started early in national politics, becoming MPs at a younger age than average and getting on and moving up the ladder fast – and that was the 18th and 19th century aristocrats, who faced few financial obstacles to political life and tended to have more gilded careers than the solid middle-class politicians. Instead of aristocratic patronage networks we now perhaps have think tank and Westminster insider bubble patronage networks now?
> *(private email)*

Second, the polarisation of our politics into factional 'silos' – largely the result of Brexit, especially in the Tory Party – has affected appointments and promotions. For example, Boris Johnson tended to favour Brexit-supporting MPs to the exclusion of clearly able Remainers like Dominic Grieve and David Gauke. Johnson even extended this partisan attitude in his award of honours, elevating Clare Fox and Ian Botham to the Lords, apparently largely on the basis of their support for this issue alone. For her part, Liz Truss's appointments to her short-lived Cabinet included extreme like-thinking economic right-wingers such as Kwasi Kwarteng.

Third, changes in the media and the growth of social media and podcasting have altered the way politicians deliver their messages in order to get noticed.

Finally (a personal judgement favouring 'centrist' politicians here, but I think more widely shared), the decline of really able people being recruited into our politics: there is nobody currently to be compared with the likes of Bevin, Macmillan, Butler, McLeod, Healey, Crosland, Hezza, Jenkins, Benn. Why should this be? I'd suggest: the general increasing perception of politicians as one of venal, narcissistic, mendacious self-seekers, again Johnson's behaviour a prime example; the poor level of MP's salaries, relative to other professions, especially business and finance; and maybe the feeling, emphasised in Martin Wolf's book on *The Crisis of Democratic Capitalism*, that the excessive and still growing levels of economic inequality appear to reflect the inadequacy of our political system to resolve this and other intractable problems. (A survey of 160 countries by the Barrie (2020) revealed that 18–24 year olds had incurred a substantial dissatisfaction with democracy over the previous decade.) The last-mentioned factor might also be a factor for some MPs, even those already in ministerial posts, to throw in the towel and abandon politics at a relatively young age.

Abandoning ship?

What is the future of ministerial promotion in the UK? Britain is often credited with helping to invent representative democracy so it is worrying to see its support decline. This is especially so when MPs seem to be among those sharing such feelings. James Forsyth read the runes on Tories abandoning ship in the *Spectator*:

> With no real prospect of a snap election before 2024, a dozen Tory MPs have already said they won't fight the next general election. One of the striking things about the retirees is how young some of them are. Their average age is below 50 which is 20 years younger than their Labour equivalents.
>
> *(Forsyth, 2022)*

He noted how Chloe Smith was only 27 years old when she won her seat in 2009 and that Dehenna Davison who won Bishop Auckland was under 30 years old and already a minister described as a 'rising star'. Davison and Smith (who briefly served in the Cabinet), both ignored the promotion ladder they might have expected to continue successfully climbing. Of course the then dire state of her party's future might have been Smith's major reason but the one she gave was that 'because of politics she hadn't led a "normal life for a twenty-something"' (Gye, 2022). Another quoted the fact that the previous 12 years had 'contained enough drama to fill several decades, let alone years. Indeed a Tory first elected in 2010 has campaigned in four GEs, two refs and Four Tory leadership contests' and was 'just exhausted' (Forsyth, 2022).

No doubt the reasons for retiring included the redrawing of constituency boundaries, which reduced their chances of winning next time, the marginality of their seats measured against likely swings to the opposition and the steep decline in the standard of living, which has increased dissent. Forsyth added a further reason: over half of Tory MPs had served as ministers and that 'once people have been a minister, they are more inclined to view their political careers as done' (Forsyth, 2023). Matt Hancock's decision not to stand in 2024–25 was understandable given his extraordinary resignation for marriage-breaking breach of Covid-19 rules and subsequent role as a contestant in the *I'm a Celebrity* reality show. Perhaps his best chance of realising his dreams is to stand as a candidate for the London mayoralty.

Sajid Javid's decision to stand down as an MP before the next election despite being a regular senior member of recent Cabinets, suggests his unsuccessful candidatures for the leadership in 2019 and 2022 were probably a factor in his calling it a day (Stacey, 2022). George Eustice, former Environment Secretary, took 15 years to make it into the Cabinet but decided he wanted to 'take the opportunity to have another career outside politics' (Culbertson, 2023). William Wragg had made a name for himself as a robust critic of Boris Johnson and had every reason to hope for promotion but maybe had tired of the hectic pace of Westminster life. David Cameron regretted the retirement of Edward Timpson, long-serving minister for Children and Families, saying 'Westminster needs to retain the skills and advice of specialists like Edward and the Conservative party too – particularly in an area where we are not famed for being as strong as he is' (ibid.).

William Hague adduces another reason why insufficient recruits to the public cause of democratic government can be found: the trend towards 'localism'. For citizens to be promoted from their 'ordinary' status to become members of the legislature, they are increasingly required to be 'more local', thus narrowing 'the pool from which they draw' (Hague, 2023b). Hague cites Philip Cowley's research showing that, at the 2019 election, 43 per cent of new Tory MPs and 52 per cent on the Labour side were former councillors. This has accentuated a trend for MPs to be drawn more from backgrounds of political activism and less from the professions – 'the mania' for localism as Professor Tim Bale describes it (ibid.), is tilting parliamentary selections against promising individuals who grow up in an area their party can't win or who can't afford to relocate, or who have led highly mobile lives rather than being immersed in local politics. 'Today's selection committees would look askance at Churchill, who represented five different seats; or Thatcher, who wasn't local to Finchley; or Harold Wilson, who crossed the Pennines' (ibid.). He concludes, ominously: 'The need to identify outstanding leadership has seldom been greater, and it is danger of not being met' (ibid.).

So are all politicians as pessimistic and disillusioned with their profession? By no means. William Hague, oddly perhaps, had already offered an answer to the question implicit in his article quoted above, by arguing that:

> The next quarter century looks set to bring the most profound political, ethical, legal and technological challenges in the history of civilisation. ... Despite everything there are many good people hopeful about becoming a politician. Oh yes. If I were you I wouldn't miss this for anything.
>
> *(Hague, 2022)*

But apart from the above changes, the route to the top has stayed basically the same as it has for 100 years. The first step on the ladder is getting selected as an MP, then it's a game of acquiring the knowledge and skills of Parliament and government and impressing the party leadership that you are someone who has the abilities and loyalty to serve the party well through a seat in the Cabinet. From this long list making it to the top job, whilst a huge leap, is nowhere near as impossible as it would be for a newly elected MP.

Andrea Leadsom also has no doubts about the value of a career in politics:

> if you ever think you are not smart or beautiful or young and ruthless or wealthy enough to become an MP, think again. Parliament is an arena to which anyone can aspire. To the cynical who feel there is no point entering politics because a lone individual can't achieve anything, think again. I know from first-hand experience that if you put your heart and soul into it, you can change the world.
>
> *(Leadsom, 2023, p.xii)*

Are we too hard on our politicians?

Rory Stewart, on his joint podcast with Alistair Campbell, suggested that:

> We have reached a stage in our politics where people who are teaching politics are no longer sure they can say to their pupils it would be a good idea to go into politics. Because in some sense the public are employers and they are very bad and abusive employers. When I was an MP I worked for the public but the public was like a boss saying you're useless, incompetent, idle and dishonest. It is a deeply, deeply dispiriting life. You want to go into a profession where you feel you've got some honour, respect and credibility and actually it is a career of perpetual humiliation. We've created an environment so unpleasant that if you can do something else, almost everyone else is going to do that something else and those who stay are people who frankly don't have too many options in the outside world.
>
> *(Stewart, 2022)*

Jonathan Yates's book, *Fractured*, is illuminating on the vanishing of 'the Common Life' that brought our grandparents together. He argues we have become much less likely to join clubs and societies, and most of us increasingly only know people like ourselves:

> Half of graduates have no friends without degrees. Most pensioners know no one under 35 (apart from their grandchildren). A fifth of Leavers and a

> quarter of Remainers have no friends who voted the other way. Half of us have no friends from a different ethnic group.

This distancing, isolating effect surely deters able people from coming forward and seeking to join the potentially noble profession of public service (quoted by Hague, 2023b).

How to improve ministerial quality in UK governance

Throughout the writing of this book, I've been aware of the criticism from many quarters that the promotable quality of UK ministers could be better. Some of these criticisms relate to lack of trust, a loss of respect for politicians and a feeling, maybe, that nothing seems to work properly and that it's the fault of a venal, narcissistic ruling elite. That these cultural currents are present, running deep and strong, is undoubtable but solutions to this state of affairs range much wider than my relatively narrow focus on promotion and the problem of a declining wish by some Britons to step on to the political stage. I am therefore going to suggest a few limited measures which I think might help improve ministerial quality.

1. *Outside recruitment*: I agree strongly with Riddell et al. in their IfG's 'The Challenge of Being a Minister', way back in 2011, which recommended that: 'At least half a dozen ministers with a political background should be appointed as ministers to broaden the range of expertise, experience and project management capacity of ministerial teams. The requirements will vary but such outsiders are particularly suited to education, health, welfare reform, defence and investment and trade promotion.'
2. *Open primaries*: This American-style practice was recommended by Alice Thomson in *The Times* who notes the Conservatives 'experimented with them between 2010–2015'. 'Tory candidates were thrown open to anyone in the constituency who wanted to vote, not just for the shrinking Conservative membership. This produced MPs of the calibre of Sarah Wollaston, Tom Tugendhat and Lucy Frazer: a GP, a soldier and a barrister who appear to have a more comprehensive skill set than many of their colleagues' (Thomson, 2023).
3. *Abandon parliamentary membership qualification for ministerial office*: Such a move would violate the British tradition of democratic accountabilitybut I would still argue it is worth consideration. This rule is not a law and has been ignored in the past – during wartime and when ministers have been temporarily appointed when defeated in a general election: it should be set aside permanently when ministerial ability is a permanent requirement of our political system. Making ministers accountable to Parliament is important but can surely be arranged fairly

easily without the need for ministers to be members of either Chamber. It seems quixotic for the UK to retain such an antique 'protected' route into ministerial office when so many other developed countries select from a very much wider talent pool.

4. *New route for mid-career spads*: Experience has suggested that former spads, a relatively new but dynamic cohort of political players, who tend to take to ministerial duties more successfully than the common run of MPs, might provide a fruitful talent stream if such 'outside' appointments are permitted. We already recruit youngsters – some perhaps too young – but my suggestion would be to target mid-career people of proven ability.
5. *End leadership elections by party members*: The practice of party members electing Leaders should be changed as it can produce executives at odds with the legislature. Most UK politics watchers won't need John D. May's Curvilinear Disparity Law to tell them that party members tend to be more ideologically extreme than either their leaders or voters (May, 1973). Democracy is hugely important but where, as in our British system, Parliament is its ultimate source of authority, it can be toxic for its majority party to be led by politicians at odds with their fellow MPs, as was the case with Boris Johnson and Liz Truss. Similar problems were caused for Labour by the election of Jeremy Corbyn in 2015. 'Sir Graham Brady, chair of the influential 1922 Committee signalled a major change of attitude on this issue at the launch of Philip Norton's history of the "1922" when he said: "In an ideal world, when the party is in government I think the parliamentary party should make the decision [on choosing the party Leader]" ' (Steerpike, 2023).
6. *Awareness training*: Before taking on ministerial office MPs should be aware of its merciless demands in terms of time, personal security and family dislocation. It was significant that Ben Wallace, someone who, according to polls could have won the Tory leadership instead of Liz Truss, declined to put his name forward for fear of the attendant damage to his family.
7. *MPs' pay*: This is a sensitive issue, especially during hard economic times but a potentially critical press should understand that MPs' salaries should not be so low compared to the private sector that they deter people of much needed ability from venturing forth into the political fray.
8. *In-service training*: Michael Heseltine confides to his autobiography (*Life in the Jungle*) that, 'Being a new boy in Parliament is unlike any other similar experience ... in the House of Commons you arrive, and you are on your own. There are no induction courses. It is presumed that, since you have persuaded people to elect you to represent them, you have some idea of how you intend to fulfil your new-found obligations' (Heseltine, 2000, pp.109–110). The advantage that spads and PPSs derive from their intense apprenticeships in ministerial offices, indicates that some kind of

in-service training featuring previous ministers and civil servants not to mention media advisers is crucially needed. I would suggest the Institute for Government might be best equipped to create and run such training courses.

9. *Leadsom's 'snakes and ladders' metaphor*: Andrea Leadsom's conclusions on promotion are worth quoting: 'The truth is that there is no real meritocracy in politics. You don't apply for a ministerial job, undertaking job interviews and proving your relevant experience; instead you get the summons and you never really know why. That, in my view, is why the game is more snakes and ladder than chess. It's a roll of the dice – finding your face fits or that you recently did something pleasing to the government that coincides with a reshuffle – it's as simple as that' (Leadsom, 2023, p.48).
10. *Longer periods of ministerial office required*: The 2020 IfG report reported the following: 'Ministers in the UK have remarkably short tenures. Since 1997, secretaries of state have stayed in post for two years on average; in some roles, junior ministers typically last little more than a year. Several departments have suffered from constant changes in leadership: for example, since 1997, there have been no fewer than 18 housing ministers. ... This compares unfavourably with some other countries – the equivalent to a secretary of state in Germany stays in office on average more than 300 days longer – as well as with private companies: top UK executives average over five years in post' (Sasse et al., 2020, pp.1–2). It is common sense to keep ministers in office longer as it is impossible for junior ministers to learn their ministerial briefs effectively given present lengths in post. This means junior ministers are being promoted before the benefits of their earlier ministerial experience have properly been absorbed (ibid.). It follows that civil servants should not be moved around so rapidly either. Sir Leigh Lewis, Permanent Secretary to the Department for Work and Pensions in a letter to *The Times* (1 September 2023) suggested, 'Good government demands good ministers supported by good civil servants for long enough to master their subject areas and lead with continuity and expertise.'
11. *Encourage comebacks*: This argument was adduced by Iain Martin in *The Times*, who suggested that, like Churchill, experienced ministers should not give up the ghost and retire but should keep on trying to make it back into the front line (Martin, 2023). Given the shortage of talent, described in this book, this seems at least an option PMs might consider. Edward Heath brought back Alec Home as Foreign Secretary in 1970, Thatcher brought Lord Carrington back in 1979, Brown recalled Mandelson to his Cabinet in 2009 and David Cameron became Sunak's Foreign Secretary in 2023. At the time of writing a number of experienced ministers might be considered for the same recall. Tories eligible for comebacks might

include George Osborne, David Gauke and Dominic Grieve, not to mention Rory Stewart. For Labour, one might mention Ed Balls, David Miliband, again, Mandelson and even a rehabilitated Tony Blair.

Do all political careers end in failure?

Enoch Powell's dictum is often quoted as if it's a recognised and established truth but I wonder if he was right? Are all those travellers on the promotion train doomed to disappointment? I would argue strongly against this delusion. It all depends, surely, on who is judging the careers here, especially politicians themselves? True, many politicians with early visions of what they want to achieve usually fall well short of them. But have they necessarily failed? Michael Heseltine famously set his sights, after making his fortune and getting married, on becoming PM. He failed in this ambition, OK, and, aged 90, will never achieve it. But has his career been a failure? I'd say far from it: he served as Cabinet minister for Defence and Environment as well as Deputy PM. He is open about loving the excitement and opportunity of his insecure profession and his memoirs suggest that, while he might regret missing out on the big one, he must certainly feel he has made a worthwhile contribution.

Tony Blair, too, had unfulfilled ambitions, which were eventually short-circuited by his nemesis, Gordon Brown. Since then, the Iraq debacle has made his career appear to be a failure. Again, his achievements of winning three elections and occupying Downing Street for a decade, can hardly be described in such terms? The same goes for Brown and Blair's predecessor, John Major. Some say Nicola Sturgeon's career has ended in failure; at the moment it looks rather like that but a decade of being Scotland's First Minister and still young enough to make a comeback? Come off it!

In my experience of studying this, admittedly strange, species, most politicians set themselves the realistically limited career objective of simply 'making a difference'. When I interviewed Michael Foot in the 1990s, he reckoned his proudest achievement was not being Environment Secretary or Leader of the Labour Party, but his 1974 Health and Safety at Work Act. Objectively, placing all one's chips on the roulette wheel of a life in politics, with its inevitable retreats, buffets and occasional humiliations, is a gamble few of us would take. However, like others in the histrionic professions, it is possible to be infected by the politics bug, with its satisfying glare of national public attention, its constant adrenal excitements akin to top level sport or acting on a West End stage and, of course, the possibility of creating for one's name a legacy in our nation's history.

Perhaps the final words of this book should belong to that lifelong advocate of more democracy. Tony Benn's reply (on a carefully typed postcard) to my letter – too busy for an interview – asking what qualities an MP should have to be considered for promotion was admirably concise:

> Dear Bill
>
> Promotion in politics depends on political alignment, sexual and geographical factors, age, party balance, personal preferences and luck. Obviously, any PM wants competence, commitment, ability to communicate and get on with others and a safe pair of hands but the system bears no resemblance to promotion in the civil service and merit does not play much of a part.
>
> Best Wishes
> Tony.

References and further reading

Note
Further to my suggested changes to improve ministerial quality in this chapter, I must highly recommend the 2024 report by an agency that has become, via its excellence, the leading source of ideas on UK government reform:

Urban, J., Thomas, A., and Clyne, R. (2024) 'Power with Purpose: Final report of the Commission on the Centre of Government. Institute for Government, 10 March. www.instituteforgovernment.org.uk/publication/power-with-purpose-centre-commission.

AZ Quotes (n.d.) www.azquotes.com/quote/1238485.

Barrie, J. (2020) 'Millennials are feeling disillusioned with democracy: This is why'. World Economic Forum, 8 December.

BBC News (1999) 'Fallout grows over Tory turncoat'. 20 December.

BBC News (2002) 'Major and Currie had four-year affair'. 28 September.

Clarke, A. (2000) *Alan Clarke* Diaries, vols I and II. Phoenix.

Culbertson, A. (2023) 'Former environment secretary George Eustice to step down at next election'. Sky News, 18 January.

Currie, E. (2002) *Diaries 1987–92*. Little, Brown.

Eagleton, T. (2022) 'The Tories will never be united'. Unherd, 16 July.

Forsyth, J. (2022) 'Why Tories are taking early retirement'. *Spectator*, 3 December.

Gye, H. (2022) 'Tories fear mass exodus of MPs as Dehenna Davison becomes latest young star to quit'. *i*, 25 November.

Hague, W. (2022) 'Would I still go into politics? That's an easy one'. *The Times*, 27 December.

Hague, W. (2023a) 'British society needs all the help it can get'. *The Times*, 1 May.

Hague, W. (2023b) 'Too much localism gives us second-rate MPs'. *The Times*, 25 April.

Hastings, M. (2019) 'I was Boris Johnson's boss: He is utterly unfit to be prime minister'. *Guardian*, 24 June.

Heseltine, M. (2000) *Life in the Jungle: My Autobiography*. Coronet.
Le Conte, M. (2019) *Haven't You Heard? Gossip, Politics and Power*. Bonnier.
Leadsom, A. (2023) *Snakes and Ladders: Navigating the Ups and Downs of Politics*. Biteback.
Lekbo (2020) 'Enoch Powell: "All political careers end in tears"'. Historum, 11 December. https://historum.com/t/enoch-powell-%E2%80%98all-political-careers-end-in-tears%E2%80%99.186927/.
Lownie, A. (2020) *The Mountbattens: Their Lives and Loves*. Pegasus.
Major, J. (1999) *John Major: The Autobiography*. HarperCollins.
Martin, I. (2023) 'Cameron's return should be a model for others'. *The Times*, 16 November.
May, J. (1973) 'Opinion structure of political parties: The special law of curvilinear disparity'. *Political Studies*, Vol. 21, Issue 2, 135–151.
McDaid, K. (2024) 'The ambitious young moderniser ended up looking out of touch'. *The Times*, 21 March.
Mullin, C. (2009) *A View from the Foothills: The Diaries of Chris Mullin*. Profile.
Neugebauer, J. (n.d.) 'In conversation with Chris Mullin'. Centre for Employment Studies Research, University of the West of England, Bristol. www2.uwe.ac.uk/faculties/BBS/BUS/Research/CESR/July_2013_Neugebauer_Interview.pdf.
Nugent, C. (2016) 'David Cameron's resignation honours list: Who is in his court?' *Guardian*, 6 August.
Paterson, S. (2022) 'Full list of Torn resignations as Boris Johnson faces PMQs'. *Glasgow Times*, 6 July.
Peat, J. (2019) 'Letter from Eton College to Boris Johnson's dad resurfaces online: And it explains a lot'. *London Economic*, 28 May.
Phillips, T. (2023) 'Stop stealing power from our elected mayors'. *The Times*, 31 July.
Purnell, S. (2012) *Just Boris: A Tale of Blond Ambition*. Aurum.
Reeves, R. (2019) *Women of Westminster: The MPs Who Changed Politics*. Bloomsbury.
Riddell, P., Gruhn, Z. and Carolan, L. (2011) 'The challenge of being a minister: Defining and developing ministerial effectiveness'. Institute for Government, 24 May. www.instituteforgovernment.org.uk/publication/challenge-being-minister.
Sasse, T., Durrant, T., Norris, E. and Zodglar, K. (2020) 'Government reshuffles: The case for keeping ministers in post longer'. Institute for Government, January. www.instituteforgovernment.org.uk/sites/default/files/publications/government-reshuffles.pdf.
Stacey, K. (2022) 'Sajid Javid says he will not stand again for MP at next election'. *Guardian*, 2 December.
Steerpike (2023) 'Sir Graham shines at 1922 shindig'. *Spectator*, 25 November.
Stewart, G. (2008) 'Nepotism on a majestic scale'. The Times, 2 February.
Stewart, R. (2022) *The Rest Is Politics*. Podcast, 18 July.
Sumption, J. (2022) 'Our system of conventions won out this time: But if Johnson had been mad as well as bad, the whole edifice could have fallen'. *Sunday Times*, 10 July.
Tapsfield, J. 'Winston Churchill's grandson Tory MP Nicholas Soames says Boris Johnson is "no Churchill" and his Cabinet is "the worst in 36 years"'. *MailOnline*, 10 August.
Thomson, A. (2023) 'Fiddling with ties while Westminster burns'. *The Times*, 1 November.

Wilcock, W. (2022) 'The greatest stitch-up since the Bayeux tapestry'. *MailOnline*, 1 August.

Wolf, M. (2023) *The Crisis of Democratic Capitalism*. Allen Lane.

Yorke, H. (2023) 'Combative Kemi, the "rottweiler" loved by the party but snapping at Sunak's heels'. *Sunday Times*, 23 April.

INDEX

Note: Page numbers in *italic* refers to figures.